SANTA ANA PUBLIC LIBRARY

D0962206

Philosophy at 3:AM

Philosophy at 3:AM

QUESTIONS AND ANSWERS WITH 25 TOP PHILOSOPHERS

RICHARD MARSHALL

OXFORD
UNIVERSITY PRESS

OXFORD

UNIVERSITY PRESS

Oxford University Press is a department of the
University of Oxford.It furthers the University's objective
of excellence in research, scholarship, and education
by publishing worldwide.

Oxford   New York
Auckland   Cape Town   Dar es Salaam   Hong Kong   Karachi
Kuala Lumpur   Madrid   Melbourne   Mexico City   Nairobi
New Delhi   Shanghai   Taipei   Toronto

With offices in
Argentina   Austria   Brazil   Chile   Czech   Republic France   Greece
Guatemala   Hungary   Italy   Japan   Poland   Portugal   Singapore
South Korea   Switzerland   Thailand   Turkey   Ukraine   Vietnam

Oxford is a registered trade mark of Oxford University Press
in the UK and certain other countries.

Published in the United States of America by
Oxford University Press
198 Madison Avenue, New York, NY 10016

Library of Congress Cataloging-in-Publication Data
has been applied for.
ISBN 978-0-19-996953-1

9 8 7 6 5 4 3 2 1

Printed in the United States of America
on acid-free paper

CONTENTS

Introduction   1

1   Brian Leiter: Leiter Reports   14

2   Jason Stanley: Philosophy as the Great Naïveté   25

3   Eric Schwitzgebel: The Splintered Skeptic   35

4   Mark Rowlands: Hour of the Wolf   46

5   Eric T. Olson: The Philosopher with No Hands   57

6   Craig Callender: Time Lord   68

7   Kieran Setiya: What Anscombe Intended and
    Other Puzzles   80

8   Kit Fine: Metaphysical Kit   91

9   Patricia Churchland: Causal Machines   101

10 Valerie Tiberius: Mostly Elephant, Ergo…   111

11 Peter Carruthers: Mind Reader   121

12 Joshua Knobe: Indie Rock Virtues   131

13 Alfred R. Mele: The $4 Million Philosopher   136

14 Graham Priest: Logically Speaking   147

15 Ursula Renz: After Spinoza: Wiser,
    Freer, Happier   157

16 Cecile Fabre: On the Intrinsic Value
    of Each of Us   168

17 Hilde Lindemann: No Ethics
    Without Feminism   178

18 Elizabeth S. Anderson: The New Leveller   188

19 Christine Korsgaard: Treating People as an End in
    Themselves   200

20 Michael Lynch: Truth, Reason, and Democracy   211

21 Timothy Williamson: Classical Investigations   222

22 Ernie Lepore: Meaning, Truth, Language,
    Reality   235

23 Jerry Fodor: Meaningful Words Without Sense, and
    Other Revolutions   247

24 Huw Price: Without Mirrors   256

25 Gary Gutting: What Philosophers Know   268

    Index   281

Introduction

THIS BOOK IS MADE up of a selection of 25 interviews taken from a series of online interviews published by the cultural magazine 3ammagazine. com over a period of about a year. The first was with Peter Carruthers in December 2011. Since then more than 70 have been published. The last one included here is the Gary Gutting interview that was posted in December 2012. The series continues.

Where Have All the Philosophers Gone?

The idea of interviewing philosophers at 3ammagazine came to me after reflecting on a curious feature of contemporary culture. An intelligentsia of public intellectuals including economists, political scientists, natural scientists and art and cultural critics is thriving in the cultural mainstream. They comment on and are seen to be part of the important advances, changes, and debates in and about the contemporary world. But my impression is that philosophers are largely absent from all this. Given philosophy's history—even its relatively recent history, when it would have been a sign of cultural illiteracy to not know about Bertrand Russell, Jean Paul Sartre, or Ludwig Wittgenstein—this state of affairs struck me as peculiar. There are notable exceptions to this, of course. Noam Chomsky is well known and significant although not so much for his work in philosophy as for his politics. The philosopher Dennett, as one of the so-called new atheists, has gained huge publicity in what have become dubbed the "Darwin Wars" defending Darwinian evolutionary theory. The Hegelian/ Lacanian Slavoj Zizek has also become moderately well known, and in the recent past Derrida attracted notoriety.

But even so, I think it is broadly the case that there is little time given for philosophical questions to be addressed by philosophers in public. Novelists and scientists seem to be much more available and popular even though, qua philosophy, their efforts are often incompetent and distinctions that undergraduates would be able to handle are often missed or misconstrued. It is as if contemporary culture largely fails to recognize that there is such a thing as a philosophical issue, and that when confronting one a philosopher may well be the best person to discuss it. This is not to say that only those trained in philosophy are philosophers. Richard Dawkins, Sean Carroll, and others have shown themselves willing and capable of philosophical thinking, and of course in the past Newton and Einstein were deeply philosophical. But even including philosophically adept thinkers from other specialist fields, it is hard not to deny that philosophy, if not erased, is largely submerged in contemporary culture. Given that contemporary philosophers are working in a much larger conceptual space than is occupied by the small list noted above, it is odd that they are at best a severely neutered contemporary presence, a situation made even more peculiar when one considers the complexity of the issues facing us on all fronts and their specifically *philosophical* challenges.

However, the internet has enabled a "long tail" of interests to thrive outside of the mainstream. Philosophers are hosting their own web pages, and others are blogging. Some of the blogs have begun to command the attention of many of their philosophical peers, and others have even managed to find readers outside of the philosophical mainstream. Brian Leiter's "Leiter Reports" blog, for example, commands a very large readership from within the academic philosophical community in the United States and elsewhere. "Bloggingheads tv," an internet channel devoted to science, politics, and culture in the United States, regularly features Joshua Knobe, the young Yale experimental philosopher, discussing philosophy and cognitive science with others working in that field. "Philosophy TV" has run a series of hour-long discussions between philosophers analyzing various contemporary topics. It is now possible to find excellent websites and blogs on many of the various fields and subfields within academic philosophy. The "Stanford Encyclopedia of Philosophy" is an open-access free site that produces high-quality entries written by experts in the subject, and many of the Wikipedia entries on philosophical topics are also substantial and written by academic philosophers. The University of Notre Dame runs a site reviewing the latest philosophy books, again written by expert scholars in the relevant fields. One of its co-editors, Gary Gutting, is interviewed about this work in this collection. Alongside all this activity can be found videos of lectures put online by various philosophy departments, which give anyone with an interest access to the very latest in contemporary philosophy and the very best contemporary philosophers. The "PhilPapers" site (www.philpapers.org) has an exhaustive list of papers written by contemporary philosophers, although some of these are behind a pay wall.

3ammagazine.com

So what interested me was bringing this exciting and substantial intellectual activity to a new demographic, one that was not primarily made up of philosophers and their students. The *New York Times* has been a rare case of a high-profile nonphilosophy site setting up a forum devoted to contemporary philosophy, and the "3 Quarks Daily" site includes philosophy in its cultural round-ups each day. But 3ammagazine addresses a very different readership from these. It is not and never has been a philosophy site (although a couple of us working for the site have philosophy backgrounds), and in fact has a slightly uneasy, sometimes even antagonistic, attitude to academia and the notion of mainstream culture generally. Its main interests have been contemporary fiction, poetry, art, and bookish culture. It tends to position itself as an iconoclastic voice raised against them and carving out a new space. If "underground" is now a better way of describing this than avant-garde, then 3ammagazine is an underground magazine. This was an important consideration. My interviews were not going to be on a philosophy site of any kind, and would be cheek by jowl with writing contemporary academic philosophy rarely shares space with. The juxtaposition was one of the things that I thought gave the project merit. Interestingly, many of the philosophers I interviewed commented that this was something that attracted them to do the interview.

That 3ammagazine is definitely not the usual place to find your contemporary philosopher is clear when one considers the history and profile of the magazine. 3ammagazine is a post-punk literary blog started by Andrew Gallix in April 2000. He continues to run and edit the site from his Parisian domicile. It is one of the world's oldest literary blogs, has a commitment to post-punk, transgressive literature, underground art, and culture, and carries the tag line "whatever it is, we're against it." It has been called "irreverently highbrow" by the *Observer* and an "on-line Fitzrovia" by the *Daily Telegraph*. Gallix, a lecturer at the Sorbonne, regularly writes lit crit pieces for the *Guardian* newspaper. An anthology of writing from its first five years was published in 2005; a city-themed book of fiction followed in 2008. There have also been readings and events organized in London, New York, Paris, and Brazil. Its "3am Asia" strand covers transgressive artists and culture, particularly from Japan. It has recently begun publishing books. Over the 13 years of its existence it has maintained a modest, prickly, and fertile presence in the new media age and is a rare longtime survivor in a digital culture where extinction is commonplace. Proudly independent of money-men and fashion, 3ammagazine is a throwback to the zines of the '80s and '90s, and further back to the '60s and *OZ*, or further back to the dissenting revolutionary pamphleteers of the 18th century. It takes ideas for walks with a whiff of lubricious brimstone.

I joined the magazine in 2001 as a contributing editor and followed the DIY ethos by doing a series of interviews with figures from areas of cult writing and music. I interviewed the likes of Stewart Home, Richard Hell, Billy Childish, Iain Sinclair, Sexton Ming, Marina Warner, Michael Moorcock, Michael Bracewell, Tony White, Zodiak Mindwarp, and Stephen Barber because I found what they were doing thought-provoking, challenging, and edgy.

Gallix introduced the idea of "mind-porn for the chattering classes," and we all tried to live up to that idea.

For those reasons, I decided in 2009 to interview the Oxford philosopher Timothy Williamson. I had read an interview done some years earlier in the collection of interviews *New British Philosophy: The Interviews* with Julian Baggini and Jeremy Stangroom. Williamson's thoughts about vagueness struck me as being odd, perverse, unbelievable—and also undeniably powerful and brilliant. It was thinking as refreshingly original as anything I knew about and exactly the sort of thing that 3ammagazine would love to publish. I approached him and, shockingly, he agreed to do the interview. The result is included in this anthology. But at the time I thought of it as a one-off and went back to the strangeness of nonphilosophers.

But in the summer or early autumn of 2011, I found I had some time on my hands and went back to thinking about putting philosophy and philosophers into the hands of a new set of readers. I searched the net, and I sent out invitations. Some of the philosophers I had read; others I had just heard about and had an inkling that they were significant in their field. Still others were just names in university philosophy departments. For a while, no one replied. I sent out another batch. Again, there was a deafening silence. I began to feel relieved because on reflection the hubris of embarking on such a project struck me. When I considered similar projects in the past, such as the brilliant Bryan McGee BBC TV interviews in the 1970s or the current online ones at "Philosophy Bites" and Chicago University's "Elucidations," all the interviewers were themselves professional philosophers with formidable pedigrees and institutional backing. What I was thinking of doing was just ridiculous. But just as I was thinking that it was far too ambitious a project for someone like me to even consider, I began to receive replies accepting the invitation to discuss their ideas. I seized hubris with both hands and went to work. I had reckoned without the philosophers themselves. If my own credentials were suspect, they were more than compensated for by the philosophers. They proved to be well able to discuss their complex ideas in simple terms that avoided reduction to the simplistic. They were encouraging, helpful, and generous with their time and ideas. Even when I was clearly misunderstanding them, they were prepared to restate the idea so that I got it, and at no point were any of them too self-important and precious not to be engaging and engaged. They were intellectuals who enjoyed their ideas, favored philosophical rigor, and welcomed interrogation and discussion. In a year I had interviewed 142 of them. They continue to be posted at 3ammagazine weekly.

The Interviews

As indicated above, the criteria used for selecting the philosophers interviewed were largely ad hoc. And the similarly ad hoc nature of responses also determined the character of completed interviews. It was certainly not intended as an overview or survey of the current state of philosophy, although I think the interviews do give an interesting snapshot of what some of our contemporary philosophers are doing at the moment across several significant fields.

However, looking over my selections, I see some recognizable criteria. I was looking for ideas that were both attractive to me and genuinely puzzling. The appeal of philosophy has always been its willingness to speak to those pressing niggles that haunt us as we make our way through life. These puzzles are often the ones that are suppressed by our day-to-day operational needs. But in the dead of night, or in moments of clarity or wonder, sometimes dread, they keep rising up. What is truth? Could we think without language? Is materialism everything? Pursuing these questions led me to pursue certain philosophers. And certain names kept cropping up. They were obvious targets. But also there were byways other figures occupied who seemed to be engaged in thoughts that were just too interesting to leave alone. These were thinkers who appealed because they had written a paper or a book with an intriguing title, or who had done an outstanding podcast, or who just seemed to have something worth listening to.

I was also studying, and these studies led me to negotiate some of the vast literature in my field. Vagueness, philosophy of language, logic, the history of these ideas all opened up new puzzles and thinkers. I contacted as many as I could. I also had heroes, philosophers who appealed because they seemed to embody in their ideas something that struck a chord with me, or whose modus operandi I admired, or ones who, frankly, I agreed with. And of course there were the famous philosophers, those who anyone working in philosophy had heard about even. An obvious criterion was a philosopher's being easily contactable via e-mail, and several well-known names were excluded simply because they weren't accessible.

Equally important to the selection were the criteria for not contacting certain kinds of philosopher. I avoided philosophers whose style I found too obscure to know what to ask them. Although all of the philosophers I interview are very smart and many of their papers and books very difficult, often technical and sometimes written in a dense style, I always felt that this was a result of the genuine complexity of their material rather than something they were aiming for. For example, a philosopher of logic is not an easy read because she's going to be using symbolic logic at some point, and at this point anyone engaging with her is going to have to work quite hard to keep up. But any obscurity and difficulty here seemed to arise essentially from the subject matter itself. I avoided writers I read as incorporating willful and avoidable obscurity, and this explains why certain thinkers were not contacted. I should also note that occasionally my bold front of bravura self-confidence abandoned me and some philosophers haven't been approached through lack of nerve. For example, Jerry Fodor nearly didn't get interviewed. When in New York I emailed him and even met with him for a coffee, intending to interview him. But I froze up and found I couldn't ask him any of my prepared questions. The interview didn't take place until many months—and many of my interviews—later. Needless to say, my fears were unfounded: Fodor was a smart, stylish, and friendly respondent.

The 25 interviews collected in this volume are just a sample of the online series. Eighteen of them are by men and seven are by women. Some of them are well established and some, such as Jerry Fodor, subject-defining in their importance. Others are new and up-and-coming. Alongside metaphysics, philosophy of mind, epistemology, logic, philosophy of science, philosophy of language, political philosophy, and ethics, topics discussed here are feminist philosophy, continental philosophy, pragmatism, philosophy of religion, bioethics, animal rights, legal philosophy, and specific philosophers such as Spinoza, Nietzsche, Dewey, and Anscombe. As with the sciences and academia generally, this increased specialization has meant that rather than a homogeneous subject "philosophy" it is better to think of a range of disciplines covered by the term. Not only is it unlikely to find any figure working in all these areas, it is becoming increasingly common to find philosophers working with nonphilosophers. In a way, the rather "potshot" approach of this project reflects the dynamism and specialization of the contemporary philosophical scene, albeit to only a limited degree of coverage.

One final comment: when the interviews were originally posted at 3ammagazine.com I wrote introductions that were designed to underline the point that these were aimed at a rather different readership from scholarly academics. I juxtaposed retro-slang and the philosophical subject matter to try to produce something that projected them into a space that distanced them from their academic milieu but placed them in the underground hinterland. In retrospect, I probably ought to have warned interviewees that this was going to happen, although latterly anyone being interviewed will probably understand that these come with the territory and take them in the appropriate spirit. And as a matter of record, several wrote saying they liked what I had called them.

The 25 Interviews

Brian Leiter opens the collection. A leading expert on the so-called Continental Philosophy tradition, Nietzsche, philosophical naturalism, and the philosophy of law, Leiter discusses these topics with customary deftness and combative aplomb. In the interview he engages with "the hermeneutics of suspicion," and analyzes the divide between continental and analytic philosophy, naturalism and realism, the dispute between Nietzsche and Marx, the current political and economic situation, legal realism, the importance of experimental philosophy, why we should tolerate religion, and the role of literature.

Jason Stanley in Chapter 2 first talks about the place of philosophy in the humanities and whether philosophy is too inaccessible, before moving on to give an overview of where philosophy of language has developed. Given that this area of philosophy has now embedded linguistics, computer science alongside philosophy, it is a good example of how philosophy is continually changing, developing, and making progress. He comments on the "titanic influence" of Saul Kripke, a philosophical giant currently working in New York and strangely obscure to many. He reflects on his work in epistemology and how he understands Ryle's distinction between knowing that and knowing how, in particular how he disputes those who would argue that knowledge of meaning is a practical knowledge.

Eric Schwitzgebel is another young and emerging philosopher working in the field of rationality, thought, and metaphysics. He works with psychologists and cognitive scientists and uses experiments as part of his approach to some of the philosophical questions he raises. He is one of the most extreme skeptics about our ability to know ourselves, and his arguments and evidence are corrosive of a comfortable self-image that introspection gives us unique access to transparent knowledge. He talks about a curious state of "in between belief," which he argues is our common state. He is the inventor of the philosophical position of "crazyism" and draws attention to the strange relationship between common sense and metaphysics. He explains why the history of philosophy is important to him, the moral behavior of ethics professors, Chinese philosophy, and whether the United States is consciousness.

Mark Rowlands begins with the curious case of Brenin, the wolf that inspired him to think about the relationship between other animals and humans and a shared heritage encapsulated in the "Machiavellian Intelligence Hypothesis." Separately, he discusses arguments for animal rights. He also looks at what a "mental process" might be and his version of the "extended mind" hypothesis. He claims intentionality as the cornerstone of everything he is arguing about, and how he doesn't think a naturalized account of it has yet been presented, even though he has tried.

Eric T. Olson is the proponent of "animalism," which argues that we are animals and that there is no metaphysical gulf between humans and the rest. He points out what this position commits him to accepting and rejecting and shows that it is a surprisingly rare position in the history of philosophy, and humankind generally. As part of this, he introduces the issue of personal identity, taking in thought experiments about brain transplants and computer-generated life and a paper he wrote entitled "Why I Have No Hands," which is part of a discussion on "partism." He also discusses the relationship of philosophy to science and why philosophy is often neglected in contemporary culture.

Craig Callender is another metaphysician, and his interests are with the nature of time and the philosophical issues arising from science, in particular physics and cosmology. He speaks about the place of metaphysics and its relationship to science and suggests that there are dangers for both if they become disconnected from each other. Indeed he suggests that knowledge of the history of philosophy and of science would show that we would be hard-pressed to make a clear distinction on many issues. As well as discussing metaphysical implications about time, he also disputes the plausibility of the idea of a multiverse, as discussed by physicist Sean Carroll and of the fine-tuned universe as put forward by Stephen Hawking. He turns to issues concerning scientific methodology and how to distinguish science from pseudo-science, and to Schrodinger's cat and why it illustrates a conflict with our ordinary experiences and the implications of this conflict.

Kieran Setiya introduces the philosophy of G. E. M. Anscombe, a major philosopher who was a friend and student of Wittgenstein and a woman. Setiya discusses her characterization of intentionality and his own work in this area, where he parts company with Anscombeans and argues that intention is a mental state. He talks about his approach to moral philosophy and the position of moral particularism that he develops.

Kit Fine is known to philosophers as one of the giants of current metaphysics. In the interview he first explains what he takes metaphysics to be. He then makes a key distinction between asking what there is and what is real, arguing that what there is is a something for science or common sense to answer, while what is real is a philosophical question. He then introduces mereology, which is the issue of how parts and wholes relate, followed by his rather negative views about the use of possible worlds in philosophy of language and metaphysics. He outlines his theory of "semantic relationism," defends the importance of philosophy, common sense thinking, queries some aspects of experimental philosophy, and believes that some questions, such as the mind-body dualism, the problem of free will, and skepticism, require more advanced tools than are available at present.

Patricia Churchland is a major naturalist philosopher whose position contrasts with many of Kit Fine's. Where Fine criticizes the American philosopher Quine for thinking that some philosophical questions could be answered by science, Churchland is a Quinean in the sense that for her philosophy and science are continuous. She is combative on this point, and her naturalism is unambiguous. She outlines her work in neurophilosophy and neuroscience. The implications of developments in our understanding of the brain for the issue of free will is summarized before she moves on to explain the implications for morality, philosophy, and religion. She also takes time to reflect on the place of women in academic philosophy.

Valerie Tiberius is another naturalist philosopher. She is interested in how we should live and, like Churchland, is involved in interdisciplinary work with psychologists and cognitive scientists as well as moral philosophers. This is more evidence that contemporary philosophy is much closer to old philosophical traditions that David Hume would recognize than many of its latter-day critics suggest. Tiberius introduces her naturalistic position before then going on to outline her theory of well-being. She offers some subtle thinking about the role of rational thinking in deciding how to live a reflectively endorsable life; she also argues that the threats of the relativism her position adopts are not as serious as many think and that because science is finding out things about ourselves this requires we change our self-image, but not to a fundamental degree.

Peter Carruthers is a naturalist philosopher working at the interface with cognitive science and psychology. He argues that we are systematically deceived about our own thoughts and draws on psychological experimentation to support his conclusions and to provide clues to the mechanisms causing the opacity of mind. He maintains that there is a single mindreading faculty that we use to perceive our own and other people's thoughts. He also talks about creativity, whether people change their minds to avoid cognitive dissonance or the feeling of having done something bad, and evidence suggesting that the self might be submerged from view, contrary to what many people believe.

Joshua Knobe is a philosopher working in both the philosophy and the cognitive science departments at Yale University and is one of the founders of experimental philosophy. He looks at the impact of people's moral judgments on their intuitions, intentional action, moral responsibility, consciousness, causation, freedom, and happiness, along with the "Knobe Effect," which is an asymmetrical feature of judgment-making named after him.

Alfred R Mele appeared in Knobe and Nichols's book *Experimental Philosophy* and was awarded a $4.4 million research grant to research free will. In the interview he discusses this project and his own position regarding free will. He examines the role of scientific experimentation in this philosophical work and disputes that there are scientific data yielding the conclusion that free will doesn't exist. He defends his own position about what free will means. He argues against the idea that perhaps the unconscious brain makes the decisions, making free will an illusion. He finishes by reflecting on experimental philosophy and the phenomenon of self deception.

Graham Priest discusses philosophical logic in his interview. He clarifies what philosophical logic is and why he thinks some key orthodox beliefs about truth and rationality are mistaken. He also outlines his own proposals for addressing this. He explains paraconsistent logic, which he proposes is required to address the mistaken belief that propositions are always either true or false. Dialetheism, his own species of paraconsistent logic, is explained, which allows for the existence of true contradictions. He talks about this and its relationship with Buddhism, Aristotle, its history, and its relation to science, false advertising, hypocrisy, Hegel, and Marx.

Ursula Renz is the only philosopher in the collection not working in either the United States or the United Kingdom. She explains where she works and what she takes to be the rewards of being a philosopher. She discusses philosophical issues regarding the "myth of the given" and connects the discussion to Kant's theory of experience and Spinoza's ethics via the work of Hermann

Cohen and Sellars. She then introduces an aspect of testimonial knowledge for post-Gettier epistemology. However, the main subject of the interview is her original philosophical work on Spinoza's ethics. This gives insights into an important part of contemporary philosophical scholarship where an important historical philosopher is shown to have continued philosophical relevance.

Cecile Fabre's interview begins with a discussion of social rights and the constitution and the relationship between democracy and social rights. She places the philosophical ideas about constitutional rights in a context and contrasts them with other types of rights. She talks about whether autonomy matters to social constitutional rights, Rawls's "Theory of Justice" and egalitarian liberalism, and then surprising consequences arising from her view of distributive justice concerning prostitution, what rights we have over our own bodies, and connected topics such as organ transplants and surrogacy.

Hilde Lindemann is also concerned with philosophical issues around ethics. She introduces feminist ethics, describing it not as a branch of ethics but rather as "a way of doing ethics that uses gender as a central tool of analysis." She analyses notions of power and identity, the rather dismal state of women in professional philosophy and the relationship between gender and subdisciplinary status within the profession. She outlines strategies of resistance to sexism, including her idea of the "counterstory," and then talks about several approaches to issues from a feminist ethics perspective. She thinks about bioethics and the dangers of linking academic research with big business. Finally she discusses her being on board with experimental philosophy but her resistance to the tendency of giving privileged status to science within naturalized philosophy.

Elizabeth Anderson philosophizes about various aspects of political philosophy in her interview. Like Lindemann, she reflects on the peculiarly poor place of women in professional philosophy compared to other disciplines. She then turns to discuss feminist epistemology and philosophy of science, elaborating her own position as a Deweyian pragmatist feminist empiricist. Dewey is introduced as a philosopher who approaches philosophical questions that are relevant to the problems people face in their lives. She then elaborates on a number of notions of freedom and egalitarianism. The aftermath of September 11 and the so-called war on terror are spoken about next, before turning to racism and the requirement of integration, which she considers "one of the most important social phenomena observed worldwide" and something that is particularly needed in the United States. She ends by explaining why she isn't a Marxist, despite being left-leaning politically, and examines the philosophical importance of the Occupy movements.

Christine Korsgaard begins her interview explaining Kant's formula of humanity, which conceives of our humanity as a source of value. She argues that despite what many philosophers think, Kant is best regarded as a naturalistic philosopher. She also introduces Kant's theory of obligations, which is based "in autonomy, or rational self-government." She goes on to outline her ideas about self-constitution and action, arguing that "action is significant because people are their actions." She then argues that Hume's notion of the battle between passion and reason makes no sense, preferring to understand the two faculties as serving different functions. She talks about practical normative concepts and why she places practical reasoning at the heart of all discussions about justice. She uses an example from Derek Parfit to raise problems with taking a predictive attitude toward our future values. She ends by dismissing claims that her Kantian, rational approach to moral philosophy can't be done; discussing moral philosophy and metaphysics as well as the dangers of saying something meaningless; and reiterating her claim about the universality of Kantian reasoning.

Michael Lynch's focus in his interview is the nature of truth and why truth matters. He gives an overview of the options that contemporary philosophers have and then goes on to say why he takes a pluralist rather than a monist view of truth, in other words, the view that there is more than one kind of truth. Having explained why he takes his position, he then criticizes deflationary theories about truth. He talks about the scope of his theory and why it is consistent with realist approaches. He speaks about moral and mathematical truth, which he considers "the two hardest test theories for any theory of truth," and about Timothy Williamson's remarks at a conference saying that many theories of truth were too imprecise to be good philosophy. Lynch goes on to briefly introduce William Alston, "a philosopher's philosopher," and then the role of reason, denying that there is any justification in thinking that reasons in the end always give way to something arbitrary. This leads to him talking about the relationship between democracy and the "space of reasons." Additionally, he criticizes experimental philosophy on the grounds that philosophy is revisionary, not merely descriptive. Finally he talks about the link between objectivity and politics and the divide between so-called Continental and Analytical philosophy.

Timothy Williamson's interview took place in 2009 and so does not take into account work done recently, including his own new book. He takes up the issue about the Analytical-and-Continental divide in philosophy but leaves it until later in the interview to fully develop his thoughts about it. He outlines his controversial epistemic theory about vagueness, defending classical logic against attempts to construct alternatives such as those discussed earlier in the interview with Priest. He then turns to his theory of knowledge, which reverses the traditional view in epistemology that starts with belief and analyses knowledge in terms of it. So Williamson starts with knowledge, and belief is analyzed in terms of its failure to be knowledge. He reflects on practical application for his views before introducing the topics of the linguistic and conceptual turns in philosophy and the development of philosophy since then. It is here that he explains why he finds Analytic philosophy attractive and criticizes those critics who have failed to keep up with what Analytic philosophers are doing. He also judges that, by way of contrast, much of Continental philosophy is stagnating.

Ernie Lepore talks about his philosophy of language and his approach to semantic minimalism. He discusses his approach to philosophy and then moves on to the influence of Wittgenstein and semantic holism on philosophy of language generally. He also talks about the work, and his relationship, with Donald Davidson. Following this, he explains the development of speech act pluralism, the view that "we say indefinitely many things when we utter a single speech sentence," which he developed with Herman Cappelen. This leads to his ideas on the role of meaning theory in explaining belief formation and his work on quotation, which he considers a special feature of language. He then turns to the issue of what a word is, the role of collaboration in his work, the relationship of mind and language, and his belief that philosophy of language is going through a kind of second renaissance (following the first, which supposedly peaked in the 1970s).

Jerry Fodor, a collaborator with Lepore, is one of the contemporary giants of philosophy. He explores his theory about the language of Thought, the work that has made him such a significant presence, reflecting on its philosophical roots and its influence. He talks about semantic holism and why he believes it is a hopeless theory, about materialist theories of consciousness, and his amazement that there are still behaviorists. He engages with issues arising from his book on David Hume and why he refuses to read Heidegger and then turns to the controversies surrounding his last book, which argued that Darwin's mechanism for natural selection was flawed. He ends by discussing a disagreement with Stephen Pinker about the scope of a modular theory of mind.

Huw Price begins his interview by talking about facts and the function of truth and then goes on to elaborate his deflationary theory of truth, contrasting it with other varieties. He continues by analyzing time (whether it has a direction) and explains a dispute with Stephen Hawking about a related issue of cosmology, as well as his thoughts about the relationship between science and philosophy. What follows is a prolonged analysis of causation. He talks about why he isn't a metaphysician and what sort of a pragmatist he is. He explains expressivism and why he rejects any assumption of a bifurcation in language between expressivism and representationalism and how he can hold to both expressivism and deflationism. He ends by thinking about philosophy's relation to experimental enquiry and some observations about philosophers changing their minds.

Finally, Gary Gutting begins by elaborating the scope of his skepticism, including the influence of Rorty on "skeptical challenges to philosophy itself." He then reflects on the divide between Analytic and Continental philosophers and believes that the divide is real and unbridgeable. He returns to this near the end of the interview when discussing the naturalistic bias in contemporary Analytic philosophy. He further considers the cognitive limits of science and in particular the focus Sellars gives to this issue. He goes on to talk about pragmatic liberalism, defending what he calls "the best of the Enlightenment" and seeing "Rorty, Taylor, and even MacIntyre as contributors to the Enlightenment project." He then introduces some thoughts on scientific realism before turning to some aspects of philosophy of religion and the ideas of Alvin Plantinga regarding arguments for the existence of God. He comments on his interest in Foucault and French philosophy, and in particular his defense of Sartre as an impressive and original thinker. He speaks about Derrida, and although he thinks we should take him seriously, that judgment comes with a health warning. He ends by reflecting on the role of the public intellectual and philosophy in the age of the internet.

The interviews are stand-alone discussions and can be read in any order. Each is accompanied by a brief biographical note and bibliography of the books written. I believe that they offer a chance for readers to deepen their understanding of distinctive and various contemporary philosophical currents. I think they are a legitimate contribution to attempts to make the contemporary philosophical scene more accessible.

1 | Brian Leiter

LEITER REPORTS

Brian Leiter is the Karl N. Llewellyn Professor of Jurisprudence and Director of the Center for Law, Philosophy, and Human Values at the University of Chicago. He teaches and writes primarily in the areas of moral, political, and legal philosophy, in both Anglophone and Continental traditions. He has written three books: *Why Tolerate Religion* (2012), *Naturalizing Jurisprudence: Essays on American Legal Realism and Naturalism in Legal Philosophy* (2007), and *Nietzsche on Morality* (2002). He has edited or co-edited a further seven books: with Leslie Green, *Oxford Studies in the Philosophy of Law, Volume 1* (2011); with Michael Rosen, *The Oxford Handbook of Continental Philosophy* (2007), *The Future for Philosophy* (2004); with Maudemarie Clark, *Nietzsche's Daybreak* (1997); with Neil Sinhababu, *Nietzsche and Morality* (2007); *Objectivity in Law and Morals* (2001); and with John Richardson, *Nietzsche* (2001). His philosophy blog *Leiter Reports* is the premier online philosophy blog in the United States. In 1989 he made a list of what he ranked as the top 25 graduate philosophy programs in the United States. Called the "Philosophy Gourmet Report," the lists have been published every year since.

3:AM: You use a striking phrase in one of your essays, "the hermeneutics of suspicion," to discuss three of your intellectual heroes, Marx, Nietzsche, and Freud. Could you say a little about what you were getting at in that phrase and how it is really relevant for the intellectual left today?

LEITER: The phrase itself derives from the French philosopher Paul Ricoeur, though I take strong issue with how he understands what such a "hermeneutics"— or method of interpretation—involves. But what Ricoeur correctly notices is that Marx, Nietzsche, and Freud represent ways of thinking about and analyzing human societies and human behavior that share certain structural similarities. First, they typically suspect that people's own self-understanding and self-presentation are misleading as to what really explains why they say what they say and do what they do. Second, these thinkers try to show that the real explanation is one that would undermine the credibility of the beliefs and values people affirm.

Take a wonderful Freudian example, which has since been confirmed by experimental work in psychology. A "reaction formation" is a psychological process in which one forms moral views in reaction to desires that one really has—so, for example, one becomes a vociferous critic of the immorality of homosexuality and gay marriage precisely because one has strong homosexual urges and desires that one finds threatening. A reaction formation is a "defense mechanism," a way of trying to protect oneself from desires one doesn't want to act upon. The typical religious or moralistic homophobe will conceive of himself as "defending family values" and "traditional marriage," when, in reality, he only mouths these moralistic platitudes because deep down he'd like nothing better than to have anal or oral sex with another man. If, in fact, it's the reaction formation that really explains his moral beliefs, then those beliefs can't possibly be justified, since they arise from a mechanism, reaction formation, that's inherently unreliable (that is, it's not a reliable way to figure out what's morally right or wrong). This bears emphasizing: if what really explains your moral attitudes is that they are a desperate psychological attempt to restrain your own desire for what those attitudes condemn, then why should anyone else take them seriously?

This kind of critical suspicion is very offensive to the dominant political culture, especially in the United States: it is considered rude and disrespectful. And so it is, but, again, that has no bearing on its epistemic relevance, that is, its relevance to figuring out what's really going on. Take Barack Obama, in whom many on the anemic American left invested their hopes. As president of the United States, his domestic policies, like those of Bill Clinton, have been largely to the right of Richard Nixon, and his primary economic advisors were the various economic soothsayers who orchestrated the deregulation of the financial sector in the 1990s that brought about the collapse of the global capitalist system under George W. Bush. His most ambitious "progressive" legislation was a health care plan originally developed by the Republican governor of Massachusetts. At every moment where Obama, if he had any moral or intellectual core, might have led, he pivoted to the right. How could the great "liberal" hope have turned out to be such a shallow apologist for and tinkerer with the status quo?

If we put aside the romance surrounding the advertising product "Barack Obama," and even put aside the more genuine emotional resonance of electing a black president given the history of vicious racism in America, the answer seems quite obvious. In the United States, no one can compete meaningfully for the presidency without many millions of dollars, and no one can raise such money without backing from the richest sliver of American society, the plutocrats. Since enough of the public can be manipulated at any time to believe just about anything—the entire history of the world is massive confirmation of that fact—it follows that only a candidate who meets the needs of the plutocracy has any chance, since only that candidate can get plutocrat money. The plutocracy has largely become more liberal on so-called social issues (for example, anti-gay bigotry), and so any Democrat who basically respects the prerogatives of the rich is a viable candidate for them. Obama is not a fool, and nor are the plutocrats: they understand each other, and the result is that Obama has had and will have more money than any of his Republican opponents, and Obama will pivot to the right on any economic issue that affects the interests of the plutocratic class. That's the hermeneutics of suspicion, and we need more of it every day.

3:AM: Linked with that last question is what makes your views distinctive about Marx, Nietzsche, and Freud. You've expressed disagreement with readings of these three thinkers that undermine the naturalism you take to be embedded in them. So postmodernist readings get short shrift from you, for example, and this feeds into the discussion about the alleged two traditions of philosophy—the Analytic and the Continental—a distinction you think is bogus. Can you tell us about how you navigate these waters?

LEITER: There are real dividing lines in the history of philosophy, but the one between the "Analytic" and the "Continental" isn't one of them, though it's interesting today from a sociological point of view, since it allows graduate programs in philosophy to define spheres of permissible ignorance for their students. A real dividing line, by contrast, one that matters for substantive philosophical questions, is between "naturalists" and "anti-naturalists." The naturalists, very roughly, are those who think human beings are just certain kinds of animals, that one understands these animals through the same empirical methods one uses to understand other animals, and that philosophy has no proprietary methods for figuring out what there is, what we know, and, in particular, what humans are like. The anti-naturalists, by contrast, are (again, roughly) those who think human beings are different not just in degree but in kind from the other animals, and that this difference demands certain proprietary philosophical methods— perhaps a priori knowledge or philosophical ways of exploring the distinctively "normative" realm in which humans live.

So on the naturalist side you get, more or less, David Hume, Ludwig Feuerbach, Karl Marx, Ludwig Büchner, Friedrich Nietzsche, Rudolf Carnap, W. V. O. Quine, Jerry Fodor, Stephen Stich, and Alex Rosenberg and on the anti-naturalist side you get, more or less, Gottfried Leibniz, Immanuel Kant, G. W. F. Hegel, Edmund Husserl, Gottlob Frege, Jean-Paul Sartre, G. E. M. Anscombe, Wilfrid Sellars (at least for part of his career), the older Hilary Putnam, Alvin Plantinga, and John McDowell, among many others. This disagreement—a disagreement, very roughly, about the relationship of philosophy to the sciences—isn't one that tracks the alleged Analytic/Continental distinction. Indeed, the founders of the 20th-century traditions of "Analytic" and "Continental" philosophy (Frege and Husserl, respectively) are both on the anti-naturalist side, and both are reacting against hardcore naturalist positions in philosophy that had become dominant on the European Continent in the late 19th century. And the first explosion of what anti-naturalists would derisively call "scientism" came in Germany in the 1840s and 1850s, as a reaction to Hegel's obscurantist idealism. Naturalism and anti-naturalism mark a profound dividing line in modern philosophy, but it has nothing to do with "Analytic" versus "Continental" philosophy.

The other distinction that I think is increasingly important is that between what I call "realists" and "moralists," between those who think the aim of philosophy should be to get as clear as possible about the way things really are—that is, about the actual causal structure of the natural and human world, how societies and economies work, what motivates politicians and ordinary people to do what they do—and, on the other hand, those who think the aim of philosophy is to set up moral ideals, to give moralistic lectures about what society ought to do and how people ought to act. On the realist side, you find Thucydides, Marx, and Nietzsche, but also Max Weber, Michel Foucault, Richard Posner, and Raymond Geuss. On the moralist side, you find Plato and Kant, but also John Rawls, Ronald Dworkin, and Martha Nussbaum, among many others. Many, but not all, naturalists are realists, since it's reasonable to think that if you want to understand the way things really are, you ought to rely on the methods of the sciences, which have been the most successful ones over the past several centuries.

On this way of thinking about the serious disagreements in the history of philosophy, postmodernism is just an embarrassing blip, largely anti-naturalist in its sympathies, but infatuated with sophomoric versions of skepticism about truth and knowledge, that both the naturalist and anti-naturalist, and realist and moralist, traditions largely repudiate. Foucault is the hard case in this story, though it always pains me to see a thinker and scholar of his seriousness lumped with poseurs like Derrida and some of the others you mention. It's important, though, to avoid the kind of cult of personality that Heidegger and a lot of post-Heideggerian philosophy depend upon. Foucault was human and fallible, so perhaps we need to recognize that he sometimes had bad intellectual judgment and picked up certain bad intellectual habits in Paris as well. But when he was at his best, Foucault diagnosed how individuals in the modern era become agents of their own oppression in virtue of certain moral and epistemic norms they endorse and thus impose upon themselves. That is Foucault's uniquely disturbing contribution to the literature whose diagnostic aim is, with Max Weber, to understand the oppressive character of modernity, and whose moral aim is, with the Frankfurt School, human liberation and human flourishing.

Now, Marx certainly didn't need to be saved by sophomoric postmodernists; indeed, Marx didn't need to be saved at all. On two central issues, Marx was far more right than any of his critics: first, that the long-term tendency of capitalist societies is toward immiseration of the majority (the post–World War II illusion of upward mobility for the "middle classes" will soon be revealed for the anomaly it was); and second, that capitalist societies produce moral and political ideologies that serve to justify the dominance of the capitalist class. Marx had three faults, to be sure: one was that he took Hegel seriously; another was that he wasn't a very good fortune teller and so wildly overestimated the pace of capitalist development; and a third is that he had no account of individual psychology, of the kind Nietzsche and Freud provide. Within academic philosophy, however, far more harm, in my view, has been done to Marx by moralists like G. A. Cohen than by any of the postmodernists. Cohen—a truly smart man, and delightful human being to boot—did two unfortunate things to academic anglophone Marxism: first, offering a philosophical reconstruction of historical materialism in its least interesting form (namely, as functional explanation, rather than in terms of class conflict); and second, in his later work, calling for a moralistic change in the consciousness of individuals, regardless of historical circumstances. This latter, Christian turn in Cohen's thought represents as profound a betrayal of Marxism as Habermas's attempt to supply it with a Kantian foundation—in this respect, both anglophone and "Continental" Marxism betray Marx's original realism.

To be sure, Cohen on historical materialism is preferable to Althusser, but that hardly matters, except for academic debates. What does matter is that class conflict is both the actual causal mechanism of historical change and intelligible to the people who are the agents of that change. Functional explanations are, by contrast, an interesting but irrelevant theoretical overlay. And the idea that Marxism should be reduced to moralistic sermons is, well, depressing, an admission of intellectual defeat.

3:AM: I guess the last question was raised because certainly here in the UK there's a sense that the political left have rather struggled to find a distinctive voice to discuss issues of inequality and injustice. In fact I think it's fair to characterize the last Labour government as being as unconcerned about plutocratic pressures as the right, and this was disappointing and shocking to many supporters of Labour. And now we have a Lib-Dem Party in bed with Tories—it's kind of ridiculous. You do have a distinctive line on all this, though, and would it be fair to say that the philosophical naturalism you argue for is the starting point for your ethical and political stance? Could you tell us about naturalism and how naturalism and politics and ethics go together in your thinking?

LEITER: The line of political development in the UK over the past generation that you describe has certainly been similar to that in the United States, though perhaps not as extreme. Just as Clinton in the United States delivered the Democratic Party wholesale to the plutocracy (so that the only issues on which it could take a real stand concerned the mistreatment of social minorities like gay men and women), so too Blair delivered the Labour Party to the slightly less rapacious ruling class in the UK. I consider this kind of analysis to follow from my realism, which I view as a subset of naturalism. As naturalists, we want to understand human beings as they actually are, and that ends up requiring realism about those human beings who are political actors. Marx is the key realist in this regard, since he understands politicians as representatives of a dominant economic class.

But naturalism and realism go no further, and this is where Nietzsche is important. For I accept Nietzsche's view (from *The Gay Science*) that, "Whatever has value in our world now does not have value in itself, according to its nature—nature is always value-less, but has been given value at some time, as a present—and it was we who gave and bestowed it." I think, with Nietzsche, that the idea that "nature is always value-less" is one upshot of a serious naturalism about the world. And as Nietzsche notes at the end of the first essay of his on the Genealogy of Morality, "The well-being of the majority and the well-being of the few are opposite evaluative points of view." This is why, to my mind, the dispute between Marx and Nietzsche is as stark as any dispute can be: they are both naturalists and realists, but Marx adopts the point of view of the majority, while Nietzsche adopts the point of view of the genius elite—not the capitalist elite, I hasten to add, since he regarded them as contemptible herd animals, like the mass of humanity. The choice between those two evaluative viewpoints isn't one that can be made on rational grounds. What worries me, as someone who mostly sides with Marx, is Nietzsche's challenge that a culture defined by egalitarian values is one in which genius will no longer be possible. I still don't know what to think about that challenge, but it's the most serious one to Marxism and to liberalism on offer.

3:AM: Can you give us your take on the current economic and political situation and what you find most valuable and interesting about the Occupy movement? I'm particularly interested in your views about the use of state violence and the endorsement of plutocratic policing to clear the protests.

LEITER: I think Robert Paul Wolff, the distinguished philosopher who has written on Kant and Marx, is quite right to note that the Occupy movement succeeded, in the space of a couple of months, in changing the national dialogue in the United States from the need for austerity and cuts to programs that benefit the elderly and the poor, to the actual reality of massive economic inequality. If 75 percent of the wealth of the richest 10th of 1 percent of American society were immediately expropriated, there would be no need to discuss cuts to spending that affect the well-being of the vast majority. This is a democracy; why isn't this a major topic of public debate? Why aren't the national media full of debates between defenders of the right of the Koch brothers to keep their billions and advocates for seizing the majority of their fortune to meet human needs? One only needs to read Marx to know the answer.

An important strategic question for the Occupy movement concerns the police. The police are, themselves, members of the 99 percent, indeed the 99.9 percent. Police labor unions remain strong, despite a three-decade-long campaign against labor unions in the United States. As unionized workers, the interests of police lie with the Occupy movement, not the plutocrats. On the day the police refuse to clear Occupy protesters from their sites, that will be the day the game is up for the plutocracy in America. It would behoove the Occupy activists, indeed any opponents of the plutocracy, to remember this.

3:AM: Which brings us to your work in legal studies and the philosophy of law. You're known for, again, developing a distinctive legal theory that you oppose to the likes of Ronald Dworkin, and you think that law is much closer to what Richard Posner describes in his *How Judges Think*. This itself is refreshingly pugnacious. Can you say what your views are, and what it [your legal theory] opposes? And why you think it is justified?

LEITER: This harkens back to the dispute between moralists and realists noted earlier, and in legal philosophy I am an unapologetic realist (like Judge Posner, who has a first-person vantage point on what it is judges really do!). The core question is, How do we understand what courts are doing? Do we take at face value the opinions they write, and see if we can reconstruct, as Dworkinians try to do, the principled grounds of their decisions, to understand them as trying to discover the answer the law always required? Or do we, instead, understand judges as political actors who exploit the many points of indeterminacy and uncertainty in the law, to reach the outcomes they deem morally and politically desirable? In the United States, it seems to me utterly incredible that anyone could look at most of the work of the appellate courts, and adopt the Dworkinian view.

Cases that reach the courts, especially those that reach the appellate courts, are precisely the ones in which the law's indeterminacies are most apparent, and judges are called upon to make moral and political judgments, not legal ones. Given that reality, decisions to confirm, say, judges on the U.S. Supreme Court should be decisions based on their moral and political views, and little else. The U.S. Supreme Court is a super-legislature, though one with a decidedly limited jurisdiction (that is, only the litigated cases that come before it). A bit of realism about courts would lead the public to realize what is at stake in every single confirmation hearing for a position on the Supreme Court; to be sure, all politicians since Reagan onward realize it, but the public is sadly in the dark.

A harder question is how far this realism about courts generalizes, though in talking to my legal realist friends in countries like Italy and Spain, my suspicion is that the narrow, but nonetheless legislative, role of courts is true most places. The English are in denial on this score, and perhaps their civil service judiciary is sufficiently disciplined that the legislative analogy is inapt. But I'm skeptical, but agnostic!

3:AM: Now, one of the interesting things happening at the moment in philosophy is x-phi [experimental philosophy]. You wrote a paper with Josh Knobe on Nietzsche and morality, and in that essay, and in your seminal book on Nietzsche's moral philosophy, you make the case for arguing that Nietzsche had three basic beliefs about humans that make this position distinctive and important (and a better description of moral agency than those of its chief rivals, Aristotle and Kant). The challenge of this is that it seems to offer a very different view of what it is to be human than is usually presented. Do you believe that a change of the human self-image is indeed what follows from this approach, and can you say what the opportunities and risks attached to this are?

LEITER: You are quite right that the Nietzschean conception of the person involves a very different view of what it is to be human. In the Nietzschean view, our conscious life is largely superficial, largely epiphenomenal—we are, as in the Freudian picture, largely creatures of our drives, many of which are unknown to us, except obliquely. But Nietzsche, unlike Freud, is not especially optimistic about the capacity for "ego" to exercise much rational influence on these drives— though it can exercise some, but only when it acquires the motivational energy of opposing drives behind it. To make matters worse, Nietzsche thinks our particular constellation of drives is a kind of biological legacy, so we are, in a kind of naturalized Calvinist fashion, set on a particular course in life long before we become aware of it; that's why Nietzsche says, famously, that "one becomes what one is without knowing what one is." So one's life, on this picture, is largely a matter of figuring out what one already is—basically the opposite of the existential picture we associate with Sartre, who was, alas, a superficial reader of Nietzsche.

I think one reason Nietzsche thinks that "illusion" and "falsehood" are essential to human life is that he recognizes no one can actually live—in the sense of get up in the morning and try to make decisions about what to do—with this picture in mind. So Nietzsche should change what philosophers call our third-person perspective on human beings, and how to understand them, but Nietzsche realized that from the "first-person" perspective (the perspective of you or me thinking about what to do), the illusion of freedom and choice is essential. But it is, to repeat, an illusion, which means we ought to rethink every normative realm dependent on those concepts.

3:AM: Now, from within the naturalism approach, I wonder if there isn't a tension between your Nietzschean idea that there are human types and empirical evidence that there isn't enough stability in any human behavior to justify saying that we can conform to type.

LEITER: You're quite correct that there is a tension between Nietzschean moral psychology, which depends on a notion of a psychological "type" or "character," and the situationist themes in a lot of social psychology, which call attention to the influence of particular situational cues on behavior. I think there are two key points to make about this apparent conflict. First, the actual empirical results make perfect sense from a Nietzschean point of view: for in all the famous case studies—including the Milgram experiments about obedience to authority—there is always some minority of subjects who are not influenced at all by the situational cues. So, in the case of the Milgram studies, there are some who simply refuse to turn up the voltage, despite being ordered to do so by the experimenter "in charge." It's quite natural to think that these were precisely the folks with character, while those who complied with even outrageous directives betrayed precisely their lack of character. Nietzsche certainly wouldn't be surprised that most "herd animals" will do what they're told! Milgram himself didn't think his experiments showed that character was explanatorily otiose in understanding behavior. Second, and this is a point I owe to Joshua Knobe and that we make in our jointly authored paper to which you allude, it may well turn out that situational cues are important to understanding behavior on particular occasions, and still be true that character type gives you the best explanation of behavior over the long haul, as it were. In the end, I suspect the situationist challenge to character-based explanations has been much overplayed, both with respect to what the actual results show and with respect to their import for a plausible moral psychology.

What happens to "reason" depends on what is meant by reason. Kant will not be happy on either the situationist or Nietzschean view. But that's because Kantians think reason can dictate our ultimate ends, not simply the means to deploy in service of ends that have no rational standing. That marks another important dividing line in the history of philosophy—about the deliverances of practical reason—and, unsurprisingly, I'm on the anti-Kantian, thoroughly naturalist and realist side of that debate.

3:AM: You have taken a distinctive approach to the place of religious beliefs in society. We're very familiar with the approach to the debate presented in terms of the science—so figures like Dawkins and Dennett and Hitchens tend to fix on the truth of religious claims to oppose religions. Your approach is different in that it's about claims constitutional, legal, and just; and these don't justify treating religious beliefs separately from any other. Is that right? Can you say something about your ideas about religious tolerance?

LEITER: This is the subject of the book *Why Tolerate Religion?* I share one thing with "New Atheists" like Dawkins et al., namely, the assumption that religions involve significant amounts of false belief. It's a bit too late in the day for that to be a serious topic of debate, since the evidence is all on only one side of that question. But I'm Nietzschean enough to realize that the fact that religion involves a lot of false belief goes no distance to deciding its value, its contributions to human well-being, its centrality to human life. If we only were allowed to believe what was true, after all, we'd give up on life pretty quickly, since, as Nietzsche likes to say, "The truth is terrible"! So I come at this from a very different angle. My initial question was whether, if you think "liberty" or "freedom" of conscience is valuable, something that ought to be protected, whether there was some reason to think that only religious claims of conscience should enjoy its benefits. And the strange reality, even in Europe—which is largely an atheistic continent now (the spectacle of the pope notwithstanding)—is that the only times the courts will exempt someone from a generally applicable law is when they assert that their religion requires them, as a matter of conscience, not to comply. We understand well enough how, as an historical matter, this came to pass: the bloody wars of religion that tortured Europe in the early modern period led to the idea that religious toleration would be a better alternative. But that's history, and the question is whether, today, there is some reason to think religious conscience is more important than any other claim of conscience. I argue that there isn't.

3:AM: You don't seem to like English departments, in the United States at least. Is this right? Is it because they seem to be in thrall to obscurantist philosophers, as you characterize them, such as Derrida? Or are you like Alex Rosenberg in his new book where he largely dismisses the study of literature per se?

LEITER: I love literature, and love the study of literature—indeed, I was almost an English major in college. One problem with a lot of American English departments in the 1980s was that they stopped teaching literature and became the repositories for bad philosophy, bad history, bad social science! Rosenberg's position is a bracing one, and a useful challenge to lazy anti-naturalist tendencies in a lot of anglophone philosophy, but it does seem to me to be based ultimately on armchair philosophy of the kind naturalists are supposed to decry. Physicalism is not a scientific result—Carnap thought it would be, but we know it isn't the case that everything that is causally explicable is explicable in terms of causal relata that are physical. So my view on this issue is certainly not Rosenberg's, as much as I admire his work. In any case, it seems to me that American literature departments have recovered quite a bit from the intellectual disaster of the 1980s, a happy development. And if I may paraphrase Nietzsche, life without literature would be a mistake!

3:AM: And finally, you have written harsh things about the state of the press in the United States, but of course it's not just the United States that has the deficit. Given the state of the world at the moment, the erosion of a strong fourth estate seems to be worrying. Are you optimistic about the future, not just in terms of press freedoms and ownership but generally?

LEITER: This is one of the few areas where the internet has made a positive difference to human freedom and well-being. The United States is obviously at one extreme in terms of the supine posture of its media, as well as its low intellectual level—and I'm not even talking here about the more-or-less openly fascist media like Fox News! But the internet now makes available the media in multiple jurisdictions, at least to anyone who looks. I often read Al Jazeera's English site, not because they are paragons of journalistic objectivity and intellectual depth but because their biases and blinders are not those of the *New York Times*. So I think one reason to be optimistic is that as the United States fades as a hegemonic power, other countries, with very different agendas, will support media that make very different judgments about what is newsworthy, what sources are credible, whose suffering counts, and so on. Fascists like Rupert Murdoch may destroy the major media in some countries, but it's a big world out there, and the internet makes it available. That's a reason for hope.

2 | Jason Stanley
PHILOSOPHY AS THE GREAT NAÏVETÉ

Jason Stanley is a leading American philosopher who works in the
philosophy of language, philosophical logic, epistemology, and early
analytic philosophy at Yale University. He has written three books: *Know
How* (Oxford University Press, 2011); *Language in Context: Selected Essays*
(Oxford University Press, 2007) and *Knowledge and Practical Interests*
(Oxford University Press, 2005). He is a well-known polemical defender
of the importance of philosophy.

3:AM: You have strong views about philosophy in general, in particular the
public perception of its place in the academic curriculum. You wrote a piece,
"The Crisis of Philosophy," where you said that in America at least, the place
of philosophy in the humanities was unclear. You've been engaged in a number
of high-profile defenses of the subject, from the *New York Times* to the rousing
debate with Carlin Romano. Can you say why you think there's a suspicion of
philosophy, and a kind of crisis, and why you defend the important place
of philosophy in our culture?

STANLEY: There has always been a suspicion of philosophy, dating back to
Socrates. The talk of "crisis" falsely suggests that there is something new about
the issue of the relevance of philosophical work. Hannah Arendt is right when
she describes as unavoidable the question, "How can anything relevant for the
world we live in arise out of so resultless an enterprise?" There is also no new
crisis in the discipline. Philosophy itself is and ought to be in continuous crisis.
There are areas of philosophy that have obvious relevance for the world we live
in. For example, it's obvious that Doug Husak's work has extrinsic value; he
uses philosophical reasoning to criticize the prison industrial complex, the great
moral failing of our country.

But ethics and philosophy of law are not my areas. I have spent my life thinking about knowledge, representation, and intelligent action, and I hold out the perhaps naïve hope that a greater understanding of the capacities that make humans distinctive in the world will end up having relevance beyond simply an expanded self-understanding. I'm also engaging in philosophy when I write about the value of philosophy. There is a grand tradition of skepticism about my field—Hume and even more clearly Nietzsche come to mind. It's sad that there are no current sophisticated defenders of that tradition with whom to engage, because it's healthy for philosophers to be forced to defend the worldly relevance of what they are doing. The fact that I work on questions that do not have *obvious* extrinsic value makes the intellectual challenge more formidable. But I think that my philosophical work is better because I take this intellectual challenge seriously. That said, I do think the estrangement between philosophy and our fellow humanities takes a particular form right now. There has been genuine progress in neighboring areas in the humanities. The progress has come through the realization of how much of the traditional humanities was done from a specific empowered, privileged perspective, either a white European male perspective or from the perspective of the state and not its inhabitants, and the realization of how taking such a perspective skewed the work.

Think, for example, of the time in the 1960s when it became clear to historians, via belated recognition of the work of Du Bois, that historical research on the Reconstruction era in the south was largely inaccurate, and the inaccuracies were due to underlying racial biases of the historians. In almost every humanities discipline, there are examples like this—cases in which it was realized that biased perspectives resulted in shoddy and inaccurate work or scholarship. The recognition of the pervasive nature of implicit (or explicit) bias in perspective, and the recognition that such bias impedes truth-seeking enterprises, was an important moment in intellectual culture. But it left the discipline of philosophy relatively untouched. That has created an even-wider-than-usual gulf between the rest of the humanities and philosophy.

Finally, as I emphasized in my *Inside Higher Education* piece, there is an additional difference between philosophy and the humanities, one that is less profound but nevertheless equally divisive. Our fellow humanists write *about* novelists and artists and musicians. In contrast, the intellectual life of most philosophers is closer to that of novelists and artists and musicians than people who study novelists and artists. There is great naïveté in the ambition to write the great American novel, naïveté that is mirrored in the ambition to solve some of the long-standing philosophical questions once and for all. It's utterly natural to view someone who is trying to write the great American novel, or is trying to explain once and for all how autonomous action is possible, as not only naïve but also ignorant (of the greatness of Melville, or the greatness of Kant). So there really is a cultural divide between the vast majority of humanists and the majority of philosophers.

3:AM: One of the things that will support your defense of philosophy is getting more people to see what you and your peers are doing. It's sometimes difficult for those outside the discipline to get a grip on the geography of what's going on that's important at the moment. Eric Schwitzgebel's just posted on his blog about how there can be philosophy of more or less anything, even dating, which kind of makes the point about how difficult it is to know where to look. Philosophy of language may be where you are best situated, so perhaps you could give a broad outline of what the main issues are in that domain at the moment. I love your comment about your piece on philosophy of language in the twentieth century for Routledge ["Pragmatics and Context: The Development of Intentional Semantics," in *The Routledge Companion to Philosophy of Language*] where you say, "I attempt to summarize philosophy of language in the Twentieth Century. It's a completely absurd task, and I fail miserably." We'll take another failure if it's as good as that one!

STANLEY: Let me begin by responding to your points about the relative accessibility of philosophical work. Even topics the significance of which is obvious to the lay public involve arguments that will stretch the patience of the lay public. For example, the significance of the topic of consciousness is very easy for the lay public to understand. But the best work on even this topic involves stretches of reasoning that are dauntingly complex. The conclusions David Chalmers draws from his views are accessible and sexy to the public. But the views of content he has that support these conclusions are deep, complex, and subtle. They are certainly not accessible to the lay public. It's the arguments he gives that make him a great philosopher, rather than the accessibility of his conclusions. As Peter Ludlow emphasized in his comments at the Philosophical Progress conference at Harvard [The Harvard-ANU Symposium on the Progress of Philosophy, September 2012], philosophers need to introduce terminology that may not have pre-established usage. A successful definition carves up conceptual space the right way. This makes philosophical work, like mathematical work, terminologically heavy. Mathematical progress depends in part on arriving at the right sort of definitions—what Frege in *The Foundations of Arithmetic* called "fruitful definitions" (the example Frege gives is that of the continuity of a function). Philosophical progress is no different. Both mathematics and philosophy are difficult to access, because they are terminology heavy in similar ways.

Philosophy of language is particularly close to mathematics in this regard, because of how close it is to mathematical logic. As I emphasized in my piece on philosophy of language in the twentieth century, philosophy of language has made so many advances because of the advances in logic in the late nineteenth and early twentieth century. Developments in logic, and in particular model-theoretic semantics, gave impetus to the discipline, and its sibling empirical discipline in linguistics, formal semantics. Right now, there is a large body of researchers sprawled across philosophy, linguistics, and computer science (and perhaps psychology as well) working on similar topics. If you take Rutgers as an example, the leading program in philosophy of language in the world, you see that our semantics research group has active faculty members in linguistics, computer science, and philosophy. I would describe the principal goal of all of our work, as with my own research in the philosophy of language, to be devoted to figuring out how much of linguistic interpretation is due to convention, and how much is due to general knowledge about the world. There was a trend in the philosophy of language starting in the 1970s to argue that what appeared to be due to linguistic conventions was in fact due to knowledge about the world and general reasoning. Probably, this divorced philosophical work on linguistic representation from thought about representation elsewhere in the humanities, where theorists were looking for symbol-like representational systems everywhere. Philosophy of language instead was devoted to emphasizing how little conventionality played a role in linguistic communication.

As I have also pointed out in the essay you mention, this was the result of quite accidental sociological features of the discipline—because of the titanic influence of Saul Kripke's work, in the 1970s and the 1980s the focus of the discipline was on defending the view that proper names that had the same reference, such as "Mark Twain" and "Samuel Clemens," had the same conventional meaning. A lot of energy in the discipline was devoted to defending this thesis. There was interesting work done here, but also some stagnation. There was a sort of template for writing a philosophy-of-language paper for several decades: start with an interesting phenomenon that seems to reveal complex conventionality (like the difference in meaning between "Mark Twain" and "Samuel Clemens," or the fact that "Every beer is in the fridge" can convey different things in different contexts), and argue that really the symbol system itself gives us very little guidance in interpretation. This really isolated the philosophy of language from many disciplines—both the humanities at large, and linguistic semantics, and even formal pragmatics in linguistics, where people were interested precisely in investigating the special features of the symbolic system.

In the mid-to-late 1990s, a group of philosophers of language with training in linguistics started to reverse the trend and focus on the special, quirky properties of symbolic systems. As a result, philosophy of language has emerged from its relative isolation. Because the focus in philosophy of language was for so long on arguing what the symbolic system *didn't* do, there was a lot of catching up to do. A lot of the interesting topics and developments, such as research into the meaning of questions, had moved into linguistic semantics, where it was a bit divorced from philosophical concerns. Now, there is a great deal of excitement in the field, as people have realized that there is so much more complexity to linguistic meaning than we had realized. Philosophers such as Elizabeth Camp have started to see that there is a case to be made that phenomena that seemed *obviously* not conventional in nature, such as sarcasm, might be conventional after all. The discovery by Andy Egan, John Hawthorne, and Brian Weatherson that epistemic modals—terms like "might" as they occur in a sentence like "It might be raining outside now" (said by someone ignorant of the weather)—behave in ways very different than standard models of meaning would predict has led to the thought that a new model of meaning might be required. Motivated by the complex properties of very simple words, philosophers and linguistic semanticists have started to formulate new theories of content, giving new life to old programs such as expressivism.

So it's a very exciting time in the philosophy of language, and has been for about a dozen years. For a long time, philosophers of language had thought that there was nothing foundational to be learned anymore from detailed work on particular constructions in language. We have now learned that this is false. Thinking intensely about the meaning of words like "might" or "if," or the relation between the meaning of questions and declarative sentences, has led to really interesting discoveries. We are at the beginning, rather than at the end, of inquiry into the complex properties of the distinctive representational system that is natural language.

3:AM: Now, one of the subjects that you keep returning to is Ryle's distinction between knowing that and knowing how. Before you tell us about your argument, which I believe is to say that knowing how is a species of knowing that, can you say what's at stake here? I think sometimes one of the problems for outsiders is that they don't pick up on the large and important issues that the detailed arguments are then engaged in sorting out.

STANLEY: There are two ways to look at my new book. The first is that I am using a defense of the thesis that knowing how to do something is knowledge of a truth to shed light on the notion of knowledge. The second is that I am using a defense of the thesis that knowing how to do something is knowledge of a truth to shed light on the nature of knowledge how and related notions such as *skill*. Philosophy, and indeed broader intellectual culture, is in the grip of a false conception of factual knowledge, one that is antithetical to much recent work in epistemology. Once one has the correct externalist conception of knowledge, a dichotomy between practical and theoretical knowledge starts to look dubious. To use an example Robert Stalnaker suggested to me, think of my knowledge that the code to an alarm is 17-32-14. I may not be able to tell you what the combination is; I just can type into the alarm pad. The knowledge resides, so to speak, in my fingers. But it's still propositional knowledge: I know that the code to the alarm is 17-32-14, but I just can't tell you. One reason the conclusions of *Know How* matter is that they free us from a constraining and misleading picture of propositional knowledge.

A second reason the conclusions of *Know How* matter is that they shed light on how much of skilled action is due to learning information about the world. Knowledge how to do something is a large part (or maybe all of) skill. I can only be skilled at basketball if I know how to play basketball. If I am right that knowledge of how to do something amounts to learning a truth, then we learn that skilled action requires learning something about the world. Even if I'm right, the question is open as to how much of the acquisition of a skill is acquiring information about the world. Does knowledge exhaust skill, or is skill knowledge together with something else? What about improvements in skill? Does that amount to additional knowledge about the world? There are a whole set of questions and positions about the notion of skill that are opened up here.

It is of the utmost importance for philosophy to gain greater clarity on what is involved in acquiring a skill, since skill and competence plays such a central role in so many philosophical projects. For example, virtue epistemologists hold that propositional knowledge relies on skills—think of the appeal to competence in the work of, for example, Ernest Sosa. The appeal to skill in Sosa's work has a reductive character: knowledge requires competence, and competence itself does not presuppose knowledge. It is important that competence does not presuppose knowledge, since competence, for the virtue epistemologist, halts the regress of justification. If knowledge how is propositional knowledge, many if not all versions of virtue epistemology are imperiled. There are many other uses of the notion of skill in philosophy that will need to be rethought if the conclusions of my book are correct. Philosophers have typically assumed that knowing how and skill are not propositional knowledge states, and used these notions in their theories. Generally, the pattern of argument is to establish some connection between the target notion to be analyzed—be it linguistic understanding, virtue, knowledge, or perception—and knowing how. The assumption that knowing how is a nonpropositional state is then brought in to solve some kind of problem, for example to halt a regress, or to provide a reductive, nonfactual basis for something. There are projects in epistemology, in ethics, in philosophy of mind, and in philosophy of language that have this character. In general, if I'm right, all of these philosophical projects have to be rethought.

The topic of the relation between knowing how to do something and factual knowledge is not local to philosophy. It has been picked up by many disciplines. For example, it is a label for a distinction in artificial intelligence, and is thought to mirror a fundamental distinction in cognitive neuroscience, between procedural and declarative knowledge. My book takes up all of these issues. For example, in chapter 7, I argue that the cognitive neuroscientific discussion of declarative knowledge is muddled. And obviously, many disciplines care about the notion of skill. The thesis of my book bears on all of this work.

3:AM: Another area of interest is that of the role of context in making meaning. Your book of essays, *Language in Context*, contains a treasure trove of your thoughts on this area. Again, though, would you just lay out why this is an important issue outside of philosophy before we look at some of your arguments?

STANLEY: My work in the philosophy of language is devoted to preserving a certain view of linguistic representation. Think of a basic nonlinguistic act of communication, such as a tap on the shoulder or a kick under the table. We do not interpret what is communicated by such acts by applying highly specific rules to structured representations. Interpreting such acts does not involve much convention. Instead, we rely on our general knowledge about the world, together with facts about the context in which the act is performed. Prima facie, linguistic communication is different. With linguistic communication, we rely on conventions governing the representations we employ. But there is a lot of reliance on general world knowledge and facts about the context of use even in linguistic communication. So the context dependence of what is communicated by an utterance of a sentence provides an argument that linguistic communication and nonlinguistic communication are not so different after all.

The purpose of my work on context is to save the prima facie distinction between linguistic communication and nonlinguistic communication, in the face of this kind of challenge. In contrast to nonlinguistic communication, I argue that the role knowledge of context plays in linguistic understanding, and production, is limited to a few conventional sources. In short, the goal of this work is to preserve a theoretically significant distinction between linguistic and nonlinguistic communication.

All of my philosophical interests coalesce around explaining the properties that make humans distinctive. My work in philosophy of language is part of this project. Sophisticated language use is one of the properties that are distinctive of our species. This strongly suggests that it involves a distinctive kind of representational mechanism. This gives me confidence to pursue the difficult details of accounting for the fact that, like nonlinguistic communication, it relies on knowledge of facts about the context of use.

I tend to assume in this work that linguistic communication is distinctive in being the application of highly specific (and conventional) rules to structured representations. I tend to assume, for example, that pictorial representation works differently. But the work of Gabriel Greenberg, now a professor of philosophy at UCLA, has cast some doubt in my mind on the distinctiveness claim. He mounts a good case that at least some kinds of pictorial representation involve many of the same features as linguistic representation.

3:AM: You won a top prize for your book *Knowledge and Practical Interests*. There you claim that my knowing something is dependent on my practical interests. So knowledge turns out to be dependent on how much it matters! This is counterintuitive—and so. exactly what I want from my philosophers! So could you explain this position. and why you argue what you do?

STANLEY: My two books about knowledge are connected. Both take on the distinction between the practical and the theoretical. In my first book, I argue that there isn't the kind of sharp divide between practical and theoretical reasoning that we learned there was in our introductory philosophy classes (when we, for example, discussed Pascal's Wager). In my second book, I take on the distinction between practical and theoretical knowledge. Both books are in the service of explaining the value of knowledge by connecting knowledge to action. My specific argument for the stakes sensitivity of knowledge, the thesis that whether or not you know something at a time is dependent upon how much the knowledge matters to you at that time, has to do with the connections between knowledge and action. For example, if I am right, then if you know something you can act on it. But whether you can permissibly act on something depends on what is at stake—whether I can act on my belief that there are nuts in my salad depends upon whether I have a fatal allergy to nuts. It is via the connection to action that knowledge gains its dependence on what is at stake. I deny that the thesis is counterintuitive. It's commonsensical to think that if what's at issue really matters, you need to do more work in order to know something. Knowing that a country poses a threat to the United States requires a huge amount of investigation, if what is at stake is the decision to go to war.

3:AM: Another area that you have intervened in is that of intention in action. There's been a lot of recent interest in this subject through the 2011 book *Essays on Anscombe's Intention*. It seems as if you take issue with those philosophers who argue for a notion of direct knowledge-action that is incompatible with causation (that is, those who move away from Davidson's interpretation; I guess McDowell is the parade case?). It's something you write about in a dispute with Jennifer Hornsby, a contributor to the Anscombe book, in terms of the phenomenology of meaning. Is that right? This is another of these big issues where the stakes are not always made clear to outsiders. But this dispute seems to be about the scope of a scientific causal explanation in human intention. Those arguing for the idea of a "direct" thing outside the scope of a causal relation almost sound like they're saying we don't need science or can't have a scientific explanation of intention. I always feel a bit lost with this because I'm sure that there's something I'm really missing here. Can you say what the big issue is with this and what your take on it is?

STANLEY: My 2005 debate with Jennifer Hornsby is but one chapter in my overall project of emphasizing the centrality of factual knowledge, properly understood. Hornsby argues that knowledge of meaning is not factual knowledge, but something else, practical knowledge. I argue, against her, that knowledge of meaning is indeed factual knowledge. Again, the significance of this debate is that it bears on the nature of factual knowledge, and the nature of skill. Knowledge of meaning is just one of the battlegrounds in the larger war about whether factual knowledge is what gives us the capacities that make us distinctively human.

3:AM: I think we can see that you are wrestling with core issues that are not orthogonal to the deep, eternal, and traditional philosophical questions. We are living in hugely complex times, and troubling ones too. The financial crisis, mass inequality, war, eco doom—there's a hell of a lot out there that, it seems, needs philosophical thinking. What do you think will be the dominant themes, contributions, and discoveries of philosophy in the next decade? Where are your interests going next?

STANLEY: I can't predict where philosophy is going next. Probably that question has as much to do with accidental sociological features of the discipline as anything else. I have been consistently working on a general picture of knowledge and agency for many years now, and increasingly find myself isolated from the hive mind in philosophy. I have been working for about twelve years on my book on knowing how, which I started as a joint project with Timothy Williamson. I took time out from this project to write my first book (which, as I've said, is related). My own work over the next several years will be devoted to exploring some of the consequences of my work, both within philosophy, for the projects of virtue epistemology and virtue ethics, and also the cognitive sciences. For example, I want to continue the research I started in cognitive neuroscience, and in general track the notion of skill across the various disciplines that study it. However, I am easily distractible. This is why I have published on so many different topics (of course my extensive project in philosophy of language is not connected to my main work in epistemology and action theory). I expect I will continue to do research on a wide variety of topics not directly related to my central philosophical life project. I'm also interested in certain topics in philosophy of language that relate to politics, such as the nature of propaganda (as in my recent *New York Times* piece). I have been thinking a lot lately of how politicians and their handlers use the special features of our symbolic system to manipulate us. It's an interesting enough topic that I can imagine eventually writing something substantial on it.

3:AM: And finally, are there things outside of philosophy itself—such as the arts, novels, and so on—that you find to be a source of inspiration and help. So has there been something you read that has helped shape your perspective on the issues you brood on?

STANLEY: The issues I brood about and the literature I read when I'm not absorbed in philosophy have exclusively to do with man's inhumanity to man. I'm not yet sure whether philosophy is my refuge, or where I think I will ultimately find the explanation.

3 | Eric Schwitzgebel
THE SPLINTERED SKEPTIC

Eric Schwitzgebel is a philosopher of moral psychology, philosophy of mind, cognitive science, epistemology, philosophy of science, and Chinese philosophy at the University of California, Riverside. He is the author of *Perplexities of Consciousness* (MIT Press, 2011) and, with Russell T. Hurlburt, *Describing Inner Experience? Proponent Meets Skeptic* (MIT Press 2007). His blog *The Splintered Mind* is a leading philosophical blog in the United States.

3:AM: I think that it's going to be helpful to put your thoughts in the context of something that you and Russell Hurlburt wrote about in your first book, *Describing Inner Experience?* where you say that despite all the advances in our knowledge about the universe we know very little about our own conscious experience. And yet we have writers of fiction, for example, telling stories where they claim to be telling us what is happening in the minds of their characters. And we make judgments of quality based on these reports; we seem to be able to say that some descriptions are richer than others and we like these. So Proust and Joyce, for example, are considered top writers because of their ability to probe the phenomenology of minds. But you think that it's bunk. We're being fooled. We are just in the grip of illusions about our own experiences. Is this right?

SCHWITZGEBEL: Proust and Joyce—and Woolf, who is my favorite in that line—are brilliant artists. But the stream of real human thought is probably much less interesting to most people than what is portrayed in their fiction. Our real stream of thought is probably no more really like the streams of thought we see in their writings than Elizabethan-era conversations were really like what we see in Shakespeare plays. It's stylized art, in a medium of words.

There are some things we know about our stream of experience. For example, if you're looking in good light at a canonically red object and you think you are having a visual experience of redness, you're probably right. But as I have argued in both of my books, I think we quickly fall into error when we try to go beyond a few obvious things. People seem to err massively when they start to think about such issues as what their imagery is like (sketchy or detailed? flat like a picture or with depth?), or their dream experiences (colored or black and white? first-person or third-person point of view?), their emotional phenomenology, or their stream of thought. You might think that you think about sex all the time and actually you think about it hardly at all. You might think you're a poor visualizer with almost no imagery experience and yet actually have lots of imagery going on. Russ Hurlburt has some terrific examples of this latter sort of thing in his work, which involves beeping people at random moments and interviewing them very carefully about what they were experiencing at those moments. My book with him is just one of his many projects. And yet ultimately I am much more skeptical than Russ is.

Early modern philosophers such as Descartes and Locke thought that we know first and best our own stream of experience, and then, based on that secure knowledge, we reach more tenuous conclusions about the outside world of physical objects. I think that's almost exactly backwards. What we know first and best are outside objects. Our knowledge of our stream of experience is much shakier, later developing, and often directly dependent on our knowledge of things outside. I know that I'm having a visual experience of red because I know I'm looking in good light at a red thing, not the other way around. And that case only works well because it's so clean. Introduce a bit of noise or weirdness, and we start to fail.

Twentieth century psychologists like Freud and Nisbett argued that we don't know our own motives very well, but neither of them really challenges knowledge of our stream of inner experience. For both of them, there's a big unconscious that we don't know about, but we still know about our ongoing consciousness. So my skepticism goes farther than theirs.

3:AM: So you've some experiments to back up your claims about this. Can you take us through some of them to get readers to understand why you're making such counterintuitive claims?

SCHWITZGEBEL: I appeal to three different types of evidence. First, I appeal to the reader's own sense of her experience. For example, right now, form a visual image of something, maybe your house as viewed from the street. Now let me ask some questions. How clear is that image? Is it clear in the center and sketchy at the periphery, or is it all clear simultaneously? Do you have to build up clarity in it over time? Is the image thoroughly colored from the outset, or do you have to add colors to it? Is the image in some sense flat like a picture, or is it more richly three-dimensional than that? Is the image stable over time, or does it shift around a lot with changes in your attention? Most readers I have chatted with, when presented with these questions and others like them, discover some questions about which they are uncertain and about which they could easily imagine people erring. Comparably sized questions about nearby external objects—whether they are thoroughly colored, stable over time, etc.— seem much easier to answer. Even if such doubt-inducing exercises aren't entirely convincing on their own, I think they help prepare the reader to find my general skeptical conclusions more plausible and palatable. Philosophers who think we have infallible knowledge of our stream of experience tend to focus on a few particular examples, like seeing red and feeling pain in vivid, canonical conditions. But those cases are highly unrepresentative, I think. When we consider real, naturally occurring experiences and carefully consider medium-sized questions about them, it becomes much less tempting to think we have excellent self-knowledge of the stream of experience.

Second, I describe the strange and suspicious diversity of opinion about the stream of experience across the history of philosophy and psychology— diversity that I think suggests error in reporting, not real differences in underlying experience. For example, in the United States in the 1950s, people used to say they dreamed almost exclusively in black and white. Now people say they dream in color. Before the 20th century, philosophers and psychologists used to say or assume that we dream in color. What's the deal? Well, I think it has to do with the fact that the 1950s were the heyday of black-and-white film media in the United States. This relationship between film media and reports of dream coloration holds cross-culturally too, as I found in a Chinese study I did with Changbing Huang and Yifeng Zhou. In the early 2000s, rural Chinese people with lots of black-and-white media exposure tended to report black-and-white dreaming, while high-wealth urban Chinese with very little black-and-white media exposure reported mostly colored dreaming. Have the media hijacked our dreams, so that when the media are black and white so are our dreams? I don't think so. For example, if you look at dream diaries in the 1950s versus the 1990s in the United States, color terms like "red" and "green" appear at virtually the same rate. My hypothesis is rather that some people are wrong about the coloration or not of their dreams, overanalogizing their dream experiences to movies. Either people reporting mostly black-and-white dreaming are wrong, or those reporting mostly colored dreaming are wrong, or both groups are wrong. (The last possibility is my favorite, but you'll have to read chapter 1 of my 2011 book, *Perplexities of Consciousness*, to see why.)

Third, I examine the instability and variability of people's reports of their own experiences in the contemporary West. For example, I interview people about their visual experiences of the periphery of vision. Over the course of the interview, people regularly change their opinions about what it's like to see. At the beginning, most people say that they visually experience a broad field of stable clarity, with indistinctness only in the margins, say 20 or 30 or 50 degrees from the center; by the end of the interview, most people say they were wrong in their original opinion and really they only experience a small point of clarity, maybe 2–5 degrees of arc, that bounces very rapidly around a hazy background. What matters here isn't who's right, but how easily people's opinions change about apparently as central and obvious a thing as the general character and clarity of visual experience. Another point of variability is in people's reports of the vividness of their imagery. Across hundreds of studies, psychologists have generally failed to find any robust relationship between people's subjective reports about their imagery experiences and their performance on cognitive tests that are widely thought to involve imagery, like mental rotation tasks and mental folding tasks. In chapter 3 of *Perplexities*, I defend the view that this lack of correlation reflects people's introspective incompetence in such matters.

3:AM: Now, out of this you have the idea that we are often in a state of in-between beliefs. Can you say what kind of a state this is, and why you call it in-between?

SCHWITZGEBEL: The best way to conceptualize "belief," I think, is that to believe something is to steer one's way through the world as though it were true. And although reaching explicit judgments about things is an important part of steering one's way through the world, much else is even more important. Suppose, for example, that you are disposed to say, in all sincerity, that all the races are intellectually equal. You will argue for this claim against all comers and really feel that you believe it in your heart of hearts. It doesn't follow that you really *do* steer your way through the world as your egalitarian utterances would suggest. You might really be incredibly biased. You might really always treat people of a certain race as though they were stupid. In that case, I don't think we should say that you really, fully believe in the intellectual equality of the races. Instead, I think, you're in a mixed-up condition in which it's neither quite right to say that you believe the races are intellectually equal nor quite right to say that you fail to believe that. I call this an "in-between" state of believing. It's in-between but it's not at all like being uncertain. You might still feel unshakably certain.

I think such in-between states are very common for the attitudes we regard as most central to our lives. Do you really believe that God exists? Do you really believe that family is more important than work? Let's not look just at what you sincerely say to yourself and others but at how you act and how you react. Let's look at your spontaneous valuations of things. Often, the match between sincere words and in-the-world reactivity is poor. And I doubt we have very good self-knowledge about any of this.

It might help repair our ignorance about such matters if we had good knowledge of our stream of experience. If I knew, for example, that I was frequently having angry thoughts about my children, or if I knew that I felt a kind of emotional soaring at the prospect of a new project at work and an emotional crash at the prospect of having to come home early to have lunch with the family—that might provide an important set of clues. But we don't know such things about ourselves, and in fact we regularly fool ourselves in such matters to protect our self-conception.

3:AM: You have come to suggest a new philosophical position, "crazyism." Can you explain your thinking here, and why we should all be crazyists?

SCHWITZGEBEL: Bizarre views are a hazard of metaphysics. If you look across the history of philosophy, all metaphysicians say crazy-seeming things when they talk in depth about such issues as the mind-body relation, personal identity, causation, and the basic ontological structure of the universe. Even philosophers who explicitly prize common sense can't seem to keep true to common sense about such matters. The great "common sense" Scottish philosopher Thomas Reid, for example, attributed immaterial souls to vegetables and said that physical objects can't even cohere into stable shapes without the regular intervention of immaterial souls. So here's the question: Why? Why are there no truly commonsensical metaphysicians? Nietzsche, Leibniz, Schopenhauer, Descartes, David Lewis—all of them say some incredibly bizarre-seeming stuff. Why is metaphysics so uniformly crazy?

My suggestion is this: common sense is incoherent in matters of metaphysics. There's no way to develop an ambitious, broad-ranging, self-consistent metaphysical system without doing serious violence to common sense somewhere. It's just impossible. Since common sense is an inconsistent system, you can't respect it all. Every metaphysician will have to violate it somewhere.

Common sense is an acceptable guide to everyday practical interactions with the world. But there's no reason to think it would be a good guide to the fundamental structure of the universe. Think about all the weirdness of quantum mechanics, all the weirdness of relativity theory. The more we learn about such things, the more it seems we're forced to leave common sense behind. The same is probably true about metaphysics.

But here's the catch: without common sense as a guide, metaphysics is hobbled as an enterprise. You can't do an empirical study, for example, to determine whether there really is a material world out there or whether everything is instead just ideas in our minds coordinated by god. You can't do an empirical study to determine whether there really exist an infinite number of universes with different laws of physics, entirely out of causal contact with our own. We're stuck with common sense, plausibility arguments, and theoretical elegance—and none of these should rightly be regarded as decisive on such matters, whenever there are several very different and yet attractive contender positions, as there always are.

I conclude that regarding the fundamental structure of the universe in general and the mind-body relation in particular as something that seems crazy must be true, but we have no way to know what the truth is among a variety of crazy possibilities. I call this position "crazyism."

3:AM: Is this what motivates you to look at the history of philosophy?

SCHWITZGEBEL: Most philosophers, when they read the history of philosophy, are primarily concerned about one of two things: working out the nuances of the interpretation of various philosophical heroes, or evaluating historical philosophers' claims for truth or falsity. That's not how I approach the history of philosophy. I'm primarily interested in what the history of philosophy tells us about the *psychology* of philosophy. Nietzsche, I think, had a similar attitude. What does it say about how philosophers think, that historical figures in philosophy would say this rather than that? What does it say about the psychological origins of our own current philosophical attitudes?

Consider my answers to some of your previous questions. I've looked across the history of metaphysics to see if any philosopher can sustain a thoroughly commonsensical broad-reaching metaphysical picture. From the fact that no one seems able to pull it off, plus some other considerations, I draw a conclusion about the necessary conflict of metaphysics with common sense. I've looked at the history of philosophical and psychological opinion about colored dreaming and noted that that opinion seems to vary contingently with available cultural metaphors for dreaming. The same media-dependent contingency, I think, influences philosophers' claims about ordinary waking visual experience, which it now seems natural to us to compare to photographs. [See chapter 2, "Do Things Look Flat?" in *Perplexities*.] I've also looked at German philosophers' rates of involvement in Nazism in the 1930s. Heidegger was no exception; many of the leading German philosophers appear to have been swept up in Nazism. From this fact about philosophers, I conclude that expertise in philosophical ethics offers little or no protection against being lured into noxious ideologies. This seems to me to be evidence that professional philosophy doesn't tend to generate lots of real practical wisdom.

Some people think it obvious that professional philosophical ethics doesn't generate moral wisdom and good behavior, but few have argued for it systematically and empirically. In fact, I have a whole series of empirical research projects on the moral behavior of ethics professors.

3:AM: The moral behavior of ethics professors? Surely their behavior is a model of virtue and rationality? Not!!!

SCHWITZGEBEL: I don't feel the cynical pull on this issue that most people seem to feel. It has always seemed to me that philosophical moral reflection—

pondering both grand moral issues and more applied issues about what to do here and now—ought to have an overall positive influence on one's moral behavior. And it seems empirically likely that professional ethicists engage in such reflection more often than do other people, and at least as well. But it has also always struck me, in personal interactions, that ethicists don't in fact behave much differently than other people.

So I went ahead and ran a bunch of empirical studies. Here are some: I looked at the rate at which ethics books are missing from academic libraries compared to non-ethics philosophy books similar in age and popularity. Ethics books are more likely to be missing. With Joshua Rust, I looked at whether professional ethicists in the United States vote more often than other professors (on the assumption that voting is a civic duty), and whether they are any more likely to respond to e-mails designed to look as though written by students. Ethicists behaved the same on both measures. With Josh and several others, I looked at courteous and discourteous behavior at philosophy conferences. Ethicists seem to slam doors, talk rudely during presentations, and leave behind trash at their seats at the same rate as do other philosophy professors. In a survey that Josh and I sent to ethicists, non-ethicist philosophers, and a sample of professors in other fields—again in the United States—we found that although ethicists were much more likely to say it was bad to eat meat they were just as likely as other professors to have reported eating meat at the previous evening meal. And although ethicists tended to say they see more moral value in donating blood, donating organs, and donating money than did other professors, the apparent rate at which they actually do those things appears to be no different overall. And of course there's Nazism, which I have already mentioned.

So I'm inclined to think that we now have systematic empirical evidence, which we didn't have before, that ethicists in fact behave no better, on average, than do other professors, at least in the United States and Nazi Germany. I'm still working on how to reconcile this finding with the practical value of philosophical moral reflection. It would be too easy to snap these results into my general skepticism about philosophical reasoning and about human rationality and self-knowledge, resulting in a diatribe against the value of philosophical ethics. But I think that's too facile. I favor a more complicated story.

3:AM: Now, one of the things you are also is a scholar with interests in Chinese philosophy and philosophers. I think many readers will be like me and confess to knowing little about these philosophers, so could you tell us about what you've been studying in this area?

SCHWITZGEBEL: One of the most valuable things, I think, about reading the history of philosophy is seeing that the broad questions explored by different thinkers are often similar: What is the nature of a person? How should we balance the apparent competing demands of morality? How much do we really know about the world? But the answers to those questions, and the approaches taken to trying to answer those questions, are often very different. And the farther one gets away from the standard canon of Plato, Aristotle, Descartes, Hume, etc., into weird minor philosophers and different cultural traditions, the more diversity one starts to see, I think.

But there is one big problem in making these cultural shifts in one's philosophical reading, which is that many philosophical traditions build upon a network of culturally specific presuppositions, especially religious ones, that are hard to get one's head around and take seriously from a contemporary secular or mainstream American-Christian perspective. This is why ancient China is particularly inviting. Although of course there is a foreignness to the ancient Chinese and things one needs to know about the period to get the most out of the texts, nonetheless the main ancient Chinese philosophers are quite comprehensible at a first pass even without any specialized knowledge of the tradition. This is especially true if one looks beyond Confucius and Laozi to figures like Mozi, Mencius, and Xunzi. Later Chinese philosophers, Indian philosophers, and Islamic philosophers are often not as approachable.

The ancient Chinese philosopher Zhuangzi is among the most interesting radical skeptics in philosophical history. The great Western skeptics—Sextus Empiricus, Montaigne, Bayle, Hume—are all interesting in their own ways, and Zhuangzi is every bit their equal, and yet different. If you're interested in skepticism and you don't read Zhuangzi, you're missing out on a valuable perspective.

The ancient Chinese Confucians Mencius and Xunzi had a very interesting debate about whether human nature is good—about the relation between morality and our natural impulses, about the universality of morality, about the developmental sources of morality and the proper course of moral education. I think we still have a lot to learn from their framing of these issues. In fact, the Mencius-Xunzi debate about human nature is how I got started thinking about the moral behavior of ethics professors.

3:AM: And I think Indian philosophy has been of interest to you as well?

SCHWITZGEBEL: I'm still struggling to get my head into Indian philosophy. It's a very difficult tradition, and I think I will never feel comfortable in it the way I feel comfortable with the ancient Chinese. When I write an article or pull together a course syllabus, I'm interested in looking at things from a broad perspective, historically, if I can do so while keeping things coherent for the student or reader. When I have the knowledge and competence to do so, and I think a philosopher outside the mainstream of the Western tradition has an interesting perspective that I can bring to bear, I will bring that philosopher into the conversation. I am not satisfied with my knowledge of the Indian and

Islamic traditions yet, however. I wish I could fission myself and lead three philosophical lives in constant contact with each other!

3:AM: You have some really wild thought experiments, and as a science fiction fan I want to ask you to talk about a couple! So, can you talk about "Strange Baby" and why it's important? When you put together these ideas do you draw on your reading of sci-fi and watching TV and films to put the experiments together?

SCHWITZGEBEL: Well, "Strange Baby" still needs some work, I think. What intrigues me in science fiction, and what I was trying to take a step toward in that blog post, is similar to what intrigues me in non-Western philosophers. A good science fiction writer can open your mind up to possibilities that you might not have considered before, can break you out of your culturally given shell of presuppositions about how the world must be. I especially like science fiction that explores possibilities around amplification of our cognitive powers and what this means for our sense of personhood and our values. Greg Egan is terrific in this way, I think, especially in *Diaspora* and *Permutation City*. Olaf Stapledon too, especially *Sirius* and *Last and First Men*. Recently I've been enjoying Vernor Vinge's portrayal of group minds in *A Fire Upon the Deep* and *Children of the Sky*, though sometimes I find his plot-to-mind-bending-idea ratio a bit too high.

If we continue on our current technological trajectory for another 50 or 200 years—which I don't regard as a given—I think the human mind and human body might become very different from the human mind and human body as we know them today. Maybe, indeed, as Egan envisions (and also futurist Ray Kurzweil), we will mostly be uploaded onto computers and able to duplicate and alter ourselves at will. Then we might look back upon natural unmodified human beings as only a baby step up from monkeys, terribly cognitively deficient.

Let me bring this back to meta-philosophy. We can barely get right the simplest of logical puzzles (see, for example, the Wason selection task or the Tversky-Kahneman conjunction fallacy). Given that kind of cognitive deficiency, how could we reasonably hope to sustain complicated, abstract philosophy page after page without serious error? How could the giant architectonics of Kant or Hegel, for example, possibly be right? If we go the way Egan and Kurzweil envision, our descendants will laugh at us—hopefully good-naturedly, with some respect for how much we were in fact able to achieve with our little monkey brains.

3:AM: The other idea was the question, "Is the United States conscious?" Great question, and yet there are serious issues at stake here. Can you let people know what the issues are and what the answer is? So, will we wake up one morning and find out that Google rules the world?

SCHWITZGEBEL: My interest in the consciousness of the United States is connected to my "crazyism," my skepticism, and my interest in breaking away from our culturally given presuppositions about the structure of the world. It also connects with my recent interest in Vinge. In anglophone philosophy since the 1960s, the dominant approach to the mind has been materialism: the view that human beings are naturally evolved beings, wholly made out of material stuff like elementary particles, with no immaterial soul of any sort. On materialistic views of consciousness, the reason that we have a stream of conscious experience is that we have brains that represent the world, that can guide us in goal-directed action, and that are massively informationally connected in complex self-regulating loops. It is that fact about the complexity of our organizational structure that is responsible for our having a stream of conscious experience so that there's "something it's like," phenomenologically, to be us, or to be a mouse, while there's nothing it's like (we ordinarily think) to be a toy robot.

But the United States appears to have all those same features! The citizens of the United States are massively informationally connected, in complex self-regulating loops—not in the same way neurons are connected, but just as richly. The United States engages in environmentally responsive coordinated action, for example in invading Iraq or in taxing imports. The United States represents and self-represents, for example via the census and in declaring positions in foreign policy. As far as I can tell, all the kinds of things that materialists tend to regard as special about brains in virtue of which brains give rise to consciousness are also possessed by the United States.

The United States is a large, spatially distributed entity. But why should that matter? Isn't it just morphological prejudice to insist that consciousness be confined to spatially compact entities? The United States is composed of people who are themselves individually conscious. But why should that matter? We can imagine, it seems, conscious aliens whose cognition is implemented not by neurons but by intricate networks of interacting internal insects confined within their bodies, where each insect has a minor animal-like consciousness while the organism as a whole has humanlike consciousness and intelligence. (Maybe such aliens are much-evolved descendants of bee colonies.) In the vast universe, it seems likely that intelligent environmental responsiveness, and consciousness, could emerge in myriad weird ways. It seems chauvinistic provincialism to insist that our way of being conscious is the only possible way. So why not regard group organisms as possibly conscious? And if so, why not the very group organisms in which we already participate, given that they seem to meet standard materialist criteria for consciousness?

It would be crazy to think that the United States is literally conscious in the same sense that you and I are conscious. But, as I mentioned before, I think we have good reason to think that something radically contrary to common sense must be true about the mind-body relationship. Maybe this is one of those weird, true things. Or maybe not. Maybe materialism is wrong. Or maybe, though it seems strange and unjustified to think so, spatial compactness really is necessary for some hunk of material to be conscious. Or. . . . I'm not sure this is something we can figure out with the tools at our disposal.

If it is true that the United States is conscious, I have no idea what to do about it. If the United States is conscious, would Exxon-Mobil also be conscious? Would disbanding a corporation or a nation be a kind of murder? I have no idea. And I guess that maybe I'm different from a lot of other philosophers in that I think it's exhilarating to find myself tossed into such confusion, with my apparent certainties evaporating beneath me.

3:AM: So, here's something that could follow from what you've suggested: if people don't really know what they're feeling, then we shouldn't worry when someone claims to be really unhappy, because hey, what do they know? They're just reading off this report from irrelevant factors. Couldn't we just stop caring because we can't trust these reports anymore? Wouldn't this be both justified and kind of horrible?

SCHWITZGEBEL: Yes, I do think skepticism can be dangerous. Who knows where the politics might lead? For example, people with severe disabilities often report surprisingly good quality of life. I'm told that insurance companies like to discredit those self-reports because then they can justify denying people treatment, saying "Well, despite their reports, five more years of life like that isn't really worth paying for." Now, I too think we ought to be really careful with quality-of-life self-reports, but it makes me nervous that my opinion is so convenient for insurance companies. Overall, though, I doubt that skepticism is more dangerous than certainty.

3:AM: Finally, if you were to give the smart but nonphilosophically trained reader a list of five books that'll blow their heads off with wonder, other than your own of course, what would they be? And your all time favorite film?

SCHWITZGEBEL: Tough call! I think everyone finds different things wonderful. Here are some of my favorites, for what it's worth, in no particular order:

Oliver Sacks, The Man Who Mistook His Wife for a Hat; Olaf Stapledon, *Sirius*; Greg Egan, *Diaspora* and/or *Permutation City*; Jorge Luis Borges, *Labyrinths*; Thomas Kuhn, *The Structure of Scientific Revolutions*.

My all-time favorite film is *My Dinner with Andre*. I watched it over and over again in college, gradually shifting sympathies from Andre to Wally. I really have no idea whether that film is any good. My perspective on it now is too personally laden with memories.

4 | Mark Rowlands

HOUR OF THE WOLF

Mark Rowlands is a philosopher of mind and cognitive science, and applied ethics, focusing in particular on the moral status of nonhuman animals and the natural environment and cultural criticism, broadly construed, and also on attempts to convince the general public of the wonders of philosophy. He has written 15 books: *Running with the Pack* (2013); *Can Animals Be Moral?* (2012); *The New Science of the Mind* (2010); *The Philosopher and the Wolf* (2008); *Fame* (2008); *Body Language: Representing in Action* (2006); *Everything I Know I Learned from TV: Philosophy for the Unrepentant Couch Potato* (2005); *The Philosopher at the End of the Universe* (2003), retitled *Sci-Phi: Philosophy from Socrates to Schwarzenegger, 2nd edition*; *Externalism: Putting Mind and World Back Together Again* (2003); *Animals Like Us* (2002); *The Nature of Consciousness* (2001); *The Environmental Crisis: Understanding the Value of Nature* (2000); *The Body in Mind: Understanding Cognitive Processes* (1999); *Animal Rights: A Philosophical Defence* (1998); and *Supervenience and Materialism* (1995).

3:AM: So you are a man who lived amongst wolves—well, one wolf, at least, Brenin—for a decade. Can you say something more about all this?

ROWLANDS: Brenin was sold to me as a wolf. But I think it is likely that he was a wolf-dog mix. The book was about the ways in which we differentiate ourselves from other animals—the stories we tell to convince ourselves of our superiority. Each story, I argued, has a dark side—each story casts a shadow. And in each case, what is most revealing is not the story itself, but the fact that we believe it and think it important. I focused on three common stories. The first is that we are better than other animals because we are more intelligent. The second is that we are better because we have morality—we can understand right and wrong—and they do not. The third is that we are superior because we, and we alone, understand that we are going to die. Intelligence, morality, and our sense of our own mortality were the three major themes of the book. I am far from convinced that any of these stories can establish or underwrite a critical gulf between us and other animals. But in *The Philosopher and the Wolf*, I was more interested in what each story reveals about us. That is, I was interested in what our valuing of these things says about us. I argued that when we dig down far enough into the roots of each of these things, we find features of ourselves that are deeply unflattering. At the roots of our intelligence we find manipulation and machination. In the roots of our morality we find power and lies. And our sense of our mortality renders us fractured creatures, unable to understand ourselves in any satisfactory way. This philosophical excavation was woven into the story of the decade or so I was fortunate enough to spend living and traveling with Brenin.

3:AM: Clearly this experience is a profound one, and you write about it as an example of the storytelling facility that you think helps understand ourselves, don't you?

ROWLANDS: When I was 27, I did something really rather stupid. Actually, I almost certainly did many stupid things that year—I was, after all, 27—but this is the only one I remember because it went on to indelibly shape the future course of my life. When I first met Brenin, I was a young assistant professor of philosophy at the University of Alabama, and he was six weeks old, a cuddly little teddy bear of a wolf/wolf-dog cub. Whatever he was, he grew up, and with this came various, let us call them, idiosyncrasies. If I left him unattended for more than a few minutes, he would destroy anything he could lay his jaws on—which, given that he grew to be thirty-five inches at the withers, included pretty much everything that wasn't screwed to the ceiling. I don't know if he was easily bored, had separation anxiety, or claustrophobia, or some combination of all of these things.

But the result was that Brenin had to go everywhere I did. Any socializing I did—bars, parties, and so on—Brenin had to come too. If I went on a date, he would play the lupine gooseberry. I took him to lectures with me at the university. He would lie down and sleep in the corner of the lecture room: most of the time anyway—when he didn't, things would get interesting. I mean, you can probably imagine the circumstances that caused me to append this little cautionary note to my syllabus: "Note: Please do not pay any attention to the wolf. He will not hurt you. However, if you do have any food in your bags, please ensure that those bags are securely fastened shut."

As a result of having to share a life with a rootless and restless philosopher, Brenin became not only a highly educated wolf—the recipient of more free university education than any wolf that ever lived—but also, I suppose, a rather cosmopolitan wolf, moving with me from Alabama to Ireland, on to Wales,

England, and finally to France. *The Philosopher and the Wolf* is the story of those years we spent together, with various philosophical musings on the differences (and similarities) between humans and other animals thrown in for good measure.

3:AM: You argue that apes are basically Rawlsian contractualist moralists, is that right?

ROWLANDS: That was the part of the book onto which the press fastened more than any other. In fact, it was the least original part of the book: a discussion of the "Machiavellian intelligence hypothesis" or, as it is now more commonly known, the "social brain hypothesis," associated with the primatologists Richard Byrne and Andrew Whiten, among others. The basic idea is that the greater mental powers of the ape emerged out of social, rather than material, pressure. That is, rather than being the result of pressure to cope with the vicissitudes of the material world, we became more intelligent largely in order to secure social advantage: through manipulation and deception of some of our peers and forming alliances with others. Our impressive cognitive arsenal is a result of this sort of process. As I pointed out, this means that manipulation and mendacity lie at the heart of the development of our intellect. Many people were unhappy with this claim, but I don't think it can seriously be disputed.

I wouldn't want to claim that apes are Rawlsian contractualists. That would assume they have abilities to engage in generalized reciprocity—and the existence of that in animals other than human is controversial, to say the least. My claim about Rawlsian contractualism was that it was a moral theory ideally suited to strangers—individuals who don't really know each other very well, and don't really care for each other very much. This sort of contractualist view grounds what we might call a morality for strangers.

3:AM: Now, this is separate from your arguments for animal rights, isn't it? Can you tell us what your basic argument is?

ROWLANDS: There is a basic argument for animal rights—at least, for the claim that animals have the basic moral entitlement to have their interests counted. It's not my argument; it's been around a long time (although I may have played some minor role in making it more precise). The argument goes like this:

1. Individual human beings possess a number of moral entitlements, including, fundamentally, the entitlement to have their interests taken into account.
2. There can be no difference in the moral entitlements possessed by two individuals without there being some other relevant difference between those individuals.

3. There is no relevant difference between human and (at least some) animal individuals, where this difference is of a sort that could disqualify the latter from the fundamental entitlement to have one's interests taken into account.
4. Therefore, some individual animals are entitled to have their interests taken into account.

The idea of having one's interests "taken into account" is not entirely clear, but is generally taken first to preclude a general discounting of the interests of animals, and second to privilege the vital interests of animals over the nonvital interests of humans. Typically, the second claim is understood as a consequence of the first: no substantial sense can be given to the idea that an individual's interests are being taken into account if their vital interests are routinely overridden by the nonvital interest of another individual.

The argument is valid. Premises 1 and 2 are largely uncontroversial. The controversial premise is, of course, number 3. The candidates for differences that might be thought morally relevant correspond to properties that are either categorical in the sense that they are possessed by all human beings or characteristic in the sense that they are possessed by most, but not all, humans. Accordingly, the defense of premise 3 is a disjunctive one. The categorical properties are, most obviously, biological ones: species membership, genetic profile, and so on. However, in other contexts, the idea that biological properties are morally relevant is quickly dismissed. The argument that males possess more entitlements than females because of their different biological composition, for example, is one that few would accept. Therefore, those whose route to the moral claims of animals is via the basic argument will typically argue that categorical differences between animals and humans are not morally relevant ones. It is not being human that is directly relevant to one's moral standing. It is what typically or characteristically comes with being human.

If this is correct, we are left with characteristic differences. The idea that these can be morally relevant is typically attacked by what has become known, perhaps unfortunately, as the argument from marginal cases. Suppose, for example, someone were to argue that animals' interests should be discounted on the grounds that they are not as intelligent as humans. The argument from marginal cases proceeds by pointing out that while this may be true of most humans, it is not the case for all (babies, young children, those with moderate to severe brain damage or in the advanced stages of degenerative brain conditions, and so on). What do we say about these humans? Do we discount their interests? Eat them, experiment on them, hunt them, make them into shoes? If we assume that the answer to this question is, or should be, "no," it means that we cannot, consistently, regard intelligence as decisive in determining whose interests are to count. The same argument applies to all the other characteristic differences between humans and animals (language use, etc).

Thus, if the argument works, categorical differences are morally irrelevant, and characteristic differences fall victim to the argument from marginal cases and, therefore, ultimately turn out to be morally irrelevant also.

3:AM: You are a philosopher of mind as well as applied ethics and animal rights. Shaun Gallagher gives rough coordinates for navigating this terrain in terms of the "Four Es": embodied, embedded, enacted, and extended. Can you quickly say what you take each of these things to mean?

ROWLANDS: Roughly: A mental process is embodied if it is composed, in part, of processes that occur not in the brain but in the wider (that is, nonneural) body.

A mental process is extended if it is composed, partly, of processes whereby a cognizing creature exploits, manipulates, or transforms relevant structures in its environment in order to accomplish a cognitive task. What makes a structure relevant is that it carries information relevant to the accomplishing of the task in question, and by acting on it the cognizing creature is able to appropriate this information.

A mental process is embedded or scaffolded in the wider environment if this environment plays an important (perhaps essential) role in facilitating this process's fulfillment of its defining function (that is, if the process relies on the environment in order to work properly).

A mental process is enacted if it is made up of a process of "enaction"—interaction, of the right sort, with the environment.

The thesis of embedded cognition is a thesis of dependence: some cognitive processes are dependent on environmental structures or processes. The theses of embodied and extended cognition are, as I understand them, both theses of composition: some cognitive processes are partly composed of wider (that is, nonneural) bodily and environmental processes. This is the way I use these terms. Others can use them somewhat differently, and the resulting ambiguity can lead to problems. I think the theses of embodied and extended cognition are the most radical and interesting (although the way I define the thesis of extended cognition makes it close to what many people have in mind when they think of enacted cognition).

3:AM: I thought it would be helpful if you could explain your position, which is partly that the mind is extended, but you want to distinguish your position from Dave Chalmers and Andy Clark's position of the extended mind.

ROWLANDS: I think that some mental processes—processes such as perceiving, remembering, reasoning—can partly extend into the environment in the sense that they are partly composed of actions that subjects perform on their environment—specifically, manipulation, exploitation, and/or transformation of structures that carry information relevant to the solution of the task the process is supposed to accomplish. Clark and Chalmers imagine the case of Otto, a person with early-stage Alzheimer's who uses a notebook to write down information he would otherwise forget. Clark and Chalmers claim (or are widely interpreted as claiming) that when Otto writes down a sentence such as "The Museum of Modern Art is on 53rd Street," this sentence is one of Otto's beliefs. Their basic argument for this claim is that the sentence functions in a way relevantly similar to the way a belief would function in a healthy person's psychology.

I deny that the sentence is a belief. I think there are several good reasons for denying this. Most importantly for me, I'm inclined to the view that intentionality is the defining feature of the mental. Intentionality is the "aboutness" of a mental state. The belief that the cat is on the mat, for example, is about a (specific) cat and its relation to a (specific) mat. This "aboutness" is what philosophers have in mind when they talk about the intentionality of thought and other mental states.

The sentence in Otto's book is not about anything in the way that a belief is about something. The sentence is just squiggles on a page; taken in itself, it could mean anything. For it to mean anything, it must be interpreted. Its intentionality or aboutness is, in this sense, merely derived. Beliefs and other mental states are not like this. You don't first encounter the belief and then have to settle the question of what it is about. To have the belief is to be aware of what it is about. This point is sometimes put by saying that, whereas the intentionality of the sentence is derived, the intentionality of a belief is original. Original intentionality is the hallmark of the mental. Beliefs have it, sentences don't. That's why the sentences in Otto's notebook are not beliefs.

I do, however, argue that a cognitive process such as remembering can be partly composed of processes of manipulating the book—opening the pages, scanning each page, and so on—in such a way to make available the information it contains. At the core of cognition, I believe, we find processes that make available information that was previously unavailable. These processes of manipulation are part of the means whereby Otto does this.

3:AM: So their version of the extended mind emphasizes location, which you don't. Yours is an amalgamated mind position, whereby you amalgamate all four Es. Is that right?

ROWLANDS: I do not think that the issue of the extended mind is one of location—and for that matter is not about the mind either. First, the thesis of amalgamated cognition is one that concerns mental (specifically cognitive) processes, not the mind. And no conclusions can be drawn from it about where these processes are—although some can be drawn about where they are not—at least not in their entirety.

The amalgamation in question is actually that of two of the Es—embodied cognition and extended cognition—not four. I regard the theses of embodied and extended cognition as two versions of the same thing and as having the same basis (the nature of intentionality). The more interesting versions of enactivism, I argue, are in fact versions of extended cognition. The thesis of embedded cognition is far less radical than the others (indeed, in recent debates, it is often used as a neo-Cartesian fallback position to attack the other positions).

3:AM: Your position strikes some as inheriting some of the same difficulties that interpretations of Clark and Chalmers have. So one is, Why does it seem counterintuitive to many but not to you?

ROWLANDS: Controversial philosophical theories sometimes have a habit of evolving into common sense. Descartes's view of the mind as something that is located inside the head provides a good example. I argue that the idea of extended cognition seems so outlandish because we have, for whatever reason, come to uncritically adopt a certain conception of intentionality as a process whereby the mind somehow reaches out into the world to grasp its objects. I argue that, on the contrary, intentionality is revealing activity, and as such is already out in the world. Revealing activity often straddles neural, bodily, and environmental processes. So from this perspective, extended cognition is utterly mundane.

3:AM: Another objection to Clark and Chalmers is: minds don't have parts, ergo, your notes can't be a part of your mind. Do you think this is right?

ROWLANDS: The thesis of extended cognition, as I understand it, should not be understood as a thesis about minds. It is one about mental processes. It does not even require that there are any such things as minds, over and above mental processes. So, the objection that minds do not have parts is wide of the mark— at least given the way I understand the thesis (others understand it differently).

3:AM: I suppose the objection to Clark and Chalmers that is most powerful is that of intentionality. Mental states have content. They are about things. In a sense, that's what defines the mental. Isn't that the thrust of the "What's it like to be a bat?" question. So the objection is that a notebook isn't mental because it hasn't got content that isn't derived from things that do have minds (for instance, us). Doesn't this make externalism tricky? And surely this is a problem even for your position, isn't it?

ROWLANDS: I agree absolutely. As I mentioned earlier, that's the primary reason I would deny that the sentences in Otto's notebook count as beliefs (or anything mental). The process of manipulating the book to make available the information it contains, on the other hand, is a complex process made up of, among other things, perception of the sentence on the page and beliefs formed on the basis of this perception. The perception and the resulting beliefs have original intentionality. Therefore, contained in this process is all the original intentionality one could want in a cognitive process. Therefore, my version of the theory explicitly accommodates—indeed, insists on—the original intentionality of mental things.

3:AM: Could you be interpreted as making a philosophical approach to the cognitive that is much closer to the intentionality arguments of Anscombe and McDowell? Your "Extended Cognition and the Mark of the Cognitive" paper can sound like saying cognition is just information processing, which is pretty naturalistic and a bit like Dennett, but you deny this is all. Is what you're doing a kind of naturalized (or naturalized-sounding) Anscombe? It seems more like you're doing a kind of conceptual analysis than the kind of thing that Dennett would contemplate. You use Brentano to discuss how the transcendental mode of presentation of an object is a way of disclosure or revelation of the world and cognition. Can you say something about all this? I guess I'm really asking, How much you are a naturalist and how much something different?

ROWLANDS: That is a very perceptive question. Yes, I do hold the rather unfashionable view that conceptual analysis is one of the cornerstones of philosophy: one of the things—not the only, by any means, but one of the things—that philosophy should be doing. The mark of the cognitive was extracted by way of a process of conceptual analysis of a certain sort—analysis of the kinds of canonical models of cognitive processes employed by cognitive scientists (for example, David Marr's theory of vision) and what these models reveal about the sort of thing cognition must be taken to be by these theorists.

To claim that philosophy is in the business of conceptual analysis is risky because it engenders much confusion. Most importantly, everyone seems to think conceptual analysis is the analysis of concepts. If I remember correctly, Timothy Williamson, in his book *The Philosophy of Philosophy*, argues against conceptual analysis on these grounds: concepts only make up a small fraction of what actually exists. Why would philosophy restrict itself to a small fraction of what exists? Embodied in this is a common but mistaken conception of what conceptual analysis is. Conceptual analysis is not the analysis of concepts. It is the analysis of things—conceptually. That is, the word "conceptual" functions as an adverb. One can analyze a thing—the same thing—chemically, physically, functionally, and so on. So, too can one analyze it conceptually. In my mark of the cognitive, what was analyzed was a type or kind of thing: cognition. And the way in which this thing was analyzed was conceptually.

Finally, the cornerstone of my view is the analysis of intentionality. I can take or leave the mark of the cognitive stuff; it is relatively unimportant to the view I want to defend (which makes it either galling or amusing, depending on what sort of mood I'm in, that almost all of the commentators have focused exclusively on it). But the analysis of intentionality—I'll be six feet under in my cold, cold grave before I give up on that. My overall view stands or falls with the account of intentionality.

3:AM: I guess the big objection that lurks is, How do you get cognitive content from this? Isn't there a general objection that you can't derive the mental content of the mental from teleofunctional accounts? Presumably you agree but think this isn't relevant.

ROWLANDS: The thesis of extended cognition is not an attempt to explain mental content. That is a task for other theories. The thesis is a thesis about the so-called vehicles of content: what sorts of things have content—and can be developed independently of an account of what gives them content. If the thesis of extended cognition is correct, these vehicles of content are not restricted to brain states or processes. But the thesis is not a theory about what gives these things content or why they have content.

I am very tempted, as I have said, by the view that the hallmark of the mental is intentionality. The clearest examples of mental items are items that are about other things—as a belief that the cat is on the mat is about the cat and its relation to the mat. That intentionality is the hallmark or defining feature of the mental is not universally accepted. But it is a common assumption, and I believe a good one. And even if intentionality is not the defining feature of the mental, it is enough for my view that it is a very important feature of many mental states. This weaker assumption is all I really need—it gives me enough to get my central argument going.

I do not know if intentionality can be naturalized. All I can say is that I have not yet seen a convincing naturalized account of it (and I include my own earlier naturalistic efforts). Theories like the teleofunctional account (an account I once endorsed) are, I now think, predicated on the mistaken conception of intentionality, which it is the task of my recent book, *The New Science of the Mind*, to unseat. That is, with the teleofunctional account, and other naturalistic attempts of that ilk, one starts with an inner state—a neural configuration of some sort—and asks what conditions must be satisfied if this state is to reach out into the world and be about something. That is the wrong place to start. The right question is this: How can an object be revealed to a subject? That is, what sorts of processes are involved in an object being revealed in a given way (a tomato being revealed as red and shiny, for example)?

The thesis of extended cognition is true if some of these processes are ones whereby subjects act on—manipulate, transform, or otherwise exploit—objects in the world. I argue that it is very implausible to suppose that revealing activity is confined to processes occurring inside skin or skull. A proper understanding of intentionality lets us see why.

3:AM: The bit of enactiveness that you integrate you develop from Husserl. Is that right?

ROWLANDS: I think the enactive approach was almost entirely anticipated by Husserl. In his work—see especially his series of lectures published as *Thing and Space*—you find an account of perceptual content developed in terms of sensorimotor expectations. In Husserl also, we find at least the beginnings of the right way of thinking about intentionality—at least, there is an ambiguity in his work that can be developed in a very important and revealing way. We find essentially the same ambiguity in his contemporary, Frege. Both Husserl and Frege attributed to what they call "sense" (German: *Sinn*) the dual role of something that is grasped in thought, but also something that fixes reference—fixes what the thought is about. I argued that this means that in any thought, sense in its reference-fixing role is non-eliminable. That is, whenever a subject grasps a sense (thinks a thought), there must be another sense that is not grasped. This sense, sense in its reference-fixing capacity, I argued, is best understood in terms of the idea of revealing activity. This underpins my argument for extended cognition. The vehicles of revealing activity are not, in general, exclusively neural but include bodily and environmental processes too. So, certainly, I would be happy to say that the roots of extended cognition are found in Husserl.

3:AM: Brenin died, and you say that although your life is better than it's ever been in some respects you feel diminished by his death. Can you say something about this? I was impressed by the almost mystical claims you make, as when you write:

> The thoughts that drive this book are ones that I have thought but, nevertheless, are in an important sense not mine. This is not because they are someone else's, although one can clearly discern the influence of thinkers like Nietzsche, Heidegger, Camus, Kundera, and the late Richard Taylor. Rather, and once again I must resort to metaphor, I think there are certain thoughts that can emerge only in the space between a wolf and a man.
>
> That space no longer exists. In our early days, Brenin and I used to take off some weekends to Little River Canyon in the northeastern corner of Alabama, and (illegally) pitch a tent. We'd spend the time chilling and howling at the moon. The canyon was narrow and deep, and it was with reluctance that the sun would push its way through the dense druid oaks and birches. And once the sun had passed over the canyon's western rim, the shadows would congeal into a solid bank. After an hour or so of easing ourselves along a

neglected trail, we would enter into the clearing. If we had timed things just right, it would be as the sun gave its parting kiss to the canyon's western lip, and golden light would reverberate through the open space. Then, the trees, largely hidden by the gloom for the past hour would stand out in their aged and mighty splendor. The clearing is the space that allows the trees to emerge from the darkness into the light. The thoughts that make up this book emerged in the space between one particular wolf and one particular man and would not have been possible without that space.

How different is this kind of philosophical reflection from that done as a professional philosophical? And do you think you'll return to that state of awareness again?

ROWLANDS: *The Philosopher and the Wolf* is a book about life; in particular, it's about growing up. I have a book coming out next year, called *Running with the Pack*—and that's about growing old. (I suppose there's a natural trilogy to be written here, but I hope I don't have to write the third part yet.) For a while, philosophers abandoned these sorts of themes. Maybe they still have; I don't know. Perhaps it was part of a perceived process of professionalization.

As Julian Barnes once remarked, we are all amateurs when it comes to our own lives, and this sort of personal examination was excised in the (poorly conceived) aim of becoming a professional discipline (which basically amounted to dealing with issues and questions that only someone with an extended formal training in philosophy could understand). I think (I may be wrong) that things are changing, and this can only be a good thing. Philosophy, in the final analysis, is the art of thinking clearly. And even if we are all amateurs when it comes to our own lives, this does not preclude thinking clearly about those lives and what is important in them.

3:AM: So, have there been books that have been influential to you as you brood on these themes? You mention Kundera and Camus. Are there others?

ROWLANDS: My professional training was solidly within the so-called analytic tradition in philosophy. Some might, therefore, think it strange that the biggest philosophical influences on me have been from what some people think of as "the other side": continental philosophers. I would include Nietzsche, Husserl, Heidegger, and Sartre—all of whom have exerted significant influence on the way my thought has developed over the years. Of course, this idea of "sides" is just nonsense. The idea that one half of philosophy can afford to proceed in ignorance of what the other half is doing—that's one of the silliest ideas philosophers have ever had (and the [silliness] bar has, it goes without saying, been set quite high).

5 | Eric T. Olson
THE PHILOSOPHER WITH NO HANDS

Eric T. Olson is an American philosopher who specializes in metaphysics and the philosophy of mind at the University of Sheffield in the UK. He is the author of two books, *What Are We? A Study in Personal Ontology* (Oxford University Press, 2007), and *The Human Animal: Personal Identity Without Psychology* (Oxford University Press, 1997).

3:AM: You've argued for animalism. This is the view that humans are animals. You point out that a surprising number of major philosophers, both ancient and modern, have denied this. Can you say something about this?

OLSON: "Animalism" says that each of us is a biological organism: an animal. All that sets us apart from other animals, beyond our being naked and bipedal and slow to mature, is our intelligence. That's a big difference: psychologically and sociologically it's an enormous gulf, even if the precise width of the gulf is a matter of controversy. But it's not a metaphysical gulf. Fundamentally we're all the same sort of thing: living organisms. Most of the big names in philosophy have said the opposite: we are *not* fundamentally the same sort of things as dogs or apes. Our bodies may be animals, but we ourselves are not. (This claim needn't presuppose the uniqueness of the human species: there may be beings standing to canine and simian organisms as you and I stand to human organisms.)

Historically, most philosophers rejected animalism because they couldn't see how we could be wholly material things—things made entirely of matter. They were convinced that no material thing, no matter how sophisticated, could ever produce thought. Thought could never arise out of any brute physical process. A thinking being would have to be at least partly immaterial, and so must we. This idea was dominant as late as the 1960s, when the main debate over our metaphysical nature was whether we are Cartesian immaterial substances or Humean bundles of mental events.

3:AM: Why do you think people nowadays argue against the view that we're animals? Is it that they fear something gets lost?

OLSON: I think a lot of people find the view demeaning. They often state it by saying that people are "nothing more than animals," which sounds like a way of saying that we're little different, psychologically and behaviorally, from chimpanzees and baboons. In short, our being animals would be incompatible with the better parts of human nature.

Another common line is that according to animalism people are "nothing more than their bodies." And it really does sound absurd to say that Bertrand Russell's body denied the existence of God, and had a famous debate about the subject with Father Copleston's body. That can make it tempting to think: animals are just bodies. But *we're* not just bodies—we're conscious, intelligent beings. So how could we be animals? The reasoning is sheer sophistry, but I'm sure it's been influential.

I see phrases like "a person's body" as weasel words. They have a corrupting influence on philosophical thinking. The absurdity of saying that Russell's body is thinking or conscious leads easily to the thought that the phrase "Russell's body" must be the name of an object that is *not* thinking or conscious. So you have the thinking, conscious thing—Russell himself—and the material thing—Russell's body—that doesn't think and isn't conscious. That's only a whisker away from Cartesian dualism. There's a lot of Cartesian thinking in the philosophy of personal identity, even if it's usually more sophisticated and better disguised than this. If there's any argument against animalism worth taking seriously, it's that animalism conflicts with attractive claims about our persistence through time.

3:AM: I guess this takes us to your interest in personal identity. Can you explain firstly what the significance of this issue is, before you give us the details of your thoughts?

OLSON: "Personal identity" can mean many things. Most people use the phrase to mean your sense of who you are and what distinguishes you most fundamentally from other people. What philosophers mean by personal identity over time is something completely different: it's about what it takes for us to survive or continue existing from one time to another. For example, I existed twenty years ago. What makes this the case? There were a lot of beings in existence in 1992. What makes some particular one of them, rather than one of the others, me? What is it about the way he relates to me as I am now? For that matter, what makes it the case that I existed at all back then? Why didn't I come into existence just this morning? Similar questions arise about the future: What sorts of adventures could I survive, and what sort of thing would inevitably bring my existence to an end?

One thing that makes these questions interesting is the possibility of cases where the answer isn't obvious. If your liver were transplanted into my abdomen, you would lose a vital organ and continue to exist (for a while) without it. The liver that was once a part of you would be assimilated into my living tissues and become a part of me. The same goes for other vital organs. But what if the surgeons were to transplant your *brain* into my head, taking with it all your mental contents? What would happen then? (Suppose they throw my original brain away.)

Maybe I would simply lose my own brain and get yours instead. I'd lose all the memories of my life and have them replaced with memories of your life— of conversations I never had, journeys I never made, and so on. The operation would give me all sorts of false beliefs: that I live in your house, work at your job, am the parent of your children. I'd be deluded about who I am; I'd be convinced that I was you. You, on the other hand, would lose your brain and stay behind with an empty skull. So a brain transplant would be analogous to a liver transplant.

But most people, when they hear this story, are inclined to say that the cases are different. What would really happen is not that I got a new brain, but that *you* got a new body. That is, you would go with your brain: the operation would pare you down to a naked brain, then move you across the room into my skull, thereby replacing all your parts but your brain with what used to be my parts. You would look in the mirror afterwards and see my face. You would enjoy the magnificent physique of a middle-aged academic. The operation wouldn't really be a brain transplant at all, but rather a transplant of everything but the brain. So no one would have his true beliefs and memories replaced with false ones, or be wrong about who he is.

The reason people tend to think that you would go with your transplanted brain, rather than staying behind with an empty head, is that the one who ended up with your brain would have your psychology—your mental properties. This suggests that our identity over time consists in psychological continuity: you are that future being who inherits your psychology in some direct way, and you are that past being whose psychology you have so inherited. That's what it is for a past or future being to be you. Views of this sort—psychological-continuity views—are the orthodoxy in contemporary philosophy.

But psychological-continuity views rule out our being animals. You can't move an *animal* from one head to another by transplanting its brain. The operation would simply move an organ from one animal to another. So if you were an animal and your brain were transplanted, you would just lose an organ and get an empty head. A brain transplant would be analogous to a liver transplant, contrary to psychological-continuity views.

For that matter, every human animal starts out as an embryo with no mental properties at all, and thus no psychological continuity. The identity of an animal over time doesn't consist in any sort of psychological continuity. If *our* continuing to exist from one time to another consists in psychological continuity, then we're not animals, but something else. (*What* else is not so easy to say.)

3:AM: So, why do you go with animalism and against psychological-continuity views? Why not accept the obvious lesson of the brain-transplant story and conclude that we're not animals?

OLSON: Well, there are some seven billion human animals inhabiting the earth—the same as the number of human people. For every one of us, there is a human animal, and for every human animal (certain pathological cases aside, perhaps) there is one of us. To all appearances, those animals do all the same things that we do: eat and drink, have conversations, surf the web. How could we be anything other than those animals?

Think about what it would mean. There's a human animal sitting in your chair and reading this now. That animal would seem to be conscious and intelligent. (It's got your brain. What could prevent it from using that brain to think?) In fact it would seem to be psychologically indistinguishable from you. So if you were not that animal but something else, there would be *two* conscious, intelligent beings sitting there and reading this: an animal and a nonanimal.

If that's not bad enough, it's hard to see how you could ever know which of the two beings you are. You may think you're the nonanimal—the one that would go with its brain if that organ were transplanted. But wouldn't the animal believe the same thing about itself, only falsely? Wouldn't it have the same reasons for believing this as you do? But then, for all you know, *you* might be the one making the mistake. Suppose you wonder: Am I the person who would go with my transplanted brain, or the animal that would stay behind? From your point of view, both answers would be equally likely. That cuts the ground right out from under the transplant argument. The thought driving the argument was that you would go with your transplanted brain. But you could never have any reason to think this: for all you could ever know, you might be the animal that would stay behind.

Unless, despite all appearances, human animals are somehow not conscious and intelligent like we are, it's very hard to deny that we are those animals.

3:AM: What does animalism say about personal identity over time, then?

OLSON: If people are animals, then personal identity over time is animal identity over time. The organism you see in the mirror is you, and you go wherever it goes. So although your sense of who you are (your "personal identity" in the popular sense) may have to do with psychological continuity; your continued existence from one time to another does not.

What animal identity *does* consist in is a large question. It certainly has nothing to do with retaining the same matter. Your being an animal doesn't mean that when all your matter has been replaced in the course of metabolic turnover in a few years' time, you'll no longer exist, and someone else will take your place. An organism is not an inert lump of matter, but a dynamic system: it survives by taking in new matter, extracting energy from it, and then expelling it. Matter flows through an organism like water through a fountain, only slower. As long as its life-sustaining functions continue, the organism still exists.

3:AM: Has the question of personal identity over time become more urgent as modern science advances to the point were we might be able to download consciousness or clone bodies with ease in some near future?

OLSON: There are people who believe that we will one day be able to create healthy adult human beings with blank brains, so that as age advances we can "download" our mental states into these beings, cheating death and giving ourselves perpetual youth. Variants of the story have us transferring to longer-lasting inorganic "bodies" rather than artificial organisms. The story is called transhumanism.

Of course, medical technology is nowhere near the point where we could actually do any of this. It's not going to happen in the foreseeable future. It's pretty doubtful whether it's even possible: whether a human brain actually has such a thing as a "blank" state, for instance, or whether an inorganic being could ever be conscious or intelligent.

But even if it really is possible, we have to ask whether the result of copying your mental states to a new human being would be you. Maybe it would be nothing more than a duplicate of you, with false memories of someone else's past and a mistaken conviction about who it is. If we copied your mental states to 10 human beings at once, at most one of the 10 resulting people could be you. The other nine would be deluded. Why wouldn't all ten be deluded?

I doubt whether the result of copying your mental states to another human being could ever be you. It certainly couldn't be if you're an animal. You can't move an animal from one human being to another by copying its mental states, any more than you can move a computer from one room to another by sending an electronic file. In fact it's hard to see what sort of concrete object you *could* move from one organism to another just by transferring information. That is: it's hard to see what sort of things we could be according to the transhumanists.

Another worry: as the story is always told, the "scanning" procedure that reads off your mental states disperses your atoms, or at least erases your brain's content. That makes it easier to believe that you're the transfer recipient, because there's no other obvious candidate for being you. But there's no reason why the procedure has to be destructive. Suppose the machine reads off your mental states without doing you any more harm than an X-ray, then copies them to another human being as before. In that case, surely, you would stay where you are and the transfer recipient would simply be deceived into thinking that he or she was you. But your relation to that person is the same in both variants of the story: in each case she gets a copy of the mental states read off from your brain. So if that person wouldn't be you in the case where the procedure is harmless, how could she be you in the case where the procedure erases your brain? It looks as if the "downloading" procedure could never extend your life. The most it could do is make a copy of you.

It's doubtful whether the transhumanist dream is compatible with any coherent view of personal identity over time.

3:AM: Returning to the science fiction stuff: you have argued about the possibility of computer-generated life, the idea that computers programmed in a certain way could become alive. You kind of doubt it.

OLSON: What I called computer-generated life is the claim, popular in the 1990s, that programming a computer in the right way might not just simulate life (in the way that computer programs can simulate weather systems), but actually create it. The controversy was about whether the result of this programming could ever be genuine life, or only something more or less similar to it. I took a different approach. I thought: you can't have life without living things. To create life, then, is to create living things—organisms.

But what sort of organism could you create just by programming a computer? An organism has to be made of something. It has to have a size and a location. So what sort of stuff could a computer-generated organism be made of? Where could it be located? How big would they be? Advocates of computer-generated life—who were scientists by training and not philosophers—had made only metaphorical gestures in this direction. So I tried to answer the questions myself. I considered all the possibilities I could think of, and they were all just about incredible. Computer-generated life looks metaphysically impossible.

I have a similar suspicion about artificial intelligence. There's been plenty of debate about whether programming a computer in the right way could produce something that counted as genuine intelligence, or only something more or less similar to it. But to create intelligence is to create an intelligent being—or else to make a previously unintelligent being intelligent. And the friends of artificial intelligence have said very little about what sort of beings they might create, or make intelligent, by programming computers. What would these things be made of? Where would they be located? I've never seen good answers to these questions. Computer intelligence may be no more metaphysically possible than computer-generated life.

I don't know whether computer-generated life is still in fashion. But because my doubts have nothing to do with the sophistication of the programming, recent developments in computer science are unlikely to make any difference.

3:AM: Anyone who writes a paper called "Why I Have No Hands" has got to be asked to explain himself!

OLSON: Half a dozen journals refused to publish that paper. One reviewer said that although it may have some value as entertainment, it wasn't serious philosophy. Since then it's generated a good deal of discussion in the journals, so I think I've had the last laugh.

Suppose we accept that there are certain particles "arranged manually," which enable me to tie my shoes and feed myself. Now we might ask: Do those particles add up to or compose something bigger—a hand? Is there anything there—any material object—besides the particles? The question may sound monumentally abstruse, if not outright unintelligible. Is there really any difference between particles being arranged manually and their composing a hand? And if there is, why should anyone care about it? But there is a difference, and it does matter.

Suppose there really were such a thing as my hand. Then there would also be such a thing as "all of me but my hand." (The wrist joint, for all its anatomical utility, has no metaphysical significance.) But this object—call it a "hand complement"—would be just as conscious and intelligent as I am. (It would differ from me only by lacking a hand as a part. How could that prevent it from thinking? *I* could think if I lost a hand.) In that case my hand complement would be a second conscious being in addition to me. There would be two conscious beings within my skin—a hand complement and a whole human being—thinking exactly the same thoughts.

But I'm the only thinker sitting here. More generally, there aren't two conscious, thinking beings wherever we thought there was just one. If that's right, then my hand complement can't be an intelligent being. And since it *would* be intelligent if it existed, there can be no such thing as my hand complement. But then there can be no such thing as my hand either. And of course what goes for my hand goes equally for my legs, my heart, and so on. A variant of the argument implies that I have no head. The entire nursery-school ontology of "parts of the body" goes out the window.

Maybe that sounds silly. But if it's not true, there must be something wrong with the argument that leads to it. Are there such things as hands but no such things as hand complements? Does something prevent my hand complement from thinking? Could I actually be my hand complement, despite the fact that it's smaller than I am? Do I share my thoughts with a vast number of other beings of different sizes? (How could I ever know which one I am?) Or does the argument's conclusion somehow not follow from the premises, despite its seemingly impeccable logic? None of those alternatives looks any better than denying the existence of hands. At any rate, those are the options. There is no easy, comfortable position here.

3:AM: You were unsettled by Hud Hudson's idea that a thing can have different parts in different places, his theory of "partism." Can you say what you think the problem is with this view?

OLSON: This is a technically demanding topic (some readers may want to skip ahead). Briefly, "partism" is designed to solve problems like the one about hands. (Hudson doesn't apply it in cases quite like this one, but we can ignore that.) Suppose again that there's such a thing as my hand complement. We don't want to say that it's a thinking, conscious being in addition to me. Partism would enable us to say that my hand complement *is* me, so that there's only one conscious being here.

But my hand is a part of me and not a part of my hand complement. How could we be the same thing? How could one thing both have and not have a hand as a part? Well, we know that a thing can have different parts at different times: if I have a bad accident at the sawmill, my hand might be a part of me today but not tomorrow. Hudson proposes that a thing can have different parts at different *places.* So the hand could be a part of both me and my hand complement (which are the same thing) at the place where that hand is located, and not a part of either being at some other place. What appear to be two things with different parts are in some cases just one thing, made up of more than one set of parts at once.

It's a very clever thought. But how can we generalize it? Here's a troublesome case: Theseus builds a ship and goes to sea. Now and then he returns to port and replaces some of the ship's worn pieces until eventually every one of them has been exchanged. Meanwhile, the local museum has been collecting the cast-off pieces, which they manage to assemble just as they were when Theseus first set sail. So there are now two ships: the repaired ship at sea and the reconstructed ship in the museum. Which of the two is Theseus' original ship?

If Hudson is right, we ought to be able to say that both are: the repaired ship is the reconstructed ship. Despite appearances, there's only one ship in the story. It simply has different parts at different places. In the museum, it's made up entirely of old pieces; at sea, it's composed entirely of new ones. So the museum guide could point to the reconstructed hulk and say, "The ship you see here has been at sea for the last month and is now approaching Corsica."

If someone actually said this, we'd take her to be referring to the ship at sea by pointing to something else that represents it, just as she might do by pointing to a picture or a model of it. But what if she insisted that the ship in the museum and the ship at sea were literally just one ship? That would be hard even to understand, never mind believe. It seems as obvious as anything can be that there are two ships (if there are such things as ships at all), one in the museum and the other at sea. Yet according to partism her statement ought to make perfect sense.

To be fair, Hudson doesn't think his theory applies in this case: even if my hand complement and I are one human being, the repaired ship and the reconstructed ship are two ships. But he has no account of why this is so, or of where his theory applies and where it doesn't.

3:AM: You're impressed by Peter van Inwagen, and clearly many of your interests seem to spin out from his *Material Beings* and his mereological investigations. Can you say what the appeal of metaphysics was? Was it the "unsettling commitments" that you liked, the risk to "common sense," the "making it strange"? Jason Stanley says that he likens philosophy to novel writing. Is this something you can understand?

OLSON: What drew me to van Inwagen's philosophy wasn't the strangeness of his views (he claims, for instance, that there are no material objects except elementary particles and living organisms—which neatly solves the problem of the ship of Theseus). It was rather the way he argued for these views. His thought has a simplicity and clarity that I've always aspired to. When he writes about something, the mist dissolves. Everything becomes plain. And once I've seen it, it often seems so natural and obvious that I wonder how anyone could see things so clearly without agreeing. I'm aware, of course, that he doesn't have this effect on everyone. But his critics rarely manage to reveal an alternative landscape of equal clarity. To my eye, they only wrap things in mist again.

Stanley's point is that philosophy is a first-order activity and not a second-order activity. Philosophers don't study Plato just because of his historical importance; that's not philosophy, but history of ideas. We do it because we think Plato might have something to teach us about the subject. We're doing the same thing he was doing, namely asking philosophical questions and trying to answer them. So philosophers treat Plato in the way novelists treat Dickens: as a colleague rather than as a mere object of study. That's the sense in which philosophy is like novel writing and not like literary criticism. But you could make the same point by saying that philosophy is like physics and not like the history of science, or like pole vaulting and not like the study of athletics. I doubt whether the connection between philosophy and novel writing goes much deeper than that.

3:AM: You've spoken of how science and philosophy can cooperate. For some, philosophers shouldn't be so close to science. For others, philosophy is redundant as science proceeds to explain away philosophy. So, how do you face down these two contrary positions to your own?

OLSON: Many scientific discoveries have a direct bearing on philosophy. For example, recent work in cosmology has revived "design" arguments for god's existence. The laws of physics turn out to involve numbers that apparently could have been different—the mass of the electron, for example, or the relative strengths of the elementary forces—but that all have to fall within an extremely narrow range of values in order for life to be possible. If these things had been left to chance (supposing that makes sense), the overwhelming likelihood is that the numbers would have had values resulting in a lifeless universe. This is something that no philosopher ever imagined from the armchair. So why is the universe "fine tuned" for life? One salient answer is that it was designed that way by some sort of god. To take another example, the science of color vision has demolished volumes of a priori philosophizing. Philosophers would be foolish to ignore this information.

To say that science makes philosophy redundant is to say that science can supply all the answers: all legitimate questions can be answered by the methods of the sciences. This claim is trivially self-refuting. The methods of science cannot establish whether every legitimate question can be answered by those methods. So the claim is illegitimate by its own standards. For that matter, the question of what the "methods of science" actually are, or ought to be, is a philosophical question. You can ignore philosophy, or try to reform it, but you can never do away with it altogether. Any attempt to dig its grave will only be more philosophy.

3:AM: One of the things some critics say about contemporary philosophy is that it is too boring, technical, jargonized, and distant from nonphilosophers' philosophical issues. You disagree, don't you?

OLSON: Those complaints could be made about any period in the history of philosophy. Most great philosophical works are dry and technical. Think of Kant's *Critique of Pure Reason*, or Hume's *Treatise*, or anything written by Aristotle or Aquinas or Hegel. If these critics were avid readers of Aristotle and Kant, and found their major works far more exciting than anything in contemporary philosophy, they'd have a legitimate complaint. But I don't think that's the case. (It's pretty hard to imagine.) I suspect that they simply find philosophy too hard. But philosophy *is* hard. That's its nature. No one would expect serious works of physics or mathematics or economics (as opposed to popularizations) to be immediately accessible to intelligent readers with no training in the subject. Why should philosophy be any different?

And contemporary philosophers don't neglect the interests of those outside the profession. It's true that if you open the pages of a journal like *Mind* or *Analysis* you're unlikely to find anything on the meaning of life, whether we have free will, or any other topic that ordinary people ever think about. But there's plenty of work being done in those areas if you look for it.

I concede that academic writing is very often harder to read than it needs to be. It tends to be larded with needless technical detail and jargon. It's interesting to ask why this is. Laziness is part of it, but the peer-review process is also to blame: it's easier to get academic work published if it's highly technical than if it's simple and clear, because simplicity and clarity make it easier for reviewers to spot the weak points. But this holds for all subjects, and has nothing to do with philosophy in particular. If anything, philosophers in the Anglo-American tradition tend to write more clearly than their colleagues in many other fields.

3:AM: Are you interested in x-phi [experimental philosophy] and what it brings to the philosophical table? Are you burning your armchair?

OLSON: The philosophical "experiments" that I'm familiar with are basically sophisticated opinion polls. This is important for those areas of philosophy that rely heavily on the opinions of ordinary people. (Philosophers call them "intuitions" because that sounds more authoritative.) If you're doing ethics, for example, you may need some premises about what it's right or not right to do. Where do you get them? The traditional procedure is to ask yourself, your colleagues, and your students, and if you find broad agreement, you take the judgment to be correct. Philosophical opinion polling appears to cast doubt on the reliability of this procedure, suggesting that the answers people give can vary widely depending on their cultural background, the way the questions are phrased, the order in which they're presented, and other factors not relevant to the truth of those answers.

This is all controversial and the results have been questioned. I haven't paid much attention because I don't put much faith in ordinary opinion. To my mind, the fact that ordinary people are inclined to say certain things when questioned about points of serious philosophical controversy is little reason to think that those sayings are true. Perhaps most people, when told the brain-transplant story, really would say that you would go with your brain rather than staying behind with an empty head. I still think they're probably wrong, because that view has consequences that on reflection I find impossible to accept. If the polling were to show that ordinary opinion is *not* actually in agreement with psychological-continuity views of personal identity, I'd be interested. But I don't think it's where those views are weakest.

I think there's a deeper reason for distrusting philosophical intuitions. I don't mind going against things ordinary people can be prompted to say about philosophical issues. But I worry when I disagree with other philosophers—people who are at least as able as I am and who have thought about the matter just as deeply. In that case it would be irresponsible for me to be confident that I've got it right and they're wrong. Fortunately there are points that we do agree about. No one disputes that if psychological-continuity views of personal identity are true, then we are not animals, and that it follows from this that the animal you live in, so to speak, is either not intelligent or is a second intelligent being in addition to you. The controversy is about whether these consequences are acceptable. Knowledge of what follows from what—of what the options are—is more solid than knowledge of which option is right.

6 | Craig Callender
TIME LORD

Craig Callender is a philosopher of science, physics, and metaphysics, with teaching interests in environmental ethics and other topics, at the University of California, San Diego. He is currently writing a book about what makes time special. He edited *The Oxford Handbook of Philosophy of Time*, (Oxford University Press, 2011) and *Time, Reality and Experience* (Cambridge University Press, 2002), and he is joint author with Nick Huggett of *Physics Meets Philosophy at the Planck Scale: Contemporary Theories in Quantum Gravity* (Cambridge University Press, 2001) and with Ralph Edney of *Introducing Time* (Totem Books, 1997).

3:AM: One of the big issues you are interested in is the scope of metaphysics. One concern about metaphysics, ever since the positivists, has been that it is too untethered from empirical testing and science, and so it is just too fanciful. Linked to this is the worry that metaphysicians just don't know enough about scientific theories to be able to provide a metaphysics connected with science. Can you say something about these connected issues?

CALLENDER: I think it's a fool's errand to try to prejudge inquiries on the basis of being too speculative or not. History is littered with embarrassing judgments stating that such-and-such is too speculative—Newtonian gravity, quantum nonlocality, relative simultaneity—only to see those ideas later vindicated. I want no part of that tradition. Nor do I wish to accuse metaphysicians of not knowing the relevant science; many know much more than I do. The more typical problem, if there is one, is that they know the science reasonably well but just don't see it as relevant to their concerns. That said, let me not shirk from the spirit of the question. You're right that I do find some contemporary metaphysics misdirected. Are roads that split and then recombine one road or two? Do hands that close into fists introduce new objects into the world? Are bunnies 4D worldliness of fur or "wholly present" 3D instances of furriness that persist through time? I just can't believe that these questions and others like them are about interesting deep facts of the world. By indexing roads, hands, and bunnies in the appropriate manner, all the problems disappear. I admit that there are some hard problems about dividing verbal disputes from genuine ones (see below). But all the background theory we have is suggesting that these disputes aren't deep or promising.

I also worry about the justification of various alleged principles of mereological metaphysics. Suppose one insists that simples (objects with no proper parts) have no spatial extension. Suppose also that our best physics posits fundamental entities that are spatially extended. What should we say? One option would be to stick with the principle and say that it turns out that the fundamental objects aren't simples, so understood. Then I have no objection, for the work is simply a study of the architecture of our concepts and not necessarily about the world. (Philosophers call this Strawsonian metaphysics, and it's a kind of anthropological exercise, one that maps the contours of our concepts.) Another option is to say that these spatially extended objects really do have parts, parts that *could*—in some metaphysical but not physical sense—break apart. Here is where I object.

Have these subentities and the metaphysical modality that goes with them earned their way into our overall system of the world? The entities and modalities posited by physics earned their way in through their empirical power, simplifying and unifying equations, and much more.

These mereological principles and attendant modalities haven't earned their way in. Mereological metaphysicians often think of their subject as almost like geometry, as having to hold but also about the physical world. If so, they need to be reminded of what happened to Euclidean geometry. What intuitively seems necessary might not be.

3:AM: What would you say to the metaphysician who might argue back and say that science often is underdetermined by empirical evidence in the present time, but who knows what will happen in the future? Isn't there a danger that worrying too much about the dangers of wild metaphysics just threatens the whole enterprise of discovery and science?

CALLENDER: I agree. Like I said above, I don't aspire to the post of grumpy, conservative arbiter of when speculation has gone too far. I don't want that mantle for all the reasons you say. Stifling wacky ideas may sometimes impede scientific progress. No lover of sci-fi such as myself would want any part of that. I love speculative science and metaphysics. Is spacetime discrete? Is it "gunky"? Is our epoch going to repeat itself? Build the models, and let's see what work they do for us. Here is an objection to what I said above. Some philosophers have said that there *could* be empirical tests of what I regard as nonissues. For example, the fundamental entities of physics might someday break apart. Would that harm my position? I don't think so, for if they break apart into extended objects then the mereologist under consideration still somehow knows, with no evidence apart from intuition, that they could break apart further. It's these "unearned" modalities that bother me.

In the case of bunnies, I've read and had it suggested to me that there is an empirical fact of whether a 4D stretch of fur and flesh is one bunny or an infinity of instantaneous "wholly present" bunnies. So I imagine hooking up some wires from a device to this fluffy pile, flipping a switch, and the pointer moving to the BUNNY or NOT-BUNNY position. It's really hard to see how this would work. What variable will co-vary with the pointer position? Mystery property X? Everything we know suggests that there is no such property, and crucially, that that property won't do any work for us in explaining anything else.

It is true that in principle we never know. Laudan and Leplin make this point in a famous paper in philosophy of science. Take two theories that look different but predict the same empirical claims, say, a theory with nontrivial spacetime curvature versus a theory with a flat spacetime where gravitons mimic the effects of curvature. There may be a temptation to regard them as notational variants, the dispute between the two as merely verbal. But they point out that it's always possible that we discover some new particles, say X-ons, and X-ons turn out to be sensitive to the difference between the two theories, for example, maybe X-ons feel curvature but don't couple to the graviton field. While one may grant this point, I don't think that it invites a free-for-all. We don't need to worry that future experiments will distinguish between a *bunny* and a *lapin*. Philosophy has not settled on a good criterion of when a dispute is verbal. Relying on that fact alone to stimulate a debate, however, strikes me as desperate.

3:AM: There's a worry as well that science is also getting too untethered and is proposing solutions as facts that are too fanciful as well. One of the familiar examples is the idea of multiple worlds and the claim that everything that could exist actually does. Is this something that concerns you?

CALLENDER: Yes, it's ironic that as metaphysics is getting accused of being too disconnected from science, science itself is positing unobservable structure that would make Leibniz blush. I'm not a fan of multiverses. To understand why, we need to get beyond the question of whether it's okay to posit some physics based on reasons of theoretical elegance. Of course it is! If we didn't focus on the simpler, more compact, more unified theories of the observable data, we would have way too many theories and no guide to the physical world. Imagine that you plot all the data points you have for your scientific domain on a graph. The number of curves that would fit this data is infinite. We need to cut this down, and the way we do it is by appealing to theoretical virtues.

The way I think of scientific theorizing is as a kind of optimization problem: Can we find the theory that best balances the various theoretical and empirical virtues? I expect many tradeoffs, both within and between the theoretical and empirical virtues. How we value the costs and benefits achieved by tradeoffs is a bit vague; that's why we don't have a simply expressible scientific method. But it's clear that no theory would accept, at one extreme, a simple list of what happens, or, at the other extreme, a "theory" that narrowed almost nothing down, such as F = ma by itself.

Given the above fuzziness, it's no surprise that reasonable people might disagree over whether a theory optimized the theoretical and empirical virtues. To me, it seems clear that the huge hit we take in extra ontology isn't worth the small gain we get in explanation. As a general point, we can additionally notice that theories will always have "unexplained explainers" or brute facts in them. We can puzzle over why they are thus and so. Then we can posit a new theory where that brute fact isn't so constrained, pull a measure out from Plato's heaven, impose that measure over all the other ways that brute "could be," and then argue that *most* of those ways lead to worlds like ours. Knowing that in principle this is always an option should make us extra cautious when we wonder whether we're getting enough for our trade.

3:AM: I guess if a physicist tells us that her theory requires weird ontologies such as multiple worlds then there's a general feeling that we folks don't have a right to challenge her. After all, commonsense intuitions are pretty rubbish when it comes to truth about the world, and so what else have we got? But you seem to think that we have philosophy and that this can be a helpful way of approaching this kind of claim, although of course someone like you is pretty well versed in the science. Is that right?

CALLENDER: Before there was physics and before there was philosophy of science, there was of course *natural philosophy*. When you read Newton, Maxwell, Thomson, Hertz, Boltzmann, and other greats, you would be hard pressed to circle what's philosophy and what's physics in these writings. There were just certain questions—are fields real or are they accounting devices? what explains entropy increase? are space and time real?—and a range of considerations for and against. The answers to these questions would draw on conceptual distinctions and scientific knowledge, however the two were classified, because these are the ingredients needed for an answer.

Specialization into distinct disciplines obviously has many benefits, but it's naïve to think something doesn't get lost too. Fallen into the cracks are a huge assortment of questions like the ones I just mentioned. These questions are deep and significant, but they are largely untouched. One can give sociological explanations for this: little grant money flows to such work in physics, the "linguistic turn" in metaphysics, and more. Whatever the reasons, there are good questions that deserve answers, and often answering them will require the skill of a natural philosopher, be she officially a philosopher, physicist, or mathematician.

I do think that philosophy has something to offer science. The information transfer can be "two-way." Due to their differences in training, philosophers often look at the same questions physicists do through different lenses, and sometimes this can help. Philosophers have training in logic, philosophy of science, metaphysics, and often history of science; with the distinctions they learn and a Socratic "follow the argument wherever it leads" ethos, they can raise questions about contemporary science that don't seem to get asked much, like whether inflation really solves, say, the horizon problem. Though some physicists I know may grimace at what I'm going to say, I do think that philosophers have helped us understand the deep commitments of spacetime theories, especially in the 1970s and 1980s, and in framing and tackling the quantum measurement problem and quantum nonlocality in the 1990s.

Many scientists thought for a very long time that relativity theory vindicated a Machian understanding of spacetime. Machianism may rise again, but the lesson philosophers have taught us is that the opposite is the case. Many scientists thought that de-coherence by itself solved the quantum measurement problem; now, thanks in part to distinctions made by philosophers, that position is seen as a nonstarter. Inasmuch as getting a clear picture of what one's theory is committed to is important for future progress, one might also see this work as significant for future progress, too.

3:AM: So, one of the big issues in science and metaphysics that you have looked hard at is time and implications running from different conceptions of time. There are several philosophically interesting and paradoxical-seeming things about time. You have recently asked the question of whether time is an illusion. So, is it? If not, what is it and what isn't it?

CALLENDER: We all seem to possess a kind of proto-theory of time. Let's call it *manifest time*. Manifest time says that time has a global, shared present that is metaphysically distinguished. This present carves the world into three, a past, a present, and a future. This present flows. It is intrinsically directed. It is independent of the distribution of matter. And so on. No matter how scientifically literate, I bet the reader shares this theory. Think of how important this conception of the world is to you! The way you live your life depends crucially on it. What you take yourself to cause, know, your very freedom and sense of self are all bound up with this conception of the world. Manifest time really is, as the philosopher Mellor calls it, the time of our lives. Yet physics tells us that this picture is more or less complete rubbish. I believe that. That is, I don't think, merely by sifting through the physics, you'll be able to recover manifest time.

Does that mean that physical time is inaccurate or incomplete? No, physical time may be all the time we need, fundamentally. However, it may be that by looking at more than physics we can explain why a creature embedded in a physical world such as ours would conceive of the world as we do in terms of manifest time. That is, I think that we can show why manifest time *makes sense* for creatures like us. I talk more about this project of getting from physical time to manifest time in the book I'm currently writing. The idea is that physics provides important constraints on any being like us, and these constraints, in concert with our psychological mechanisms, means of communication, macroscopic environments, and senses of selves, all together explain why we conceive of the world in terms of manifest time.

Is manifest time an illusion? In one sense, yes: manifest time is not accurately representing physical time. But there is a sense in which a world without perceivers lacks colors; only when perceivers are around do colors obtain. (Alternatively, maybe the colors exist as dispositions to look colored if an appropriately configured perceiver is present.) Either way, we don't regard colors as illusions. Maybe some aspects of manifest time are like this, in which case we wouldn't judge them as illusions. Embed a creature like us in a world like ours and that triggers a sense of flow, say. Once you break down manifest time into its various components, it becomes a bit tricky whether we ought to say it's illusory. What I can say is that I don't think manifest time maps onto the fundamental picture of time we have from physics.

3AM: You recently took up arms against Sean Carroll developing an idea of a multiverse to explain the low entropy. You make this a parade case of the kind of ontological speculation that is too expensive. Having to posit such a huge untestable ontological commitment to explain something like low entropy at the big bang, you just don't think is worth it. Is that right? Are there other ideas coming from physics that worry you in the same way?

CALLENDER: Philosophers are raised reading Socrates, who tried to be a gadfly to conventional wisdom. Here I'm just trying to be a similar kind of pest to a prevailing opinion in physics. Scores and scores of our best physicists say that one of the great unresolved problems of physics is that it doesn't explain the initial low entropy state of the universe. I want to express some healthy skepticism about this claim.

At least two thoughts motivate this skepticism. First, suppose we judge the constraint on initial conditions to be lawlike. (I think that there are some powerful arguments for this.) Then all the universes that don't begin in a low entropy state are, strictly speaking, unphysical and have zero probability. The initial state is then hardly monstrously unlikely (hence demanding explanation), but rather has probability 1! Second, won't the problem just creep up on you again? The new theory that explains the initial state of the universe will have unexplained explainers in it too. Every theory does. Then presumably one of the great unsolved problems of the new physics will be to explain those unexplained explainers. How deep in unobserved physics do we go before we say, "Enough"? Note that I'm *not* saying that physicists shouldn't posit models that explain the low entropy initial state. Often in the history of science one sees physicists motivated by something they find unnatural in the existing theory, even if the existing theory handles the phenomena pretty well. Einstein's initial motivation for relativity was like this. He saw in electromagnetism an asymmetry in the theory not reflected in the phenomena—and he bristled at this asymmetry. Others didn't. Einstein then invented an alternative theory that eventually crushed the original.

But I think it would have been wrong to say, prior to relativity, that we *knew* that the asymmetry between moving magnets and magnets at rest was a deep unsolved problem of physics. No, it was a curiosity of a successful theory that was a clue for developing a new, and as it turns out, better, theory. Similarly, I don't think we know that the initial low entropy is a problem for the standard picture of physics. The problematic aspects of the posit are overstated. Whether it emerges as a clue to something better is something we shall see.

3:AM: You also disagree with people like Stephen Hawking about the fine-tuned nature of the universe. Is Hawking just speculating rather than doing science?

CALLENDER: I think that most of the fine-tuning arguments one sees are nonsense. The idea is something like: a physical parameter P is finely tuned if the probability of P taking a value compatible with life is low. Its low probability is then supposed to call for explanation via new physics. Forget the vagueness of what we mean by "life." That's a serious problem, but a deeper one is that we typically have no warranted probability metrics to support these judgments. Where are these judgments of unlikeliness coming from?

Maybe this objection seems like a technicality, but it isn't. Most of the parameters people talk about being finely tuned are things like force strengths and particles' masses. In most cases these are nomic, that is, lawlike, features. So to get a probability metric over a bunch of nomic parameters, one needs, it seems, a kind of meta-law, a law over laws. That is, one needs a law that tells us the probabilities of P taking on various values. But why would we ever need this, and what possible evidence could we ever muster in favor of one rather than another?

Suppose someone argued that light going 300,000 kilometers per second was crucial for life. Is the speed finely tuned? Given that the speed of light is a law, no! It *had* to be that way. However, that doesn't stop the determined, for they can invent a theory of theories that includes a probability metric that assigns a 1 percent chance that the speed of light is 300,000 kilometers per second and then conclude that light's speed demands explanation. What possible warrant could there be for that theory of theories and metric? I was never a strict empiricist, but reading this literature makes me want to be. I reach for Hume, the great Scottish philosopher, and one of my favorite passages in the *Dialogues Concerning Natural Religion*. Hume has the skeptic Philo say:

> ...the subject in which you [Cleanthes] are engaged exceeds all human reason and inquiry. Can you pretend to show any such similarity between the fabric of a house and the generation of a universe? Have you ever seen Nature in any situation as resembles the first arrangement of the elements? [If so]...cite your experience and deliver your theory.

Now, of course, as I said above, one can use a hunch about what's natural or not as motivation to develop a theory. I'm not an arbiter of hunches, and the history of science teaches us that scientists have used quite a variety of hunches successfully. But hunches about tuning shouldn't masquerade as arguments.

3:AM: I guess this leads to the issue of whether you think scientists overstate what their theories actually commit us to. Jerry Fodor quips that the last people he asks when trying to work out the philosophy of biology are biologists. Is there a danger that the scientists might not be philosophically sophisticated enough to handle the scientific knowledge they have?

CALLENDER: That doesn't keep me awake at night. Some scientists are tremendously sophisticated philosophically, and it's true, some are not. Gosh, look at the interpretational mess Bohr and Heisenberg contributed to with their more philosophical writings. The treatment of the quantum measurement problem in textbooks, popularizations, and elsewhere is a scandal. Maybe there is something to be said for being too close to a theory to appraise it carefully....I don't know. But overall I think many scientists are very good at philosophy: the later Einstein, John Bell, Bob Geroch, John Maynard-Smith. And philosophers certainly can't get on their high horse when it comes to these matters. Did they do any better on the quantum measurement problem until they started reading Bell?

What worries me most in this neighborhood is, contra Fodor, the *separation* between philosophy of science and science. To go with your Fodor quip, but coming from the other side, one might add Feynman's famous claim that philosophy of science is as important to scientists as ornithology is to birds. The two quips seek a kind of separation between the two fields that I find unhealthy and unnatural. And both strike me as ironic, for Fodor's work is often best when connected to what scientists are saying, and Feynman, despite frequent jibes at philosophy, was very philosophical—as anyone who has read him will attest. Feynman is right, a bird can *get by* without ornithology; however, wouldn't a bird equipped with ornithology be in a vastly superior position relative to other birds? For answering the sorts of questions I work on, it's important to talk to scientists and philosophers. One wouldn't want to take lessons on a foundational issue from an uninformed or unreflective scientist, but neither would one want to do so from that kind of philosopher.

Another worry I have in the neighborhood of your question is whether science is being communicated to the public in a responsible way. On the one hand, we have all these new and great venues for popular science. Look at the top-notch exposition and production values in the latest Brian Greene series on PBS. But on the other hand, a lot of the work today seems so much more sensationalistic than in the past. Compare the brilliant George Gamow books that were popular a generation ago (*One, Two, Three...Infinity*, etc.) with current ones and you'll see what I mean. If the speculative ideas are advertised as such when they come, no problem. But we obviously don't want a public voting on science policy who believe that physics is only about multiverses and multiverses of multiverses; nor do we want the public thinking string theory is (yet) as secure as relativity.

3:AM: Methodological naturalism claims that philosophy should work in a way that is consistent with scientific methodology. But you don't actually think there's a scientific methodology, do you? So, do we need to revise methodological naturalism? Or else aren't we in danger of the claim to be a naturalist becoming a little too vague to be useful?

CALLENDER: Good question. I don't think that there is a *particular* scientific methodology, but I do think that there is a difference—along a spectrum—between scientific and unscientific methodology. Look at all the pseudo-scientific garbage that is being thrown at us daily, for example, power wrist bands that make you energetic, magnetic therapy wraps, most vitamins, detox therapy. Just going through a CVS [pharmacy] gets it thrown in your face. What's the difference between the methodology behind this stuff and behind the theory of the electron? Not always one single feature, like Popper thought (falsifiability). But as Philip Kitcher, John Dupré, and others have stressed, maybe there is a set of criteria that makes something scientific. Each field has particular metrics for how to handle the tradeoffs among various criteria, so I think it's often hard or even practically impossible to articulate a simple criterion. Often it's easy: the tests on wrist power bands aren't blinded, aren't independent, aren't over a statistically significant sample. Sometimes it's hard: could you tell while it was happening that cold fusion would be bunk but high-temperature superconductivity would be a tremendous achievement? Even if hard to state, I don't think the claim behind methodological naturalism need be contentless. But as you say, it may sometimes be too vague to be useful. If the philosophical case is like the power wrist bands, then I think it is clear enough to use; if it's trickier, then perhaps not.

3:AM: It always seems puzzling to me that Schrödinger's cat story is forever being used as an example of something that is supposed to clarify what the quantum universe is like, because I can't make sense of the claim that the cat is dead and isn't dead until someone observes it. So I don't believe anyone except Graham Priest can either, because it claims that true contradictions exist. But everyone does. So, where am I going wrong?

CALLENDER: No, you're right, Schrödinger's cat is a problem, not an answer. Schrödinger devised the thought experiment to highlight the trouble of thinking that the whole world behaves as subatomic quantum particles do. The key to explaining quantum phenomena is letting particles enter into superpositions, states that compose contrary properties. If *everything* is quantum mechanical, however, then in principle everything—cats, tables, you—can superpose. The problem with this isn't that these states comprise true contradictions. They don't. The problem is that the states appear to conflict with our ordinary macroscopic experience of determinate objects.

Why isn't Schrödinger's cat a true contradiction? It could be, in a sense. The "quantum logic" program offered something like this picture. But I don't think that program was successful as a physical theory, and many controversial assumptions go into reading superpositions like that. I prefer instead to just think of a superposition as a third kind of state. There is the state of the cat dead, the state of the cat alive, and the state of the cat in a superposition. If you want a picture, imagine a state represented by a unit vector along the x-axis in a plane, a state represented by a unit vector along the y-axis, and then a state represented by a third vector that turns out to be equal to the sum or difference of the other two. Three vectors, three states, zero contradictions. Understood this way, the problem is the empirically motivated one, and we needn't call on Graham Priest for rescue just yet.

Of course, figuring out why the heck we have determinate macroscopic experiences when we're in superpositions, if we're in superpositions, is the million dollar question. Here there are basically three answers: (1) many determinate experiences somehow "emerge" from this superposed state; (2) quantum mechanics is incomplete, and the completion adds determinate nonsuperposed stuff; or (3) we're not in Schrödinger catlike superpositions, for quantum mechanics is modified so that these states collapse in an appropriate way. I have no idea which answer is correct. But I feel that I best understand option two, so I tend to sympathize with it.

3:AM: Eric Schwitzgebel has argued that all metaphysical positions part company from common sense at some point. As a leading metaphysician, could you tell us about some of the metaphysical strangeness that you actually think may well be true? Sometimes philosophers give the impression that there's nothing too amazing about the world beyond some of it being really big or really small, but there are very weird possibilities, aren't there?

CALLENDER: I think that the example I work on—tracing the emergence of "manifest time" from its origin in physical time—is a great example. Our manifest impression of time departs quite radically from the fundamental reality, once that is properly understood.

But let me describe four other weird possibilities. One: Flashy Worlds. Suppose that the "flash ontology" for quantum mechanics is true. Invented by John Bell and used to great effect by Roderich Tumulka, the flash ontology is a contender for interpreting the world described by GRW [the Ghirardi-Rimini-Weber theory], one of the more promising interpretations of quantum mechanics. According to a flash ontology, the "be-ables" of the theory—the ontology, the stuff that exists—are distinguished spacetime events correlated with the spontaneous localization of the quantum wavefunction. That's it— just these flash events and spacetime. If this picture is right, the universe is much more sparse than ordinarily conceived. Tables, chairs, and cats are constellations of sparse collections of flashes, not features of some continuously existing stuff. When the wavefunction is evolving and not undergoing a GRW localization, there is simply nothing there—no flashes. If I prepare an electron in the void and send it to you, when you measure you'll produce a flash, a real thing; but until that point, there was nothing there. We're used to the idea that tables are mostly empty space filled with matter; but here the matter itself is replaced by mostly empty space too!

Two: Flashy Causal Set Worlds. One idea in quantum gravity, associated especially with Rafael Sorkin and Fay Dowker, is that spacetime emerges from a collection of events produced by a probabilistic "sprinkling" process. One can imagine joining Bell's flash ontology with the causal set picture to eliminate the background continuous spacetime. All there is in such a world would be a sparse collection of flash events. From this sparse collection, tables, chairs, cats, and even spacetime would all emerge. The universe would look continuous and filled in when really it is just a bare collection of flashes.

Three: No Time. Thanks to relativity we're used to the idea that there is, fundamentally, no space or time but only spacetime. Many approaches in quantum gravity go a further step. They break spacetime up into space and time again and then get rid of time altogether. Of course, the appearances are recovered. What looks like change and time "reappear" only at certain approximations. But it's certainly very counterintuitive to think of change as in some sense emergent.

Four: Spatial Topology Change. Relativity makes this hard but not impossible. The idea is that the topology of space changes with time. Imagine that space is connected and then at some point becomes unconnected; then one has what is sometimes called "trousers" spacetime. Or maybe the universe all of a sudden becomes a big torus—a four-dimensional donut—or a Poincaré dodecahedron. There are rigorous constraints on what can happen according to the laws, but some cool possibilities remain open.

3:AM: I guess as a long-term *Dr. Who* fan I have to ask you, as our man about time, whether time travel could happen.

CC: The idea is logically possible, even if it could get weird. Here is a quote you'll like from the guy who "fixes" time travel mistakes in [Charles] Yu's *How to Live Safely in a Science Fictional Universe*:

> Other people are just looking for weird. They want to turn their lives into something unrecognizable. I see a lot of men end up as their own uncles. Super-easy to avoid, totally dumb move. See it all the time. No need to go into details, but it obviously involves a time machine and you know what with you know who.

Weird doesn't mean impossible. If it did, then TV-for-dogs wouldn't exist. Maybe time travel is physically possible. I don't have any special insight here. General relativity allows many models that allow time travel. So in that sense, sure, why not? When you start adding conditions, however, it becomes harder and harder to find such models. You want the Tardis to create the spacetime path on which Dr. Who goes back? Then that means you want a time machine, and it's much harder to have a spacetime with a time machine in it than just a spacetime with some paths that might take you backward in time. You want a "realistic" matter-energy distribution? Then it's harder still. You want the spacetime to have certain "reasonable" features, like no holes or weird topological identifications? Then harder still. I don't think these conditions necessarily shut the window of possibility. Hardness doesn't necessarily mean unlikely. Still, the opening starts to look depressingly small, however, and maybe that's telling us something. Whether future physics opens the window wider, I can't say. Perhaps it will vindicate the Doctor when he says that "People assume that time is a strict progression of cause to effect, but *actually*... it's more like a big ball of wibbly wobbly... time-y wimey... stuff."

7 | Kieran Setiya

WHAT ANSCOMBE INTENDED
AND OTHER PUZZLES

Kieran Setiya is a philosopher of ethics, epistemology, and the philosophy of action with further interests in metaphysics, philosophy of mind, and the history of philosophy, at the University of Pittsburgh. He is the author of *Knowing Right from Wrong* (Oxford University Press, 2012) and *Reasons Without Rationalism* (Princeton University Press, 2007), and he co-edited with Hille Paakkunainen *Internal Reasons: Contemporary Readings*, (MIT Press, 2012).

3:AM: I want to ask you first about your work on intentional action and then discuss your approach to moral philosophy. Could you first just introduce us to G. E. M. Anscombe and her book *Intention*, which Donald Davidson called the most important work on this topic since Aristotle? Now, that might be a surprise to many outside of the philosophical community. Anscombe is not a household name, unlike her teacher and friend, Wittgenstein. Indeed it may well be the case that people are more likely to have heard of Davidson than Anscombe. Yet she was a formidable thinker, very original, and a woman. Could you say why you find her work impressive and important to you, and maybe say why you think she isn't yet a household name?

SETIYA: Anscombe begins her book by making an obvious connection: intentional action has something to do with reasons. When you act intentionally, you can ordinarily say why you are doing whatever you are doing: "because I am writing a book"; "in order to impress my friends"; "because he killed my brother." This connection has been common ground in the philosophy of action, though the details are contested. Anscombe's originality lies in two things.

First, that she was addressing this topic at all. In an essay published the year after *Intention*, Anscombe argued that "it is not profitable for us at present to do moral philosophy; that should be laid aside at any rate until we have an adequate philosophy of psychology, in which we are conspicuously lacking." If you want to know what it is to act well, hadn't you better know what it is to act intentionally at all? If you want to know what the virtues are, hadn't you better know what a trait of character would be? When Anscombe wrote *Intention* in the 1950s, the theory of action was not a going concern. She made it into one—though there are still moral philosophers who ignore or neglect philosophical psychology. Anscombe conceived *Intention* as a first step in filling the gap.

Second, Anscombe's own account of intentional action involves some pretty striking claims. One is that we have a kind of spontaneous knowledge— knowledge that does not rest on observation or inference—not only of our own mental states but of what we are doing, what is actually happening out there in the world. Another is that intentional action and its explanation by reasons resist assimilation to explanation by efficient causes or natural laws, the only kinds that are countenanced by natural science. There is more in heaven and earth than is dreamt of in the reductive naturalist's philosophy.

Why is Anscombe not a household name? Few philosophers are; they mostly write for each other, in ways that are hard to access for those without a philosophical education. But Anscombe is difficult even for professional philosophers; she is notorious for it. There's a lot in her work I don't understand, and I find it painful to read. Unlike Davidson, who is also difficult, her ideas don't form a system one can readily generalize; they don't have uses or applications that would give them a presence outside of philosophy. And they run against the intellectual spirit of the times, which is reductionist and naturalistic to a fault. Even in philosophy, Anscombe's influence has been limited. The reprinting of *Intention* 10 years ago did something to change that, but I don't think she will ever have the impact of more systematic figures.

3:AM: So, the problem of intention is interesting, but its significance is sometimes difficult to grasp. To me it seems that the issue is about finding a place for intentions, those things that answer the "why" question, in a way that is consistent with the realm of nature where *why* questions don't arise. Mind and world have to be part of the single scientific enterprise, and intentions are peculiarly resistant to this enterprise. Jerry Fodor once wrote in a review of John McDowell's *Mind and World* that

> conflicts between the scientific image and, for example, the claims that moral theories make, or theories of agency, or theories of mind, are real possibilities. If they arise, it's the other views that must give way; not because the "scientific method" is infallible but because the natural realm is all the realms there are or can be. All that ever happens, our being rational included, is the conformity of natural things to natural laws.

Do you think this is the reason intention is so important a topic, and why it is also so difficult?

SETIYA: Right, here you are picking up on one of the big claims of Anscombe's book: we can't reduce intentional action to the occurrence of an event whose efficient cause is a mental state; and the explanation of action by reasons is not explanation by natural law. Intentional action doesn't seem to fit within the scientific image of the world. How can we put them together?

But Anscombe's other claim is just as compelling and equally mysterious. How can we have spontaneous knowledge of what is happening outside our own minds? How can I know, not on the basis of observation or inference, that I am managing to voice these words, not just meaning to do so? Although it may seem puzzling, the idea that we have such knowledge reflects some pretty mundane facts about intentional action. As Anscombe points out, if you don't know that you are doing something—"What? I am talking out loud as I type?"— you can't be doing it intentionally. Likewise, if you only know you are doing something because you happened to notice it, or if you infer or predict that you are doing something on circumstantial evidence, you can't be doing it for reasons. It appears to follow that if you are doing something intentionally, or for reasons, you know you are doing it, and your knowledge doesn't rest on self-observation or theoretical inference. There are tricky exceptions to this, but I think it captures something deep about the ordinary case of intentional action and that we need to make sense of it somehow.

So, those are two reasons "action theory" is philosophically engaging: it presents puzzles about the manifest image of the world and about the scope and nature of self-knowledge. Solving these puzzles would tell us something deep about our place in nature. But action theory also matters for the reason I gave a moment ago: because intentional action is a central focus of moral philosophy. At our most ambitious, we might hope that a proper conception of agency would be a foundation for ethics, a source of ethical principles in something like the way a proper conception of a functional kind—knowledge of its function—would tell us what it is for that kind of thing to function well. At our less ambitious, we might hope that a proper conception of agency would help us to avoid moral and ethical mistakes. That is basically my view.

3:AM: You have approached intentions from the perspective of actions. So, how do you go about explaining intentionality in action?

SETIYA: By temperament, I am attracted to compromise; I tend to see some truth in both sides of a dispute. (In philosophy, the result pleases no one.) Like Anscombe, I think we have spontaneous knowledge of what we are doing intentionally, at least in the ordinary case. To express this knowledge is to express one's intention in acting: "I am typing at the computer"; "I am writing a book." But I draw a conclusion with which true Anscombeans would be unhappy: that intention is a mental state, involving belief, which motivates intentional action. Like Anscombe, I think acting for a reason is "having an answer to the question 'Why?'"—an explanation of what one is doing that gives one's reason for doing it. This explanation belongs in the content of one's intention. "What are you doing?" "I am typing at the computer." "Why?" "Because I have a deadline to meet." Unlike Anscombe, I don't think this requires a kind of explanation that is irreducibly different from the ones invoked by natural science. A lot of my work has been devoted to showing how we can domesticate Anscombe's insights about knowledge in intention and knowledge of reasons, how to make sense of them without metaphysical or epistemic extravagance.

3:AM: How does your approach answer a scientistic challenge, say, from the likes of Alex Rosenberg, who might argue: look, there are no *why* questions in science, because nature isn't purposeful. So explaining intentions is explaining something that really isn't there. Intentionality is just an illusion that evolution has selected for.

SETIYA: It is one thing to doubt that there is teleology or purpose in nature, if one excludes psychology: talk of functions in biology is metaphorical or false. It is another to doubt the teleology of intention and intentional action, to take an eliminative stance to psychological explanation, as such. That is a notoriously difficult view to comprehend. Its advocates cannot regard themselves as believing its truth or as defending it for reasons. They cannot make sense of what they are doing.

My attitude to the metaphysics of mind—how intentional psychology fits into the scientific image—is one of relaxed indifference. I don't have a reductive view to offer. But unlike some, I don't see in-principle objections to reductionism, as there might be if the kind of explanation involved in psychology were radically different from explanation elsewhere—for instance, if it had to invoke irreducible norms of reason and rationality. I have argued that this isn't so. In consequence, the issue of reductionism is much less pressing for me than it is for others. If psychology needs to be reduced, it can be; if it can't be, I am much more confident that it is real than that it needs to be reduced.

3:AM: One aspect of your approach, and that of Anscombe and Davidson and McDowell, that makes me lose my way is its commitment to science and rationality (on the one hand) and the claim that a teleological explanation is somehow obvious, transparent, not open to observation or inference, but just a brute thing (on the other). If this other thing was spooky and unscientific then I'd find it easier to grasp, but you don't want rationality and the mind to be spooky. It's as if dualism would make more sense of what you're doing really, but you're committed to natural laws that won't permit spooks. I wonder if you could help suggest why this whole philosophical approach can strike some readers as being difficult to grasp. After all, Wittgenstein and Anscombe both are pretty terrific writers who are intense, terse, and often difficult to follow.

SETIYA: I think you are on to something important here, which I have tried to anticipate in pulling apart the two threads in Anscombe: spontaneous knowledge of what one is doing intentionally, and the idea of irreducibly normative or teleological explanation, which is found, in different ways, in Anscombe, Davidson, and McDowell. I am sympathetic to the former, not the latter. That is one of the ways in which I am, as you say, not a "fully committed Anscombean."

There is a question for the "fully committed" that you frame, very helpfully, as an objection: What is so great about replacing the Cartesian dualism of mind and body with a dualism of the "space of reasons" and the "space of natural laws"? (The language derives from Wilfrid Sellars.) The answer, I take it, is that the objections to Cartesian dualism made by Davidson and McDowell are not arguments for reductionism. A simple way to put this: for these critics, the problem with Descartes is not dualism, as such, but a mistake about the sort of duality we confront. The Cartesian tries to substitute kinds of stuff for kinds of explanation or understanding and consequently obscures the nature of the mental. This leads to further mistakes, about privacy, self-knowledge, and other minds.

There is a different motivation for questioning Descartes, perhaps more prevalent these days, which is reductive naturalism. If this is your point of departure, distinguishing the space of reasons from the space of laws will seem to miss the point: there is only one kind of explanation, just as there is only one kind of stuff. That might explain the obscurity or elusiveness to which you are responding. Of course, Anscombe and Wittgenstein are difficult to read for other reasons, too: their writings are epigrammatic, condensed, and multivocal in ways that make them frustrating and hard to pin down.

3:AM: Your work on morals is fascinating. James Conant and Cora Diamond controversially argue that Wittgenstein didn't produce two opposing philosophical theories. They suggest a greater continuity between the *Tractatus* and the *Philosophical Investigations*. And Conant links him to Kierkegaard and a shared attempt to produce works that would help people live a good life. The therapeutic approach opposes a fully realized, propositional formula or set of principles to achieve this. They talk about "soul sickness." This seems to be a starting point for understanding your own approach to moral philosophy and the question, "Why should I be good?" Am I right in suggesting this connection?

SETIYA: That's an interesting angle. I would separate two aspects or kinds of philosophical therapy: one aims to change how people live, the other treats philosophical problems not by giving answers but by exposing them as illusory or confused. I am wary of the first ambition, but I cautiously embrace the second. One of the central ideas of my first book, *Reasons Without Rationalism*, is that a common understanding of the question "Why be moral?" is misconceived.

If you are asking "Why be moral?" you might be asking whether "moral virtues," such as justice and benevolence, are really virtues, whether they are really ways of being good. That is what Callicles does in Plato's *Gorgias*. But it has seemed to many philosophers that the question can be interpreted in another way, as conceding that you have to be just and benevolent in order to be good, and asking "Why be good?" Why should I act as an ethically virtuous person would act, if that is not what I want to do? I argue that the second question makes no sense. It assumes that we can interpret the concept "should" as denoting a standard for action distinct from the standard of ethical virtue or good character, a standard by which they can be challenged. What could this standard be? A while back, I mentioned the ambitious thought that principles of reason might derive from the nature of agency, that a criterion for how we should act might fall out of what it is to act intentionally. In *Reasons without Rationalism*, I show that we can make sense of "Why be good?" as a substantive question only if this ambitious project can be made to work. And I argue that it can't. There is no standard for how one should act apart from the standard of ethical virtue or good character. In that sense, the question "Why be good?" is a target for philosophical therapy, not direct response.

3:AM: So, your position is a version of moral particularism. Before saying what it is and how you argue for it in *Reasons Without Rationalism*, can you say something about the two dominant approaches to moral philosophy that your position opposes, namely, the deontic reasoning approaches and the consequentialist approaches? You recently wrote a paper entitled "Does Moral Theory Corrupt Youth?" which I think helps us grasp some of your ideas.

SETIYA: The term "consequentialism" in fact originates with Anscombe, though its meaning has been transformed. The basic idea is that, for consequentialists, whether an act is right or wrong depends entirely on its consequences, what it happens to bring about. What is more, the consequences must be evaluated "impersonally": it can't matter to right and wrong action whether you are the agent of an outcome or how you relate to it, only what the outcome is, described in ways that do not mention who you are. In this sense, utilitarianism is the paradigm example of a consequentialist moral theory. What matters is the sum total of utility, or pleasure over pain, regardless of whether it's yours. "Deontologists" reject consequentialism: they formulate rules and principles that try to articulate when and why it is wrong to bring about what is, from an impersonal standpoint, the better outcome. For instance, it might be wrong to kill one person in order to save five, even though more people live. Imagine a physician who decides to operate on a healthy patient, taking his organs and causing his death, in order to give life-saving organ transplants to five other people. This seems grotesquely wrong. As you can tell if you think through the example, it is not easy to state principles that explain why, and not always clear when they conflict with consequentialism. These debates become very intricate very fast.

3:AM: So, what is moral particularism as you construct it, and how does it improve on the alternative approaches?

SETIYA: What interests me is not so much the content of particular consequentialist or deontological views and the differences between them, but the approach to moral thinking that is characteristic of the moral theorists who develop such views. The methodology looks like this: start with "moral intuitions"—moral claims that just seem true, or that reflect what Rawls called one's "considered judgments"—and try to build a systematic body of principles that balances fidelity to intuition with simplicity, power, and explanatory depth. Where this system supports moral intuitions, they are justified; where it conflicts with them, they are undermined; and it can tell us what to do where intuition is silent. The overall picture is a generalization of Rawls on "reflective equilibrium."

Looked at in one way, the model I have just described can seem inevitable, and it is often treated that way in moral philosophy. What can we do but start from what seems right to us or what we confidently judge? And where should we go but towards ever greater coherence? But I think it is profoundly flawed. One way to see this—the way I pursue in the paper on corrupting youth—is through a dilemma, which can be put like this. Question: In constructing an ethical view, should we give other people's intuitions the same weight that we give our own? If so, the path of reflective equilibrium will take us from conflicting intuitions to skeptical results. But that is a mistake. If I meet someone whose intuitions tell him that self-interest is the only ethical virtue, I shouldn't lose faith in morality; nor does it matter if the people whose intuitions tilt this way are numerous, or if their views have the same internal coherence as mine. On the other hand, if we give our own intuitions more weight, when we have no independent reason to suppose that they are more reliable, we fall into a kind of "epistemic egoism." It is as if we are assuming, without evidence, that we are more likely to be right, that moral reality is more available to us than to those with whom we disagree, regardless of what beliefs we actually form!

In my view, the idea of reflective equilibrium as a theory of justification for moral belief turns on a confused analogy of moral thinking with scientific theory. The problem is that moral intuitions are not like observational data; systematic coherence does not play the same role in ethics that it plays in science. This is one of the ways in which my view is particularist: it is opposed to a certain kind of theory construction in moral philosophy.

As a footnote, I should say there are other conceptions of particularism in ethics. The term is most closely associated with Jonathan Dancy. He claims that the possibility of moral thought and judgement does not depend on the provision of moral principles or the codifiability of the moral landscape. This has some affinity with the opposition to theory I just described, but it is not the same thing. On one interpretation, Dancy's point is metaphysical: it doesn't follow from the nature of ethics that its content can be codified. That might be true, but I think it's largely irrelevant. Even if ethics could be codified, that wouldn't vindicate the epistemology of the moral theorist; and even if it can't, the epistemology might be right. On a second interpretation, Dancy's particularism is a doctrine in moral psychology—that practical reasoning is possible— and can go well, without relying on moral principles. I think that's true, and I argue for it—in fact, for a more radical claim—in *Reasons Without Rationalism*. But again, it's distinct from my objection to moral theory and from the epistemological turn of my most recent work.

3:AM: So, how do we know what it is to be good, if we can't use moral theory? What if my model of virtue is Pol Pot, a mass-murdering political tyrant? Without moral intuitions to rely on, how can you show that I am making a mistake? Your forthcoming book is called *Knowing Right from Wrong*. Does it answer this question?

SETIYA: Sort of. The book attempts to show how moral knowledge is possible in the face of radical disagreement. A pivotal thought is that the standards of justification in ethics are "biased towards the truth." There is no ethically neutral, Archimedean point from which to assess the justification of ethical beliefs. Instead, the basic measure of such beliefs is the standard of correct moral reasoning—a standard that is subject to ethical dispute. When I am confronted with someone who believes that self-interest is the only ethical virtue, it is not just that I am right and he is wrong, but that I am reasoning well about ethics and he is reasoning badly: my beliefs are warranted and his are not. This story doesn't rest on epistemic egoism, since what justifies me is not that my beliefs are mine, but that they are based on reasoning that tracks the truth.

So, yes, I have a story about how I can be justified in thinking that I am right about ethics and that those who disagree with me have got it wrong, if I am in fact right. What I don't have is a way to show that they are making a mistake— except by appealing to standards that they won't accept. It would be nice if we could do that, but we can't.

3:AM: It seems that your approach has consequences for how we might learn to be good. Do you think that this is the case, and that it would make us have to reevaluate our whole selves in a way that the other moral systems don't?

SETIYA: In *The Sovereignty of Good*, Iris Murdoch said that moral philosophy must answer the question, "How can we make ourselves better?" I find that challenge haunting because it is not at all clear to me that it can. One way to see the problem is this: if I am right about moral epistemology, deep mistakes about the content of morality entail mistakes about how to engage in moral reasoning that will obstruct any rational improvement in one's moral view. In effect, there will be moral blind spots.

A useful comparison here is with a standard problem for ideology critique: any hegemony worth its salt will ensure that its ideology includes epistemic principles that prevent it from being debunked even by what is in fact compelling evidence. So what can you do? There is no way to gain leverage for a movement of the necessary kind.

In a way, then, the answer to your question is yes: in order to become good, when we are not, we have to reevaluate our whole selves, our standards for how to reason as well as our particular moral beliefs. But that is a problem, not a solution—in part, a political problem. And again, it is one by which I am stopped short. What I take up in *Knowing Right from Wrong* are more abstract, less practical issues about the nature and source of ethical knowledge, and its relationship to substantive human nature.

3:AM: Another figure you have found important, and again this is a topic I think helps flesh out your approach, is Melville's Bartleby. Can you say what it is about this figure that you find appealing?

SETIYA: Bartleby is something of an inkblot: it is possible to read into his deflated agency a whole array of philosophical puzzles, about perceiving the reality of other people, about integrity and truth, about alienation and capitalism. On the reading that most grips me, Bartleby presents a picture of intentional action that severs its connection with reasons: "I prefer not to" is not an answer to the question "Why?" In the end, though, I suspect that all of these readings are false. In a beautiful book, *The Silence of Bartleby*, Dan McCall refutes a whole slew of interpretations. He sees the very desire for symbolic capture as a kind of violence against Bartleby that takes his silence away from him. It is Bartleby's silence, his refusal to justify himself, or to be interpreted by us, that I value most of all.

3:AM: John Searle recently complained that although he found much of contemporary philosophy clever, and much of it arguing things that were likely to be true, he didn't find much of it illuminating. Are there other philosophers—contemporaries as well as those of the past, who you find illuminating?

SETIYA: I don't agree with Searle. I find a lot of recent philosophers illuminating—so many that it is hard to name just a few. In metaphysics, I have learned most from Cian Dorr and Kit Fine; in epistemology, from Ralph Wedgwood and Timothy Williamson. The moral philosophers to whom I return most often, apart from Anscombe, are Thomas Nagel in *The Possibility of Altruism*, Iris Murdoch, and Bernard Williams. My greatest historical influence, by far, is David Hume, with the proviso that everything you think you know about him—that he is an instrumentalist, a skeptic, an early emotivist—is wrong.

When I went to graduate school in the mid-'90s, I thought I would work on metaphysics with David Lewis. In my second year, I took a seminar with Harry Frankfurt (now famous for *On Bullshit*) in which we read Christine Korsgaard's book *The Sources of Normativity*. Frankfurt was relentlessly and amusingly critical. I took it upon myself to defend her views. In any case, I was hooked. My topic changed from the nature of persistence through time to the intersection of action theory and ethics. Although I have ended up as a critic of Korsgaard, myself, I am deeply indebted to her work.

3:AM: And finally, outside of philosophy, what books, films, music have you found inspiring or suggestive for you? Are there any particular works that have directly or indirectly influenced your philosophical arguments?

SETIYA: I got into philosophy as a teenager through reading H. P. Lovecraft, who wrote pulp fiction in the '20s and '30s and who pioneered the now-familiar trope in which apparently supernatural phenomena are exposed as alien science. It's a philosophical move, and Lovecraft was interested in philosophy. I began to read the thinkers he liked—an eclectic mix of Lucretius, Nietzsche, and Bertrand Russell—and went on from there. For all its flaws, I still think Lovecraft's short novel *At the Mountains of Madness* is quite wonderful. There are also visual artists whose work I have found inspiring: Antony Gormley, among others. His explorations of embodiment and agency strike me as extraordinary instances of philosophical art.

3:AM: Frederick Stoutland, who has sadly died, made a fascinating personal confession during writing the introduction of the book *Essays on Anscombe's Intention*, in which your essay appears. He said that the writing of the introduction led him to change his mind about some of the arguments of Donald Davidson, and that in a subsequent essay he was much more sympathetic to Davidson than in the introduction. Of course, the fact that he said this in the introduction is already a little paradoxical. But it led me to wonder whether you have ever changed your mind through engaging with an idea, not just a little, but decided that you had been wrong. I guess I'm interested in this because Stoutland's change of mind struck me as rare. And surely it shouldn't be. What do you think?

SETIYA: That is a wonderful question! When I first came into contact with philosophers, I was stunned by how opinionated they seemed to be. I had expected tremendous self-criticism and thus self-doubt; what I found was an excess of confidence. Now, some of this is stylistic, the thought being, I suppose, that a good way to test ideas is to advocate them forcefully in blunt discussion with forceful advocates of alternative views. But some of it is pathological. And I honestly doubt whether the confrontational style is worth it. Even when dispassionate, it can be unpleasant and unconstructive. (I say this without the pretense of being innocent, myself.) In any case, this style makes it more professionally embarrassing to change one's mind, which might in part explain why philosophers don't, or don't appear to, very much. A more respectable motivation is that it is hard to do philosophy without fixed points. If everything is up for grabs, the intellectual vertigo is too extreme. The only way to get anywhere is to take some things for granted, which then become so entrenched in one's thinking that it is impossible to dig them up.

If I had to cite a case in which I have changed my mind in a substantive way, it would be this. Until quite recently, I was sure that there is no hope for a relativistic understanding of ethical truth. At the same time, I believed that ethics could be objective, and objectively known, without God. In philosophy, this is pretty orthodox: things cannot be made right or wrong by God's arbitrary whim; and if his will is not arbitrary, it must appeal to independent standards of right and wrong. While I still doubt that God is involved in the metaphysics of morality, I now believe he matters epistemologically. Although its framework is atheistic, the secret doctrine of *Knowing Right from Wrong* is that there can be knowledge of absolute ethical facts only if that knowledge is explained by God.

Since I don't believe in God, I am more open than I ever was to the prospect that ethical facts are objective without being absolute—independent of particular societies, but not wholly independent of us—and I am much less confident in rejecting social relativism. I find these conclusions uncomfortable, and I am not at all sure of them; they reflect a radical shift in how I think about a fundamental part of moral philosophy.

8 | Kit Fine
METAPHYSICAL KIT

Kit Fine is a leading philosopher of philosophical logic, metaphysics, philosophy of language, and ancient philosophy, in particular Aristotelian logic and modality, as well as writing papers in linguistics, computer science, and economic theory at New York University, where he is the Silver Professor of Philosophy and Mathematics. He has written *Semantic Relationism* (Blackwell, 2007); *Modality and Tense: Philosophical Papers* (Oxford University Press, 2005); *The Limits of Abstraction* (Oxford University Press, 2002); *Reasoning with Arbitrary Objects* (Blackwell, 1986); and *Worlds, Times, and Selves* (with A. N. Prior, University of Massachusetts Press, 1977).

3:AM: You are a leading metaphysician and take a distinctive approach to this branch of philosophy. So, what do you think metaphysics is, and how do you approach it? You tend to approach it as an a priori subject, and this raises the interesting question as to how is it possible for you to find things out about the world from your armchair. And what can it do that math can't? Your book *The Limits of Abstraction* develops out of curiosity about Frege's work on the foundations of mathematics and abstraction, and this suggests that metaphysics and mathematics are related in some degree. But are they really, beyond their a priori status?

FINE: Metaphysics is the philosophical study of the general nature of reality. It asks questions like: What is the nature of space and time? What is the relation between mind and body? Do abstract objects exist, or is everything concrete? I believe that metaphysics is like mathematics in being a priori; it comes to its conclusions without the benefit of any particular experience, but in contrast to mathematics, it is concerned with the general categorical features of reality and not with the purely mathematical or "structural" features. It is a mystery how we can acquire knowledge of this sort from the armchair, and perhaps even a mystery how we can acquire mathematical knowledge from the armchair, but I am in little doubt that we can in fact obtain such knowledge.

At the very least, for many of the questions of interest to metaphysics— such as the existence of abstract objects—it is unclear how empirical inquiry of the sort with which we are familiar in science could be even remotely relevant. In my monograph *The Limits of Abstraction*, I did employ mathematics. But the mathematics there is in the service of metaphysics and of philosophy more generally. The questions ultimately of interest to me are philosophical, such as, What is the nature of numbers? How do we refer to them? How do we know they exist?

3:AM: You grapple with metaphysical questions ordinary folks like to think about too. So, you have written about ontology, about what is real. We ask whether numbers exist, or chairs, or atoms, and you suggest that there is an inherent confusion that haunts answers to this question. The confusions involve mistaking ontology with quantification. And this is due in part to Quine, who thinks the question is scientific when it isn't. You say, "He asks the wrong question, by asking a scientific rather than a philosophical question, and he answers the question he asks in the wrong way, by appealing to philosophical considerations in addition to ordinary scientific considerations." Can you say something about these confusions?

FINE: This is a big topic, but let me expand a little. Even "ordinary folks" may wonder whether there really are numbers or chairs or atoms or the like. Perhaps the world is entirely concrete or consists entirely of microscopic particles or is merely a construction of our minds. But what are we asking when we ask such questions? For surely we can all agree that there is an even prime (2) and an odd prime (say, 3) and so there are numbers. Or we can all agree that we are sitting on some chairs and so there are chairs. Or we can all agree that there are water molecules, each of which is made up of two hydrogen atoms, and so there are atoms. The answer to all of these questions appears to be obviously "yes," and so do we even bother to ask them?

Quine thought that in asking such questions we were indeed asking "quantificational" questions. For the case of each kind of object in question, we were asking whether there was an object of this kind. However, he thought that the answer to this question was not as obvious as one might have thought, and that subtle philosophical considerations might be involved in attempting to answer it. In the case of chairs, for example, we might establish that there were no chairs by showing that every statement apparently about chairs could be paraphrased into one that was about particles.

I think that this is a mistake. In asking these ontological questions, we are not asking about what there is, but about what is real. Are numbers real? Or chairs? Or atoms? The quantificational questions are relatively straightforward; they are to be answered by common sense or by science. Philosophy does not come into it. But the questions about reality are deeply philosophical, and it is only through having a conception of reality, a philosophical Weltanschauung, that they can be answered.

3:AM: So, you work to draw a distinction between existence as a quantifier and existence as a predicate. You reject that the question requires us to think of existence as a quantifier and instead argue that it is in these settings used as a predicate meaning something like "real." Is that about right? Can you spell this out for us so we can grasp why this helps us answer our questions about what exists? Do we end up being naturalists?

FINE: Part of the problem here is that terms like "exists" and "real" are used in many different ways, especially in philosophy. For me, the fundamental question of ontology is not "what is there?" but "what is real?" But what do I mean by "real"?

As a first stab, I would say that what is real is what one must make reference to in giving a description of reality. Thus suppose you were a Platonist and thought that reality included facts about numbers, such as that $2 + 2 = 4$. Then numbers for you would be real. This is to explain the real in terms of reality. But what is reality? Here perhaps the best I can do is to explain the role of reality in metaphysical thinking.

Reality is what accounts, in the most perfect way possible, for everything that is the case. Suppose, for example, that I thought that the existence of a chair consisted in nothing more than certain atoms arranged in the shape of a chair. Then this would strongly suggest that reality did not include the existence of chairs, since I could account for their existence in other terms. It is not at all clear, if one were to pursue this method of inquiry, that one would end up being a naturalist. For it is not at all clear that one can account for everything else in terms of the naturalistic facts.

3:AM: This is part of all sorts of debates, reductionism versus eliminativism, and realist versus anti-realist arguments. To some outside mainstream philosophy, these debates can seem a bit forbidding and technical, but they are actually about issues that very often as children we start to ask and continue being puzzled by, aren't they? Can you say something about how philosophers are currently wrestling with these deep questions and perhaps explain why sometimes the discussions can become difficult for outsiders to grasp?

FINE: There is a great deal of emphasis right now on just what the questions are. What are we asking when we ask, "So numbers exist?" This branch of metaphysics even has a name: "meta-ontology." And so it is no surprise, given that there is no agreement on what the questions are, that there is no agreement on how they are to be answered.

But one approach to these questions, which I myself favor, is to ask "what grounds what?" In what does the existence of a chair consist? Or in virtue of what is an action right or wrong? These questions are meant to get at the ontological ground of the phenomena in question, and it is thought that by working out what grounds what we can get at what is "real" or "fundamental."

I suspect that the discussions are difficult for outsiders for a number of different reasons. One is that the discussions are sometimes quite technical; they might involve consideration of the logical role of the quantifiers, for example. Another is that they can involve subtle philosophical distinctions—between what there is, for example, and what exists or what is real. But the main reason is probably not peculiar to ontology: it is just that analytic philosophy as a whole has become highly specialized, with its own concepts and presuppositions, which can be very difficult to understand without some formal training in the subject.

3:AM: A metaphysical question that philosophers have been grappling with for some time is the question of mereology, of the relationship of wholes to parts, both in space and time. Again, this is one of those questions that as a child you worry about. It raises all sorts of questions that I think are basic, like how can something that changes be the same? Persistence of identity is one of those loaded issues that never go away. You're a key player in contemporary arguments about this. So can you say something about how you think we should go about thinking about the problem. Perhaps you can use the example that you have written about where we are to "consider a piece of alloy and a statue that always coincide. Are they the same (the monist position) or not the same (the pluralist position)?"

FINE: Yes, the concept of part is an important concept both in ordinary life and in metaphysics. My own view is that contemporary philosophers have had an unduly restricted conception of part. They have thought that the parts of an object are like the divisions one might make in space. Suppose, for example, that I have a rectangular surface. Then I might divide it into the upper half and the lower half, or the left half and the right half, or the diagonal half from top left to bottom right and the diagonal half from bottom right to top left, and so on. For these philosophers, all parts are like that.

But consider a sentence such as "John likes the movie." Then this has two main parts: the noun phrase "John"; and the verb phrase "likes the movie." The verb phrase, in its turn, has two parts: the verb "likes"; and the noun phrase "the movie." And, finally, the noun phrase "the movie" itself has two parts: the determiner "the"; and the noun "movie." Thus the sentence has a complicated hierarchical structure (which linguists set out in a tree). But there is nothing in the spatial model that could account for this hierarchical structure; everything is flat. In my view, the hierarchical part-whole structure that we find in a sentence is everywhere about us—in atoms, molecules, chairs, trees, cities, and the like—and philosophers have come to an erroneous conception of the nature of these entities through having an erroneous conception of their parts.

Consider the example of the statue and the alloy of which it is made. They are not the same since the statue will cease if squashed into a ball while the alloy will still exist. But what then is the relationship between them? On the flat model of part, it is hard to say since there is just one region there, equally occupied by the statue and the alloy, and so how can they be different? But on the hierarchical model there is no difficulty, since the alloy might constitute a whole, the statue, at a higher level.

It is as if we were to say that the noun "fire" properly constituted the one-word sentence "Fire" with the sentence itself at a higher grammatical level than the noun itself, or if we were to say that Socrates was a part of singleton Socrates, the set whose sole member is Socrates, even though there were no other "material" by which the member and the set might be distinguished. So just as the word "fire" can constitute the sentence "Fire," which is not identical to the word, or the individual Socrates can constitute the singleton Socrates, which is not identical to the individual, so the alloy can constitute the statue.

3:AM: Another terrific argument philosophers are currently engaged in thinking about is the idea of possible worlds. This is a logical tool for handle counterfactuals, but it has metaphysical consequences as well, doesn't it? For example, you argue that Aristotle was close to being committed to some sort of Megarian view that every possible world is one where the possible and the actual coincide. However, you make a distinction between understanding "world" as "witness" and "locus." Although formidably technical in detail and proof, I think the argument is drawing a picture that is, again, mind-expanding. Can you tell us about this argument? I think it broadens the scope of how we might think about issues about modality that, again, are pretty primitive and universal, like "Could I have been someone else?" or "What if I had been born a lizard?" Standard fare for many a bored teen and for anyone with a scintilla of wonder in them.

FINE: Yes, there has been a heavy emphasis on possible worlds in the philosophy of language and metaphysics. I think that to a large extent this emphasis is misplaced, that the work done by possible worlds would be better done by other means.

So instead of saying that necessarily Socrates is a man, it would be more illuminating to say that Socrates is by his nature a man, putting the emphasis on the nature of Socrates rather than what is necessary. Or again, instead of understanding the counterfactual "if the match were struck it would light" in terms of what would happen in the closest worlds in which the match is struck, it would be more illuminating to talk about the consequences of a situation (not a whole world) in which the match is struck.

The distinction between worlds as "locus" and as "witness" concerns a subtle point in the interpretation of Aristotle. Let me briefly explain what I had in mind. I can say "Possibly, you might have been a lizard." But why the "might"? For the possibility in question is not that you might be a lizard but that you are a lizard. I suggest that the first modal locution, "possibly," locates the world in which you are a lizard and that the second modal locution, "might," bears witness to its being such a world, one that realizes a possibility. I then appeal to this distinction in explaining some puzzling things Aristotle says about the logic of modality.

3:AM: Your book *Semantic Relationism* begins with a puzzle that you note has been puzzlingly not noted as a puzzle by many. The puzzle is how are we able to say the same thing from one occasion to the next. The puzzle becomes clearly important when we consider a population who can't say the same thing from one occasion to another. And if extended to thought, we wonder how we can think the same thought on different occasions; then again, not being able to do so would put paid to memory. So it's a capacity that is unremarked upon but remarkable, and you develop your theory of "semantic relationism" to explain it. This theory is designed to replace a view that resemblance is the key to understanding how we can repeat ourselves. Can you tell us what your theory is and why it is far better than the resemblance view?

FINE: Take two lines and suppose they are parallel. Then in virtue of what, if anything, are they parallel? One possible answer is that they are parallel in virtue of having the same direction. In other words, there is a certain feature of lines, their direction, and two lines are parallel in virtue of having this feature in common. This is the resemblance view. Now it is not at all clear that it is correct.

One might well have thought that lines do not possess an "intrinsic" direction and that far from understanding parallelism between lines in terms of their direction one should understand direction in terms of parallelism, that direction is what is common to parallel lines.

Now consider the analogous case of synonymy, or saying the same thing. You say "Obama is president" and I say "Obama is president" and we are thereby same-sayers. But in virtue of what, if anything, are we same-sayers? Almost every philosopher who has considered this question has wanted to adopt the resemblance view. They have wanted to say that we are same-sayers in virtue of saying the same thing. In other words, there is something I say and something you say and it is in virtue of this thing being the same that we are same-sayers.

The basic idea behind semantic relationism is that this tempting thought is mistaken—that, just as in the case of direction, what is said is to be understood in terms of same-saying rather than the other way round. One advantage of the relationist view over the resemblance view concerns the question of why the sentence "Hesperus is Phosphorus" is informative while the sentence "Hesperus is Hesperus" is not, given that they appear to say the same thing, that a given planet is the same as itself. The relationist can admit that they say the same thing in the sense of having the same intrinsic meaning, while denying that they stand in the same-saying relation. Just as two lines intrinsically the same in terms of length can be relationally different in terms of parallelism, so two sentences intrinsically the same in meaning can be relationally different in terms of same-saying.

3:AM: Some journalists and nonphilosophers have been rather carping of certain types of philosophy, saying that its trivial, nitpicking, and no longer doing what philosophers of old did. They also complain that they can't read it anymore because it is technical and difficult to grasp what is at stake. Reading your work, what can seem philosophically abstruse issues and technically dense arguments open up startlingly fresh and new imaginative vistas, don't they? How would you characterize the point of doing philosophy?

FINE: Philosophy is no more interesting than its questions. What is the nature of space, of time? What is the relationship between mind and body? How do we know it's not all a dream? If you're not interested in the questions, then you're not going to be interested in the subject, and you might as well turn to something else. It might appear surprising that these questions, which we can all appreciate, should lead to work that is so difficult to understand. But consider Fermat's Last Theorem. All of us with a modicum of mathematics can understand the theorem, but very few of us can follow the proof. I am not suggesting that the disconnect between the questions and the answers is as great in philosophy as it is in mathematics, but I do not think one should be surprised if seemingly innocent questions should lead, step by step, into ever-greater levels of complexity and difficulty.

3:AM: Eric Schwitzgebel argues that metaphysical theories at some point must part company with common sense. He labels this position "crazyism." Are you a crazyist in this sense?

FINE: No, I'm a non-crazyist. I'm firmly of the opinion that real progress in philosophy can only come from taking common sense seriously. A departure from common sense is usually an indication that a mistake has been made. If you like, common sense is the data of philosophy and a philosopher should no more ignore common sense than a scientist should ignore the results of observation. A good example concerns ontology. Many philosophers have wanted to deny that there are chairs or numbers or the like. This strikes me as crazy and is an indication that they have not had a proper understanding of what is at issue. By recognizing that these things are crazy, we can then come to a better understanding of what is at issue and of how the questions of ontology are to be resolved.

3:AM Experimental philosophy asks that philosophers leave their armchairs. So they would ask perhaps whether math really is a priori, say, or whether principles of abstraction do work like Frege said they did, and then they'd experiment on the folks to find out. So what is your view about the role of non–a priori approaches to metaphysics?

FINE: I am not especially enamored of my armchair and would be happy to leave it if I thought that it would be of help in answering the questions of interest to me. But I fail to see how it could be. Consider the question of whether mathematics is a priori or whether principles of abstraction of the sort proposed by Frege might provide a foundation for a significant part of mathematics. How could asking people possibly be of any help in answering these questions? Physicists don't ask people to look down telescopes, and mathematicians don't ask them to assess the plausibility of their axiom. And so why should it be any different for philosophy? Or, take another analogy. We don't ask folks to read X-rays since it takes skill and training to know what to make of them—to understand whether a particular blotch, for example, has any real significance. It is no different, it seems to me, in regard to the intuitions of philosophers. One needs skill and training to know what to make of them, and it would be a terrible retrograde step to rely instead on the untutored judgments of ordinary people.

3:AM: You're also concerned to pursue questions that you think we've got the right tools for. You give as an example the case of economics, where they started to use the tools of physics in order to get precision and went disastrously wrong until Keith Arrow sorted out the mess. So, are there areas in philosophy at the moment that you think are pretty futile to pursue, or examples from the past to illustrate what you think?

FINE: Yes, you have to know when to ask a question. Until recently, there was no point in trying to prove Fermat's Last Theorem; the mathematical tools were not available. And similarly in philosophy. But great judgment is required in order to know when is a good time to ask a question. You have to match the tools available against the difficulty of the problem; and it is very easy to overestimate the power of the tools and to underestimate the difficulty of the problem. In my opinion, many of the questions philosophers currently consider are not worth pursuing—not because they are of no interest but because we do not yet possess the tools to make any real progress with them. These include the mind-body problem, the problem of free will, and the problem of skepticism. I feel that contemporary philosophers asking these questions is like the ancient Greeks asking about the constitution of matter or the nature of the cosmos. Good questions, to be sure, but no point, at the current stage of inquiry, in trying to answer them.

3:AM: Have you ever changed your mind on a significant point through thinking hard about something or listening to someone else's argument? It seems rare in philosophy and this is rather peculiar, isn't it, if philosophical enquiry is about being open-minded?

FINE: Yes, I have changed my mind on a number of issues, and one thing that has surprised me is that I have become more Kantian in my thinking. I used to hate Kant and everything he stood for, while recognizing that he was one of the greatest of philosophers. But I have now come round to some of his ideas, especially in the philosophy of mathematics.

Yes, it is relatively rare for philosophers to change their minds—and perhaps somewhat disturbing. Perhaps one reason is that decisive refutation is so unusual in philosophy, and most of us have the tendency to stick to our opinions unless we are given some pretty compelling reasons to change them. A related reason is that good ideas in philosophy are like good wine; it needs to mature to be at its best. So we spend a lot of time letting our ideas mature, and before you know it, it's too late to do anything else!

3:AM: After the low period of the Positivist attack on metaphysics, the subject seems to be in the ascendency again. Is this your feeling about the subject, and how do you account for its resurgence?

FINE: Yes, it is in the ascendant. Why? Perhaps the main reason is that you cannot keep a good question down. You can be told that certain questions are meaningless and even be given apparently compelling arguments for thinking that they are, but if they strike you as meaningful then you are not going to be convinced.

Suppose that a friend of yours has been in a serious accident and you wonder whether they have died. A philosopher then tells you that it is a meaningless question and even gives you apparently compelling arguments (where do you draw the line between life and death?). Are you going to stop worrying? Of course not. And the same is true for many of the questions of metaphysics. I personally could not care a toss for the many arguments that philosophers have presented for thinking that certain metaphysical questions are meaningless, even if I could not see what was wrong with them. If, on careful reflection, a question just struck me as meaningful, then this intuitive evidence of meaningfulness would far outweigh any philosophical argument to the contrary.

3:AM: Having said that, there seems to be a kind of philosophy envy coming from the physicists these days. So, Hawking recently said that philosophy is dead because physics explains it all, which I took as an act of desperation on behalf of a scientific community that doesn't do well in drawing very sophisticated inferences from their data. What do you think about this?

FINE: I haven't read Hawking on this but I assume (or, at least, I hope) he just had cosmology in mind and not the whole of philosophy. Perhaps he is right that there are certain questions in cosmology that were once thought to be belong to philosophy but should now be thought to belong to physics. But even here, I suspect that philosophy can be of great help—not, of course, in doing physics, but in interpreting physical theories and relating them to the questions of interest to us.

3:AM: Are there any books or films outside of philosophy that you have found illuminating for your work?

FINE: No.

9 | Patricia Churchland
CAUSAL MACHINES

Patricia Churchland is UC President's Professor of Philosophy Emerita at the University of California, San Diego, and is an adjunct professor at the Salk Institute for Biological Studies, San Diego. She is a philosopher of neurophilosophy, philosophy of mind, science, and medical and environmental ethics. She is the author of *Braintrust: What Neuroscience Tells Us About Morality* (Princeton University Press, 2011); *Brainwise: Studies in Neurophilosophy* (MIT Press, 2002) and *Neurophilosophy: Toward a Unified Science of the Mind-Brain* (MIT Press, 1986). She is co-author or editor of *On the Contrary: Critical Essays 1987–1997* (MIT Press, 1998) with Paul Churchland; *The Mind-Brain Continuum* (MIT Press, 1996) with R. R. Llinás; *Neurophilosophy and Alzheimer's Disease* (Berlin: Springer-Verlag, 1992) with Y. Christen; and *The Computational Brain* (MIT Press, 1992) with T. J. Sejnowski. She was awarded a MacArthur Fellowship in 1991.

3:AM: What made you want to be a philosopher? Were you a brooding child in the armchair or one prone to want to experiment and find things out? Was it philosophy first, or science first with you?

CHURCHLAND: I had no idea what philosophy was until I went to college at UBC. I first read Hume and Plato, so naturally I was under the misapprehension that philosophers are trying to figure out what is true, and that contemporary philosophers are mainly trying to figure out what is true about the mind. Of course Hume and Plato *were* trying to do that, hence my misapprehension.

I made the assumption, wrong of course, that conceptual analysis was a brief preliminary on the road to finding out about the nature of free will, consciousness, the self, the origin of values, and so forth. Eventually I realized that for contemporary philosophers conceptual analysis per se was an end in itself. For some, it was somehow supposed to lead to the truth about these phenomena, not just to tidy things up a bit. By then I was in graduate school in Pittsburgh, and when I was in a seminar studying Quine's book *Word and Object*, I realized the implications of naturalizing epistemology and of Quine's claim that philosophy and science are continuous.

I discovered that Quine understood the problem with the claims about a priori truths and necessary truths more generally. Analyzing a concept can (perhaps) tell you what the concept means (at least means to some philosophers), but it does not tell you anything about whether the concept is true of anything in the world. But many philosophers in the second half of the 20th century really seemed to think that they were laying the foundations for science by laying down the conceptual (necessary) truths. I asked one: show me one example where 20th century conceptual analysis laid a foundational plank for any empirical science—*any empirical* science. No answer.

3:AM: Your approach to philosophy may strike some as being not really philosophical. This is because you place neuroscience at the heart of your approach. Can you say something about why you think this approach has caused some people to worry that it undermines the claims of philosophical enquiry proper and how you respond?

CHURCHLAND: Philosophical enquiry *proper*—mmm, is that the sort of thing Aristotle and Hume were doing, or the sort of thing that Kripke and Gettier were doing? Let me sound curmudgeonly for a moment: if I want to know how people use words, I will go to sociolinguists, who actually do science to try to find those things out. If I want to know how we learn and remember and represent the world, I will go to psychology and neuroscience. If I want to know where values come from, I will go to evolutionary biology and neuroscience and psychology, just as Aristotle and Hume would have, were they alive.

Theorizing is of course essential to make progress in understanding, but theorizing in the absence of knowing available relevant facts is not very productive. Given how long philosophers have been at conceptual analysis (I mean the 20th century stuff), and how many have been doing it, what can we say are the two most important concept results of all that effort? By "important" here, let's mean "has a significant impact outside philosophy on how people understand something." Otherwise, as Feyerabend said, we are just talking to ourselves, taking in each other's laundry. Incidentally, the analytic claim that knowledge is "true justified belief" does not accord with how ordinary people in fact use the word "know." So, whose concept is being analyzed? When philosophers try to understand consciousness, much of what they claim is not conceptual analysis at all, though it may be shopped under that description. Actually, they are really offering a theory about the nature of consciousness. When that theory is isolated from known facts, it is likely not to be productive.

3:AM: So, I guess we can very safely say you are a naturalist philosopher. The trouble is, there seem to be many varieties of naturalism. Could you say something about how you'd characterize your general position?

CHURCHLAND: Perhaps I've already partly answered this. My current interest is in moral values, and to address where values come from—self-maintenance values and social values—many sciences are relevant; evolutionary biology, anthropology, psychology, neuroscience, political science, cultural history.

3:AM: You argued that although neuroscience is important, it doesn't mean that psychological explanations become redundant. You say that we wouldn't know what neuroscience needed to explain without psychology. Can you say more about this, and also the connected point about whether we can reduce folk psychology to neuroscience?

CHURCHLAND: There are many levels of organization in nervous systems. Hence we aim to explain mechanisms at one level in terms of properties and dynamics at a lower level, and to fit that in with the properties at the higher levels. If you want to study learning and memory, it is useful to take advantage of behavioral data concerning forgetting curves, the relation between doing and learning (in contrast to merely seeing and learning), and so forth. In fact much of the behaviorist literature on learning (conditioning, extinction, etc.) has turned out to be extremely useful to neuroscientists who want precise descriptions of a phenomenon that needs to be explained. What is reinforcement learning, and what are its mechanisms? We now know much more about the neurobiology of the reward system than we did two decades ago, and we know it is as crucial as pretty much all forms of learning, except perhaps priming.

The neuroscience of vision has been powerfully guided by psychological experiments of vision, including those focusing on illusions of color, constancy, stereo, motion, motion capture, and so on. Masking, where a signal is presented and followed immediately by a noisy signal, has been important in the study of consciousness because if the time between the two stimuli is short, you do not experience the first stimulus. Stan Dehaene has used this to ask this question: What is the difference in the brain between the condition where you are conscious of the stimulus and where you are not? He uses imaging and EEG techniques to make progress on this, and the results are promising. Others are probing the differences in the brain during sleep and being awake, between being awake and in coma, and so forth.

Early studies of sleep and dreaming were crucially dependent on waking subjects up during sleep to find out whether they are dreaming or not. Using that strategy, it was found that when the eyes are rapidly moving (REM sleep) people are usually dreaming; when the eyes are not moving, there may be some mentation, but little in the way of visually rich dreams. Some of our critics claimed that we thought that psychology was useless. These were generally people who had not read our books but just talked to other people who had [also] not read our books.

3:AM: So, can you give readers an overview of what you take to be the relation between the mind and the brain?

CHURCHLAND: In all probability, mental states are processes and activities of the brain. Exactly what activities, and exactly at what level of description, remains to be seen. But studies of decision making in the monkey, where activity of single neurons in the parietal cortex is recorded, you can see a lot about the time-accuracy trade-off in the monkey's decision, and you can see from the neuron's activity at what point in his accumulation of evidence he makes his decision to make a particular movement. It is surely also important that the differences between coma, deep sleep, being under anesthesia, on the one hand, and being alert on the other all involve changes in the brain.

3:AM: Now, philosophers like Dave Chalmers, for example, argue that even when all the data are in on how the brain works, the nature of consciousness will remain elusive. Any functional/causal explanation of how the brain works could without obvious absurdity be duplicated in a world without consciousness. That's the kind of argument, isn't it? So, how do you answer that sort of challenge? Are you saying that it's just empirically lucky that consciousness turned up in our world, even though it didn't need to, or are you saying that given what we know about the brain, consciousness was necessary? Or do you just think that this issue is not interesting anymore?

CHURCHLAND: Well, anyone can make that prediction. But how does he *know* that? He *doesn't*. It *is* a prediction. Remember, in the heyday of vitalism, people said that when all the data are in about cells and how they work, we will still know nothing about the life force—about the basic difference between being alive and not being alive. Well, they were completely *wrong*. Chalmers is making a prediction about the future of science, a very strong prediction, and unless he has a crystal ball, I am pretty sure he is just guessing. The neuroscience of consciousness is not going to stop in its tracks because some philosopher guesses that project cannot be productive.

In any case, it is important to know that significant progress has been made on the problem since Chalmers's prediction. Personally, I am less attracted to guesses about what cannot be done, than about making progress on a problem. If you give up because you announce the phenomenon cannot be explained, you are missing out. I do not spend time arguing against Chalmers because it is a waste of time. Better to use your time productively. Get on with it.

3:AM: You've written about the possibilities that machines might be able to think. You doubt that classical AI models will work, but machines that mimic the brain might work. Can you say something about this?

CHURCHLAND: Brains are not magical; they are causal machines. It is important to understand, however, that many questions, including many fundamental questions, about brain functions are still unanswered, so until we get a little further, it is not likely we can make a machine that is even as smart as a rat brain—or even as clever as a fruit fly, come to that. For example, we do not understand how information is integrated across modalities, or how retrieved information affects perception or decision making. Surprisingly, basic questions about how exactly neurons code information are still unanswered. Because the field is still very young and very immature, it is hard to see how certain problems will be solved.

3:AM: Another big issue your work tackles is free will. The more we get to know about the neuroscience, the more it seems that doubts come creeping in that we're really at the mercy of our physiologies. You discuss cases of tumors and sex molesters and different populations of voles where chemicals in milk seem to cause good parenting. So what are the implications for free will as neuroscience uncovers these connections?

CHURCHLAND: Many mammals and birds have systems for strong self-control, and it is not difficult to see why such systems were advantageous and were selected for. Biding your time, deferring gratification, staying still, forgoing sex for safety, and so forth, is essential in getting food, in surviving, and in successful reproduction. Suppression of impulses that would put you in danger is obviously an important neurobiological function. Studies on rats in Trevor Robbins' lab in Cambridge show that many are capable of deferring gratification, of forgoing a small reward to wait for a big reward, of goal maintenance, and so forth. Some rats are not as proficient as other rats, so there are individual differences. Of course, circuitry and chemicals are part of the story of self-control as well as the story of decision making in general. Where control breaks down or is dysfunctional, we want to understand what the changes are. In the case of addictions, some answers are coming to light. Psychologists also are studying ways in which self-control can be improved in children and in adults who are impulsive, and this research has very practical results.

When the very abstract question of free will is put in this context, I am no longer sure exactly what the question is. If it means *can we have self-control*, then obviously the answer is yes. If it means *can we create a choice with no causal antecedent*, in all probability the answer is no. But the second question is not very interesting.

3:AM: Your latest book, *Braintrust: What Neuroscience Tells Us About Morality*, seems like an extension of the Nietzschean project as identified by Brian Leiter in his 2002 book *On the Genealogy of Morals*. You are arguing that instead of following the guidance of religion and traditional morality, we should instead investigate the naturalistic basis of our morality. Is that a fair summary of what you're doing?

CHURCHLAND: I want to understand what changes in the mammalian and avian brains made sociality possible; more specifically, what made cooperation and altruism possible. The book thus focuses on the changes in the mammalian brain that first involved extending care to offspring, then to kin, mates, and so on, depending on how the species evolved in its environment. Of course, problem solving and executive control also are very important. In contrast to Parfit, I think it is implausible in the extreme that moral wisdom involves a special kind of apprehension of Platonic truths and the application of "supreme principles" grasped with this special faculty. Once you look at the problem biologically, that approach looks like the deadest of dead ends. [See Philip Kitcher's review of Parfit in the *New Republic*.]

3:AM: What you do that Nietzsche couldn't is give us the science. So, you give oxytocin as a key ingredient for trust relationships, for example. You have some cool examples in your book. Can you say something about all this?

CHURCHLAND: Much circuitry and many chemicals are involved in mammalian social behavior, but I do think Nietzsche would think the account, as we have it so far, makes good sense. It is important to understand that while oxytocin may be the hub of the evolution of the social brain in mammals, it is part of a very complex system. Part of what it does is act in opposition to stress hormones, and in that sense release of oxytocin feels good—as stress hormones and anxiety do not feel good.

3:AM: Some philosophers might take issue with your approach by saying that even if what you say is true, morality is about what we ought to do, and so knowing the chemical base of behaviors and attitudes is helpful but shouldn't be used to guide behavior. What do you say to that kind of argument against your position?

CHURCHLAND: Well, of course, knowing about oxytocin and the circuitry it works with does not tell us whether or not a flat tax is preferable to a graduated income tax, or how the drug laws should be revised, and so forth. I make that point in the book. I do not think neuroscience will weigh in on what makes us happy or how to improve our institutions. But knowing about the neurobiological and evolutionary basis for social behavior can soften the arrogance and self-righteousness that often attends discussions of morality. It may help us all to think a little more carefully and rationally.

On the other hand, so far as I can tell moral philosophers do not possess special moral expertise—they are not, as philosophers, more morally wise than regular people in other trades and professions. By and large, the philosophers who say we must maximize aggregate utility end up with all the usual problems every undergraduate can list at a moment's notice, not least of which is that what makes people happy is apt to vary with their values, not to mention that calculating aggregate utility is NP-incomplete, or as close as makes no difference. Other philosophers who shop some version of Kant's categorical imperative seem equally stubborn about sticking to their guns regardless of the difficulties. *So* if moral philosophy is a normative business, perhaps some new strategies might be worth considering. On the other hand, I think some moral philosophers who work in practical settings such as hospitals are doing sensible and significant work.

3:AM: Although some see your approach as threatening their self-image, another reading of your approach is that it is profoundly reassuring. You are saying that our brains are ensuring that we flourish and live happily together. Can you say something about this and whether you personally are encouraged by what your research is discovering?

CHURCHLAND: I am not quite sure how anything I have said might threaten someone's self-image, though I do appreciate that if you have always thought in Cartesian terms, if you have always assumed you had a soul that would go to heaven after the body died, then you might feel disoriented for a while. Anything that shakes up your common ways of thinking can feel funny for a while; imagine those who read Harvey and realized that animals' spirits for life are not concocted in the heart—that probably animals' spirits do not exist at all. The heart is a meat pump. Oh no—my self-esteem is withering! Galileo seemed to have scared a few people merely by noticing that Jupiter had a moon.

3:AM: You're a top philosopher and have recently been officially recognized as a "genius." But I wonder whether your philosophizing has led you to have doubts about positions you hold, whether you even changed your mind the more you found out or thought about a subject. I'm interested in this because someone might think that the purpose of philosophizing was to find out stuff rather than retrench. Do you think that philosophers really do have open minds when they go philosophizing, or is your impression that they are pretty much stuck in an opinion and tend to stick to it?

CHURCHLAND: Let me just say about the MacArthur prize, that it was very welcome, not least because so many of the heavyweight philosophers totally dumped on the book. Many philosophers hated the very title, and they hated the Quinean ideas behind it. Even philosophers who did not mind psychology claimed the brain was irrelevant because it was the hardware, and we only need to know about the software (*so* wrong). So, the MacArthur gave me a kind of legitimacy, and I was a little more accepted, if grudgingly.

I should add that other philosophers were very supportive, such as Clark Glymour, Owen Flanagan, Alex Rosenberg, Bob Richardson, to name a handful. I think some philosophers are quite open-minded, and really are in the field to make discoveries and answer real, as opposed to merely semantic, questions. Nevertheless, many philosophers were totally threatened by the idea that conceptual analysis, whatever the heck that is, was not enough.

If you want to understand the nature of something, to find out the truth, that is one thing. If you want to play semantics, make up wild thought "experiments," that is another thing. I am not so interested in the latter, though I do appreciate that it can be fun, however unproductive. I have, of course, changed my mind about many things, as the science moved forward. I used to suspect that in the brain, time is its own representation. I now think the problem is so much more complicated. Initially I was rather impressed by the experiments showing that on complex problems, subjects who are distracted do better in getting an answer than either those who answer immediately or those who spend time reflecting on the problem.

The interpretation of the results was that the unconscious has a bigger bandwidth and hence can do a better job than conscious processing in the case of complex problems. However, as other labs tried to replicate the early results, many difficulties came to light. Now I am not so sure what to believe. I was also mildly skeptical about unconscious attention, but a number of psychophysical results have just about convinced me. (See Leopold and Logothetis, for example.) I used to think possible worlds semantics was interesting; I now think it is utterly uninteresting. Ditto for twin earth, and all that stuff.

It now seems that the brain has a "small world" architecture—or at least the cortex does. Everything can connect to everything else in a few synaptic steps. This will be important as we work on the problem of integration.

3:AM: One of the difficulties of the philosophical position you argue for is that it can get tangled up with political debates over the existence of god. Evangelical atheists make it hard to discuss the issue without having to find arguments of theology too, and some think that the arguments with theology have been counterproductive. What do you think about this?

CHURCHLAND: It seems probable that humans have been on the planet, with much the same brain, for about 250,000 years. For most of that time, until about 10,000 years ago, there was nothing like organized religion. Undoubtedly, such humans had social practices for resolving disputes, reconciling after disputes, caring for others, carrying out trade, and so forth. These may not have been articulated as rules but were picked up by the young as they imitated those around them. So social behavior, moral behavior, preceded formulated laws and organized religion, by about 200,000 years or so.

Monotheism is even newer, and Christianity newer yet again. That is quite interesting. As is the fact that many Confucians and Buddhists and Taoists may have religious (way-of-life) practices, without believing that there is a person-like god who hands down commandments. And such people are no less moral than those who do believe in a God-the-Lawgiver. That does make you ponder. If you want to put me in a category, you can say I am a pantheist, in the sense that I care about nature and the planet. I find great solace and joy in nature, and I am totally thrilled by the idea that I share so much, genetically and otherwise, with all mammals, and much with all animals. It gives me a deep sense of connectedness.

3:AM: Finally, you are a genius and a woman. In philosophy, women seem to find it hard to succeed, despite notable exceptions like yourself. Is this something you recognize? And if so, how do you account for the peculiar problem of philosophy and women? Is there anything you think would help the situation?

CHURCHLAND: I am not sure how to answer the question of women on philosophy. I should perhaps mention that at the beginning of my career, Paul [Churchland] and I made the very deliberate decision not to publish together, not to publish collaboratively. The reason was very clear: if we did, people would almost certainly attribute the ideas to him and mere stenography to me. (Someone actually did that regarding the book *The Computational Brain*, which Terry Sejnowski and I jointly wrote. So my fears were not idle, alas.) Part of the problem for women circa 1965 was that philosophy was very combative. If you were a woman and gave as good as you got, they wrote you off as a ball-buster; if, on the other hand, you did not engage in a tough way, they wrote you off as a wimp. So either way—ball-buster or wimp—you were hosed.

Now, this is less true in philosophy, but it is still largely true in politics, or so it seems to me. In my first job, I discovered that if I held my own in an argument, the men afterwards would say this: "Well, she sure cut your balls off." I think that gives you a sense of how philosophy, masculinity, and verbal combat were connected in 1970. It was an unfortunate and unproductive combination, and it has been a great relief to see the conventions of philosophical conversation much civilized over the last two decades. I have to say that I have never seen in a discussion in science at a seminar, for example, the viciousness and mean-spiritedness that I regularly witnessed in philosophy. Some still practice it, but it less common and *much* less acceptable. The massive range bulls on the hills above the farm used to behave in much the same way: snort, charge, butt heads, paw the ground. I tended to think it was pretty funny. Given that the combat factor was so significant, I was lucky to be tall, lucky to be married to a large male, and lucky to have had a rural upbringing so that I knew to take no crap from man nor beast.

It also helped that I was taken entirely seriously in neuroscience, and being a member of Terry Sejnowksi's lab for many years allowed me to learn the conventions of scientific debate and conversation. So when at meetings philosophers would yell at me "You are not really a philosopher at all, snarl, snarl," I was having a pretty hearty chuckle inside. Or as Tina Fey would say, I did not care. I knew it did not matter. I think the field of philosophy has changed over the last 40 years, and it is much better for women now than it was in 1969, when I got my first job. Nevertheless, throughout my career there were men who, hating me or my work or both, put obstacles in my way when it suited them. Others, especially in science, went out of their way to be supportive.

10 | Valerie Tiberius
MOSTLY ELEPHANT, ERGO...

Valerie Tiberius is a philosopher of ethics, moral psychology, well-being, and wisdom at the University of Minnesota. She is the author of *The Reflective Life: Living Wisely with Our Limits* (Oxford University Press, 2008).

3:AM: What made you into a philosopher? Were you always asking troublesome big questions, or was that something that happened over time, gradually, until you felt you couldn't stop?

TIBERIUS: My dad is an educational psychologist who was a philosopher at heart. Bertrand Russell and John Stuart Mill were two of his favorite philosophers, and there were a lot of their books around when I was growing up. I suppose he taught me the joy of asking troublesome questions. He also taught me that the reason we didn't go to church was because we were atheists and the reason we were atheists was the problem of evil. When I got to college I was delighted to find people thought about these kinds of things and called it work.

3:AM: You're known for your approach to morality. You have developed a theory of the reflective life and reflective values. To understand it, it's important, I think, to set it in context and to contrast it with what it opposes. So firstly, can you say something about the issue of naturalism and morality, which is a vital aspect of your approach? At the beginning of your book you cite the psychologist John Haidt, who suggests that Plato's metaphor of the chariot and the charioteer ought to be replaced by the metaphor of the elephant and the rider. These are metaphors about the power of our reasoning, and Haidt's point, which you agree with, I think, is that our reasoning powers are pretty feeble compared to the lumbering nonreflective self. Can you say something about this, and why this is so important to moral philosophy?

TIBERIUS: In philosophy, naturalism means a lot of different things. What I mean by it, basically, is that everything we want to understand has to be understood without invoking anything spooky. So I think that if we're going to make sense of ethics or morality, we can't talk about nonnatural properties of goodness or rightness that are somehow in the fabric of the universe but not made up of the stuff that everything else is made up of. We naturalists also have to avoid talking about principles of reason that somehow exist independently of us and our practices of reasoning. For a naturalist, having an accurate picture of what we are really like is extremely important, since what we are like (and what the world is like) is all there is.

The point about our reasoning abilities has a more particular kind of importance. Now, I think our reasoning powers are feeble compared to what we have sometimes assumed, but I still think they're pretty darned important. What I think is most important is to recognize that we're not as rational as we assume and we don't know as much about ourselves as we think we do. Once we face these facts, I think our reasoning will be improved.

3:AM: Now, the approach you take contrasts with other approaches in several ways. One important approach you reject is one that tries to work out a theory of the human good, or well-being, or happiness, or whatever, which we can then apply to answer the question about how we should live. Can you say why this approach won't do? There are quite a few philosophers who have taken this approach you reject, so, as you say in your book *The Reflective Life*, why are you changing the subject?

TIBERIUS: The truth is that I don't think working out a theory of well-being is the wrong way to go—in fact, I've done a lot of work on this topic myself! But in *The Reflective Life* I wanted to talk about living a life as opposed to what a good life looks like from the outside, so to speak. I just think that the question of how to live is an important question in its own right and, while it's related to the question of how to define well-being, different problems and solutions come up when you focus on the first person question.

3:AM: Some might think that you are approaching the issue in an Aristotelian way. After all, he considered people as part of nature and then asked what makes humans flourish given this nature. But yours is not an Aristotelian approach, and I think it will be helpful if you can explain why yours is quite a different approach despite the joint commitment to naturalism. I think your criticism of Kwame Anthony Appiah's approach was that it was closer to Aristotle than you think useful, even though it took seriously the challenge of naturalism to ethics. Am I right in thinking that?

TIBERIUS: That's a good point. I probably do have more in common with Aristotle than I have admitted. The big difference is that I think Aristotle assumes that nature is in a way inherently normative. That people and animals and plants have a natural telos or goal that it's good for them to reach. I don't think this: there are no values in nature in the sense Aristotle thought. Values are, on my view, incompatible with nature, but they don't come directly from nature without the intervention of valuers. So, to put it simply: I think Aristotle would say that in a world with no sentient beings (nobody to care about whether anything goes one way or another) there would still be some value, because plants would be able to reach their natural ends. I don't think this. I think in a world with no valuers (and I'm fairly open-minded about who counts as a valuer) there would be no values.

3:AM: So your approach is what you call a first-person, process-led approach. Is that right? Can you say something about this?

TIBERIUS: Yes, that's about right. Basically, I'm interested in talking about how to live rather that what to get. I'm interested in (and I think it's important to talk about) how to get from A to B, how to think about our choices, how to think about what matters to us, how to overcome the obstacles we have to pursuing what really matters to us, and so on.

3:AM: So from the perspective you outline, we're largely controlled by non-rational impulses. We don't have a good grip on what we're doing, what we're thinking, what we're wanting. Like Hume, we're a slave to our passions. We're riding an elephant, as Haidt suggests. This is backed up by cognitive science, which seems pretty secure. So to some it may seem that to be able to live a reflective and wise life is a hopeless task for a creature like this. You ask the question, "How should you live?" and some might think we know too much about ourselves for the question to have any point. But you disagree: you think we can answer the question. You start by discussing three features of a first-person process. We're to aim at reflective success, we're to use norms that are not derived from unachievable ideals, and we're to recognize the importance of our passions and experiences for both information and motivation. Can you tell us more about this?

TIBERIUS: Hume's view was that reason is the slave of the passions, and there's a sense in which I agree with him about this. I agree that values are not dictated by reason; they come, ultimately, because of our passions. But this does not mean the same thing as saying that we are the slaves of our passions. We do have lots of nonrational impulses, but we also have the capacity to reflect, reason, and change our minds. We may not be able to steer the elephant in the short term, but I think we can get our elephants going in better directions over the long term by cultivating certain good reflective habits. These habits involve some reflection, but they also involve (as you point out) passion and experience.

I do think that perfect wisdom is an unachievable ideal, and I agree that we aren't going to improve our lives by force of rational will. But this doesn't mean that we don't need to ask the question, "How should I live?" The fact is that most people do ask this question! And if you do ask it, what's your option? One option is to give yourself over entirely to instinct, feeling, and desire and to abandon all hope of exercising any kind of reflective control over how things go for you. Another option is to think really hard all by yourself, devise a purely rational plan for living, and then try to enact it. I advocate a middle path. We should reflect about what kind of life we want to live, on what kind of life will allow for a good self-assessment (this is reflective success—it's the "pat on the back" standard!). But when we do this, we should draw on our experience and listen to our emotions. Then, when we try to live up to our ideas about how we live, we should continue to pay attention to experience and feelings, since our plans might not really fit us very well once we try them out.

3:AM: The four conditions you say are very important for a life of reflective wisdom are perspective, flexibility, self-awareness, and optimism. You say that these are the key to contemporary life, contrasting them with more traditional settings. A striking element is your insisting that optimism is important in this context. Can you tell us about these elements and why they are so important?

TIBERIUS: Perspective and flexibility are important because we need to appreciate all the values that could contribute to our lives going well, and we have tendencies to pay too much attention to things that don't have that much value (we ruminate on silly things and take for granted what really matters), and we get stuck in a rut where we only experience one kind of value (for example, we become so obsessed with work that we can't enjoy the little time we have with friends). I think the pressures of contemporary life, particularly in North America, make these problems very pressing.

I define *optimism* as a kind of hopeful attitude about human nature. I think optimism is important because so many of our projects depend on other people in various ways that it will be difficult for us to sustain our commitment to them, and enjoyment in them, if we think that "people suck." For example, if you play sports and you think that all your teammates and competitors are mean, selfish, nasty people, I think you won't get as much out of the activity. The value of optimism about human nature is even more obvious when you think about the importance of close relationships with friends and family to our happiness. I will say that I'm the least certain about this chapter (on optimism) of all the virtues I discuss in my book. I wonder now whether we couldn't just be cynical (I take cynicism about human nature to be the vice that's opposed to optimism) about some people but not others, so that we can have our cake and eat it too. There's some reason to think most of us are not capable of constraining our cynicism in this way, but I'm not as sure as I once was.

3:AM: The neat thing about your approach is that you think asking "How should I live?" is a pragmatic question that needs to be understood as being answerable without perfect information, perfect rationality, or full moral virtue. We're mostly elephant after all! You link the approach to Hume and Rawls and Charles Taylor. Hume seems particularly important in that he connects evaluative authority to contingent human nature. (You don't, however, defend the Hume who claimed that practical reason is instrumentalist, do you?) This is the crux of your approach, isn't it, that we shouldn't think we need an impossible ideal to live well using reflective virtues? And this helps explain why process is so important, and we shouldn't be trying to set up standards of authority outside of this process. Is this right?

TIBERIUS: Yes, exactly. That's a nice way of putting it. And it's true that I don't follow Hume in thinking that reason is purely instrumental. I think we can be reflective about our ends too. We can wonder if something we value for its own sake is really good for us. I do agree with Hume that there aren't rational principles from which we can derive and answer, but I think that we can reflect on the question using our rational capacities and come up with a satisfying answer.

3:AM: This virtue wisdom, in your view, can't be codified according to rules or principles. In this you agree with philosophers like McDowell and Nussbaum. But you disagree with them that it's analogous to perception. Rather, you break it down into a set of skills that accord with what we know about our psychology and the limits of our rational capacities. Is this right? So why can't it be codified, and why isn't it like perception? Can you say something about this?

TIBERIUS: I find the perception metaphor a little bit mysterious, which is why I wanted to avoid it. What exactly is being perceived? And what is the defect of someone who doesn't "see" the right answer? I'm not sure what's helpful about thinking of this as a perceptual defect. What can't be codified, on my view, is the decisions that a wise person will make in different contexts. I don't think we can capture all these decisions in a neat set of rules.

3:AM: But someone might suggest that by putting so much on the facts about us (psychological and cognitive facts especially) there are two risks to your theory: What happens if we find out new things about ourselves that suggest the reflective life is quite impossible? And another problem someone might raise is, How can *ought*'s be derived from *is*'s? Just because we are predisposed to live harmoniously (backed up by all we know about the psychological and rational cognitive facts about ourselves), can't we still ask, "Should we?" And if we can't, then are you not actually doing away with morality?

TIBERIUS: These are great questions! I have sometimes been genuinely worried about the first. So far, I don't think the evidence favors the pessimistic view, though. I don't think the psychological evidence shows that we are incapable of reasoning or responding to the reasons that we find. On the second, I don't think *ought*'s can be derived from *is*'s directly. Some ought has to be assumed in the inputs to get oughts as the outputs. The ought that I assume is a value—the value of living a reflectively endorsable life. What I say in the book is that to people who really honestly don't value this at all, I have nothing to say. That may seem like a disappointing answer, but I think it's the best we can do. I also think that almost everyone does care about living such a life, once they understand what it is. No one wants to regret how they've lived their lives or feel dissatisfied with how they did or think that the path they took was entirely unjustified or senseless.

3:AM: Can reflective wisdom endorse evil things as well as good, by your account? So isn't it imaginable that Pol Pot, for instance, might have done exactly what he did according to his own reflective wisdom? If we think we have a moral ideal such as "Thou shalt not commit genocide," for example, we can criticize him. But how do I criticize Pol Pot from this perspective? Doesn't your position leave us very much in a relativist bind?

TIBERIUS: Yes. This is a bullet I am forced to bite. Because I distinguish a prudentially good life (a life that is good for the person who is living it) from a morally good life, and because my view about the prudentially good life is subjectivist, I don't have the resources to make it impossible that an evil person could be living a reflective life (a good life for him or her). I do think, though, that these kinds of cases aren't going to be as common as we might fear, because of what most human beings are like.

3:AM: The approach seems to give authority to emotional responses, for example, as well as just rational ones (when the circumstances permit). This is very different from traditional theories where the rational mind has been given sole authority to arbitrate on questions of what it is right to do. So, this approach seems to have the potential to recognize the full scope of how human animals make up their minds. In this it seems very much like the Nietzschean view, as set out by Brian Leiter, where normative commitments are a mix of where nature put them and how we sort them. But truth is not a highest ideal; nor is moral goodness. There is no "higher ideal," it's whatever is practical for the circumstance and preferable for the personality type. Is this right?

TIBERIUS: Well, I'm not a big fan of Nietzsche. I like the point about recognizing the full scope of how human animals make up their minds. I do think that it's a virtue of my view that it includes the emotions in important aspects of life from which they might previously have been excluded. But I wouldn't sign on to the idea that there is no higher ideal than what is preferable for a personality type. My work has been about living a good life from your own point of view, and in this work I have been fairly quiet about morality. But there are other ideals besides ideals of personal or prudential value. I think there are moral values, and that these values sometimes give us overriding reasons to do things that might frustrate other aims that we have. Morally speaking, I think (as many people do) that we ought to be kind to each other, that we ought to stand up for justice in our societies, that we should be helpful and generous when we can afford to be, and so on. I also wouldn't sign on to thinking that truth isn't an ideal. Truth is an important aim in the context of scientific investigation, and in ordinary life we should aim to believe things that are true.

3:AM: Why do you think we need to reflect anymore? Why, once the grip of the old moral principles has been shown to be ungrounded, can't we forget all the languages and thoughts of normativity? What would be lost? I guess I'm wondering why naturalism isn't eliminativist as well as reductionist.

TIBERIUS: I think I get what you're trying to say, but you've attributed some ideas to me here that I don't share. I don't think the grip of old moral principles has been shown to be ungrounded. I don't think there aren't really any standards or rules. I've been talking about what it is to live a good life for a person. I haven't been trying to articulate a moral theory; nor have I been trying to destroy moral theories!

In answer to the question about why naturalism isn't eliminativism and why we shouldn't just abandon the language and thought of normativity in favor of just observing what we will in fact do, let me say this: normative language and thought also evolved with us (along with our nicely coordinated affective natures), and we need it. Think about a time that you confront a genuine question about what to do. Say you discover a friend's boyfriend is cheating on her and you need to know whether to tell her or not. Or you discover a friendly co-worker stealing from the office. Or you get pregnant (or get your girlfriend pregnant) and wonder about the option of abortion, and so on. What do you need? I think you need a reason to act.

Imagine that you ask advice from an eliminativist naturalist who thinks we can get rid of all this normative talk about reasons and rights and wrongs. Such an advisor might point out that in 55 percent of cases like the one you're in, people (to stick with the first example) tell the friend the truth. Or maybe they would say, "In cultures A, B, and C, people tell; in cultures D, E, and F they tend not to." Or, maybe they'll tell you that given your history, there's a 65 percent chance that you won't tell. Do any of these observations help you make up your mind? They wouldn't help me. I'd want to know how the reasons of honesty, helpfulness, and kindness apply in this case, and how they can be weighed against each other if they conflict.

I guess what I want to say is that we can chill out pretty well until something goes wrong, until there's a conflict, until we don't know what to do. Then we need to think in normative terms. Maybe there are people who can avoid this—people who just do things without any thought to why they're doing them or what counts in favor of doing one thing rather than another, without any thought about what the best course of action would be. I'm certainly not like this. I suspect not many people really are.

3:AM: Your approach would seem to require a different kind of education of morals (perhaps of everything) and a broader, richer conception of what humans are. This may strike some people as odd because it's often a criticism of some versions of naturalism that it diminishes the image of the human animal. Do you think that, properly understood, science is adding to the potential of living the good life because we can understand ourselves as just animals at last? And how radical a change of self-image for humans does this approach bring about?

TIBERIUS: I would say that, properly understood, science is adding to the potential of living the good life because it helps us better see the kind of animals we are. We are animals with powerful feelings and subconscious motivations, but we are also reflective animals who talk in normative terms and care about doing things for good reasons. Of course we are "just animals," but this doesn't mean that we are just a bundle of uncontrolled motivations. We are more than that, because of our complicated brains, though nothing that we are is something supernatural. I don't know how radical a change this is. I don't find it that radical, but I wasn't raised to believe that we have nonnatural souls. I do find it requires a change of self-image to realize that I'm not in control of what I do as much as I thought I was, but I don't find this to be a fundamental kind of change. It's a matter of degree.

3:AM: You start one of your papers with the great question, "Should you brush your dog's teeth?" This shows that your approach is very lively, unstuffy, and engaging. This is more than just style, isn't it? Is it important to you that the questions addressed are ones people recognize as their own—are in a sense domestic rather than too grand? How much does this reflect your belief about how philosophers should approach their work? Experimental philosophers seem to have a knack of approaching much of their material like this. Are you one of them?

TIBERIUS: Thanks! I do think it's important to bring philosophy "down to earth," to engage with real questions that matter to people other than philosophers, and not to lose sight of things that really matter. But I don't think this divides experimental philosophy from traditional philosophy. Some experimental philosophy is fairly esoteric and some traditional philosophy is well grounded in the big questions. Currently the term *experimental philosophy* is usually used to refer to philosophers who actually employ empirical methods. Typically, this takes the form of survey research to gauge people's intuitions about concepts. "Empirical philosophy" is philosophy informed by the empirical sciences. I consider myself an empirical philosopher (or empiricist, or empirically informed philosopher). There might be a correlation between philosophers who are willing to engage with the empirical sciences and philosophers who keep the big, important questions in mind, but it isn't a perfect correlation. One thing I've noticed is that philosophers who engage in interdisciplinary work are better at talking about their work in ways that nonphilosophers can understand, which might give us a leg up in terms of being part of a larger conversation.

3:AM: And finally, what are the books, music, or art things (if any) that you have found illuminating while you've been thinking all this?

TIBERIUS: Some of the novels I refer to in the book: *Bel Canto*, by Ann Patchett; *The Poisonwood Bible*, by Barbara Kingsolver; and *Remains of the Day*, by Kazuo Ishiguru. Hume's *Treatise*, of course. Alan Gibbard's *Wise Choices, Apt Feelings*; Christine Korsgaard's *The Sources of Normativity* (more of an influence on past work, but still important); *The Pursuit of Unhappiness*, by Dan Haybron, *The High Price of Materialism*, by Tim Kasser; *The Robot's Rebellion*, by Keith Stanovich, *Welfare, Happiness, and Ethics*, by L. W. Sumner; *Strangers to Ourselves*, by Timothy Wilson; *The Moral Psychology Handbook*, edited by John Doris—I was part of the collaborative research group that put this book together and that project was very influential.

I don't think my work is explicitly influenced by art or music, but I do love to look at art and listen to music and I'm sure this has some kind of subconscious influence. I also find talking to my friends and family a very important source of ideas and insight.

3:AM: And finally, can you give your top five recommended reads that will get people to understand better the issues of contemporary moral philosophy?

TIBERIUS: This is a very difficult task. Contemporary moral philosophy is just far too big a topic for me to think about, so if you don't mind, I'll focus on books about happiness, well-being, and the good life. Even narrowing in this way, it's hard to limit myself to five (of course, I'd also recommend the books mentioned in my answer to the previous question). Timothy Wilson's *Strangers to Ourselves*, which is by a psychologist but is a fantastic discussion of the psychological research on self-knowledge and the adaptive unconscious. Dan Haybron, *The Pursuit of Unhappiness*. Rosalind Hursthouse, *On Virtue Ethics*. Richard Kraut, *What Is Good and Why*. L. W. Sumner, *Welfare, Happiness, and Ethics*.

11 | Peter Carruthers
MIND READER

Peter Carruthers at the University of Maryland is a leading expert in the philosophy of mind, the philosophy of psychology, and cognitive science and has developed theories on consciousness, knowledge of our own propositional attitudes, the role of natural language in human cognition and modularity of mind, as well as written about the mentality of animals, the nature and status of folk psychology, nativism, human creativity, and theories of intentional content, and defended the notion of narrow content for psychological explanation. He is the sole author of *The Opacity of Mind: An Integrative Theory of Self-Knowledge* (2012); *The Architecture of the Mind: Massive Modularity and the Flexibility of Thought* (2006); *Consciousness: Essays from a Higher-Order Perspective* (2005); *The Nature of the Mind: An Introduction* (2004); *Phenomenal Consciousness: A Naturalistic Theory* (2000); *Language, Thought and Consciousness: An Essay in Philosophical Psychology* (1996); *Human Knowledge and Human Nature: A New Introduction to an Ancient Debate* (1992); *The Metaphysics of the* Tractatus (1990); *Tractarian Semantics: Finding Sense in Wittgenstein's* Tractatus (1989); *Introducing Persons: Theories and Arguments in the Philosophy of Mind* (1986); co-author with George Botterill of *The Philosophy of Psychology* (1999); co-editor with Stephen Lawrence and Stephen Stich of *The Innate Mind, Vol. 3: Foundations and the Future* (2007); *The Innate Mind, Vol. 2: Culture and Cognition* (2006); *The Innate Mind: Structure and Contents* (2005); co-editor with Stephen Stich and Michael Siegal of *The Cognitive Basis of Science* (2002); co-editor with Andrew Chamberlain of *Evolution and the Human Mind: Modularity, Language and Meta-Cognition* (2000); co-editor with Jill Boucher of *Language and Thought: Interdisciplinary Themes* (1998); and co-editor with Peter K Smith of *Theories of Theories of Mind* (1996).

3:AM: You're a philosopher whose work interfaces with cognitive science. Can you introduce yourself and how you've ended up thinking that philosophy and psychology complement each other? Were you a philosophical child or was it something you grew into, or did something happen to turn you into one?

CARRUTHERS: I got into philosophy as a teenager hoping that it would make me think and reason more clearly, and because I wanted to know the meaning of life. I guess it did help with the former. But I simply stopped thinking about the latter once I met my wife in my second year in college. I was also always interested in figuring out how the mind works, and applied to university initially to pursue a dual degree in philosophy and psychology. But this was back in the '70s, and the psychology classes were all about rats and behavioral conditioning, which I found deathly dull. So I switched to pure philosophy. It was only a dozen or more years later that I started reading work in cognitive science again, initially through the writings of philosophers like Dan Dennett and Thomas Nagel, which draw on psychological results. Their stuff was so much more exciting and interesting than the Wittgenstein texts that had formed the basis of my philosophical training that I gradually found myself switching direction. I have since come to think of myself as a sort of theoretical psychologist (by analogy with theoretical physics, which takes other people's data and tries to make sense of them). I also believe very strongly that good philosophy needs to be empirically informed, at least.

3:AM: Could you give an overview of where you think the connections are between the disciplines? Many folk will think that psychology and philosophy are not asking the same kind of questions, but you seem to believe that they do overlap. How do you see this situation?

CARRUTHERS: I think the difference is largely one of scope. Thus many of the questions that occupy cognitive scientists are quite fine-grained, about this or that mental phenomenon. (But not always: many cognitive scientists, too, are troubled by the issue of how consciousness can exist in a physical world.) In contrast, many of the questions that occupy philosophers are quite general: Do mental states form part of the furniture of the universe, or are they a sort of useful fiction? Are mental states causes of physical phenomena? And so on. From this perspective, philosophy and cognitive science can flow into one another: with philosophy taking data and fine-grained theories from cognitive science and attempting to integrate them into a wider theoretical framework, and with cognitive science sometimes looking to philosophy for help in providing such frameworks, or perhaps for some useful distinctions.

3:AM: Linked to this, are you then part of the experimental philosophy movement that gets linked with Josh Knobe and others?

CARRUTHERS: No. It requires a long apprenticeship to design and implement experiments effectively. While there has been some good work done by people in the experimental philosophy movement, whenever I talk to psychologists about this stuff I find myself embarrassed for my discipline by their reactions. I'm not averse to philosophers being involved in experiments, of course, but it is probably wise always to do it in collaboration with someone who has had the necessary training.

3:AM: One of the interesting things you argue is about introspection. You take a rather counterintuitive view that what we introspect is not infallible. Can you say what this position is and why it's controversial? There have been some cool experiments about this that you write about; readers would be interested in some of these, I think.

CARRUTHERS: What I actually claim is something much stronger than this. For many philosophers today allow that introspection is fallible, and it is subject to errors resulting either from pathology or inattention. What I claim is that we make systematic errors about our own thoughts, and that the pattern of errors reveals something about the mechanisms that normally give us access to those thoughts. (Compare the way in which visual illusions are used by cognitive scientists to give us insight into the mechanisms involved in visual perception.) In particular, I claim that people make errors whenever they are provided with cues that would lead them to make a similar error about the thoughts of a third party. This suggests, I think, that they are using the same mental faculty for both (often now called the "mindreading" faculty), relying upon the same sorts of cues.

For example, people who are induced to nod their heads while listening to a message (ostensibly to test the headphones they are wearing for comfort and staying power) express greater confidence in the message thereafter than those who have been induced to shake their heads while listening. This is just what we would think when observing other people: if they nod while they listen we assume they agree, and if they shake their heads while they listen we assume they disagree. Likewise, right-handed people who are induced to write statements with their left hands express lower confidence afterwards in the statements that they have written than people who write with their right hands. This is because the shaky writing makes the thoughts look hesitant. (And people who look at the written statements of others will make just the same judgments about the writers' state of confidence.)

People are completely unaware that they are always interpreting themselves in just the same way that they interpret others, however. Indeed, they think that they are directly introspecting their own thoughts. (I argue in my book *The Opacity of Mind* that there are reasons the mindreading faculty should have been designed in such a way as to produce this illusion.) As a result, people will smoothly and unhesitatingly confabulate about their thoughts, telling of thoughts that we know they didn't really have.

For instance, in one study people were presented with pairs of pictures of female faces, and asked to pick the more attractive one. When they did so, the pictures were laid face down on the table for a moment, before the chosen picture was handed to subjects and they were asked to say why they had chosen it. However, in some trials, through the experimenter's sleight of hand, the picture that they were then looking at was the one they had rejected, not the one they had chosen. The results were quite remarkable. First of all, hardly anyone noticed! Moreover, they went on to tell why they had chosen that picture, often citing factors that we can be quite sure were no part of the reason for their choice. (For example, saying, "I like her earrings," when the woman in the chosen picture hadn't been wearing earrings.) When people's answers in the actual-choice and sleight-of-hand conditions were analyzed, the experimenters could discover no differences between the two. People's reports had the same degree of emotional engagement, specificity, and so on, and were expressed with the same degree of confidence. I take this study, and many others like it, to show that people have no direct access to the factors that determine their liking for things.

3:AM: In your new book you put forward a theory: Is it the idea that there's not introspection and perception of the world but a single thing that does both?

CARRUTHERS: Not quite. I do argue that there is no introspection of our own thoughts (our judgments, beliefs, intentions, decisions, and so on). But what I argue is that there is a single "mindreading" faculty that enables us to perceive our own thoughts as well as the thoughts of other people. This faculty evolved initially for social purposes, enabling us to anticipate (and sometimes to manipulate) the behavior of other people, as well as to better coordinate cooperative activities. But it can likewise be turned on the self, relying on the same channels of information that are used when interpreting the behavior of others. Sometimes we attribute thoughts to ourselves by literally perceiving our overt behavior. But often we rely on sensory cues that utilize the same perceptual channels, such as our own visual imagery, or our own inner speech.

3:AM: Another big subject you've looked at is creativity. You have a theory that creativity isn't a uniquely human thing but is due to a relatively simple mechanism that even moths have. Can you say what your theory is and what evidence you've found supporting it?

CARRUTHERS: I should say that my work on this is much more tentative and exploratory than my work on self-knowledge. And it is a theory of just one component of creativity, namely, the "generative" component. Thus it is common for theorists to distinguish between two phases in creative activity. One is generative, when new ideas are thrown up for consideration. The second is evaluative, when these ideas are considered, explored, developed, and (if they are judged worthy) expressed or implemented.

There is quite a bit of work suggesting that the generative process is stochastic, or semi-random, in character. For example, the most creative individuals also tend to be the most productive individuals, and such people have more "duds" or failures than others, just as they have more successes. What I have done is to suggest that this process may co-opt and reuse much more ancient mechanisms for the stochastic generation of actions. For it is known that many species of animal can engage in "protean" behavior (especially when fleeing from a predator). A fleeing gazelle, for example, will execute an apparently random sequence of twists and turns and leaps in the course of its flight. There is a good reason for this: the best way to make your actions unpredictable to a predator is to make them as close to genuinely random as possible. (It is for this reason that the submarine commanders in the Second World War would throw dice to determine the pattern of their zigzag patrols, to make themselves unpredictable to the submarine-hunting vessels up above.)

So the paradigm example of creativity, from this perspective, is fast online improvisation in jazz. Those who study such performances report that the players seem to be stochastically selecting among well-rehearsed notes and phrases, while operating within a set of local constraints (such as permissible keys). And notice that jazz improvisers will often report that they are surprised by their products, suggesting that they were unplanned but rather proceeded directly from stochastic selections among actions.

3:AM: What are the consequences of your theory for, say, our views about the creative artist or scientist? Do you think it diminishes the significance of creativity by making it kind of mechanical and simple? Should we appreciate music less or differently from before, if your theory is understood and accepted?

CARRUTHERS: No, I don't think the theory should have any of these consequences. Creativity doesn't have to be deeply mysterious in order to be valuable. And much of the real work of the creative artist occurs downstream of the initial generative phase, when the ideas are evaluated and implemented, or upstream when knowledge is being acquired or skills are being developed and rehearsed.

3:AM: Your new book looks at a whole range of issues about the opacity of mind. One of these issues is cognitive dissonance and its interpretation. Can you explain why this is an important subject and why you come to a fairly surprising theory about this?

CARRUTHERS: These data count powerfully against the existence of direct introspective access to our judgments and beliefs, in my view. But this will take a little while to explain. Bear with me. The basic finding is a long-standing one: people who have been induced to write what are called "counterattitudinal" essays (arguing against something they are known to believe) will thereafter shift their reported attitude in the direction that they have argued if (but only if) their freedom of choice in writing the essays is made salient to them. In the "low choice" condition, for example, subjects might be told something like this: "Thank you for agreeing to participate in this exercise. A university committee is considering a rise in fees next term, and needs examples of arguments on both sides of the issue. We would like you to write an essay laying out the arguments in support of a fee rise. Thank you for your cooperation." In the "high choice" condition, in contrast, the experimenter might say, "Of course it is entirely up to you whether to write this essay" (most still comply; if they don't do so immediately, the experimenter might say, "We would be very pleased if you would; it is important to have examples of arguments on both sides of the issue, and we don't have enough on the side of raising fees; but of course it is entirely up to you"). Alternatively, subjects might be asked to sign a consent form on top of the essay sheet that reads, "I hereby participate in this activity of my own free will," or something of the kind.

The effects in experiments of this kind tend to be highly significant and quite robust, even about matters (such as fee levels for university students!) that subjects regard as of high importance. In a typical experiment "high choice" subjects might shift their reported attitudes from "strongly opposed" to the fee increase to only "slightly opposed" or even "slightly in favor" (whereas "low choice" subjects shift their reported attitudes not at all). We know that this has nothing to do with the quality of the arguments produced by the two groups, because there are no such differences. We also know that the "high choice," but not the "low choice," subjects are put in a bad mood by the end of the essay writing, and that once they have reported their change in attitude they are no longer in a bad mood.

The traditional explanation of the finding is in terms of "cognitive dissonance." The idea is that people sense the inconsistency between their freely undertaken advocacy of a fee increase and their underlying attitude, and this makes them feel uncomfortable. Since they cannot change what they have done, they thereafter change their attitude, thus removing the feeling of discomfort.

But we now know that this explanation isn't correct. For "high choice" subjects will shift their reported attitude just as much even if they write a pro-attitude essay (arguing against a fee increase, for example), provided that they believe that their action will have bad effects. This was beautifully demonstrated in a study in which subjects were told of the recent (fictional) discovery of a "boomerang effect." They were told that the committee making the decision would be reading a significant number of essays before deciding. Essays read late in the sequence would persuade in the normal way. But essays read early in the sequence would boomerang: an essay arguing for a rise in fees would be apt to convince the readers not to raise fees, whereas an essay arguing against a rise in fees would be apt to persuade the readers to raise them. The subjects were only told about the order in which their essay would be read after writing their essays. Seemingly drawing a number out of a hat, subjects were told that their essay would either be read second, or second-to-last.

In this experiment, "high choice" subjects who wrote counter-attitudinal essays showed no change in attitude in the boomerang condition (whereas they showed the usual degree of change in the no-boomerang condition). In contrast, "high choice" subjects who wrote pro-attitude essays in the boomerang condition shifted significantly. Although they had written essays arguing that fees should not be raised (which is what they believed), they thereafter reported thinking that it wouldn't be bad if they were. The real cause of the phenomenon, then, is the sense that one has freely done something bad (since what one has done seems likely to cause fees to rise), not that one has freely done something inconsistent. Moreover, we also now know that subjects don't change their underlying attitude in advance of being given the questionnaire on which to express it. For subjects will also use denials of responsibility to reduce dissonance, or they will deny that the issue is an important one. And if they are given a number of such options, they will use whichever one is offered to them first, without using any of the others.

So the true explanation of the phenomenon, in my view, is this. Subjects are feeling bad because they see themselves as having freely done something bad (not necessarily on a conscious level, of course). When presented with the attitude questionnaire, they imagine responding in various ways: "Should I circle the 2 [on a 9-point scale, meaning 'strongly oppose'], or the 3, or the 4, or the 5?" Imagining themselves circling the 5 (the neutral point) presents their essay-writing action to them as being not bad (because the fee rise that they might have helped to cause would not then be thought to be bad). So they experience a little flash of pleasure at the thought of taking that action rather than the others, and so they go ahead and do it. Seeing themselves say that they aren't opposed to a fee increase, they believe that is what they think, and hence their negative mood disappears. This is because they are no longer appraising what they have done as bad.

Note that this explanation only works if subjects don't have introspective access to their real antecedent belief about the matter. For if they did, then at the same time that they circle the 5 they would be aware that they are lying, and this would make them feel worse, not better. Note, too, that a question about one's attitude is precisely the sort of thing that ought to bring it to consciousness, if such a thing can ever happen. But plainly it doesn't, since otherwise the effect wouldn't occur. Hence these findings provide powerful evidence, in my view, that beliefs can never be directly introspected.

3:AM: What other issues do you think are central to your approach to understanding the mind and ourselves?

CARRUTHERS: Perhaps the main issue concerns the architecture of the mind as a whole, especially its "central" portion that deals with abstract thoughts (nonperceptual judgments, decisions, and the rest). Philosophers are virtually united in believing that there is a sort of central arena in which these thoughts can become activated and interact directly with one another, and I think most people tacitly accept something similar. But there is a lot of work in cognitive science to suggest that this picture is radically mistaken. Granted, there is a central arena of sorts, but it is a sensory-based one, realized in the "global broadcast" of attended sensory information to many different areas of the brain. This attention-based global broadcasting mechanism has been co-opted in humans and some other animals to form the basis of a working memory system. Hence we can call up, sustain, and manipulate visual images in this workspace. And likewise we can generate items of inner speech that become globally accessible in the same sort of way. These sensory-based representations can carry conceptual content. So one can hear oneself as saying (to oneself) that one should make a trip to the supermarket, or whatever, just as we hear meaning in the words of other people. But an item in inner speech is not itself a judgment, or decision, or any other form of thought. Rather, at best, it expresses and is caused by such a thought (although in fact we know that the relationship between speech and the underlying attitudes is complex and pretty unreliable).

Of course we hear ourselves as entertaining specific sorts of attitude, too, through the interpretive work of the mindreading faculty, just as we perceive other people as judging that it is about to rain (as they fumble with an umbrella while looking at the clouds), or as deciding that it is time to leave, or whatever. But on reflection, we should no more think that we have direct noninterpretive access to our own attitudes than that we have such access to the attitudes of other people. What we really have access to is sensory-involving events of various sorts. And the only "arena" in which all our attitudes can interact in a global way is indirect, through their contributions to the contents of sensory-based working memory.

I think we intuitively identify ourselves with the conscious events that we experience as occurring in working memory, and we tend to believe that these events include such things as judgments and decisions. But in my view, they don't, and these sensory-involving events are merely the effects of the activity of the self, rather than constituting the self. This occasions a radical change in perspective on ourselves. For the self and its attitudes is something completely submerged from view, directing and orchestrating the show of sensory events that parade before us in working memory.

3:AM: So, in terms of our image about ourselves, how do your theories change what might be the folk belief about ourselves, and how far does it preserve this image? I guess one big area is that of human values, which some see as being threatened by this approach to human ethics. So, would it be fair to place you squarely in the Hume, Nietzsche, naturalism camp?

CARRUTHERS: I haven't really begun to explore the implications of my recent work on self-knowledge for human ethics. But the theory does suggest that our folk conception of ourselves is radically in error. This is because, outside of the broadly sensory domain (perception, imagery, inner speech, emotional and bodily feelings, and so on), none of our mental states is ever conscious. In particular, there are no such things as conscious nonperceptual judgments, no such things as conscious intentions, and no such things as conscious decisions. (And this holds, I argue, irrespective of what sort of theory of consciousness one endorses.) So our conception of ourselves as conscious agents is radically wrong. Rather, although there are many conscious events that contribute to agency, there is no such thing as conscious choice or conscious decision.

3:AM: How much nonprofessional reading helps you with your thinking, for example, science fiction, novels, art, music—are there cultural things that you find helpful in formulating your thoughts and ideas?

CARRUTHERS: I have barely read a novel since my wife and I had kids! (Although I used to read a lot.) All my reading time now is devoted to philosophy and cognitive science. I visit the Smithsonian museums fairly often (we live just outside Washington, DC), but I don't think my interests in art and music have the slightest connection with my work. Nor, come to that, do my interests in sport. (I am an American football fan, and regularly attend my college's games.)

3:AM: Finally, it seems that we're living in complex and tough times. Philosophers like yourself seem to be working in areas of real importance, working out why we think what we do and how we do it, etc. So, how might the stuff you are doing help us understand better the challenges of the complex world we're in?

CARRUTHERS: There is a great deal of good and potentially useful work that has been done by studying areas of human weakness, as well as policies or techniques that might enable better decisions to be made. One has to do with institutional defaults. In some areas of Europe, for example, there is no short-age of organs for those needing transplants, whereas here in the United States the shortage is chronic. The difference? It turns on whether the law requires people to opt out of being an organ donor (as in some countries in Europe) or to opt in (as in the United States). Yet the two rules are equally consistent with the principle of respect for people's freedoms and religious beliefs. There are similar findings regarding the effects of standard plate sizes on the amounts that people eat, and so on. In fact I am teaching a new course at the moment entitled, "Know Thyself: Wisdom Through Cognitive Science," which looks at a range of findings from the cognitive sciences and attempts to extract practi-cal morals (or rather, it gets the students to try to extract those morals). But in the most general terms, I think it is crucial that people should realize that they don't know themselves nearly as well as they believe they do. This is what *The Opacity of Mind* is about. We should be much more humble in our attitudes to our own powers of reasoning and decision making, and much more open to learning about the factors that really have an impact on the outcomes, for the most part outside of our awareness.

12 | Joshua Knobe
INDIE ROCK VIRTUES

Joshua Knobe is an experimental philosopher interested in morality, intention, causation, consciousness, free will, and linguistics working in both the philosophy department and the cognitive science department in Yale University. The "Knobe Effect" is the name given to the claim that ordinary people's views about the world are infused with moral considerations. He has edited a book with Shaun Nichols, *Experimental Philosophy* (Oxford University Press, 2008), and has appeared many times on the online news, science, and current events channel blogginghead.tv.

3:AM: So, how did you start? You have brought a freshness to academia; how come?

KNOBE: From very early on I was interested in philosophical questions, but I always had a fear of academia. I thought that if I ever became an academic I'd became this dried-up person and spend my life writing about something that no one would ever read or care about. And I'd write about it for a few years for a few other professors who'd obsess over it, but it would make no difference. So then after I was an undergraduate I was still very interested in philosophy, but instead of going to philosophy school I did a whole bunch of weird jobs. I was working with homeless people and teaching English in Mexico and doing translations in France. So then, over time I began to feel that I wasn't getting anywhere, and I'd always had this interest in philosophical problems and they wouldn't go away. So in the end, I decided to return to academia, and I eventually did return to grad school.

3:AM: What kind of philosophy interested you at the time, given that experimental philosophy didn't exist then, obviously!

KNOBE: At the time before I went to grad school, the kind of philosophy I was interested in was very much the traditional philosophy. I was obsessed with Nietzsche and Kierkegaard, and so I wanted to investigate and do the kinds of things that they were doing. So that was what my sense of what philosophy was all about. But at the same time, I was doing all this research in psychology. I had published a bunch of papers with someone who had been a grad student at the time when I was an undergraduate student. And we were working away at these psychological projects. But at that time, I saw this work as being sort of a thing on the side and separate from my real interests, which I took to be my philosophical interests. And then when I got to grad school, something kind of weird happened. Someone started to write a commentary on the stuff that we had been doing in the psychology journals. But this person was in philosophy and wanted to treat these psychological papers as being of *philosophical* importance. So he'd be saying, you know, I think you're right about this, wrong about that, maybe this needs better evidence. But he was treating it all as if it had philosophical significance.

So as I looked through his criticisms, and one thing I was really struck by was how some of the things he said we were right about struck me as being wrong. I started thinking that we were not actually right about those things. And then I wanted to go and *show* that we were wrong! But I had the idea that this time, when I try and do it, I'd publish it as philosophy. I'd call it a philosophy paper. So then I did more studies to try and show that we had been wrong about what we'd said earlier in the psychology journals. And this time I sent them to philosophy journals, and that's when I got the idea of doing experiments, but qua philosophy.

3:AM: So you've really got your feet in two camps.

KNOBE: I am a philosopher of two different things. So I have a weird job. I'm a philosopher both of cognitive science and philosophy. So I have two offices and different students in both departments.

3:AM: Are you treated differently depending on which office you are in? Do people make different sense of what you have to say depending on whether they take you to be working as a philosopher or a cognitive scientist?

KNOBE: Absolutely. You know it's really interesting. It's not that I do separate papers, so I have cognitive science papers and then philosophy papers. It's that the very same work, the same papers, will be treated as incredibly controversial and polarizing in philosophy whereas in cognitive science they're just some interesting contributions to cognitive science. There's something rather strange about the way this can happen.

3:AM: So, can you say a little about the kind of experiments you've been doing? For instance, there's the experiments investigating intuitions about free will that you've written about, which might strike readers as being a strange thing to try and run experiments about.

KNOBE: Yes, well, since the very beginning of philosophy and the Ancient Greek period philosophers have been debating about whether free will is compatible with determinism. So the question is, If everything we do is completely determined, if each thing we do is completely determined by what happened beforehand, then can we still be morally responsible for the things we are doing? And some people say, "Obviously not! If everything is determined then we couldn't be morally responsible for them." But some people say, "No, that's no problem at all. Whether you are morally responsible has got nothing to do with whether you are determined. These are just two completely separate issues." So what we were interested in was what were the psychological roots of this conflict.

So we were interested in finding out what it is within people that is drawing them to the one side or to the other side of the issue. So we thought: maybe it's people's abstract theory that is drawing them to the idea that someone who is determined cannot be morally responsible. And that it's people's more immediate emotional responses that are drawing them to the view that people who are totally determined can be morally responsible. So we tried to devise these questions that would make people think about the issue either from a more abstract, theoretical perspective or from a more concrete, emotional, immediate perspective.

So, I guess the study you already know is the one where everyone was told about this universe, Universe A, where everything was determined. And then some people were just asked in the abstract: In Universe A, could anyone be held to be morally responsible for anything they do? And people said overwhelmingly, "No, absolutely not." We got the same response in America, in Japan, in India, in Colombia. Everyone was saying the same thing, giving the same answer: "Definitely not! You cannot hold anyone morally responsible. No one can be morally responsible in this universe."

But then in the other condition, we asked a more concrete question. So we said, "Consider this one guy, his name is Bill, and he lives in this determinist Universe A. So this guy, Bill, he falls in love with his secretary. So he decides to leave his wife and family. Then he sets up an incendiary device to burn them all to death." And then we asked whether they thought this one guy, Bill, was morally responsible for what he did. And in this case people say "Totally!" That guy Bill is morally responsible even though he lives in Universe A. Everyone said this. But in the other condition, everyone said that *no one* in Universe A could be morally responsible. So it seems as if people who have been made to think about it in this more emotional way are giving one answer and people being asked to think about it in a more rational, more abstract way, are giving the exact opposite answer. And so this is a significant difference and helps us to think about why we believe what we believe.

3:AM: But then you found that *engineers* didn't conform to this, was that right?

KNOBE: Now, this was strange. The philosopher Arudra Burra tried this out on a bunch of engineers, and they were the only ones who had the point of view that it was compatibilist in the abstract case. So people of all different cultures and all different groups, they had the opposite intuition except for the engineers, who have this view that determinism is no problem at all for moral responsibility, and we would be fine if it turned out that determinism was true.

3:AM: Why did Kierkegaard and Nietzsche attract you initially and how would you link those two to what you're doing with experimental philosophy?

Knobe: Well I'm really interested in moral intuitions and how people come to form the ideas that they do, and these are questions that interested Nietzsche and Kierkegaard. They were doing exactly the sorts of thing that we are trying to do with our approach—except that we are using empirical data from experiments to help us work out our answers. So I don't see experimental philosophy as a break from the philosophical tradition; it's rather that recent philosophy has been untypical of what philosophy has been like for most of its history.

3:AM: So, this would link in particular to your reading of Kierkegaard from back when you were starting out, with his interest in Naturalistic religious beliefs and so on?

KNOBE: I hadn't really considered that, but now that you raised it I can see that that might be a very interesting connection.

3:AM: This seems to offer a challenge to philosophers who want to say that our beliefs and concepts are not relative but can be fixed and discussed without knowing any of this experimental data. So, is philosophy being made redundant because of your work?

KNOBE: Not at all. I wouldn't agree with that. Maybe what should end is the idea that there is a rigid distinction between philosophy and everything else. That distinction isn't an historical distinction; it's a fairly recent invention. If you go back to Karl Marx or John Stuart Mill or other thinkers from the nineteenth century, they were very interested in questions of economics and psychology and philosophy, and they just didn't worry about the idea that we have to draw some big careful line between these different fields. If we've got to end anything, it's certainly not philosophy, which has an incredibly rich and valuable history. It's just this relatively recent idea that philosophy has to be cut off from all these other disciplines.

3:AM: Is it that there's a continuum from physics to the arts, to literature, say, where the difference is more a difference in degree than kind?

KNOBE: That's a nice way of thinking about it. So, if you say there's clearly some kind of distinction between philosophy and literature, we can say there's a continuum where at one end of it you're clearly doing philosophy and at the other end you're clearly doing literature, and that will be helpful. But if you say that we have to establish this rigid line between philosophy and literature, so that everything is either one or the other and nothing can be a mix of the two, then you're doing something that is not helpful at all.

3:AM: So, what else other than philosophy and cognitive science is feeding into your work?

KNOBE: Well you know, my wife and I have been together now for twenty years, and for the whole time she's been involved in indie rock. I feel that she has given me the sense of all these other possible virtues—virtues that aren't always recognized in academia, but they are really essential to rock and roll. The sense of rawness and excitement. And this sense, especially in indie rock, of having a community that is collaborative and supportive of each other. The idea that if you're on a bill with another bunch of bands, you should try and support the other bands on the bill. I feel that the people I am working with in my little area of philosophy, experimental philosophy, have taken on this indie ethos.

13 | Alfred R. Mele

THE $4 MILLION PHILOSOPHER

Alfred R. Mele is the William H. and Lucyle T. Werkmeister Professor of
Philosophy at Florida State University and director of the Big Questions in Free
Will Project (2010–2013). He has written *Backsliding: Understanding Weakness of
Will* (2012); *Effective Intentions: The Power of Conscious Will* (2009); *Free Will and
Luck* (2006); *Motivation and Agency* (2003); *Self-Deception Unmasked* (2001);
Autonomous Agents: From Self-Control to Autonomy (1995); *Springs of Action:
Understanding Intentional Behavior* (1992); and *Irrationality: An Essay on Akrasia,
Self-Deception, and Self-Control* (1987); and co-edited with R. Baumeister and K.
Vohs *Free Will and Consciousness: How Might They Work?* (2010); co-edited with
M. Timmons and J. Greco *Rationality and the Good* (2007); co-edited with J. P.
Rawling *The Oxford Handbook of Rationality* (2004) and *The Philosophy of Action*
(1997); and co-edited with J. Heil *Mental Causation* (1993).

3:AM: So, when did you start having philosophical thoughts? What kind of
child and youth were you? Was it something specific that happened or you
read or saw that started it all happening?

MELE: My old high school friends tell me that I was very philosophical back
then. In my opinion, their memory is biased by what they know about me now.
I loved reading science fiction when I was a kid. It undoubtedly prompted some
philosophical reflection that I didn't recognize as such at the time. But that was
a long time ago; memory fades. I became hooked on philosophy in college. A
course on ancient Greek philosophy did it. I was bowled over by Plato's—and
especially Aristotle's—amazing combination of breadth and depth. I wound up
writing my dissertation on Aristotle's theory of human motivation.

3:AM: You are a leading philosopher interested in free will. You were recently awarded a grant of $4-plus million to study the subject. That's fantastic!

It's a traditionally metaphysical philosophical problem, but recently it has been studied more as a scientific issue. So, although on the face of it the grant looks as if philosophy is being endorsed, this might not be so obvious if we take that into consideration. A grant for a study into philosophy less connected to scientific methodology, for example, wouldn't get the money. So, what does this grant tell us about the current status of philosophy in general?

MELE: Yes, a $4.4 million grant just for philosophical work on free will would exist only in a remote possible world (to use some philosophical jargon). But the explanation of this fact really is very simple. Scientific research on free will is way more expensive than ordinary philosophical research on the topic because scientific experiments are expensive and philosophers normally need only some time away from teaching to concentrate on research and writing. The Big Questions in Free Will (BQFW) project is funding a total of eight two-year science projects on free will at an average cost of about $340,000. Of the 24 people on the winning teams, seven are philosophers. One of the guiding ideas of the BQFW project is that experiments on free will conducted by teams that include scientists and philosophers might be particularly promising (for reasons I'll get into later). Our philosophy and theology grants are for a maximum of one year. In 2011, there were six winners at an average cost of a bit over $50,000. This level of funding is adequate when there are no lab expenses, no research assistants, etc. There's a second round of competition this year.

3:AM: Having said that, the project you direct, Big Questions in Free Will, might be construed as being linked only to science. Yet it includes not just science and philosophy but theology too. Theology might be thought to be an interesting domain for a tough-minded philosophy project, so can you say why we shouldn't be surprised by finding it in this exciting work?

MELE: The BQFW project is funded by the philosophy and theology wing of the John Templeton Foundation. There is a lot of interesting theoretical work on free will not only in philosophy but also in theology. Work of both kinds merits support. Incidentally, the first-round winners in the theology of free will competition are all "tough minded" philosophers.

3:AM: You of course have written several books about aspects of free will. So, I guess we really do need to know what you think about free will: Is it real, and do we have it?

MELE: Is free will real and do we have it? That depends on what you mean by "free will." Suppose Joe asks me whether resident aliens exist. I'm thinking about people like my friend Flori, a Romanian citizen living in the United States. So I say yes. But he's thinking about beings from other planets who reside on Earth. So he infers that I believe in the existence of such beings. Sometimes it's important to say what we mean by an expression before we make claims about existence. What does "free will" mean? Several different answers are in circulation both inside and outside the academic world. According to some people, free will is housed only in nonphysical souls; it's a supernatural power. According to others, whether or not souls exist, free will doesn't depend on them. People in this second group divide into two subgroups. Some will tell you that the ability to make rational, informed, conscious decisions in the absence of undue force—no one holding a gun to your head—is enough for free will. Others say that something important must be added: if you have free will, then alternative decisions are open to you in a deep way that I will say something about. Sometimes, perhaps, you would have made a different decision if things had been a bit different.

For example, if you had been in a slightly better mood, you might have decided to buy two boxes of Girl Scout cookies instead of just one. But this is not enough for the kind of openness at issue. What is needed is that more than one option was open to you, given everything as it actually was at the time— your mood, all your thoughts and feelings, your brain, your environment, and indeed, the entire universe and its entire history. Somewhere along the line— during a *BigThink* interview I did, I believe; but possibly earlier—it occurred to me that we can think of the three different views of free will that I just sketched on the model of standard fuel options at gas stations. Some people opt for premium gas. It's analogous to the soulful conception of free will that I described. Others prefer midgrade gas, which corresponds to the idea of free will that features deep openness and is noncommittal about souls. And still others are happy with regular gas, an analogue of the remaining view of free will—the one that highlights rationality and the absence of force and is noncommittal about deep openness.

I won't explore these views here; there's not enough space for that. (Readers interested in philosophical assessment of views of free will might like my *Free Will and Luck*.) But I don't want to duck the question. So, is free will real? If we understand free will as the analogue of regular gas, yes. If we understand it as the analogue of midgrade gas, it's hard to say. As far as I can tell now, it's an open scientific question whether the brain works in a way that provides for the kind of openness I described. What if we understand free will as the analogue of premium gas? If I could think of a good reason to understand it that way, I'd give you an answer.

3:AM: It's interesting that you write about how, although philosophical theories have often not taken into account recent empirical evidence coming from cognitive science and neuroscience, for instance, you also worry that these scientific approaches fail to recognize the various models of free will developed in philosophy and theology. Can you give an example of this issue and how you think we should proceed? There will be some that say that philosophers who try and work it out from their armchairs are wasting everyone's time; others will say that science is too limited in what kind of explanations it can offer to ever get to grips with something like free will. How do you think this standoff should be handled? Or is it a phony war, really?

MELE: I'll try to give you a direct answer after providing some background. In my 2009 book *Effective Intentions*, I assessed some much-discussed scientific arguments for the thesis that free will does not exist. The general structure of these arguments is simple. In stage 1, data are offered in support of some featured empirical proposition or other—for example, the proposition that conscious intentions are never among the causes of corresponding actions. In stage 2, the featured empirical proposition is combined with a proposition that expresses some aspect of the author's view about what "free will" means to yield the conclusion that free will does not exist. What I argued in *Effective Intentions* is that the data do not warrant various empirical propositions featured in these arguments. If my arguments are successful, the scientific arguments are shown to be unsuccessful before there is any need to examine propositions about the meaning of "free will." Sometimes I hear that I am missing the real threat to free will posed by experiments of the sort I discuss—for example, Benjamin Libet's work on decisions. The real threat, I am sometimes told, is bound up with what philosophers call *substance dualism*, a doctrine that includes a commitment to the idea that every human person is or has a nonphysical soul or mind. (So we're back to the analogue of premium gas.) This alleged threat is based on two claims: first, given what "free will" means, having free will requires being or having a nonphysical soul or mind; and, second, the experiments at issue provide powerful evidence that such souls or minds don't exist.

I don't conceive of free will in a dualistic way. But a number of scientists say they do. For example, in a 2008 article in *Current Biology*, Read Montague writes:

> Free will is the idea that we make choices and have thoughts independent of anything remotely resembling a physical process. Free will is the close cousin to the idea of the soul—the concept that "you," your thoughts and feelings, derive from an entity that is separate and distinct from the physical mechanisms that make up your body. From this perspective, your choices are not caused by physical events, but instead emerge wholly formed from somewhere indescribable and outside the purview of physical descriptions. This implies that free will cannot have evolved by natural selection, as that would place it directly in a stream of causally connected events.

Here Montague represents free will as something that depends for its existence on the truth of substance dualism. Anthony Cashmore, in a 2010 article ("The Lucretian Swerve: The Biological Basis of Human Behavior and the Criminal Justice System"), asserts that "if we no longer entertain the luxury of a belief in the 'magic of the soul', then there is little else to offer in support of the concept of free will." And he makes the following claim: "In the absence of any molecular model accommodating the concept of free will, I have to conclude that the dualism of Descartes is alive and well. That is, just like Descartes, we still believe (much as we pretend otherwise) that there is a magic component to human behavior." Joshua Greene and Jonathan Cohen, in a much-discussed 2004 article ("For the Law Neuroscience Changes Nothing and Everything"), claim that "most people's view of the mind is implicitly dualist and libertarian" without offering any hard evidence for the truth of this assertion. They also contend that "neuroscience has a special role to play" in the development of "moral intuitions that are at odds with our current social practices" because "as long as the mind remains a black box, there will always be a donkey on which to pin dualist and libertarian intuitions." (A libertarian conception of free will is roughly my analogue of midgrade gas. When you combine it with dualism, you move up to premium.)

In his new book, *Who's in Charge? Free Will and the Science of the Brain*, Michael Gazzaniga says that free will involves a ghostly or nonphysical element and "some secret stuff that is YOU." Obviously, this isn't a report of a scientific discovery about what "free will" means; he is telling us how he understands that expression—that is, what "free will" means to him. Given what Gazzaniga means by "free will," it's no surprise that, in his view, "free will is a miscast concept, based on social and psychological beliefs... that have not been borne out and/or are at odds with modern scientific knowledge about the nature of our universe." However, he rejects the idea that moral responsibility depends on free will, and he makes a case for the thesis that moral responsibility exists.

I'll have more to say about this soon. In my 2006 book *Free Will and Luck* and elsewhere, I defend a position on what "free will" means. My position is thoroughly naturalistic. I certainly don't view free will as something that depends for its existence on the truth of substance dualism. If a philosopher and, say, a biologist who disagree about what "free will" means were having a cordial discussion about their disagreement, it would not be surprising if, before very long, one of them said that the other was using "free will" in a specialized way that is out of touch with ordinary usage. Such a claim is worth testing, and soon I'll say something about a test I conducted. Biologists know that the simple fact that they are biologists doesn't give them any special insight into what the expression "free will" means. (Some biologists may believe that philosophers don't have any special insight into the meaning of "free will" either, and they may offer as evidence the great amount of disagreement among philosophers about what "free will" means.) They can be led to entertain the thought that their understanding of that expression may be an artifact of their own personal upbringing and to consider the hypothesis that they are out of touch with ordinary usage of "free will." In experiments with human participants, scientists definitely prefer to have a sample size larger than one person; and any scientist can see that if the way he or she goes about determining what "free will" means is simply to consult his or her own feeling or intuition about the meaning, then—to the extent to which it is important to avoid being mistaken about the meaning of "free will"—he or she should seek a better method. (The simple, navel-gazing method is not recommended for philosophers either, of course.)

There is an interesting body of work in psychology and experimental philosophy on what nonspecialists mean by "free will." In some work that will be published this year, I make a small contribution of my own. In one study, I invited participants to imagine a scenario in which scientists had proved that everything in the universe is physical and that what we refer to as "minds" are actually brains at work. In this scenario, a man sees a $20 bill fall from a stranger's pocket, considers returning it, and decides to keep it. I ask whether he had free will when he made that decision, and 73 percent answer yes. (In a related condition involving a compliance drug, only 21 percent of participants say the person has free will at the time.) If these participants are playing along, we have evidence that a majority of English speakers do *not* see having a nonphysical mind or soul as a requirement for free will. In this, they differ from Montague, Cashmore, Greene, Cohen, Gazzaniga, and some others.

I might add that many people think that what they call "free will" is required for moral responsibility. People with this view of things who think of free will in the dualistic way Gazzaniga does, will—unlike him—think of moral responsibility as something that requires "some secret stuff that is YOU." But other people with the view that moral responsibility depends on free will may agree with Gazzaniga's naturalistic conception of responsibility and conceive of free will in the same naturalistic way (see *Effective Intentions*). If it turns out that Gazzaniga's own magical conception of free will is a minority conception, then, in defending the existence of moral responsibility, he may also unwittingly be defending the existence of free will (at least, as many people conceive of free will).

I've decided to say a bit more about Gazzaniga's new book here. In it, he sells our mental life short at times. For example, he writes: "When we set out to explain our actions, they are all post hoc explanations, using post hoc observations with no access to nonconscious processing." Is it true that we *never* succeed in explaining actions of ours partly in terms of *conscious* processing that preceded them? As it happens, I read Gazzaniga's book on a flight to a conference in Munich. People who invite philosophy professors to conferences rarely are willing to spring for a seat in first class, and this occasion was no exception. I like extra leg room on planes. So right after I buy a ticket in coach online, I look for an exit row seat—first on the aisle and then next to a window. If I find a seat I like, I snatch it up. I do all this consciously. (I don't know how to look for exit row seats unconsciously, though I'm sure computer programs can do it.) And I do it because, at the time, I have a conscious preference for extra leg room on long flights, and I know—consciously know—how to get the extra room without paying more than my hosts are willing to spend. If someone had asked me to explain why I chose the seat I chose—or why I was sitting in that particular seat—I could have offered a fine explanation partly in terms of a conscious preference I had when I was going about the business of selecting a seat. And, of course, this explanation would not invoke a nonphysical mind or soul, any more than Gazzaniga's own position on emergent mental properties invokes one. Why does Gazzaniga sell our mental life short? Perhaps because he is overly impressed by some of the experiments he discusses—well-known experiments by Benjamin Libet and more recent work by Chun Siong Soon and colleagues. I discussed Libet's work at length in my 2009 book, but a 2008 *Nature Neuroscience* article by Soon and colleagues was published while the book was in press; and because I did not discuss it there, I continue to get e-mail messages about it. I'll say something about that article here.

On the basis of brain activity as measured by blood flow, Soon and colleagues were able to predict with 60 percent accuracy about seven seconds in advance of a button press whether a person would press the button on the left or the button on the right. People were supposed to decide on a button and then press it straightaway. They all did this many times, knowing that nothing hinged on which button they pressed. What does the early brain activity at issue signify? Perhaps just an unconscious bias toward a particular button. In any case, there is no reason to prefer either button over the other. So if the person were asked why he pressed the left button this time, he should say something like, "I just randomly picked it, because I'm following your instructions." Because there is no place in the experiment for conscious reflection about which button to press, there is no place for an explanation of the button pressing in terms of conscious reasons for pressing it.

The same general point applies to Libet's studies; his subjects are arbitrarily picking a moment to begin flexing a wrist. In the case of my selecting an exit row seat, things are very different. I know I have a reason—a good one—to select such a seat rather than an ordinary seat in coach. And because I do, I consciously look online for an open seat in an exit row. By the way, given what I have told you, you can predict with close to 100 percent accuracy what I will try to do next time I buy a coach seat on a long flight; and you have achieved this degree of accuracy for free, just by consciously attending to what I wrote. I said I'd try to give a direct answer to the question at hand. First, as the background I provided indicates, neuroscientific arguments for the nonexistence of free will may be badly misdirected if the conception of free will at work in them is the analogue of premium gas. Philosophical models of free will and experimental philosophy are directly relevant here.

Also, anyone—including philosophers—can study the data produced by studies that are supposed to show that there's no free will and make an informed judgment about how well or poorly they support such claims as that conscious intentions are never among the causes of corresponding actions or that conscious reasoning plays no role in producing decisions. Of course, philosophers can benefit from scientific work too. Libertarianism about free will embraces the midgrade conception of free will and asserts that free will is real. Any evidence there may be about whether the brain works in ways suitable for the truth of this libertarian thesis would obviously be directly relevant. Philosophers' claims that libertarianism is true made solely from the armchair do not seem promising, but this also is true of scientists' claims about what "free will" means that are made solely from the armchair. Fortunately, neither group is restricted to the armchair on these topics.

3:AM: Can you tell me a bit more about that 2008 study by Soon and colleagues?

MELE: Sure. Soon and coauthors write: "We found that two brain regions encoded with high accuracy whether the subject was about to choose the left or right response prior to the conscious decision." They report that "the predictive neural information...preceded the conscious motor decision by up to 10 [seconds]." Science writer Elsa Youngsteadt [in "Case Closed for Free Will," *ScienceNow Daily News*, April 14, 2008] represented these results as suggesting that "the unconscious brain calls the shots, making free will an illusory afterthought." In this study, as I mentioned, the encoding accuracy actually is only about 60 percent (50 percent being chance, of course). Using only a fair coin, I can predict with 50 percent accuracy which button a participant will press next. And if the person agrees not to press a button for a minute (or an hour), I can make my predictions a minute (or an hour) in advance. I come out ten points worse in accuracy, but I win big on the matter of time. An interesting issue here is what is in fact indicated by the neural activity that Soon and colleagues measure. My money is on a slight unconscious bias toward a particular button on the next go—a bias that may contribute to the participant's having about a 60 percent chance of pressing that button next. In any case, the threat to free will here is an illusion.

3:AM: Linked to the last two questions, the opinion of folk, that is, nonphilosophical people, seems to be an important datum for researchers in this area. You've an article upcoming called "Folk Conceptions of Intentional Action." So, why should what folk think about the issue of free will be important in this domain? After all, when physics comes up with descriptions of the universe that no folk could ever have, we don't send the physicists back to the drawing board. What's so different here, especially since science seems to be given such a big role in the investigation?

MELE: There are questions about what ordinary terms mean and questions about what exists. For example, we can ask, "What does 'free will' mean?" And we can ask "Does free will exist?" How the latter question should be answered depends on how the former should be answered. As I see it, how lay folk use the expression "free will" is directly relevant to the former question. I wouldn't try to figure out whether free will exists by asking lay folk whether it exists. But I do think that facts about how lay folk use the expression "free will" are relevant to some debates about what that expression means.

3:AM: Experimental philosophy is an exciting new way of doing philosophy, isn't it? How do you assess the approach to philosophy being developed by Josh Knobe and others? I presume you are part of this; am I right? Does it mean that traditional philosophical methods of enquiry (crudely, sitting in the armchair) are redundant?

MELE: Yes, I am part of it, even if experimental philosophy is only a small part of what I do. I have conducted experimental philosophy studies of intentional action (some with Fiery Cushman), weakness of will, self-deception, and free will. I find that I mainly use the methods of experimental philosophy when I find a certain view about some concept or other plausible, and then I read that this seemingly plausible view is out of line with ordinary usage or with "the folk concept." I don't see my work in experimental philosophy as a threat to traditional philosophy or its methods. I see it as complementing traditional philosophy.

3:AM: In your book *Self-Deception Unmasked*, you discuss the role of emotion in belief formation. Can you tell us what you think the roles of emotions are in this, and how this links with the notion of self-deception? And are we self-deceived a lot?

MELE: Here's how *Self-Deception Unmasked* begins: "A survey of university professors found that 94 percent thought they were better at their jobs than their average colleague" (Gilovich 1991, p. 77)! Are university professors exceptionally adept at self-deception? Perhaps not. "A survey of one million high school seniors found that...all students thought they were above average" in their "ability to get along with others...and 25 percent thought they were in the top 1 percent" (ibid.)! One might suspect that the respondents to these surveys were not being entirely sincere in their answers. Then again, how many university professors do you know who do not think that they are better at what they do than their average colleague? Self-deception, as I think of it, is (roughly) motivationally or emotionally biased false belief. Obviously, only 1 percent can be in the top 1 percent, nothing like 94 percent of professors can be above average for their profession, and so on. So, assuming that the people surveyed are reporting what they in fact believe, there are lots of false beliefs here. And why would they overestimate themselves on these matters? Part of the answer would seem to lie in what they want to be true: that they are very good at their job or extremely easy to get along with. It is likely that their wanting something to be true of them biases their self-estimations.

So, yes, I think there's quite a bit of self-deception in the world. In what I have called "straight" self-deception, people are self-deceived in believing something they want to be true. Philosophical and psychological work on self-deception has focused on this phenomenon. Apparently, there also is a theoretically more perplexing, if much less common, kind of self-deception— a "twisted" kind. An example might be an insecure, jealous husband who believes that his wife is engaged in an affair even though he has only flimsy evidence for that proposition and does not want it to be true that she's so engaged. The question how instances of twisted self-deception are to be explained is largely an empirical one. In chapter 5 of *Self-Deception Unmasked*, drawing partly on empirical literature, I develop a pair of approaches to explaining twisted self-deception: a motivation-centered approach, and a hybrid approach featuring both motivation and emotion. My aim is to display our resources for exploring and explaining twisted self-deception and to show that promising approaches are consistent with the position I defend on straight self-deception. The issue is too complicated to go into here.

3:AM: So, when your work is done and the big question is answered, will we have all the answers we require? And do you anticipate that we'll have a different view about ourselves as a result? What do you think the implications of your work will be, especially in how we might need to rethink ways of doing politics, for example, and thinking about blame, punishment, and the like?

MELE: The BQFW grant winners so far include people who say free will exists, people who deny that it exists, and people who are undecided about this. In addition, the grant winners are tackling free will from lots of different angles. Among the topics under investigation are what goes on in the brain when people make decisions, the effects of people's beliefs about free will on their behavior, and what lay folk mean by "free will." The grant winners will participate in a trio of conferences. Now, we investigate things and we assume things. Certain assumptions that some researchers may make—for example, that "free will" means something essentially dualistic, or that brain science really can't tell us anything about free will—will actually be investigated by other researchers. And I'm hoping that everyone's work on the topic will be enriched by the interaction at the conferences. I'm also hoping for—and expecting—significant progress on the topics studied. But I'm realistic about deep, complicated issues that have worried extremely bright people for a couple thousand years: we won't reach a consensus on all the important questions about free will. As for implications about politics, punishment, and the like—let's wait and see.

3:AM: And finally, are there books that have been important to you that our smart but not necessarily philosophically trained readers should be reading this year? Could you give us a short reading list?

MELE: My own books are important to me, but I won't list them. Thinking back about the books I read in 2011, I can tell that I spend much more time reading articles than books and about as much time reading science as philosophy. OK, I'll quit stalling. Here's a thought. If I had to recommend just one book on free will for smart readers who might not have any philosophical training, I'd recommend Robert Kane's *The Significance of Free Will*. It's a serious work of philosophy that's written in a way that should help smart people feel what's deep, exciting, and puzzling about free will. I'm not saying I endorse his position on free will—I don't (on this, see parts of my *Free Will and Luck*, for example). But I do endorse his way of thinking and writing about free will. The philosophical work I enjoy reading most engages me in a way that motivates me to think hard about the issues as I read. Kane's book will do that for smart, patient readers.

14 | Graham Priest
LOGICALLY SPEAKING

Graham Priest is a dialetheist-paraconsistent philosopher interested in
logic, logical paradox, and metaphilosophy at the University of Melbourne
(where he is the Boyce Gibson Professor of Philosophy). He is also
Distinguished Professor of Philosophy at the City University of New York
(CUNY), a regular visitor at St. Andrews and a fellow in residence at
Ormond College. He has written *Doubt Truth to Be a Liar* (Oxford
University Press, 2006); *In Contradiction: A Study of the Transconsistent*
(2nd ed., Oxford University Press, 2006, originally published 1987);
Towards Non-Being: The Logic and Metaphysics of Intentionality (Oxford
University Press, 2005); *Beyond the Limits of Thought* (2nd ed., Oxford
University Press, 2003, originally published 1995); *An Introduction to Non-
Classical Logic* (Cambridge University Press, 2001); and *Logic: A Very Short
Introduction* (Oxford University Press, 2000).

3:AM: You're famous for denying that propositions have to be either true or
false (and not both or neither), but before we get to that, can you start by
saying how you became a philosopher? Were you always someone who had
these questions about how we thought and how the world was, or was it
something completely different that got you into the rather strange world of
philosophy?

PRIEST: Well, I was trained as a mathematician. I wrote my doctorate on
(classical) mathematical logic. So my introduction into philosophy was via
logic and the philosophy of mathematics. But I suppose that I've always had
an interest in philosophical matters. I was brought up as a Christian (not that
I am one now). And even before I went to university I was interested in the
philosophy of religion—though I had no idea that that was what it was called.
Anyway, by the time I had finished my doctorate, I knew that philosophy

was more fun than mathematics, and I was very fortunate to get a job in a philosophy department (at the University of St. Andrews), teaching—of all things—the philosophy of science. In those days, I knew virtually nothing about philosophy and its history. So I have spent most of my academic life educating myself—usually by teaching things I knew nothing about; it's a good way to learn! Knowing very little about the subject has, I think, been an advantage, though. I have been able to explore without many preconceptions. And I have felt free to engage with anything in philosophy that struck me as interesting.

3:AM: Now, you're interested in the very basis of how we think. You are saying that assuming that every proposition has to be true or false (and not both or neither) is a mistake. So you are asking questions that are deeper than the ones about which is the best way of getting truth. Nevertheless, truth and rationality are targets of your arguments. Is that right? Could you say something about this?

PRIEST: Well, first a clarification. I'm not interested in the way that people actually think (at least not professionally); that's a matter for cognitive psychologists. Next, dialetheism (the view that some contradictions are true) does not imply any kind of relativism. I believe just as much as you do that when we ask questions there are true answers (in cases where there is a fact of the matter), and that there are some ways of trying to figure out what these are that are better than others. In that sense, neither truth nor rationality are targets of my work. As I argued in *Doubt Truth to Be a Liar*, dialetheism is quite compatible with very orthodox views about truth and rationality. What my work does target is a certain mistaken claim about truth. Contrary to orthodoxy in Western philosophy, some claims are true and false, that is, they have a true negation. Nor is this irrational. Indeed it is arrived at in the most rational of ways: by seeing where the evidence and arguments about paradox, motion, the limits of thought, and so on, take us.

3:AM: So, paraconsistent logic is a logic that tries to work out how we might formally understand treating some propositions as being both true and false at the same time. You argue that Aristotle's the guy who defends the "law of non-contradiction" and that his defense is suspect in various ways. Can you say why?

PRIEST: The only significant and extended defense of the Principle of Non-Contradiction (PNC) in the history of Western philosophy (that I am aware of, anyway) was by Aristotle in *Metaphysics, Gamma*; and indeed it is badly flawed. There is one major argument, and scholars cannot even agree on how it is supposed to work, let alone that it works. The other arguments are mostly beside the point, targeting the view that all contradictions are true, or that someone can believe that all contradictions are true.

Now, in the standard logic of our day, any contradiction entails everything. Thus, from "it is and it isn't raining," it follows (quite counterintuitively) that you are a frog. A paraconsistent logic is one where this principle of inference fails. A paraconsistent logic is clearly necessary if one wishes to handle inconsistent information in any sensible way. Dialetheism is the view that some claims are both true and false; that is, that for some sentences, A, both A and ~A are true ["~" is a logician's way of writing "it's not the case that"]. Any dialetheist must subscribe to a paraconsistent logic; otherwise they would be committed to the claim that everything is true, which, presumably, it isn't. Dialetheism is in no way committed to the claim that every claim is both true and false. (One should note that many contemporary logicians think that a paraconsistent logic gives the correct account of validity, but for reasons that have nothing whatever to do with dialetheism. Indeed, Aristotle's logic, syllogistic, was paraconsistent, though he was no dialetheist.) On a standard dialetheist semantic picture, there are but two truth values, true and false; a sentence may have just one of these, or both. (And on some accounts, one might add "or neither" as well.) Paradoxical sentences like "This sentence is false" have both. But run-of-the-mill sentences such as "the cat is on the mat" (for a particular cat and a particular mat) have only one truth value.

3:AM: So, paraconsistent logic contrasts with the assumptions of classical logical. Now, this logic, developed in the modern era by people like Frege and Russell, seemed to suggest that what it was doing was giving a very abstract description of how we really think. It was almost as if they were giving the abstract formula for a kind of biological reflex. We were creatures that had evolved to have these features of cognition that the classical logicians were codifying. But you take a very different view. You place the development of classical logic in a historical framework and basically say that it is just a cultural artifact, stylized and context-specific as, say, the development of noir in film or Romanticism in literature. You are working in Australia, and it seems Australia finds your views amenable. Europe is comfortable with the deviant logic of Hegelian, Marxian dialectics, and so on. The Anglo-American tradition is rooted in classical logic, although in the UK there's Dummett and his intuitionist logic. So, how far do you think that logic is linked to place or culture, and how much of disputes between philosophers might be explained by different assumptions at this base level? What is the story we should have about the status of logic according to you?

PRIEST: Well, for a start, I don't think that logic has anything to do with the way that people actually reason. Standard work in cognitive psychology (for example, the Wason Card Test) shows that people often reason invalidly in systematic ways. Logic is about the norms of correct inference. But the word *logic* is ambiguous. It can mean our theories of inference, or it can mean the subject of these. Compare "dynamics." Sometimes this means a theory of how things move (as in "Newtonian dynamics"). Sometimes it means how things actually move (as in "the dynamics of the earth").

So for "logic." In the sense that "logic" refers to our theories of the norms of correct reasoning, it is clear that these are, like all theories, constructed at particular places and times and bear the historical traces of these. You don't need to know much about the history of logic in this sense to know how much it has evolved in Western philosophy over the last 2,500 years (and continues to evolve). And of course, there can be rival and competing theories in logic; there always have been. As for whether logic, the subject of the theories, the norms themselves, change, that is not so obvious. Can claims of the form "this follows from that" actually change their truth value? This is a hard question. I am inclined to think not; but to justify this view would take a lot more space than is appropriate here.

3:AM: Now, what may puzzle someone who hears the arguments for having true contradictions is what then happens to rational thought. So, one way I might wish to expose your faulty thinking is to lead you to a point where your argument implies a contradiction. Theists often find themselves faced with accusations that their belief about God implies God is both interventionist and noninterventionist, or immanent and nonimmanent. When you get to the idea of the Christian trinity, where God is one person and three people simultaneously, you kind of think that this is decisively problematic. But you seem to be saying that there is no problem. How can any argument be defeated, on your view?

PRIEST: A quick answer is that a view can be defeated if it can be shown to lead to something rationally unacceptable. For example, if my views could be shown to entail that I am a frog, I would give them up. Why is that consequence unacceptable? Well, because there is no evidence for it, and good evidence against it.

But more should be said. Some contradictions are true; it does not follow that all are. Some contradictions are rationally acceptable; it does not follow that all are. There is a lot more to rational acceptability than mere logical possibility. That you are a frog is a logical possibility, but to believe it would be grounds for certifiable insanity. A rational person, as Hume put it, apportions their beliefs according to the evidence. So what happens if I have some set of beliefs which entails A, and you demonstrate to me that ~A? Logically, it is possible to accept A and ~A, but absent special considerations, this would seem to be ad hoc and rationally unappealing. True contradictions would seem to be, after all, unusual. Is there any rational reason to suppose that this is one of them?

Take some concrete examples. You mention God. If there were a God of the Abrahamic kind, then God would no doubt be a most unusual object. Maybe God can be three and one. But a standard version of the problem of evil argues that if there were a God of this kind, there could be no gratuitous suffering in the world. Suppose the argument is sound. Anyone who thinks that there is no gratuitous suffering in the world does not appear to be living in the same world as I am. Could I accept that there is and is not gratuitous suffering in the world? That would seem to be crazy—just as much as supposing that the local supermarket has and has not milk on its shelf. This is not a claim about some strange object like God, but about a perfectly mundane situation. Moreover, if it really is true that there is no gratuitous suffering in the world, this makes nonsense of much of standard morality. I should not be compassionate to those who appear to be suffering this way, for example; they are not. This contradiction hardly seems acceptable.

3:AM: Now, you are an extreme case of a paraconsistent logician. You are a dialetheist. You claim not only that logic can accommodate a proposition being both true and false, but you also say that you think true contradictions exist in the world. Now, in this you move from claims about logic and reasoning to metaphysics. This will strike some people as being strange. They may say it's one thing to say that it's best to think about the world using these rules of inferences, but quite another thing to say that the reality of the world is structured in the same way as our reasoning. If our minds have evolved in a haphazard way to merely get around our part of the biosphere, then it would be surprising that this process actually tracked reality or truth. And experimental data suggest we are only weakly selected for cognitive truth or consistency. So, are you like Plato and think that our thoughts do cut nature at the joints, and how do you respond to the naturalist philosophers?

PRIEST: I don't think that this question has much to do with dialetheism. It is a quite general question about the adequacy of our cognitive apparatus. Let us suppose that this has evolved with the rest of our biological apparatus. It seems to me that there are good evolutionary reasons to suppose this apparatus gets things right, at least in gross terms. To state the obvious, a cognitive system that told its bearer that there was no problem when a sabre-tooth tiger was advancing would not last long. (I'm not sure what recent evidence you are referring to.) Of course, the results of scientific investigation take us much further than our basic cognitive apparatus. But even here, there is reason to believe that we are doing a decent job of determining the truth. If we weren't, we presumably wouldn't have had the rather spectacular success in technology that we have had. (Not that I can take much credit for that personally!) One might think that metaphysics is different from physics, but I don't really see a principled difference. We make theoretical investigations of the Way the World Is.

If our investigation of the evidence leads us to believe that something is true, then we have good reason to believe that the World Is That Way.

3:AM: I wondered if any of the recent work by x-phi has supported your views. So, for example, Eric Schwitzgebel seems to be finding experimental evidence has led to him endorsing the idea of "in-between beliefs" and adopting a paraconsistent logic. What is your attitude to this idea that outside of the armchair there's supporting evidence for your views?

PRIEST: Well, if you ask most analytic philosophers, they will tell you that it is clearly absurd to accept an explicit contradiction. In fact, the evidence of x-phi now turning up suggests that most people do not find it absurd at all. (There is some more evidence to this effect found by Dave Ripley.) I must say that this concurs with my own impressionistic evidence. Sometimes I meet people at parties and am asked to explain what I do. When I talk about accepting contradictions, most people cannot see why this should be at all interesting. They think it's pretty obvious that most people do this and are perfectly reasonable in doing so. But do I take it that this supports my view? Not really. After all, at one time most people believed that the sun went round the earth. They were just wrong. Only serious theoretical investigation can sort these matters out. The results do provide a welcome reply to dogmatic philosophers who reject the possibility of any sane person happily believing a contradiction, though.

3:AM: Now, as I indicated earlier, there are examples of the kind of dialetheic position you hold embedded in certain well-known religious beliefs. Buddhism, for example, is pretty relaxed about contradiction. I once tried out an argument with a Buddhist and he was sanguine about having to hold contradictory propositions. Meinong is also known, I think, for holding to the idea of true contradictions existing. So, can you say whether you find that your position underwrites a new way of looking at the world and our place in it? For instance, do you think that the position is inclined to be less judgmental, more understanding, say, in the realm of ethics and in the management of disputes? Would the world be better if we were all more paraconsistent, even dialetheistic? And wouldn't science struggle?

PRIEST: Lots of questions here. First, endorsing the PNC is certainly highly orthodox in Western philosophy. Even before the current dialetheic phase, however, there were dissenting voices. Heraclitus and Protagoras endorsed contradictions—at least according to Aristotle. Some medieval theologians, such as Nicholas of Cusa, held God to be a contradictory object. In modern philosophy, the clearest dialetheist is Hegel, who said in his *Logic*, for example, that for something to be in motion is not for it to be in one place and one time, and another at another, but at one and the same time to both be and not be at a place. The case of Meinong is less clear. He certainly says things that look as though he is violating the PNC, but there is room for exegetical evasion.

Turning to the Eastern philosophical traditions: the PNC is less orthodox, though it has certainly had plenty of defenders there too. Buddhist philosophy (or philosophies: there are as many different traditions in Buddhism as there are in Christianity) is a particularly interesting case. The canon is certainly rich with the assertion of contradictions, but it is not clear that these are not just rhetorical devices, or that the apparent contradiction cannot be defused in some other way. In fact, I hold that some of these contradictions are meant to be taken seriously, in at least some of these traditions; but the point is contentious. About 10 years ago, I gave a talk (with Jay Garfield) at the Tibetan University at Sarnath in India, advocating this view. The audience contained Buddhist monks and other Buddhist scholars. When we got to the claim about contradictions, half the audience were nodding sagely; half were holding their heads in their hands in horror.

Anyway, one can hardly say that dialetheism is a new way of looking at the world; it has a good history—though it may be new to contemporary analytic philosophers. Is it a more irenic position, though? I doubt it. Suppose one person maintains A, and one person maintains ~A. Someone who comes along and suggests that A&~A is likely to find both parties disagreeing with them. After all, the person who accepts A will characteristically reject ~A (and symmetrically for the person who accepts ~A). That is the real locus of disagreement. Ethical disagreements make the matter even worse. Suppose, for example, that one party holds that abortion ought be illegal, and another holds that it ought to be legally permissible. Even if it were to turn out to be both, there would still be an issue about what to do in practice. That is where the rubber would really hit the road.

And as to whether science would struggle: it would not. The corpus of science is inconsistent nearly all the time. Witness the inconsistency between quantum mechanics and general relativity. Even individual theories can be internally inconsistent, such as Bohr's theory of the atom. Scientists are quite used to living with contradiction. Perhaps, in the past, these contradictions have been resolved eventually. Being a dialetheist does not remove this option; it just adds others. The question is only, What is the best scientific theory to accept? If it turns out to be an inconsistent theory, so be it. Thus, for an hypothetical example, suppose that we had a theory of the micro world according to which micro objects really do behave in a contradictory fashion; however, all the actual observable predications of the theory were spectacularly verified, and none were refuted. Then it would be rational to accept this theory. Nor, while the situation remained thus, would there be any reason to revise it.

3:AM: Now, what would you say to those who think that actually you're kind of cheating, or at least that you're guilty of false advertising? So, like physicists who make claims about vacuums and then we find that they are using the term in a way that allows there to be something in the vacuum, so too with your contradictions. Once we get into the detail, what people thought was on offer is much more nuanced and not really as full-blooded as might have been expected. So, Roy Sorensen argues this when he defends his view of vagueness. He thinks that the contradictions that you endorse aren't really the kind of contradictions that we need to worry about. What do you say to this kind of criticism?

PRIEST: The view you mention goes back to a paper by Charles Chihara about 40 years ago. Views of the kind in question have been defended more recently by Roy Sorensen, Matti Eklund, and others. The view is to the effect that our language is inconsistent, in the sense that anyone who grasps the meaning of certain of its constructions (such as vague predicates or the truth predicate) is committed to endorsing or believing certain contradictions. These are not true, however. The cognitive states in question are just a by-product of language mastery. This is certainly not my view. Dialetheias are true (spell out the details of truth in whatever way pleases—satisfying the T-schema, corresponding to reality, verified, or whatnot), with all that this implies. There is no danger of the view collapsing into what seems to me to be this somewhat half-hearted view. Indeed, the danger is in the other direction. To be forced to endorse some contradictions but to deny their truth risks collapsing into bad faith of the worst kind.

3:AM: Another worry might be one that I think haunts some of my earlier questions. We want beliefs and so on to guide us. And when I'm disagreeing with someone, I kind of need to think that if I'm right and she disagrees, then she's wrong. And vice versa. So, when rational peers disagree the problem is a genuine one of finding who got it wrong. I can imagine plutocrats and general hypocritical bastards all over thinking that this is a logic for them because the commitment to consistency is removed. They can say one thing and think another without sanction. Ricoeur's "hermeneutics of suspicion," where philosophical programs to unmask hypocrisies used to defend vested interests, including the arguments of Marx to unmask the upper classes and so on, seem to be programs that won't thrive.

PRIEST: Let's start by fixing some terminology. To say that a claim is false is to say that its negation is true. To accept something is to believe it, to put it in one's "belief box" as it were. To reject something is to refuse to put it in the box. Now let's get some facts straight. Frege notwithstanding, to reject a claim is not to accept its negation. Most people sometimes find themselves in the situation of believing contradictions, things of the form A and ~A. When they do so, they may well revise their views. Perhaps this is usually the correct thing to do. However, in that state, they accept ~A but do not reject A. The same is true of dialetheists who wittingly and consciously endorse some statements of the form A and ~A. And those who take some sentence, A, to be neither true nor false reject A without accepting ~A.

Now, a disagreement between two people occurs when, for some A, one accepts A and one rejects A. The question, then, is who is right. Dialetheism does not affect this matter. A dialetheist may accept something of the form A&~A. A nondialetheist will reject A&~A. (They may accept ~(A&~A) as well; but that may not distinguish them from the dialetheist, who may do the same.) In any case, if one party holds that A (and only that A) and another holds that ~A (and only that ~A), someone who endorses A&~A is unlikely to resolve the dispute; both parties will probably disagree with them.

Now, hypocrisy. One standard meaning of a hypocrite is someone who tells other people that they ought to do something but does not do it himself. Dialetheism has nothing to do with this. Another form of hypocrisy is stating that you have views that you do not have (to reap the benefit)—though this might better be called lying. Someone who believes A&~A but asserts only A is not in this camp. They do, after all, believe A. They might be lying in a different sense, though. There is a conversational maxim to the effect that one should assert the strongest relevant information in one's possession. Thus, someone who asserts that A when they believe that A&~A might well mislead in virtue of the fact that they are not telling the whole truth. But dialetheist or not, someone who does not accept something, but asserts it to try to get people to believe that they do so, is simply lying. And someone who accepts A is not going to make peace with someone who rejects A simply by adding ~A to their beliefs. Dialetheism provides no easy way out for a person who finds themself in a confrontation with someone who rejects their views.

3:AM: On the other hand, the dialectic position of Marx, based on his Hegelianism, is one where contradictions between thesis and antithesis lead to synthesis at the next level, in a process of never-ending dialectic. This in some way seems close to your position. So then, the hermeneutics of suspicion is supported by your approach, and not threatened at all. Your position seems to both threaten and endorse this kind of program. This might be satisfying for a dialetheist-paraconsistent philosopher. What do you say about all this?

PRIEST: I don't think it threatens it, as I have just explained. As for Hegel and Marx, I think, indeed, that they were dialetheists. They endorsed some contradictions. (Though they both had a tendency to call contradictions some things which are not contradictions in the logician's sense; but some of the things they called so were.) This is a somewhat contentious view, but I have defended it elsewhere. ["Dialectic and Dialetheic," *Science and Society* 53, 1990.] Dialecticians, then, are dialetheists. Dialetheists do not have to be dialecticians, however (though they may be). Dialectics tells a story about how development of a certain kind (in our concepts or in reality) is driven by contradictions which arise. This dynamic story is no part of dialetheism as such.

3:AM: You wrote *Sylvan's Box*, about an empty box with something in it. It's a great example of metaphysical literature. Can you say what made you write this and what you think readers have made of it? This leads us to thinking about imaginative literature and film and music. Your work is formidably technical, but its implications seem to line up with some of the great imaginative literature and films that play with paradox and contradiction. Do you read metaphysical literature and science fiction, watch films, and so on? Have any been of help/inspiration your thinking? And if you had to give us a list of your top five books for someone who was smart but not necessarily philosophically trained, what would you recommend?

PRIEST: Gosh! I'm afraid that I'm not really one of the literati. I go to the movies when I get a chance, but I rarely read nonfiction. I listen to a lot of music, though. Especially opera. When I wrote *Sylvan's Box*, I wanted to write something to the memory of my old friend, Richard Sylvan, who had died shortly before that. However, the main philosophical motivation was provided by the fact that someone had said to me that it was impossible to have a really inconsistent fiction: you have to reinterpret apparent contradictions somehow. I thought that was obviously untrue, so I wrote the story to show it. To interpret away the contradictions in the story is to misunderstand it (or at least to give it a highly nonstandard interpretation). I think that most people who have read the story have taken that point. I believe it changed David Lewis's mind about the matter, for example. Are there other philosophical lessons that one can take away from the story? Probably, but I'll leave that matter to the creativity of the readers.

Since I don't really read fiction, I don't think I have been influenced by it in any way. On the odd occasions I do read, I like fiction that explores philosophical ideas. The novels of Sartre and Dostoevsky are obvious examples. I also love the short stories of Borges. These are the closest thing to philosophy-fiction, if there is such a genre. The same general point goes for movies. Anyway, I would not dream of recommending any of these works to people (with or without philosophical interests) unless I were very sure of their tastes. What people like in these matters is so subjective (which is not to say that what is good is subjective). Opera is rarely philosophical in any sense (though it tends to move me more than any other form of art). Wagner's operas, especially the Ring Cycle, do have philosophical undergirding, though. I recommend Bryan Magee's *The Tristan Chord: Wagner and Philosophy* if anyone is interested in that matter.

15 | Ursula Renz
AFTER SPINOZA: WISER, FREER, HAPPIER

Ursula Renz is a philosopher working in the Austrian University of Klagenfurt and at Zurich University whose interests include epistemology, Kant, Spinoza, Wilfred Sellars, and 20th-century philosophy. She has written two books, *Die Erklärbarkeit von Erfahrung. Subjektivität und Realismus in Spinozas Theorie des menschlichen Geistes* (2010) and *Die Rationalität der Kultur. Zur Kulturphilosophie und ihrer transzendentalen Begründung bei Cohen, Natorp und Cassirer* (2002). She has edited "Hermann Cohen: Gastherausgeberschaft einer Schwerpunkt-Nummer der *Deutschen Zeitschrift für Philosophie*, 2/2011; *Baruch de Spinoza. Ethica more geometrico demonstrata. Collective Commentary*. Ed. by Michael Hampe, Ursula Renz, and Robert Schnepf. Leiden u.a. (Brill); "Im Erscheinen. Natürlichkeit und Natur bei Spinoza. Schwerpunktheft der *Deutschen Zeitschrift für Philosophie* 3/2009; Hrsg. von Andrea Esser und Ursula Renz. *Klassische Emotionstheorien*. Hrsg. von Hilge Landweer und Ursula Renz; Special Editorial Team der Studia Spinoza 16 (2008), *Spinoza and Late Scholasticism*. Hrsg. von Robert Schnepf und Ursula Renz. Zu wenig. Dimensionen der Armut. Hrsg. Ursula Renz und Barbara Bleisch (2007); *Baruch de Spinoza. Ethik. Klassiker Auslegen*. Hrsg. von Michael Hampe und Robert Schnepf unter Mitwirkung von Ursula Renz (2006). Her book on Spinoza won the 2010 *Journal of History of Philosophy* prize.

3:AM: When did you decide to become a philosopher? Were you a philosophically curious child, or was philosophy something you came to later?

RENZ: As far as I can tell, I was a philosophically curious child. I always wanted to understand what was going on with and around me. When I was a teenager, we once had to take a test. We got a list of verbs and had to pick out those describing the activities we would most like to do in our future job. Among the verbs I selected figured prominently "to understand," "to grasp," "to analyse," "to comprehend." Unfortunately, I had no idea what kind of profession this could amount to. Philosophy was never an issue in my parents' house, and we had no philosophy classes at high school (or no classes which deserved this name). So, it was only when I went to university at the age of twenty that I got in touch with philosophy. There, however, another problem arose. Philosophy classes were attended often by professionals such as doctors, lawyers, psychologists who were all more educated and eloquent. This was extremely inspiring, but it took me a while against this background to become self-confident enough to think of my own understanding of things as being valuable in any sense.

3:AM: I'm based in England, so I wonder if you could tell the readers a little about the place of philosophy in your culture.

RENZ: Let me specify first what culture we are talking about. I am a German-speaking philosopher, but I am actually living in two places which are out of Germany, in Klagenfurt, a small and provincial town in Austria, and in Zürich, the financial capital of Switzerland. In neither of these places has philosophy ever played a major role in cultural life or society. Klagenfurt is a lovely small city in Kärnten, which is an economically poor, but lovely, region close to Slovenia. It is known for three things: it's situated in a beautiful landscape, it has a rich literary tradition, and it suffers from a problematic history of oppression which has still a problematic influence on regional politics. In Zürich, by contrast, it's primarily money that matters; there is a lot of money there, and you also need more than in most places to make a living there. There is a saying, used rather sarcastically, that in Klagenfurt even the air is philosophical. It draws back to the enlightenment philosopher and patron Franz Paul von Herbert, who was born in Klagenfurt and emigrated later to Switzerland. I sometimes wonder what he thought about the air in Switzerland….

3:AM: You have written a book on Spinoza that won the *Journal of the History of Philosophy*'s prize for the best book published in that field for 2010. Before turning to the content of that, I just wanted to ask you about the rewards of philosophy—what are they, why do you philosophize, what's the payoff, and how did you feel receiving such a prize?

RENZ: I am a little bit reluctant to sell philosophy as something that is attractive as such. But to philosophically minded people, it has indeed a lot to offer. Let me start with a comparison. As an activity, philosophy is extremely challenging and thrilling, comparable with climbing or hiking. Solving a philosophical problem or finding a convincing answer to a philosophical question is like trying to get on to the top of an impressive mountain. You have to deal with hard stuff; you focus on one particular mountain, while watching many others; it needs all your skills and technique to get to the top, but it also requires discipline and sometimes even dedication. Arriving there is extremely satisfying, but there is always the risk that you won't arrive.

There are also other rewards in philosophy, which have to do with the training it offers. Academic philosophy is an excellent training of your analytical skills, and over time these may provide you with a more differentiated view on many facets of life. To be able to identify differences which otherwise you would have felt only in a confused way is another important payoff of philosophy. I must say, I do not share the disenchanted attitude of many academic philosophers that philosophy may not give any answer to existential questions. Of course, we do better to abstain from expecting easy, simple, and quick answers, but sometimes philosophy may provide a deeper understanding of certain problems which is quite valuable sometimes even for daily life. Finally, there is the special reward for philosophers who work in the history of philosophy that you get in touch with great philosophers of the past. Sometimes you find allies in them, sometimes it's simply fascinating to discover foreign accounts, but in any case it's a rewarding, enlightening experience.

Of course there are also those rewards stemming from recognition. These are important, as in any profession. However, saying this, I do not only think of prizes and the like. I also get lots of recognition in my teaching. It is wonderful to see students becoming enthusiastic about philosophy. I am not a good teacher, however, if I am not actually inspired by my research. That's why it's so important that professors find enough time to spend with their own research. What was it like when I got the prize? At first, I couldn't believe it. Then I felt a deep thankfulness. It was a completely unexpected reward. I still am thankful.

3:AM: In your essay "Philosophie als Transzendentalphilosophie" (I just wanted to be able to say that!) you are engaging with modern developments out of Kant. The argument concerns the "myth of the given" and how Kant's concept of experience relates to this, and then what later philosophers made of this. Can you first say what you take the Sellarsian "myth of the given" to be, and how it relates to Kant's *Critique of Pure Reason*? And why are these issues so significant? I think that sometimes the general public misses the significance of what philosophers argue about because they aren't told how the seemingly esoteric disputes relate to them.

RENZ: When philosophers talk of the "myth of the given," they usually attack a certain way of thinking about the epistemic function of the sensory content. The phrase *myth of the given* is a polemical expression which is to denounce a certain kind of argument presupposing that in sense experience some knowledge is just given to us. This is, they say, a fallacious assumption, for it confuses two notions of sensory content. If we conceive of the sensory content of experience in terms of "sense data" which are simply given to us in sensing, we cannot refer to it in order to ground empirical knowledge. They do not categorically preclude that we probably have sense data in this primitive sense, but this does not imply that one has knowledge. If, on the other hand, we conceive of sensory content in a more complex manner such as that it involves seeing a thing as such and such, then it is not simply given to us, for it depends on the exercise of conceptual capacities. But these capacities are shaped by concepts used in former training, and these concepts may be right or wrong. That's why according to Hermann Cohen all contents of human thought including sensory experience are subject to transcendental analysis, that is, we have to discuss them upon the grounds that justify them.

3:AM: Cohen with Sellars agrees that Kant is offering a new holistic account of experience, but you contrast their positions at other points. Am I right? Can you explain this?

RENZ: Let me start with a small observation: Cohen's important and rich book on Kant's first critique is entitled *Kants Theorie der Erfahrung*; one of the first and most important texts Sellars wrote about Kant was his paper "Some Remarks on Kant's Theory of Experience." Maybe this is pure coincidence, but I presume that Sellars knew at least the title of Cohen's book. What's more interesting, though, is that Cohen and Sellars, while speaking quite different philosophical idioms, defend the same interpretation of the *Critique of Pure Reason*.

First, they both take the merit of Kant's first critique to be conceptual in kind. The crucial innovation of Kant's transcendental philosophy, so their shared opinion goes, does not consist in any kind of new grounds for knowledge claims. Instead, he developed a new concept of experience, and hence of empirical knowledge. Second, they both took the essential moment of Kant's new concept of experience to consist in the idea that every token of experience belongs to a system constituting one's experience as a whole. Experience comes as a whole and is not composed of self-subsistent mental atoms. This is what I called a holistic account of experience. Finally, they also agree that empirical science plays a major role in Kant's views on experience.

However, even more important than the particular commonalities in their views on Kant is the inspiration Kant's transcendental provides in the development of their own philosophical approaches. Both are committed to a transcendental approach in a very radical way; they both assume that philosophy has to be transcendental philosophy in order perform its task. If the aim of philosophy is "understand how things in the broadest possible sense of the term hang together in the broadest sense of the term," as Sellars claims, it has to become transcendental philosophy.

3:AM: Interestingly, you argue that both Cohen and Sellars assume that an irreducibly normative ethics is compatible with scientific realism. And you say

Cohen is trying to set up a task for ethicists to reject mythic underpinnings of morals and develop a new, purely anthropological ethical vision. Can you say more? It sounds as though they're being a bit Spinoza-like in their approach.

RENZ: Put in this way, this is misleading. Cohen's is a sharp critique of Spinoza's ethical approach. The reason for this becomes obvious, if we consider how differently they conceive of the relation between ethics and anthropology. Following a widespread view of Spinoza, one of the basic claims of the *Ethics* is that ethics, as a philosophy discipline, has to rely on anthropology. This was also Cohen's understanding of Spinoza, and in many respects it is mine as well. That's why in the third part of the *Ethics* he is developing a theory of affects, before, in parts four and five, he deals with ethical issues. In Cohen's ethics, by contrast, the relation between ethics and anthropology is reversed. Ethics is not grounded in anthropology. On the contrary, it is, in Cohen's own wording, a "theory of the concept of man" which is to derive from the idealistic grounds of Kantianism. The result is not an anthropology in the usual sense of the word, but rather some kind of humanistic ethics, which seeks to capture our intuitions of what matters in morality in a nonreductionist way.

Let's now add Sellars to this picture. Generally speaking, Sellars is closer to Spinoza, or the widespread view on Spinoza I have just sketched, than Cohen. Cohen was, after all, a very religious man, and one might question whether he would have liked my comparison with Sellars. Sellars on the other hand would probably not have refrained from being compared with Spinoza or, I guess, with Cohen. One of the central points of his approach consists in his view on the irreducibility of normativity. He maintains scientific realism and concludes that scientific insights will overrule most of our ordinary anthropological convictions. But he denies that this calls for a naturalization of normative claims.

On the contrary, he assumes that the crucial aspects of our ordinary conception of man are related to the notion of personhood, where persons are bearers of duties and rights. This corresponds in a certain way with the relation between the basic claims behind Cohen's logics or epistemology and his ethics. In his logics, Cohen expresses a strong commitment to some kind of scientific realism. At the same time he claims that the task of ethics is to develop a theory of the concept of man which is anti-naturalist in spirit. To put it in a nutshell: one could say that both assume that normative claims constitute a principal limit to the reach of scientific explanation.

It is illuminating to discuss also Spinoza's naturalism against the background of this picture. It is striking that Spinoza does not treat ethical and epistemological normativity in the same way. He has a radically deflationary view on moral normativity, but not so, to my mind, on epistemic normativity. There is a dis-analogy in this respect which is often missed, when Spinoza is characterized as a naturalist. His ambitions were in many respects naturalist, but his epistemology is not at all a form of naturalized epistemology. Cohen too, I think, has missed this point.

3:AM: Another area you've written about is about how far and in what way our individual knowledge depends on the testimony of others. We're living in a world where we're soaked in blogs and sources of testimony from all over. This is clearly an important topic. You say that while testimony of others is often a source of information, we are not simply entitled to knowledge claims based on testimony. Is that right? (I confess my German is useless, so I could have misread this.) Can you say more about the conditions that you think should be satisfied to give testimonies epistemic authority? Again, I wonder if this issue is not one that grew out of your studies of Spinoza.

RENZ: Not really. I started to work on this issue when I had to prepare for the oral exams of my habilitation (a kind of higher doctorate which is usually required in the German countries in order to be eligible for full professorship). You have to give a talk about a topic which is rather new for you and defend it in a discussion with professors of all fields of the humanities. I chose to give a talk on testimonial knowledge, because I expected that this is a topic which allows one to see and to explain the relevance of the basic problems discussed in post-Gettier epistemology. I then realized that most philosophers, who defend the idea of testimonial knowledge, neglected the reasons why many early modern epistemologists rejected it and maintained individualist conceptions of knowledge. I started to wonder whether there is not a possibility to defend an individualist view on knowledge without embracing epistemic, rationalist, or empiricist fundamentalism.

3:AM: Of course, it's for your work on Spinoza that you are best known. To introduce us to this philosopher, can you say some general things about why he is a particularly important and special thinker to you? And why contemporaries should know about him?

RENZ: Spinoza was a very rigid and autonomous thinker whose works exhibit a strong sense of systematicity. What I mean is the following: Spinoza is always very clear about the implications of a certain claim for claims in other fields. Hence I do not think that the systematicity of Spinoza's works is simply due to his usage of the geometrical method. On the contrary, his usage of the geometrical method is, in my view, a matter of the exposition of this systematicity, rather than of proof. Still, his usage of this method shows that he had firm ideas of how things cohere with each other. To get an understanding of these connections is extremely instructive, even if one does not follow him in all his points. Moreover, Spinoza's is as rich as it is rigorous, one can find interesting and challenging views on almost everything: metaphysics, religion, knowledge and science, morality, social life, and politics as well as, of course, all kinds of mental phenomena.

3:AM: You were incredibly ambitious in your book on his masterwork *Ethics*, writing about it as a systematic whole rather than doing what others usually do, which is to pick themes and arguments and focus on those. So, did you do that because you think something is lost if it is treated piecemeal and the architecture of the work is ignored? Can you say why you approached him as you did, and how this is different from others?

RENZ: What I did was the following: I developed a wholly new interpretation of Spinoza's philosophy of mind according to which the *Ethics* can be defended against the Hegelian charge of the disappearance of finite subjects. In order to do this, I had to get a grasp of the *Ethics* as a whole. In elaborating my view, however, I did a lot of piecemeal analysis of particular concepts, claims, and arguments; and I also engaged in very close reading of particular passages. Surprisingly, I have found a lot of textual evidence and argumentative support for my rather unusual reading. So, it was the overall intention and not my method which was particularly ambitious.

3:AM: You think Spinoza is out to show that we can explain our subjective experience and that this is important because the explanation makes us wiser, freer, and happier. Is that right?

RENZ: Yes, this is the central contention of my reconstruction, and I have to add that this claim is directed against the idea that the *Ethics* aims at some kind of Eleatic monism according to which the perspective of finite subjects is unreal. To my view, this amounts to an unsatisfying account of Spinoza's philosophy. In any case, it would not make any sense to call such an account "ethics." We have to keep in mind that, according to Spinoza, there is nothing good or bad for God. I also cannot see how an Eleatic reading fits Spinoza's political theory and social philosophy, which accentuate the ideal of the free individual. It was because of this dissatisfaction that I was looking for another way of reconstructing Spinoza's metaphysics and philosophy of mind.

3:AM: A theory of the human mind then seems to be essential to Spinoza's approach. Can you say something about this?

RENZ: Let's have a look at the organization of the *Ethics*: the parts on the mind and on the emotions constitute some kind of bridge between the metaphysics of part one and the more practical parts four and five. The idea behind this structure is easy to grasp: according to Spinoza, the first thing we have to do is to clarify the ontological concepts such as being, causation, or modality.

These concepts should allow explanations of nature that undermine all kinds of anthropomorphism. Once this is done, we can start analyzing human life, and in particular human mentality. Spinoza seems to think that we have to understand how the human mind is working and how it produces all the qualitative differences of our experiences, before we can continue with a discussion of ethical issues such as social life, freedom, and happiness.

3:AM: Descartes is perhaps the great contrasting philosopher, with his mind-body dualism. Can you say how Spinoza contrasts with Descartes? Was rejecting Descartes part of what Spinoza was explicitly doing in this work?

RENZ: There are many differences between Descartes and Spinoza of which the rejection of mind-body dualism is only the most prominent. Other important differences concern epistemological issues. Descartes is an epistemological fundamentalist, and his rationalism is tied up with what is also called "innativism." He thinks that in order to acquire true knowledge we have to rebuild the whole system of knowledge. In doing this, we have to rely on a few indubitable ideas, so called "innate ideas" which are essentially distinct from ideas which are either acquired or fictitious. In his early works Spinoza seemed to be impressed by Descartes's epistemology, but later he rejected the notion that we can separate innate ideas from acquired or fictitious ideas. Finally, there are differences in their theories of emotions which are too numerous to be dealt with here. Nonetheless, we should not merely focus on the differences between Descartes and Spinoza; there is also much continuity. Many of the differences just mentioned grew out of Spinoza's attempts to further develop Cartesian concepts.

3:AM: You relate Spinoza's metaphysics and philosophy of mind to contemporary discussions about the mental as explicable entities in their own right. Can you say how Spinoza's ideas are still relevant in thinking about this realm?

RENZ: It is not a particular idea, but rather the underlying strategy of the *Ethics* as to why I think Spinoza is an interesting point of reference in this discussion. Contemporary discussions on this issue usually rely on the following alternative: we either have to explain the mental in terms of the physical, or we must accept that subjective experience is something inaccessible to all kinds of rational explanation. For Spinoza, this alternative is misleading. If we want to explain subjective experience, we cannot be satisfied with the identification of the physical processes underlying the mental life. Instead, we have to understand how meaning is produced, and to do so we should also examine the influence of language or history. Spinoza's approach is thus not reductionist, but it seeks to involve, on the contrary, all kinds of causal factors.

3:AM: Spinoza gave imagination a central role in all our perceiving and representing, didn't he? Can you tell us about this?

RENZ: Let me emphasize first that Spinoza's concept of imagination is much wider than one expects when talking about imagination, for he dismisses the categorical distinction between sensation and perception on the one hand, and imagination on the other. Imagination is underlying both processes of having impressions from outside and of fantasizing about external things from inside. This is completely counterintuitive, for we make this difference in daily life and this, moreover, rather automatically without any special effort. Furthermore, we think that we can fantasize at will, whereas this is not possible with veridical processes like perception or sensation. We therefore assume that veridical processes like perception or sensation, and imagination, are completely different processes. Spinoza dismisses this categorical distinction, for several reasons. First, he does not think that fantasizing a thing is a more "voluntary" act than perceiving it. To him, both processes are rather a way of undergoing affections, than of bringing something about. Secondly, he thinks that there is something true involved in all our ideas; we simply have to analyze them rightly to see this. On the other hand, there is much imagination—or to put it more bluntly, construction—involved in our perception.

3:AM: Now, throughout your account of Spinoza you provide reasons for thinking of Spinoza as being systematically rational and having no need for theological categories. Yet the fifth part of *Ethics* talks about the eternity of the human mind. So, how do you understand what Spinoza is arguing here?

RENZ: There are of course many theological concepts used in the *Ethics*. The crucial question is if they are really essential to the basic metaphysical or psychological claims of Spinoza, or not. I think that in many of Spinoza's seemingly theological statements the theological vocabulary can be eliminated without loss. Now, you ask whether this is possible also with respect to part five of the *Ethics*. Let me emphasise that there are many different claims contained in part five, which have to be carefully distinguished. I cannot do this here in detail, but one of the points of my book was to show that most of these claims can be translated into epistemological claims. The notion that there is some part of our mind which is eternal can, for instance, be equated with the claim that in principle all our subjective experience can be expressed in terms of completely true, eternal truths. Understood in this way, the term *eternity* is denoting a possible epistemic achievement.

There is another point, which is to be distinguished from the doctrine of the eternity of the human mind, and which to my view is a bigger challenge for a nontheological interpretation, that is, the claim that in the *amor Dei intellectualis* we are blessed. Spinoza explains this by saying that in having complete knowledge of some item of God, or nature, it is not only the case that we love God but also that he loves us back. I must confess I cannot see how we can make sense of the idea that God loves us back without employing some traditional theological vocabulary. So there is some incoherence in this respect, but this incoherence is a problem for all readings, those who take Spinoza as a naturalist philosopher and those who read him as a theologian.

3:AM: Self-knowledge and explanation as therapy seem to be at least partly what Spinoza thinks justified his system in the *Ethics*. But you have written independently about the limited use of philosophy as therapy. So, are you not sympathetic to Spinoza's conception of philosophy? And how does your interpretation of him as an epistemic individualist square with his political, intrasubjective commitments?

RENZ: In the article you are referring to, I discussed some assumptions one has to hold in order to make sense of the notion that philosophy could be some kind of therapy. I showed that this notion is relying on the idea that we may alter or even change our mental states by reflecting on our concepts. I argued that this is possible to the extent in which our mental states are cognitive or representational states. The point where I depart from Spinoza is thus not his idea of philosophy as such, but the idea that all kinds of mental states are completely representational. Furthermore, I warned against the following mistake: we can ascribe to philosophical reflection some therapeutic effect, but we cannot infer from this that reflection is the essence of psychotherapeutic processes. Psychotherapy may involve some kind of philosophical reflection, but its effectiveness depends primarily on the relationship to the therapist. My skepticism concerning the limited use of philosophy as therapy is thus less a principal departure from Spinoza's conception of philosophy than it expresses some worry towards mistaken ambitions of philosophers in a field where we lack competences. To handle a therapeutic relationship requires another kind of professionalism than to think about concepts.

As to your second question, I cannot explain this in detail. I just want to point out that it is completely wrong to assume that my individualist interpretation questions in any sense Spinoza's political commitment. On the contrary, to my view we cannot understand many tenets of his political theory, unless we reject the Hegelian or Eleatic picture of Spinoza's metaphysics as wrong. And I think this is an important legacy of the enlightenment in general. To my mind, the notion of individuality is often merged with the idea that individuals are completely autarkic, isolated entities. This is not at all what I claim.

3:AM: Was Spinoza a naturalist, given his ambitions for science and his minimal (nonexistent?) theological commitments? In this, was he more iconoclastic than say Leibniz, Hobbes, and Descartes? I guess the question is, Just how radical were his ideas?

RENZ: This is difficult to say right away. Radicalness is a category the application of which requires a close analysis of the relation of an approach to the ideas maintained in its environment. Now, although these philosophers shared many ideas, we should be careful not to underestimate the differences of the contexts in which they lived and worked as well as of the precise use they made of certain ideas. Furthermore, we should not mistake radicalness with iconoclasm. I would say, for instance, that Spinoza is more radical, but less iconoclastic, than Descartes.

16 | Cecile Fabre
ON THE INTRINSIC VALUE OF EACH OF US

Cecile Fabre is an Oxford University philosopher interested in political philosophy, ethics, legal philosophy, and the philosophy of war. She is the author of *Social Rights Under the Constitution: Government and the Decent Life* (Oxford University Press, 2000); *Whose Body Is it Anyway? Justice and the Integrity of the Person* (Oxford University Press, 2006, paperback ed. 2008); *Justice in a Changing World* (Polity Press, 2007); and *Cosmopolitan War* (Oxford University Press, 2012).

3:AM: When did you decide you were going to be a philosopher? Was it always part of your way to think philosophical thoughts, or were events crucial in your philosophical formation?

FABRE: I can't really pinpoint a moment when I decided to become a philosopher. It wasn't really an "on the road to Damascus" epiphany; rather, it became clearer and clearer to me, over time, that although my first academic love was history, I was more engaged with normative questions. If I had to write a historical commentary of, for example, a speech by Lenin, as part of my history module on the Russian Revolution, I would analyze the fundamental moral and political principles at play in that speech, rather than worry about what might have led Lenin to say what he said when he said it. By the end of my bachelor's degree in history, which I took at La Sorbonne, I knew that I wanted to become a philosopher.

That said, the first absolutely crucial moment, in that process, happened in my last year of high school: in France, philosophy is compulsory in the Baccalauréat and I was fortunate enough to have an absolutely outstanding teacher, Barbara de Negroni—in fact, one of the best teachers I have ever had—who first planted the seeds. She herself is particularly interested in moral and political philosophy, and it is under her guidance that I took my very first steps in those fields. The timing was particularly good: it was in 1989, the bicentenary year of the French Revolution, and I was living in Versailles, of all places.

The second, foundational moment, happened in 1992: I had just started a master's in political philosophy at the University of York, under the tutelage of Peter Nicholson, Susan Mendus, and John Horton: this was an eye opener. I discovered the analytical tradition, which is so different from the continental way of doing philosophy; more importantly still, I discovered a different academic culture here—one in which students are very strongly encouraged to challenge their teachers' views and to try and articulate their own. Within six weeks of starting the course, I decided to stay in the UK to do a doctorate.

I ended up in Oxford—the third major step—and had the spectacular good fortune to be supervised and mentored by some of the very best political philosophers this side of World War II—in particular the late Jerry Cohen. He more than anyone taught me how to "do" political philosophy; more importantly, he taught me how to follow an argument to its conclusion, however unpalatable the latter; he also showed me, and countless others, how important it is to be able to say, in public, "You are right, and I am wrong." It might not seem much—yet that lesson has been invaluable.

3:AM: Your doctoral thesis became the book *Social Rights Under the Constitution*. It's a subject that maybe has eluded some of us: whereas civil and political rights are protected under most constitutions in the world, social rights aren't. So, welfare state provision is not part of constitutional protection. Can you first say more about this situation and how it came about?

FABRE: As it happens, social rights are protected under the French constitution— or constitutions in the plural I should say, for we have had quite a few. Then again, there is a much stronger, or at least a more explicitly endorsed, statist tradition in France than in the English-speaking world, which in part explains why we do have those constitutional rights, and the Anglo-Saxon legal and political tradition resists them. By the same token, insofar as civil and political rights respectively seek to keep the state at bay (don't infringe on freedom of speech) or to control it (citizens get to decide who is in power), you can see why that tradition—at least in the United States—has been more hospitable to constitutionalizing them.

3:AM: You think that this is a bad situation. You want social rights to be constitutional. I think the reasons you give are framed by what you call the "two major issues of contemporary political philosophy: the issue of democracy and the issue of distributive justice." Can you say something about this and how your argument develops from this context?

FABRE: I am not sure that I would still call democracy and distributive justice the two major issues of contemporary political philosophy: toleration, the problem of political obligation, and war come to mind as well. That said, the reason I started on this question—constitutionalizing social rights—lies in a puzzle: the more elaborate and demanding your conception of distributive justice (that is, of how, to whom, and when material resources such as money ought to be distributed in our society), the less space there is for democracy to function. Suppose you say "justice requires that all individuals have the same amount of resources." Any decision made by the democratic majority which fails to distribute resources in that way counts as unjust. It would seem, then, that we cannot be both committed democrats and committed proponents of justice—at least, of demanding justice. Something "has got to give," to put it in a very nonphilosophical way, and the question is what, precisely, must give: justice, or democracy? The book in effect argues that democracy must give in to social rights.

3:AM: You claimed in the book that your argument was pretty much the first, along with a thin version from David Miller. Thomas Nagel had said constitutional social rights were a good idea but gave no defense. John Rawls too had stated that the social minimum should be entrenched but then fell silent. Ronald Dworkin was just silent. Joseph Raz had discussed civil and political rights but avoided social rights. Why was it such a muted philosophical subject, and have things changed since you published your book?

FABRE: The main reason, I think, why Anglo-American legal and political philosophers have either avoided the issue, not fully defended constitutional social rights, or argued against them is the deeply entrenched conviction that judicial review as carried out by the U.S. Supreme Court is not an appropriate or effective instrument to protect those rights. I don't think that things have changed that much in that part of the world; gratifyingly, however, the collapse of communism in Europe and other forms of dictatorial regimes in other parts of the world, notably Latin America or indeed South Africa, has led constitutional scholars there to think afresh. I must confess that I have not kept up to date with this particular literature in the last ten years, but I do know that there has been renewed interest there in constitutional social rights. Whether courts are indeed the best forum in which to bring about social justice is something which we might be able to ascertain in a couple of decades, when the judicial and constitutional dust has settled.

3:AM: Rights, autonomy, and a minimally decent life are the three core components of your argument defending constitutional rights. What do opponents argue against your views, and which argument do you find the most dangerous to your position?

FABRE: Some critics dispute the very idea of rights; others endorse rights but reject constitutional rights. My colleague at Oxford, Jeremy Waldro, is the foremost and most sophisticated proponent of the view that equal respect for persons entails a strong commitment to democracy—which commitment is incompatible, he claims, with constitutional rights. Insofar as I share the view that we all owe one another equal respect, his argument, if he is right, is devastating for my conclusion. Fortunately (for me at least!) I don't think he is right, but still.... Others, finally, reject the view that justice only requires that individuals have prospects for a minimally flourishing life. They claim that a just society is one in which people have as much as one another, or that priority should always be given to those who are worst off. These views are much more demanding on agents than my own; and if they are right, then it seems to me that we might have to give up on constitutionalizing justice, out of deference to democracy.

3:AM: I guess one of the issues coming out of cognitive science and philosophy of mind rather than political philosophy has been the question of free will and agency. Naturalist philosophers such as Alex Rosenberg and x-phi-ers have presented evidence to show that autonomous agency is an illusion but that this supports distributive justice. How do you meet this kind of objection? And suppose that somehow the evidence supporting this position was overwhelming; would you change your views about the desirability of social rights?

FABRE: This is a powerful challenge to my autonomy-based argument for constitutional social rights, but I still would endorse the latter. For even if we are not in fact autonomous, whether or not our life goes well, whether we are happy, in pain, whether we do indeed have the material wherewithal to implement the conception of the good life which we are predetermined to want remains important: not all roads to justice start from autonomy. That said, I do think that theorists of distributive justice could do much worse than to study the free-will problem assiduously—especially those theorists known as luck egalitarians, who believe that people are not owed help, as a matter of justice, if they are not responsible for their predicament. If there is no such thing as free will, then everyone is owed help. I used to think quite strongly that responsibility did have an important role to play in determining who does have and who lacks a claim at the bar of justice: now, I am not so sure.

3:AM: Your third book was *Justice in a Changing World*, which is an extended meditation on Rawls's *Theory of Justice* and the various debates that it has generated since being published. Can you say first of all why Rawls is so important? It links to your earlier thoughts about the welfare state, doesn't it?

FABRE: Rawls's *Theory of Justice* is one of the three most important works in political philosophy in the Western canon (the other two being Plato's *Republic*—which of course is about much more than political philosophy—and Hobbes's *Leviathan*.) Thanks to Rawls, it became possible once more to think about those crucial issues (resource distribution, freedom, fairness) both in normative terms and with a high level of analytical clarity. While his works are not as directly discussed as they used to be, all of us in our field one way or another position ourselves vis-à-vis Rawls, even if we do so often unconsciously. This book of mine, *Justice in a Changing World*, was written as a textbook for advanced undergraduate and graduate students: it couldn't not address Rawls. And in any event, as you say, I have a strong, abiding interest in distributive justice and the ethics of the welfare state; if only for this reason, engaging with Rawls has always been necessary.

3:AM: In your book you discuss how the scope of justice has to be extended from Rawls's original position to encompass justice between generations, justice between cultural groups, national self-determination, territorial justice, justice between foreigners, immigration, and reparations for past injustices. In your view, are all these equally significant, or is there a hierarchy of justices?

FABRE: A lot depends on what you mean by "hierarchy." If you mean "Which issue is the most pressing as a matter of public policy?" then I would say that justice between foreigners and immigration are the most important: a world in which millions of people avoidably die every year is unconscionably unjust. But if you mean "Is it morally more important to argue in favor of justice across borders, or in favor of justice between generations, or in favor of national self-determination?" then I don't think that there is such hierarchy.

I don't think that there is a hierarchy of justices, as it were, within distributive justice. As to whether or not the demands of distributive justice are more compelling than the demands of restitutive justice: perhaps. At the very least, whether one gives priority to helping someone in need whom one has not harmed, and giving back what we owe to someone one has harmed, partly depends on the extent of the need, the magnitude of the loss, etc.

3:AM: Rawls is what you call an egalitarian liberal. You contrast the position with two main rivals: communitarianism and libertarians. What are the main contrasts as you see them between these three positions, and what makes egalitarian liberalism more just than the other two positions?

FABRE: Egalitarian liberals believe not only that individuals have fundamental rights to important freedoms such as freedom of speech, freedom of movement, and so on, but also that they are owed material assistance, as a matter of justice—on the basis of need, or on the basis of being worse off than others.

In other words, they believe that the welfare state, which is funded through coercive taxation, is just.

For libertarians, by contrast, justice requires that individuals' rights over their body and person (rights of self-ownership) be respected; this includes full, exclusive rights over the product of their labor. For libertarians, in other words, coercive taxation for distributive purposes is tantamount to an act of theft. The difference, or differences in the plural, between egalitarian liberals and communitarians are somewhat harder to draw, if only because there are many different strands within communitarianism with which to contrast different strands of liberalism.

However, it is fair to say that egalitarian liberals believe that individuals are the primary locus of concern and respect, that they have the capacity to challenge the prevailing social and cultural ethos of their community, and moreover that they should exercise that capacity; communitarians, on the other hand, conceive of individuals as mostly and deeply embedded in a network of social and cultural values and relationships from which they cannot, and ought not to strive to, escape.

As an egalitarian liberal, I reject both communitarians' emphasis on the value of a communal ethos qua communal ethos, and libertarians' rejection of the welfare state. *Pace* communitarians, it is good that we should be able and willing critically to reflect on communal values (which does not mean, necessarily, rejecting them, but rather, and at the very least, questioning them); *pace* libertarians, if individuals are the fundamental locus of concern and respect, then they are owed assistance—they are owed, for example, not to be left to starve to death (at the very least).

3:AM: How do you see recent protests such as the Occupy movements? Are the complaints against plutocracies and the perceived unfairness of a tiny minority having so much power and wealth compared to vast majorities being so poor and weak symptoms of the lack of the kind of egalitarian liberalism you are discussing? Are you hopeful that politics is moving in the right direction?

FABRE: Those complaints are definitely, and absolutely, symptomatic of our collective moral failure to implement egalitarian liberalism widely understood. But I am not hopeful at all that politics is moving in the right direction: the latest budget in the UK, to give but one example.

3:AM: In your book *Whose Body Is It Anyway? Justice and Integrity of the Person*, you take the idea of distributive justice and subject it to intense scrutiny. Were you surprised by where your arguments took you in this? Or were you already holding pretty controversial views on certain areas of this subject before refining the arguments laid out in the book?

FABRE: I was surprised by some of the turns which my arguments took—though not all. For example, for as long as I have thought about this, I have held the view that we simply do not have the right to hold on to our organs after we are dead, as well as the view that prostitutes are not doing anything wrong. But I was not prepared for having to endorse the view that, in some cases at least, the coercive taking of live body parts is permissible, indeed required at the bar of justice; or the view that organ sales are not, per se, morally wrong. In writing that book, I had to confront some of the most uncomfortable intuitions I have ever had—which was very tough at times, both intellectually and emotionally. But this is also what I love about philosophy: that it is wholly existential.

3:AM: So, in this book you ask what we should be allowed to do and what we shouldn't be allowed to do with our bodies, and also what society should be allowed to do with them too. Again, you begin your argument from a rights-based sense of justice, so the argument connects with your previous thinking. But it is unusual to find such an argument being directed at the body. As you write at the start, "In the prevailing liberal ethos, if there is one thing that is beyond the reach of others, it is our body in particular, and our person in particular." Your book challenges this, doesn't it? Can you say what you are arguing?

FABRE: In a nutshell, my claim is this. Many people live a less than minimally decent life, die even, because we do not give them the money or material goods which they need. Likewise, many people live a less than minimally decent life, die even, because we do not use our body, and person, in the required way: we do not rescue them from drowning, we do not provide them with medical services, we do not give them the organs they need. Now, most people claim that the first is an unjust state of affairs (so we should set up a welfare state out of coercive taxation), whereas the second is not unjust (so we are morally permitted not to provide the relevant services and organs.)

In his seminal *Anarchy, State, and Utopia*, Robert Nozick, who is a libertarian, claims that this is an incoherent position: the coercive distribution of money and the coercive distribution of personal services/body parts stand or fall together. Of course, Nozick thought that liberal egalitarianism was misguided precisely because it had to endorse the latter. My aim was to show, first, that Nozick's "stand or fall together thesis" is sound, and second, that on an independently plausible (and relatively modest) account of liberal egalitarianism, one could endorse the coercive taking of services and body parts (under certain conditions) without thereby treating agents as objects, slaves, etc.

3:AM: There are obvious controversies in what you are arguing. So, for example, can you say what your argument commits us to in terms of organ transplants and farming? You don't believe they should be illegal, do you?

FABRE: I certainly do not think that organ transplants should be illegal; nor do I think that organ farming should be—in fact, it might well serve to remedy chronic shortages.

3:AM: I guess what might strike many as really surprising is that you think that prostitution should not be illegal but that it should be protected as a right. Many feminists will join forces with libertarians and say this can't be justified. But you think it can. So what is the argument for defending prostitution in terms of justice and the integrity of the person and human flourishing?

FABRE: You are right that many feminists would vehemently oppose my views; but some would not, on the contrary—and those in fact would align themselves with libertarians (since for libertarians we have the right to dispose of our body as we wish.) The justice-based argument for defending prostitution goes something like this: insofar as prostituting oneself does not harm others, and insofar as a just society is one which respects agents' autonomy (the latter being constitutive of human flourishing), it is also one in which prostitutes ought to be left free to decide what to do with their body (in matters of sex).

I should say, though, that the case of pimps and clients is more complex: to the extent that clients and pimps objectify the prostitute, then they act wrongly—indeed unjustly. But (and this is crucial) it does not follow that the state may coercively prevent them from buying and procuring sex: there are many unjust practices and conducts which, for various reasons, the state ought not to criminalize (when parents give unequal amounts of pocket money to their sons and daughters, just on the basis of gender), and I believe that this is one such case.

3:AM: What do you say to those who argue that prostitution is constitutionally harmful to flourishing and personal integrity, that it is unavoidably so? I presume, then, you would argue that the right to prostitute yourself be withdrawn, but only in those instances where it could be shown to be intrinsically harmful. Wouldn't pimps worth their salt just deny the intrinsic harm and the onus would then be to prove they were wrong, which wouldn't be good, would it?

FABRE: Even if prostituting oneself is intrinsically harmful to one's flourishing and personal integrity, that fact alone does not entail that there is no such thing as a right to prostitute oneself. For a start, it is helpful to scrutinize a bit more closely what we mean by "not having a right to prostitute oneself, or to visit prostitutes, or to procure prostitutes." We might mean "doing something which is morally wrong." In this case, we would need to distinguish the claim that prostitutes act wrongly by undermining their own integrity from the claim that their clients and/or pimps act wrongly by contributing to this state of affairs. I do think that the latter claim is true in most cases, but I am not persuaded at all that undermining one's personal integrity is morally wrong, particularly when one does not harm others in so acting and when one has very good, compelling reasons (for example, economic necessity) to do it. Alternatively, by "not having the right" we might mean that prostitutes, their clients, and pimps ought to be interfered with and punished for engaging in prostitutional relationships. To make that claim of pimps, and perhaps even clients, is one thing; to make it of prostitutes, who again more often than not are driven, not to say coerced, into prostitution is another thing altogether.

Notice that, in my response, I accept the objection's premise: that prostitution is intrinsically harmful. I am not persuaded that it is (though prostitution as it typically occurs, under duress, for example, is). I am not persuaded, in other words, that the act itself of selling or buying sexual services is necessarily vitiative of one's flourishing and integrity. My response to the pimp would be this, however: even if prostitutional sex does not undermine flourishing and integrity, nothing can justify the treatment which pimps standardly mete out against prostitutes.

To finish on this point: here is a thought which I have always found interesting. If the wrongness of pimping consists, at least in part, in procuring a service without taking part in its production, and profiteering from it, then the same goes for a great many economic relationships in capitalism.

3:AM: You also think surrogacy should be a right too. The way this works, sometimes at the moment, is that rich people buy the children of poor people. It's hard to see how a right of parenthood could be treating a child as a unit in a financial transaction, so how do you defend this?

FABRE: This is a difficult question. Let me start with the really tough concession which, in my view, any defender of surrogacy must make, namely, that there is a sense in which surrogacy does consist in buying and selling a child. In the book, I try and show that arguments to the contrary fail.

The question, then, is what follows from that concession. If buying x entails that one may treat x as a commodity (as something which we can in turn sell at will, destroy, abuse, neglect), then surrogacy would be grievously wrong. However, when we buy or sell stuff, we only buy and sell the independently defended rights which it is possible to have over it. To make this less abstract: though I bought my house from another person, I did not buy from him the right to burn that house to the ground at will, since he did not have that right himself in the first instance. Likewise, when we buy a fish, or a cat, or a horse, we do not thereby acquire the right to treat them as commodities. The same goes with children born from commercial surrogacy agreements.

3:AM: I think anyone reading your work can see that you are confronting some of the toughest questions facing humanity with compassion, but without sentimentality. You don't duck implications of ideas of human rights, of extending the scope to ensure greater egalitarianism and justice. But as you look at the world at the moment, are you hopeful that humanity has the capacity to respond to your arguments? Rawls is sometimes read in terms of neo-Marxism. Do you find any left-field alternatives to your own vision of egalitarian liberalism, such as Zizek's Stalinism or Simon Critchley's anarchism, at all interesting?

FABRE: I am not that hopeful about the future, to be honest. At the same time as progress has been made regarding the rights of women, minorities, indeed children, we have endowed ourselves with unprecedented capacities for collective self-destruction. Insofar as neither Stalinism nor anarchism strikes me as morally viable alternatives to some form of liberalism, all that we can hope for is to muddle through with the latter as an imperfect guidance to conduct ourselves, both as citizens and in a private capacity.

3:AM: Finally, for the politically literate readers here at 3:AM, are there five books you could recommend that we'd find enlightening?

FABRE: Assuming that your readers would have read Plato's *Republic*, Hobbes's *Leviathan*, and Rawls's *Theory of Justice*, I would list the following, in no particular order: the first volume of Churchill's history of the Second World War (admirably written, and an inspiring display of willpower and cunning in the face of adversity); Michael Walzer's *Just and Unjust Wars* (I am currently working on the ethics of war, but even for the nonspecialists, this is one of the best philosophical books of the 20th century); Tolstoy's *War and Peace* (it's got everything: war, love, private and collective grief, and a deep, deep love of humanity); Eliot's *Middlemarch* (for she shows us that in the end, what really matters is the ordinariness of our daily moral life); Kant's *Groundwork of the Metaphysics of Morals*.

I mention the latter because it is both one of the most important books in moral philosophy—if not the most important—but also because, or mainly, Kant's abiding commitment to the fundamental equality of all human beings resonates through every single one of its pages. It is full of mistakes, of course; in particular, its egalitarian commitment is somewhat vitiated by Kant's attitudes to women. This last point notwithstanding, I find that book extraordinarily moving—the philosophical equivalent (to my mind) of J. S. Bach's music. In the same way as Bach's rigorous, almost mathematical phrasing at its best reaches sublime spiritual heights, Kant's rigorous, demanding philosophy at its best reaches to the deepest, in fact spiritual, commitment to the intrinsic value of each and every one of us, irrespective of race, gender, social class, and community membership. I can think of no greater ideal to aspire to.

17 | Hilde Lindemann
NO ETHICS WITHOUT FEMINISM

Hilde Lindemann is a philosopher of bioethics, the ethics of families, the social construction of identities, and feminism at Michigan State University. She is a former editor of *Hypatia: A Journal of Feminist Philosophy*. She is co-editor with Marian Verkerk and Margaret Urban Walker of *Naturalized Bioethics: Toward Responsible Knowing and Practice* (2009); sole author of *Holding and Letting Go: The Social Practice of Personal Identities* (2012); *Damaged Identities, Narrative Repair* (2001); *Stories and Their Limits: Narrative Approaches to Bioethics* (1997); *The Patient in the Family: An Ethics of Medicine and Families* (1995); and *An Invitation to Feminist Ethics; Feminism and Families* (2005). She has coauthored with James Lindemann Nelson *Alzheimer's: Answers to Hard Questions for Families* (1996) and with Marian Verkerk and Margaret Urban Walker, *Naturalized Bioethics* (2008).

3:AM: You're a leading professor of philosophy, working primarily on feminist bioethics. So, were you always a philosophizing type of person, wondering about the meaning of things and so forth, or has this career been something of a surprise? Or is it that you just couldn't ignore certain aspects of the way life seemed to be organized that struck you as being absurd and unfair?

LINDEMANN: I was initially trained in German literature and theatre studies, though I always liked doing philosophy (and philosophers—I married two of them). I started out working as a freelance copyeditor for several university presses, because that was work I could do with one hand while diapering my babies with the other. But when I was well into my forties, my husband and I talked our way into jobs at the Hastings Center, a highly respected bioethics research institute just north of New York City. Jim was hired as their associate for ethical studies and I became an editor at the *Hastings Center Report*. And because it was that kind of a place, I started doing work in bioethics too, and then Jim and I wrote a book together, *The Patient in the Family*. At that point I decided I'd better get a Ph.D. in philosophy if I was to get serious about a career as a bioethicist, so I did.

3:AM: One of the several important contributions to philosophy has been your work in feminist ethics. To some this will be a new field, so could you begin by outlining what the basic geography is of this field? Alison Jaggar sees it as a response to the way traditional ethics has let women down in five areas: its interests are male-biased, it trivializes private realm morality such as housework issues and child rearing, it treats women as morally shallower than men, its values tend to be traditionally more male than female (so autonomy over interdependence), and it favors traditionally male ways of reasoning over female ways (rules over relationships). Is this about right?

LINDEMANN: Alison Jaggar is almost always about right. If I were to expand, I'd say that feminist ethics is not a branch of ethics, but a way of doing ethics that uses gender as a central tool of analysis. The idea is that gender is an abusive power system: it consists of social institutions and practices that systemically privilege men's interests, preoccupations, and concerns over those of women, while at the same time requiring women to be subservient to men. The practices and institutions give rise to attitudes, values, vocabularies, and ways of thinking that purport to justify the social order and help keep it going. Feminist ethics identifies the shared moral understandings that sustain these social arrangements, asks questions about who benefits from them or has to be pressed into service to make them function smoothly, and makes normative judgments about whether a particular way of living is actually the best way for everybody who shares in it.

3:AM: You have some very subtle approaches to many of these aspects of the subject that need careful explanation if they are not to be misunderstood disastrously. An obvious way feminism gets attacked is by those who say it's a war on men, when the starting point is that, if there's a war going on, it's men who started it and men who prosecute it. Feminism is self-defense. How bothered are you about the way feminism is presented, or is the argument that feminism is too aggressive, or what have you, just an excuse made by anti-feminists to avoid the issues?

LINDEMANN: I think it's a great mistake to see feminism as a war on men. Men aren't responsible for the subordination of women; they just benefit from it. It's not politically useful to set men up as the enemy, because that alienates people whom we need as allies. And it perpetuates the victor-vanquished, master-slave relation that's the whole problem in the first place. If the gender system is ever to be dismantled, it won't be by declaring war on men. It's much better to affirm lots of differences among people without insisting that differences have to be ordered into power hierarchies.

Many people, including women, attack feminism as too aggressive or too man-hating or (this one kills me) no longer necessary because we now live in a postfeminist era. These are all ways of avoiding things that are uncomfortable to face squarely, although my "postfeminist" students mostly just haven't had any firsthand experience of the ugliness of sexism yet. In any case, if you are on the privileged end of any abusive power system it's easy not to notice that things aren't so hot for people in other parts of the system; that's part of what it is to be privileged. Given the understandable reluctance to confront one's own complicity in injustice, and given how these power systems are epistemically rigged so that we aren't supposed to notice the abuses that are going on over there in the corner, it's no wonder feminists aren't popular. But we're necessary. Can't do good ethics without us.

3:AM: Another difficulty is to work out how to avoid treating gender difference using "man" as the standard against which "women" is then measured. Even the Jaggar list I suggested earlier seems to have that problem a bit. So, how do you deal with that kind of worry?

LINDEMANN: What you're talking about is androcentrism: the assumption that "man" is paradigmatic for human beings. By the logic of androcentrism, if men are the norm, then women are abnormal, deviant, they don't measure up. And yes, feminist critique that starts from men, centers on men, uses men as the reference point for what is wrong, is arguably tainted by androcentrism as well. It's a hard habit to break, but if you think of gender as an abusive system that subordinates women just for being women, the moral analysis can stop focusing on men and shift to the failings of the system.

3:AM: Another problem is one that you note when you write about the Cranford Community Hospital and Eton College sponsoring a Nurses Recognition Day. The woman you are writing about there, Virginia Martin, wasn't sure she wanted to get involved because she figured (and I'm quoting your book), "If you needed a Recognition Day, it must be because you knew you weren't recognized, and why would you want to draw attention to that? Doctors don't bother with recognition days." I know quite a few very strong women who feel the pull of this kind of thought, that feminism can look like special pleading, an admission of weakness. What do you say to them to address this worry?

LINDEMANN: I know plenty of strong women like that, myself. The worry is a political one: never offer the enemy your jugular or you'll get it ripped open. Some feminists won't, for example, talk about rape "victims," because they don't want to contribute to what they see as a culture of victimization;

they talk about rape "survivors," instead. But I don't think survivor talk does justice to many women who have been raped. For one thing, being raped can leave you with massive feelings of powerlessness; you don't at all feel you survived intact. For another, if you have to be a strong survivor, the onus of responsibility is on you, not your rapist. But I do understand the desire for respectful recognition that's just extended as a matter of course, instead of having to be insisted on. It's humiliating to have to insist.

3:AM: So, it's the relation of power that you take as a key issue in the discussion of feminism and understanding of gender. You argue that it is through understanding these power relations that the idea of a feminist ethics is developed. In your 2001 book *Damaged Identities* you write: "A person's identity is damaged when a powerful social group views members of her own, less powerful group as unworthy of full moral respect, and in consequence unjustly prevents her from occupying valuable social roles or entering into desirable relationships that are themselves constitutive of identity." You go on to discuss other consequences that follow on top of this, including "deprivation of opportunity" and "infiltrated consciousness." Can you say something more about this?

LINDEMANN: Our identities serve as tokens in our social transactions, in that they indicate how others are supposed to treat us and how we are supposed to behave. These "supposed tos" are both socially and morally normative, and what they prescribe sets limits on what we can do, including what social goods we can claim. There are plenty of studies showing, for example, that girls don't get called on by their teachers as often as boys do, that women don't get as many of the most prestigious jobs, that their ideas are often credited to their male colleagues, and so on. That's largely because the stories that constitute the "woman" identity portray women as stupider, more emotional, and more light-minded than men. And if they act smart or ambitious, they get dismissed as bitchy or shrewish and are treated accordingly. I use the term "infiltrated consciousness" to refer to the state somebody is in when the morally degrading terms the power system reserves for a particular social group have to some extent entered into the group member's own sense of who she is. It constricts her agency. She'll act more in accordance with how those stories tell her she's supposed to act, accept more of the obstacles to living well that the power system puts in her way.

3:AM: To look at recent studies into the state of women in philosophy, do women philosophers have damaged identities in your sense? Could you say something about this? I guess a question that arises from this is how much of current philosophy is therefore constructed in ways that make this happen, and is therefore abusive.

LINDEMANN: According to the National Center for Education Statistics, only 20 percent of all postsecondary teachers of philosophy are women, and only 16 percent are in tenure-track jobs. A common explanation is that women just aren't very interested in the topics philosophy concerns itself with, but I don't buy it—you can do philosophy on anything. The real problem is that women aren't welcome. It's hard to sort out cause and effect, but there's a strong correlation between how women are viewed and disciplinary boundary policing. A few years ago I was at a metaethics workshop, and over breakfast a male colleague and I made a game of ranking the different specialties in philosophy according to how prestigious they were—a ranking with a precise inverse correlation to gender. Here's the list we came up with:

Philosophy of Mind, Philosophy of Language, and Metaphysics: The alpha-dominant philosophy, done by Real Men
Epistemology and Philosophy of Science: Done by manly enough men
Metaethics: Done by men who aren't entirely secure in their masculinity
Ethics, Social, and Political Philosophy: Done by girls
Bioethics: Done by stupid girls
Feminist philosophy, of course, is not philosophy at all

All of which is to say, women don't get much respect; in my language, their identities have been damaged. And the consequences can get pretty nasty.

Rebecca Kukla put it nicely when she was guest-blogging on *Leiter Reports* in October: "We get shut out of professional opportunities, harassed, discouraged from participating in 'hard' subdisciplines or applying to top jobs and graduate programs, openly belittled, presumed to be sleeping with our directors/letter-writers/co-authors." Women graduate students are ridiculed in seminars, by professors as well as men students, for asking questions that don't have the right kind of edge to them, and if they develop the edge they get treated as men-wannabes. When they go on the job market they get interviews because most universities require that good-faith efforts be made to recruit women, but somehow, mysteriously, the best-qualified people in the candidate pool turn out to be men. We're routinely omitted from the keynote lineup of major conferences, and when conference organizers get called on this, the favorite excuse is, "We asked a woman but she couldn't come"—as if only the first woman they approached could possibly be enough of a draw to be a featured speaker. We're expected to do more committee and administrative work, and we're paid less well than our male counterparts. Sexual harassment is pretty widespread. So yes, you could say the discipline is abusive.

3:AM: One way in which you argue we should resist and change abusive power is through what you call an analytic and practical tool, the counterstory. It is through these counternarratives that we can achieve what I think Martha Montello first called "narrative repair." Can you say how you characterize this notion of the "counterstory" and perhaps give some examples of how it works, and where it has been successful?

LINDEMANN: As I employ the concept, a counterstory is a story told for the purpose of uprooting the widely circulating identity-constituting stories that depict members of a particular social group as morally subpar. These are stories of resistance that say, "I'm not who you say I am, and I deserve respect." They range all the way from Harriet Jacobs's *Incidents in the Life of a Slave Girl* to Walt Disney's *Tangled* (Rapunzel as action hero), but most of them aren't written down—they're the story you tell yourself when your boss gropes you, or when somebody shouts a racial slur at you, or when, if you use a wheelchair, the store clerk asks your able-bodied friend what size you wear instead of asking you. The "we're here, we're queer, get used to it!" counterstories that reidentify gays and lesbians seem to be gaining traction, although they still have a long way to go. And transgendered people's counterstories are beginning to get uptake among the cisgendered, so that's progress too.

3:AM: This is not an approach that is disconnected with currents in both literary theory and philosophical ethics. So, for example, you mention the philosopher Jonathan Dancy as one of the people who helped you develop this idea. Is that right? We might wonder: Do philosophers who draw on narrative to explain ethics need to answer the question of exactly what theory of narrative are they drawing on? After all, there are many ways of telling stories, so to say "narrative will help" is too vague. You wrote in *Stories and the Limits: Narrative Approaches to Bioethics* that it was in the late eighties that moral philosophers such as Bernard Williams, Michael Stocker, Lawrence Blum, Jeffrey Blustein, Annette Baier, and Margaret Urban Walker started approaching ethics through narrative. And you link this move to Williams's observation that impartialist systems of morality "elbow out much that gives meaning to life, including anything that could inspire us to take any moral goal system seriously." But narrative theory in English departments was pretty controversial at the time, and philosophically weak, don't you think? So, did you avoid getting dragged into the bad-tempered culture wars of the time with your approach? Can you say where in broad terms your approach connects with ethical theorizing in philosophy? Who are the theorists that you draw on and develop?

LINDEMANN: One of the reasons I didn't pursue a Ph.D. in English literature is precisely that narrative theory struck me as bad-tempered—and even worse, sloppy. When I was editing bioethics case studies at the *Hastings Center Report*, I was fascinated by how the cases could elicit different moral judgments, depending on how they were told. Stories are always selective, and sometimes I felt that the most important details had been left out; I would want to take the story apart and retell it from the point of view of the night nurse, or the patient's little brother.

But whether a given story is a good one depends on what it's supposed to be doing. If it's meant to display a morally puzzling situation, it's got to be accurate and include everything that is morally salient, so that it faithfully mirrors the moral shape of the situation. I think Dancy is particularly good on this. I favor his account of how moral reasons operate: a moral consideration that functions as a reason in favor of doing something over here might reverse its valence over there in that other situation. But, while the reasons really are there and really do work that way there, you might need practice seeing what they add up to. That's why it's often helpful to engage in moral reflection with others; they might see something you missed. Their description of the shape also takes a narrative form and can serve to correct your story.

I suppose I'm an antitheorist, of the Annette Baier–Walker–Williams stripe. Walker has been hugely influential in my thinking about morality as something we do together, and I also return over and over again to Wittgenstein's *Philosophical Investigations*. I learned a lot from my dear friend Sara Ruddick, whose work in care ethics and peace politics is simply first-rate.

3:AM: There are so many aspects of this that you address. But some are really hard. In the book of essays *Feminism and Families*, which you edited, Shulamith Firestone discussed the role of families and concluded that families were so damaging for women that her considered advice was to "shun them." And you thought that this was poor advice, writing, "Most of us were reared in families, and many of us went on as adults to form new families of our own." But when you consider the issue of genital surgery for girls in the United States, this use of fetal dexamethasone, which raises several disturbing ethical issues, you think girls should just live with the problem. But isn't that as unrealistic as Shulamith Firestone's advice about families? I guess the general question that these issues raise is just how far counternarratives must go to have practical and ethical traction when health care is the issue.

LINDEMANN: There's a physician in New York who has been giving dexamethasone to women as soon as they know they are pregnant with a second child, if they have previously borne a child with congenital adrenal hyperplasia (CAH), an intersex condition. If the fetus turns out to be female, and if she has CAH, the dex will keep her genitals from looking too masculine. And because it's given as soon as these women are pregnant, about 90 percent of the fetuses that are exposed to it aren't candidates for it; only one in eight fetuses started on this treatment are actually females with CAH, and of those who are, 20 percent won't benefit from the treatment.

That might be okay if the drug were completely benign, but there's evidence that fetal exposure causes problems with working memory, verbal processing, and anxiety. Is it really a good idea to inflict these problems on 90 children who can't get any benefit from the drug, just to keep 10 others from having funny-looking genitals? As for surgery in infancy to normalize genitals, it turns out that this can require repeated operations and often interferes with sexual pleasure because it deadens nerves. And of course, an artificially created vagina has to be kept open, which means inserting painful expanders that a young child may experience as sexual violation. The problem with both these remedies is that they have serious side effects, and they are done solely because people have a hard time tolerating bodily differences. I wouldn't want to say to anyone that they should "just" live with it, but I do think the parents of these babies should try hard to accept the way they look and teach their children to do the same. In the immortal words of Mr. Rogers, after all, some are fancy on the outside, but everybody's fine.

3:AM: Now, you are also a distinguished bioethicist. A big concern is the link between those working in the pharmaceutical and biotechnology industries and academia. For many looking in, financial motivation seems to be the overriding factor deciding the research agendas. Can you say something about how you view this situation?

LINDEMANN: Short answer: with a great deal of suspicion. When, in the early 1980s, universities got into bed with big pharma and the biotech companies, many academics and even more administrators began to forget what universities are for. Those of us inside the academy are supposed to create knowledge, it's true, but not so that private corporations can profit by it. I'm old-fashioned enough to think knowledge is valuable for its own sake, rather than for the sake of a company's bottom line. The way the profit motive drives university research agendas has had a truly demoralizing effect on all my academic friends, and it's not just in the sciences. We philosophers are under increasing pressure to find external funding, and if the funders aren't interested in what we happen to want to think about, we feel like we aren't doing our share to keep the university afloat.

3:AM: One of the corrosive aspects of the relationship between research programs and money is whether it is possible to have independent academic enquiry and discussion of these matters. Many university professors are on the payroll of large companies, and the worry is that they can't be independent enough. You recently had some worries about an academic journal's relationship to such industries, and you resigned. Is that right? Can you say something about this?

LINDEMANN: I was on the editorial board of a high-impact bioethics journal, and I was worried about where the money to run the journal was coming from.

It was impossible to get a straight answer out of the editor, and the journal's website didn't display the information either. There were some other shoddy editorial practices that bothered me too, and I finally just lost all confidence in the editor, so I resigned. Since then I learned that he's now president for bioethics at a biochemical company that cultures, grows, and banks adult stem cells derived from a patient's own body fat. He still runs the journal.

3:AM: A really interesting development in philosophy recently has been Josh Knobe's experimental philosophy, which asks that philosophy leave its armchair and test out its ideas empirically. How far are you sympathetic to this approach? It seems as though there are striking experiments about moral agency, for instance, coming out of this and related to work in cognitive science that would be corrosive to many of the sexist justifications for agency that need opposing. I guess this question is whether, alongside considerations of the social discourses of power in play, feminist ethics and ethicists generally would benefit from considering this naturalized approach to ethics.

LINDEMANN: I recently co-edited a collection called *Naturalized Bioethics: Toward Responsible Knowing and Practice*, so I'm already on board here. But where I and my co-editors part company with most naturalized moral epistemologies is that they tend to naturalize moral knowledge to the sciences, whereas we don't see why that kind of knowledge should have privileged status. Social science may be the most reliable way of giving us genuine knowledge about how morality arises and is passed on in human communities, neuroscience can tell us how our neurological capacities make moral behavior possible, and so on. And the sciences might well, as you suggest, give us fodder for debunking sexist justifications, but what they can't do is tell us whether a particular form of morality is morally preferable to another.

And if you're going to naturalize moral knowledge, there doesn't seem to be any reason why scientific knowledge shouldn't just take its place alongside anything else we think we know. Historians can show us how morality changes over time; novelists, poets, playwrights, and other artists can help us see the intricate ways in which it works out—often painfully—in everyday life, or show us how it might change for the better. We need biographers to tell us about admirable, unsatisfactory, and ordinary lives. We need to reflect on our own experiences of social and institutional life. Sometimes, we need to ask people, "What are you going through?" and then we need to listen carefully to the answers.

3:AM: Looking at the landscape for both feminism and bioethics now, are you hopeful or depressed? What do you think are the big challenges facing us all as we move forward, and have you any thoughts of where we'll be a decade hence?

LINDEMANN: There is still so much work to do in both areas, but I'm cautiously hopeful. What so often has happened to the work of women in philosophy is that it gets a hearing in its own generation, but then subsequent generations forget all about it. Did you ever hear of Damaris Cudworth, Lady Masham? She was a great friend of John Locke's (Locke even left his estate to her son) and there was a voluminous correspondence between them, much of it dealing with philosophical topics. But it's Locke who is remembered, not she. Likewise, people remember that Queen Christina of Sweden invited Descartes to come tutor her and that he died of pneumonia because she insisted on early morning tutoring sessions, but nobody remembers that Christina was a philosopher in her own right. These days, it's feminist philosophers who don't get much recognition, and I hope that subsequent generations won't forget them.

Matters are different in bioethics—that's where, if you're a philosopher, you can still find a job. But I'd like to see bioethicists do two sorts of things that, at the moment, I don't think they are doing very well. One is to engage in a little more activism, especially in cases where they can see patient abuses going on. Most bioethicists don't see that as their job at all, but their insider-outsider perspective positions them well to speak up. I also wish that clinical ethicists were better trained to teach health care providers, their patients, and the patients' families how to engage in collaborative moral reflection. Many clinical ethicists seem to think they're supposed to solve the ethical problems they're called in on as consultants, but if morality is something we do together, it's the parties to the problem themselves who have to construct a way forward that everybody can live with, and the ethicist's job is to show them how to do that.

I'm a lousy prognosticator—I'm not even sure where I'll be living a decade hence, much less where these two fields are headed—so I won't try to make any predictions.

3:AM: Finally, are there any books that you have read that you have found inspirational and helpful from outside of philosophy that we would find enlightening?

LINDEMANN: Jane Austen's six novels are important in my life; I reread them every five years or so. Virginia Woolf's *A Room of One's Own* and *Mrs. Dalloway*. Caryl Churchill's plays. Anything Tom Stoppard ever wrote. And, of course, all of Dorothy L. Sayers's murder mysteries.

18 | Elizabeth S. Anderson
THE NEW LEVELLER

Elizabeth S. Anderson of the University of Michigan is a philosopher interested in ethics, social and political philosophy, philosophy of the social sciences, and feminist theory who has written about democratic theory, equality in political philosophy and American law, racial integration, the ethical limits of markets, theories of value and rational choice, John Stuart Mill, John Dewey, and feminist epistemology and philosophy of science. She has written *The Imperative of Integration* (Princeton University Press, 2011) and *Value in Ethics and in Economics* (Harvard University Press, 1993). *The Imperative of Integration* won the American Philosophical Association's 2011 Joseph B. Gittler Award.

3:AM: When did you decide to become a philosopher? Was it a surprising choice for you and those who knew you?

ANDERSON: My father got me started reading philosophy when I was in high school. We read parts of Plato's *Republic* and Mill's *On Liberty* together. We also read and talked about free-market economics: Henry Hazlitt's *Economics in One Lesson* was among my favorites. Political discussion dominated family dinner conversations. At Swarthmore College I originally majored in economics. I was always more interested in foundational issues and political economy than in mathematical model building, however.

Reading Amartya Sen turned me decisively toward philosophy. He showed how getting clear on foundational issues in economics, and making sure that one is using empirical concepts that track normatively relevant concerns, was essential to getting economics to answer questions that matter. But once one gets one's concepts and tools in good working order, and uses them to understand the actual world (not just the possible worlds of a priori market models), laissez-faire doesn't look so good any more. His nonideal, pragmatist, empirical approach to normative issues, particularly with regard to the proper uses of markets, was a major influence on my intellectual development. His critique of the concept of preference in economics was a turning point that led me to major in philosophy. No one was surprised when I decided to make a career out of it.

3:AM: It seems unavoidable to confront the treatment of women in professional philosophy. Your work is not primarily about this, but it's a huge issue, isn't it? In the interviews with Patricia Churchland and Hilde Lindemann, the issue is identified as a problem. What's your take on this? Why is academic philosophy seemingly a worse place for women than in the rest of the humanities? And most other places in the academy?

ANDERSON: It is stunning how far behind philosophy is, not just compared to the other humanities but to most other disciplines—including economics, chemistry, statistics, biochemistry, and molecular biology—in the representation of women. Even mathematics and astrophysics have more women. No theory of biological sex differences can credibly explain this.

Women were certainly not flourishing at the University of Michigan philosophy department when I joined it as its only female professor in 1987, filling a line that had been occupied by three female predecessors. All of them had been denied tenure or left when they saw what the result would be. I entered a department that was full of righteous denial that the flourishing of women there was a proper concern. My department has made huge strides on gender issues in the past decade, but the field still has a long way to go. Sally Haslanger has written some of the most important work on gender bias in philosophy. That even overt sexism is common in philosophy is well documented.

The puzzle is, Why is gender bias greater in philosophy than in other fields? I suspect that gender symbolism, however absurd this is, plays a role. Gender symbolism is the tendency to project gender categories onto inanimate things and abstract ideas, as when we think of pears as feminine and bananas as masculine. Gender symbolism is pervasive in academic disciplines and subfields and helps predict the distribution of men and women across fields. The humanities are "soft," hence "feminine," hence imagined to be more suited to women—and indeed women are coming to predominate in most of the humanities, as judged by Ph.D.s granted. But within the humanities, philosophy is relatively "hard," hence masculine, hence imagined to befit men, so women are scarce. And within philosophy ethics is relatively "feminine," so is it that surprising that women are disproportionately concentrated there?

That's only one dimension of a big complicated issue and far from the whole story, given that fields such as chemistry and statistics have better representation of women than philosophy, although they are symbolized as masculine. We need to consider dynamic issues as well. Sociologist Paula England has found that as more women enter a field, men run away from it. This can lead to tipping points, in which fields such as art history and psychology become dominated by women. But we are still only at the most primitive stages of answering the comparative question.

3:AM: You are known for your work in feminist epistemology and philosophy of science. So, can you first say what the motivations for such an approach were in philosophy and who the pioneers were?

ANDERSON: I have argued that feminist epistemology and philosophy of science is a branch of naturalized, social epistemology focusing on the causes and consequences of gendered ideas and practices on the presuppositions, content, methods, concerns, cognitive authority, uses, composition, and organization of diverse fields and modes of inquiry. It's what you get when you join naturalizing trends in epistemology and philosophy of science with feminist concerns, such as the ones that underlie your previous question about the relative paucity of women in philosophy. Pioneers in the field include Linda Alcoff, Louise Antony, Lorraine Code, Patricia Hill Collins, Donna Haraway, Sandra Harding, Nancy Hartsock, Sally Haslanger, Evelyn Fox Keller, Elisabeth Lloyd, Helen Longino, Maria Lugones, Charles Mills, Lynn Nelson, Nancy Tuana, and Alison Wylie. This is far from an exhaustive list; I apologize for errors of omission.

3:AM: So, what are the basic components of feminist epistemology and feminist science? Is Harding's tripartite classification of empiricist, standpoint theory, and postmodernism still the menu of frameworks for this approach?

ANDERSON: Harding's classification remains a useful entrée to the field. Very roughly, feminist empiricism advocates the use of empirical methods to analyze, uncover, and avoid sexist and androcentric biases in inquiry. Feminist standpoint theory claims that women, or feminists, have privileged access to certain truths or epistemic authority over certain questions concerning women's oppression and women's interests. Feminist postmodernism questions the unity of the category "woman," stresses the importance of intersecting identities (of race, class, age, nationality, and religion with gender) in analyzing the processes and products of inquiry, and adopts interpretive approaches to scientific theories that highlight the contingencies of their conceptual frameworks and presuppositions.

In practice, these approaches have converged. We can empirically investigate claims of gendered epistemic authority, as Alison Wylie has shown, and sometimes we find very interesting results. Intersectional analysis also enriches empirical investigations of questions of interest to feminists. And feminist empiricists such as Helen Longino have also identified contingencies in scientific theories that open up opportunities for alternative explanations of observed phenomena. However, it is hard to summarize this field briefly. I advise readers to consult my *Stanford Encyclopedia of Philosophy* entry for an overview.

3:AM: Where do you position yourself?

ANDERSON: I would call myself a pragmatist feminist empiricist, where my pragmatism is decidedly in the tradition of Dewey, not Rorty or Quine.

3:AM: Of course, the feminist epistemology approach has its critics. The charge of political correctness has been made by people such as Susan Haak, Noretta Koertge, and Robert Almeder, and you note that this is the most important charge. These are serious philosophers, so you have to take them seriously. What are the serious charges they make, and how do you defend the approach?

ANDERSON: The most serious charge made by Haak, Koertge, and Almeder is that feminist epistemology grants a license to feminists to reject empirically supported hypotheses that are politically inconvenient, and to advance empirically unsupported hypotheses that are politically convenient to feminist agendas. They also complain that feminist epistemologists cynically reject the quest for objectivity and truth as power plays, and uncritically value supposedly "feminine" ways of knowing, even when not all women think in these "feminine" ways and even when thinking in these ways would reinforce women's subordination.

There are three things that are striking about their critique, and the critiques of other outsiders to the field. First is how little they have read of feminist epistemology and philosophy of science. Their critiques, when they succeed in striking any target at all, "beat dead horses killed long ago in debates internal to the field," as I argued in a review of their criticisms. More often, they simply throw around false accusations. Elisabeth Lloyd and Helen Longino, for example, defend robust accounts of objectivity in science. Second is how spectacularly detached they are from engagement with actual scientific theories, methods, or practices when they purport to lecture feminist philosophers of science about the nature of science.

The leading feminist epistemologists and philosophers of science, by contrast, demonstrate their points through detailed examination of particular scientific theories, practices, and controversies. Third is how detached they are from academic norms of rational discourse, which demand responsiveness to critique. They keep repeating the same false accusations, completely ignoring feminist responses to their criticisms. There is a level of obtuseness and hysteria here that is quite shocking. It's like trying to engage people who claim that Obama is a Muslim jihadist terrorist.

3:AM: You've written about John Dewey. What do you find in Dewey that is admirable? Is his approach something that feeds into your idea of what philosophy and philosophers should be doing?

ANDERSON: Dewey's philosophy is grounded in the actual problems and predicaments people face in life. Consider the fact that his famous ethics text, written with James Tufts, begins with an anthropological and historical discussion of the moral practices of ancient peoples around the world, and how they were tied to the characteristic problems such societies needed to solve.

Reflective moral thinking draws from how people experience their problems and attempt to solve them, and aims to help them improve their ways of thinking about problems and solutions. The call to philosophers to engage actual problems arising in human practices is, of course, a hallmark of feminist theory—to start theorizing from the problems and experiences of women. And it is a hallmark of contemporary philosophy of science—to start theorizing from the actual thought and practices of scientists and the challenges they encounter. The deep affinities among these philosophical perspectives help explain why so many feminist philosophers are drawn to the philosophy of science, and to pragmatism.

3:AM: Race and inequality as well as feminism are what have driven much of your philosophical work. In your debate with Jason Brennan and David Schmidtz, you attack the idea that negative freedom is enough to guarantee a just society. This is a powerful point. Can you elaborate here what you were getting at?

ANDERSON: There are at least three important conceptions of freedom: negative freedom, opportunities (options actually accessible with the skills and resources at one's disposal), and personal independence (not being subject to the arbitrary will of another person). There are tradeoffs among these freedoms. Legally enforced private property rights themselves represent a massive diminution of negative freedom (the state will use coercion to exclude people from using others' property), justified by the fact that this will massively improve people's opportunities. Traffic rules serve the same function.

I argue that we should evaluate the rules of property and distribution as akin to traffic rules, in which it is obvious that numerous tradeoffs of negative liberty for the sake of expanding opportunities are justified. Social insurance offers a case in point. Universal health insurance trades off some negative liberty (everyone must pay into the system) for a vast increase in opportunities (everyone has access to affordable health care). The cost in negative liberty is trifling compared to the gain in opportunities.

It is telling that every country in the world that has achieved universal access to affordable health care has made use of extensive state action to do so. There are collective action problems here, notably adverse selection in the health insurance market, that unregulated private enterprise cannot solve. Similarly, modern property rules forbid certain kinds of racial discrimination, as in the sale and rental of housing, and refuse to recognize contracts into slavery and debt peonage.

Such rules function to block private property from being used as an instrument for racial and caste subordination. What's really at stake here is a choice between feudal property and forms of private property compatible with a democratic society of equal citizens. Libertarians fail to recognize the supreme importance of the difference between feudal property and a property regime compatible with a free society of equal persons, none of whom must live in subjection to the arbitrary will of others.

3:AM: So, your position is an egalitarianism that privileges social relations over mere distributive equality. You began discussing this in your book *Value in Ethics and Economics*. What's wrong with distributive equality? It's not that you don't want distributive equality but that you don't want it to limit what egalitarianism means. Is that right?

ANDERSON: Right. You get a much sharper understanding of any political theory by focusing on what it is opposing. Throughout the history of egalitarianism, the enemy has been social hierarchy—social relations of domination and subjection, of stigmatization, of unequal standing. Egalitarians have mobilized against monarchy, aristocracy, colonialism, slavery, patriarchy, feudalism, plutocracy, caste systems, racism, class domination, and stigmatization and marginalization based on sexuality, disability, and bodily appearance. Equalizing distributions across individuals, or moving in that direction, is often a useful strategy for dismantling unjust social hierarchy and sustaining egalitarian social relations.

But this has been neither the sole aim nor the fundamental point of egalitarianism. Moreover, many egalitarian aims don't involve the equal distribution of anything. Feminists seek reproductive autonomy for women. There is no good that is being distributed equally when this egalitarian demand is met. The Civil Rights Movement sought an end to racial segregation in public accommodations—a goal explicitly contrasted with "separate but equal" precisely because mere equal distribution of goods was insufficient to break down the racial caste system.

Distributive equality is pointless apart from its role in expressing and sustaining equality of social relations and blocking unjust social hierarchy. Some egalitarians today, such as Larry Temkin, think egalitarians should value equal distributions of happiness across individuals who live on different planets, even if they have no interactions. I think such a distributive picture of equality abstracts from everything that makes equality worth caring about.

3:AM: So, you want ideals of social relations instantiated. When did this social movement understanding of egalitarianism develop?

ANDERSON: The idea that human beings are fundamentally equals from a moral point of view is ancient. I suspect it can be traced all the way back to the origins of monotheism, in the idea that we are all equally creatures of God, all made in God's image, all in principle equally eligible for salvation. However, for most of history most monotheistic churches have promised equality only in the next life; in this one a thousand reasons were invented to uphold various forms of social, political, and religious hierarchy.

That's ideology; what about practice? Functionally egalitarian communities have also existed for a long time. Hunter-gatherer societies are functionally egalitarian because they produce no surplus. Once societies began producing surpluses, it took ideological commitment to live as equals. In ancient civilizations, this was generally achieved only in ascetic religious cults.

Religious communes were egalitarian not out of political ideals but usually for ascetic reasons: say, everyone had to take a vow of poverty to get closer to God. What was missing from the ancient world was a practice of universal political equality of all members of society based on an underlying idea of moral equality.

Egalitarianism as a social and political movement demanding equal social relations in this world is a distinctively modern phenomenon that I trace to the Levellers in the English Civil War. They sought a universal male franchise, representation of districts in proportion to population, and the abolition of feudal privileges, including abolition of the monarchy and House of Lords. We can even see the beginnings of feminist political demands in the 1640s, but it has been characteristic of the history of egalitarian social movements that they start off making demands on behalf of a subset of the oppressed and only expand under pressure from those excluded.

3:AM: In a sense, your arguments for egalitarianism are far bigger than just redistribution. Can you say what you are critiquing and what your ideal would be?

ANDERSON: Egalitarians have always been much sharper about what they hate than about envisioning a positive alternative. Egalitarian critiques of feudalism, racism, patriarchy, imperialism are trenchant, and humanity has certainly progressed through movements to abolish the worst forms of social inequality, such as slavery and the legal subordination of married women. But social inequality survives in obstinate habits and implicit biases even after its legal infrastructure has been abolished. It has been difficult to forge complete, positive alternatives.

We have learned from experiments in living what sorts of egalitarian systems don't work very well. Various types of communal living have been repeatedly tried and repeatedly failed. Comprehensive centralized state-managed economies have been disastrous. Other experiments have been highly successful—democracy, social insurance, universal education, human rights. While these are all continuing works in progress, we can have confidence that further steps along these lines are good for humanity.

3:AM: You wrote a great essay on the aftermath of September 11 in the United States. It again broadened out what you thought were the issues at stake in this huge event. Your disappointment with Obama and the political landscape highlights the values you are arguing for and against. Can you say something about your views on this?

ANDERSON: September 11 was a traumatic event that empowered the Executive to take unilateral, unaccountable actions that violate people's rights. Obama has been comparable to or worse than Bush in asserting an unreviewable power to assassinate U.S. citizens secretly declared to be involved in terrorism, to prosecute whistleblowers, and to engage in mass monitoring of private citizens. When intelligence agencies comprehensively monitor our phone calls, emailing, texting, web browsing, and use of social media, and can track our motions in detail, the right to privacy has been reduced to a nullity.

The U.S. government claims success in the war on terror, but the connection between that and mass violations of U.S. citizens' privacy is unproven at best. Most of the terrorism convictions obtained since September 11 appear to have been due to FBI agents whipping up antigovernment fervor among disaffected incompetents, bribing and prodding them to engage in violence, and providing them with all of the leadership, organization, planning, and equipment needed to do the act.

If terrorism has to be ginned up to be discovered, chances are there isn't much of a threat there to begin with, certainly not so much as to justify a massive expansion of the national security state. Some people claim that the innocent have nothing to lose from comprehensive government snooping. I disagree. Security of private life from the probing eyes of the state is a good in itself. In addition the probability of false accusation skyrockets under mass surveillance, since spies need to justify their jobs by fingering suspects. It will take a mass movement for civil liberties to reverse these trends.

3:AM: Your new book is required reading. Why does racial integration remain an imperative?

ANDERSON: My book *The Imperative of Integration* opens with a diagnosis of one of the most important social phenomena observed worldwide. This is that systematic inequalities of power, social esteem, opportunities, and wealth tend to track social group identities, whether of class, caste, race, gender, religion, ethnicity, language, or family line.

The identities of disadvantaged groups vary across societies (although women are disadvantaged everywhere), but the cause is everywhere the same. Systematic group inequality is the result of advantaged groups gaining privileged access to goods critical to social advancement, and closing ranks so as to protect their relative monopoly. In other words, it is the result of the self-segregation of the advantaged. Self-segregation thus causes socioeconomic inequality.

It also undermines democracy. People privileged by segregation tend to be insular, clubby, smug, ignorant of the disadvantaged, inattentive to their interests, and full of negative stereotypes about them. When such people dominate positions of power and authority in society, the institutions they run are similarly negligent or even hostile toward the interests of the disadvantaged. Segregation thereby perpetuates inequality and undermines democracy. In my book, I survey extensive empirical evidence that integration can help remedy these problems, taking black-white integration as my central case study.

3:AM: Do you find widespread resistance to this in the United States?

ANDERSON: Black-white racial segregation is by far the most stubborn form of segregation in the United States today. It is far greater than segregation of any other racial or ethnic group, and far greater than class segregation. The legacies of slavery and Jim Crow have proven to be extremely difficult to overcome, with antidiscrimination law and affirmative action making only modest and slow inroads into the problem.

Nevertheless there are grounds for hope. The simple act of voting to elect a black person for public office appears to soften racial bias. President Obama's election may thus have more than symbolic value. More importantly, the experience of integration makes people more likely to choose integrated settings later in life. There may therefore be a silver lining in our otherwise disastrous wars in Iraq and Afghanistan.

The U.S. military is the most deeply integrated of all large U.S. institutions. Millions of young adults have passed through its ranks in the last decade. This is liable to have integrative effects, as is the revitalization of American cities, which are being populated with young adults with more cosmopolitan attitudes.

3:AM: It seems clear that feminism, feminist epistemology, and science, and integration, liberty, and equality, are being bound together in your work. And that's one of your complaints, isn't it, that by splintering the ideals and keeping them apart we lose what the overarching ideal is?

ANDERSON: I don't claim that freedom and equality are identical ideals. Pluralism of values is a deep feature of political life. Nevertheless there are several points of convergence between freedom and equality. Recall that one conception of freedom is personal independence: freedom from subjection to the arbitrary will of others. Subjection to another's arbitrary will is also known as a relation of domination, which is a chief target of egalitarian critique.

Moreover, egalitarian socioeconomic policies, such as free, universal education and social insurance, function to open up opportunities for all, and thereby provide escape routes from personal dependency. We also should not forget the role of competitive markets in opening up opportunities. When workers have multiple employers to choose from, they are less prone to abject subordination than in a company town. Similarly, access to multiple sources of credit helps people avoid debt peonage.

3:AM: So, do you think your arguments endorse any particular political arrangement? Is liberalism able to address these issues, or a form of Marxism or anarchism?

ANDERSON: I am a liberal of a decidedly left-leaning anti-Marxist type. Marxism was a disastrous political experiment. The collapse of the USSR and the Eastern European bloc was good riddance for the world. Anarchism has never found a way to solve the problem of bad actors. Anarchists, like libertarians, have boundless faith in people's reasonability and willingness to respect human rights. That faith is unjustified. If you want to know what anarchism looks like, don't imagine a libertarian utopia. Take a look at Somalia.

3:AM: It seems there's a world going to hell, and anti-egalitarian reality and justification seem very prevalent. That's depressing. At the same time, the Occupy movements and the Arab Spring are examples of hope. Do you think these are significant in the long run, and are you optimistic or pessimistic about the future?

ANDERSON: The Occupy movement has succeeded in putting issues of inequality back into political consciousness. Importantly, the movement has stressed how the rules of the economic game are unfairly rigged to favor the wealthy, and not just on the outcomes. This means that we need to go well beyond taxation-and-redistribution schemes to look more closely at the underlying rules.

Financial deregulation, the weakness of corporate governance, destruction of labor unions, closure of the courts to class action lawsuits by aggrieved workers and consumers, regulatory capture by private interests, weak protection of workers' pensions, excessive protection of intellectual property monopolies, and public disinvestment in higher education all play significant roles in the growth of inequality.

Nor can a credible case be made that any of those developments are in any larger public interest, say, of economic growth—quite the contrary. Financial deregulation, for example, has led to profound and systematic instability and the deepest world recession since the Great Depression. Corporate executives are no more productive than their predecessors decades ago, who made a small fraction of their salaries. The elimination of class action lawsuits simply gives corporations opportunities to commit fraud and other illegal acts on a mass scale, because the cost of arbitration is too high when each case must be adjudicated individually. Weak protection of workers' pensions has allowed firms to drain funds when stock markets boom and refuse to refund them when they bust.

Austerity measures are reducing seats at public community colleges and universities, thereby closing the doors of economic opportunity to hundreds of thousands, perhaps millions, of young people, at substantial cost to the stock of human capital essential for future growth. The destruction of labor unions has meant there is virtually no counterweight to business interests in Congress and state legislatures, leading to the erosion of workers' rights and bargaining power. Excessive IP protection in academic publishing is increasing college costs and student indebtedness.

And the baleful effects of regulatory capture are too obvious to need spelling out. The U.S. public is getting some sense that the game is rigged, but we need relentless focus on the details of how the game is rigged to get progressive results. Ironically, Tea Partyers also complain that the game is rigged unfairly. But their analysis of how this is so focuses ire on the disadvantaged, such as food stamp recipients and undocumented immigrants.

Right now the momentum in the Arab Spring appears to have been mostly captured by Islamist parties, although they were not the ones to set off the protests. This is not propitious for democracy or equality. Progressive social movements need to take the long view. It took about 400 years from the Levellers' demands to the fruition of representative democracy based on a universal franchise in nation states. Forging democracy is a long, tough slog. The hope is that once people have tasted it even partially, they tend to want more.

3:AM: Finally, are there any books or films that have enlightened or inspired you outside of philosophy?

ANDERSON: Douglas Massey and Nancy Denton, *American Apartheid*, got me thinking seriously about racial segregation and its implications for inequality. Charles Mann's *1491* makes pre-Columbian New World history come alive. His *1493*, an ecological and commercial history of the "Columbian exchange"—the consequences of the world circulation of organisms and goods between New and Old Worlds—is equally stunning. On film, I'm going to recommend a forgotten classic that deserves a fresh viewing: Audrey Hepburn's *A Nun's Story*. It's a compelling film about a nun's struggles in the face of her moral reservations against following through on her vow of obedience, given the sorts of orders she was issued.

3:AM: And finally can you recommend five books we should be reading?

ANDERSON: Stephen Darwall, *The Second Person Standpoint*, provides a definitive account of claims of moral rightness, including claims of justice, in terms of social relations of mutual accountability, and a must-read for anyone interested in the foundations of deontology and social contract theory. Debra Satz, *Why Some Things Should Not Be for Sale*, offers very wise reflections on the promises and limitations of markets and revives the rich moral perspectives of classical economists such as Adam Smith and David Ricardo. Miranda Fricker, *Epistemic Injustice*, extends concepts of justice to the realm of how we treat knowers, and thereby joins a relational theory of justice to issues of feminist epistemology. Amartya Sen, *Development as Freedom*, offers a vital perspective on global justice and its connections to an opportunity-based conception of freedom. Finally, George Orwell, *The Road to Wigan Pier*, an egalitarian classic, is still well worth reading today.

19 | Christine Korsgaard
TREATING PEOPLE AS AN END
IN THEMSELVES

Christine M. Korsgaard is Arthur Kingsley Porter Professor of Philosophy at
Harvard University. Her interests are in moral philosophy and its history,
practical reason, agency, personal identity, and human-animal relations. She is
a leading authority on the philosophy of Kantian ethics. She is the author of
Self Constitution: Agency, Identity, and Integrity (Oxford University Press, 2009),
The Constitution of Agency (Oxford University Press 2008), *Creating the
Kingdom of Ends* (Cambridge University Press, 1996), and *The Sources of
Normativity* (Cambridge University Press, 1996), which was an expanded
version of the Tanner Lectures she delivered in 1992.

3:AM: You are perhaps the most important contemporary Kantian moral
philosopher. In your early book *Creating the Kingdom of Ends* you write:
"Reflection...commits us to the conception of our humanity as a source of
value. This is the basis of Kant's *Formula of Humanity*, the principle of treating
all human beings as ends-in-themselves." This is the core to your approach to
morality, isn't it?

KORSGAARD: The specific idea of humanity as a source of value comes
from Kant, but it represents the kind of idea that attracted me to Kant in the
first place. I have always been suspicious of the idea that values simply, and
without further explanation, exist; that they are, as people say, part of the fabric
of the universe. I am what philosophers call a "naturalistic" philosopher, in the
sense that I assume that the universe is basically the one that the physical sciences describe, and that the existence of anything other than basic material
things requires an explanation: sometimes a scientific explanation, but sometimes a different kind of explanation altogether. I am not what philosophers
call a "reductive" naturalist, because I believe that there are good explanations

of the existence of lots of kinds of things that the physical sciences have no truck with—or rather, that the physical sciences can only approach by way of these other explanations.

For example, functional or purposive objects—furniture and tools—exist only in the perspective of beings who have the purposes in question. The physical sciences can explain the matter of a hammer, but to explain its form and function you have to talk about the way creatures who sometimes have to pound on things look at the world. I think values are like that—they exist because people, and in a certain way the other animals too, have to value things. Ultimately, there are values because of the way people (and the other animals) have to value themselves and each other, if they are going to value anything at all.

Philosophers may be startled when I suggest that Kant is a naturalistic philosopher, because he talks about a distinction between the "noumenal world" and the "phenomenal world," reality and appearances, which makes it sound like he believes in some realm beyond the natural world. But actually, Kant is the best naturalistic philosopher, because he believes that the existence of pretty much anything that isn't obviously part of the natural world can be explained in terms of the human perspective and human needs, including our cognitive needs as creatures who try to form a conception of the world. He thinks that even reason itself must be explained in terms of our needs as self-consciously cognitive and active beings. And Kant seeks explanations of these "nonnatural" things that aren't "reductive" in a slightly different sense of the word than the one I mentioned above—explanations that don't make them turn out to be less deep or important, or in some way cheaper, than we thought they were.

But that answer makes it sound too much as if it is only, so to speak, the metaphysics that attracts me to Kant's *Formula of Humanity*, and that isn't true. I also think Kant gets it right here morally, or almost right. I think Kant was correct in pointing to the idea that people should not use each other as mere means, as something that is at the core of our moral relations with each other. And it is right to think that the real source of all value in the world lies in people and animals. Kant left the other animals out, which is why I say he only almost got it right.

3:AM: You've recently written the introduction to the new edition of Kant's *Groundwork*. Can you say why you think Kant's approach to morality remains extremely relevant?

KORSGAARD: Partly for the reasons I just mentioned. And partly for a reason that Kant himself insisted on: his theory that obligation is based in autonomy, or rational self-government, gives us the only adequate account of why we have moral obligations. According to Kant, the only way we can actually be obligated to do something is if we ourselves recognize it as a law that we should do that thing—and so, in effect, command ourselves to do it. Kant's philosophy is an articulation of the view that grown-up people live under their own self-government, and that morality is the ultimate expression of that fact. We are, in St. Paul's famous words, laws to ourselves.

3:AM: I suppose one of the things that strike me as being peculiar about Kant is that he thinks that even if I do good things all the time but am not morally motivated (so I just happen to like being nice) then my actions are morally worthless. How does he justify this position, and do you agree with him?

KORSGAARD: "Moral worth" isn't a synonym for moral value in general; Kant isn't saying that such actions have no value at all. Moral worth is the specific kind of goodness that characterizes the will, the faculty of choice. Kant brings the issue up because he believes that by reflecting on what exactly constitutes moral worth, we can discover what the moral law is. The idea is that a good will is the will of a person who does the right thing for the right kind of reason, so by thinking about how a person with a good will makes choices, we can discover how we ought to make choices—what the right kind of reason is.

What Kant discovers is that a person of good will does the right thing because he recognizes that there is a law, that is, a claim on him, to act in a certain way. And that leads to the formulation of the categorical imperative, which tells us to act only on principles that we can regard as laws. And yes, I agree with him. If you feed me when I am starving, or keep your promise to me, only because you "like being nice," but you do not acknowledge that I have any claim on you, or that you owe this to me, then your actions are without moral worth. You have not reflected deeply enough on the relations in which you stand to other people, and what you owe to them.

3:AM: The normativity of self-constitution is a key idea in your philosophy, isn't it?

KORSGAARD: It's not the normativity of self-constitution. It's that a particular form of self-constitution is the source of normativity.

All living things are self-constituting, in the sense that they are engaged in a constant process of making themselves into themselves. Living things are made of fragile materials which are always decaying or being used up, and they constantly take in new materials and transform those materials into themselves—that is, into their own parts and organs and energy. In fact, a living thing just is such a process.

Human life is a form of life, and I believe that the things that make human life so different from that of the other animals can be traced to a special feature of the way we carry on this process of self-constitution. There is an aspect of our identity—I call it practical identity—which we construct self-consciously. By that I don't mean that we go around thinking "okay, now I am constructing my identity." I mean that when we decide what to count as reasons for our actions and what principles of action to commit ourselves to, we are also deciding who to be. What makes this possible is the fact that human beings have a particular form of self-consciousness, which makes us aware of the grounds of our beliefs and actions—in the case of actions, the motives that prompt them, in the case of beliefs, the perceptions, the evidence, the arguments that make them seem compelling. The other animals believe and act as their nature prompts them, but they lack the kind of control over their nature which our awareness of the grounds of our beliefs and actions gives us. Being aware of their grounds, we cannot commit ourselves to belief or action unless we can endorse those grounds. To endorse them is to treat them as reasons. That's why human beings need to have reasons for what we believe and what we do.

In the practical case, the case of action, we get these reasons from the roles and relationships that life makes available, and perhaps some we carve out for ourselves. That you are someone's mother or friend, that you have a certain occupation, that you have enrolled yourself to fight for some cause, are all sources of reasons and obligations for you. There are two things interesting about this kind of identity. One is that we carve it out for ourselves and are responsible for it, and the other is that it is normative, or value-laden. That is, having a certain practical identity is something that we try to live up to, that we succeed or fail at, that makes us good or bad.

That's something I think is special about being human—having a normative self-conception, wanting, as we say, to respect yourself, thinking of yourself as worthy or unworthy, rating yourself. It's a condition that gives a strange extra dimension to human life, both a special source of pride and interest and a profound cause of suffering. Some of the other animals seem to have moments of pride, but they don't seem in general to think of themselves as worthy or unworthy beings. Some of them certainly want to be loved, but I don't think they worry about being lovable. So having a normative form of identity that you carve out for yourself is one of the most distinctive features of being human. It is because we are self-constituting in this way, I believe, that human beings are governed by rules and laws and norms.

3:AM: You say in your book *Self-Constitution* that humans are condemned to choice and action. And that action is self-constitution. Can you say more about what you mean by this and why action is so significant?

KORSGAARD: Action is significant because people are their actions. If I push you from behind, having been blown over by a strong wind myself, and we fall like a pair of dominos, that's a misfortune. But if I push you from behind, to hurry you along so that I can go faster, or to save you from a truck that's about to hit you, that's me. Philosophers have always insisted on the point that people are supposed to be responsible for their actions, but what I have in mind is something almost more primitive than that. We take people's actions personally: for example, we think we are allowed to love and hate people for their actions, while we think it's wrong to love or hate someone (just) because of his physical characteristics, or where he comes from, or what's happened to him. And this is related to the fact that people are supposed to be the source of their actions in some special way.

Some philosophers think that special way is that people are the causes of their actions. Other philosophers think that people are the sources of their actions because actions have mental causes, like desires or intentions. They think that causal chains that run through our mental lives somehow reflect what we are more intimately than causal chains that run through our physical lives (like the one that leads from the strong wind blowing me over to my pushing you from behind). I think that people are the sources of their actions in the sense that we constitute our identities as agents when we act.

There are two thoughts working together here, and it will help if I separate them. One is that we make ourselves into agents when we act. I know that sounds odd; I'll come back to it. The other is that we make ourselves into the particular agents who we are by the content of what we choose to do. That one is easier to understand, of course. When I take on a role, and act on the reasons and obligations associated with it, I make it part of my identity to have that role.

How do I at the same time make myself an agent? When an agent acts, she deliberately brings about a change in the world by determining her own movements. So the question of how I make myself an agent comes down to the question of how I make my movements efficacious, and how I make them my own. I make my movements efficacious by choosing the right means to my ends. That's why action is governed by the principle of taking the means to our ends. I make my movements my own by acting on the principles in which I believe, the ones I think of as laws. That's why action is governed by the categorical imperative, which tells us to act on those principles we can regard as laws. So as I see it, human action has an essentially moral dimension. The argument for that is kind of complicated, but here's a fairly colloquial way to put it. We think of any creature as acting when its movements are determined by its mind. Even simple creatures like insects are agents who do things because their movements are determined by their perceptions, by sights and sounds and smells. But for human beings, being determined by the mind means being determined by thinking. And your movements are most your own when they are determined by your own thoughts about what you ought to do. So when your movements are governed by your deepest thinking—by the principles that, on reflection, you believe are the right ones to act on, and that you identify with—then they are most genuinely your own. So by acting on principle, I make myself an agent.

3:AM: In *The Constitutional Model* you talk about what Hume calls "the combat of passion and reason." Could you explain the contrast and why you find the constitutional model the more compelling of the two?

KORSGAARD: According to the combat model of the soul, reason and "passion" (as the 18th-century philosophers like to put it) compete for control of our actions. We act morally and rationally when reason wins. This conventional picture makes very little sense, however. How is an agent supposed to choose between reason and passion, when reason itself is the faculty of choice? Or if the agent does not choose between them, but is simply overwhelmed by one of them, why do we attribute the resulting action to the agent at all? (It's no accident that we speak of being overwhelmed by passion, but not of being overwhelmed by reason.) For that matter, if they serve the same function—providing motives to act—how is the difference between reason and passion any different from the difference between two different passions? According to the constitutional model, which I derive from Plato's famous comparison between the city-state and the soul, reason and passion are not competitors for the same role, but rather serve different functions—roughly speaking, passion proposes and reason disposes. Our emotions, desires, and passions suggest things we might do, but reason decides. If they are in conflict, passion is getting out of line and trying to usurp reason's function, which is the government of the self.

I prefer this model because it makes better sense of our psychic economy. Reason and passion do different things; they are not just sources of different kinds of motives. But I also like it because the comparison between the city-state and the soul helps to clarify the nature of self-constitution, especially the part about making yourself into an agent. It's easier to see how a city-state makes itself into an agent than how an individual person does that. A group of people make themselves into a city-state by adopting principles together, by making shared laws. And when they make themselves into a city-state, they are making themselves into a collective agent, whose actions are governed by its laws.

3:AM: In one of the essays in the collection *The Constitution of Agency* you argue that contemporary moral philosophy is mistaken in viewing its concepts as essentially descriptive rather than constructivist. But some argue that your way of understanding constructivism doesn't distinguish it from pragmatists who define truth in terms of usefulness or realists who use descriptions to solve practical problems. How do you respond to these critics?

KORSGAARD: I argue that practical normative concepts—concepts like "right," "good," or "just," which have implications for what we do—are essentially placeholders for the solutions of certain problems that people have to solve. Speaking a bit roughly, "good" names the solution to the problem of what to aim for, what goals to have; "right" names the solution of the problem of what to do, "just" names the solution of the problem of what we may legitimately expect from one another in social and political life.

One advantage of looking at things this way is that it explains what two philosophers who disagree about what, say, justice is are disagreeing about. Say one thinks justice is maximizing the greatest happiness of the greatest number, and another thinks justice is protecting each person's liberty to the greatest possible extent compatible with a like liberty for others. Why are they disagreeing about "justice" rather than merely talking about two different things? Well, because they are disagreeing about the principles that determine what we may legitimately expect from one another in social and political life.

The difference between my view and that of the realist is that I think that finding the solutions to these problems is essentially a matter of practical reasoning, not a matter of finding out certain truths about the world—say, finding out what things have intrinsic value and are therefore "really" worth aiming for. I think we solve these problems by a kind of thinking that is continuous with ordinary practical deliberation, that is, by asking, What should I do and how should I do it? As for pragmatism, before we can know what is useful, we must know what is good, so the pragmatist standard cannot come into play until after the kind of question I am talking about gets settled.

3:AM: A striking conclusion you argue for in that essay and one that runs through much of your work is that reason is no despot. This is because "we identify with the voice of reason." Is there a worry that this is too refined and unworldly a view of what actual people are like?

KORSGAARD: "Reason" and related terms like "rational" can be used in either a normative or a descriptive way. When we use these terms normatively, "reason" is synonymous with "good reason." When we use the term descriptively, a reason is some consideration on the basis of which we decide to do something. In that sense, there things you do for good reasons, things you do for bad reasons, and things you do but not for reasons at all—like, say, scream when you see a monster at the window. (It's not like you think, "Oh, a monster. I guess I had better scream now.") It's because we use the terms both ways that we can say "that's a bad reason" (descriptive use) and "that's no reason at all" (normative use) and mean essentially the same thing.

So a first point is that when I say that we identify with reason, I am using "reason" in a descriptive sense. The fact that we do some things automatically rather than on consideration doesn't challenge the claim that we identify with reason, since we don't always identify with such reactions—in some cases we apologize for them and say we couldn't help ourselves. And the fact that we do many things for bad reasons doesn't show that we don't identify with the voice of reason either. It only shows that often we can't hear it very well.

As I mentioned when I talked about the contrast between the constitutional model and the combat model, we sometimes say we were overwhelmed by passion when we have acted badly, but we don't say we were overwhelmed by reason when we have acted well. That's not just because acting well doesn't require an excuse. It's because when you do what you wholeheartedly believe you had excellent reason to do, you identify with the action, and don't wish to chalk it up to some force working within you rather than to yourself.

3:AM: In "Integrity and Interaction" (chapter 9 of *Self-Constitution*) you tell the story of Derek Parfit's Russian nobleman, who in his youth was a socialist planning to redistribute his wealth, who worries that when he gets old enough to do this he'll have changed his mind and become conservative. So he decides to act now to make a contract to bind his later self. Only his wife can revoke this contract, and he asks that she will not ask him to revoke it even if his later self pleads with her to do so. You disagree with Parfit on this, don't you? Can you say what you take the issue to be and how you resolve it?

KORSGAARD: "Disagree" isn't exactly the right word here. Parfit uses the example to illustrate the way we might think about someone who predicts that his values will change, and how we should think about the identity of such a person over time. Parfit suggests that both the nobleman and his wife might think of the nobleman's later self as a different person. In an earlier paper, I argued that there is something already amiss with taking a merely predictive attitude towards your own future values. Our values are, after all, up to us— they are not something that simply happens to us—and that goes with the ways in which our practical identity is up to us.

In the passage you refer to, I am using the example to make a slightly different point. It is an important part of Parfit's own argument that the example is not supposed to be like the famous story of Odysseus tying himself to the mast to avoid doing something irrational when he hears the Sirens sing. The younger nobleman does not regard his later self as being irrational, merely as being different. I think that's a problem. I argue first that it is impossible to interact properly with someone who takes this attitude towards himself—the nobleman puts his wife in an impossible position, since she must either wrong his younger self by breaking her promise to him, or wrong his older self by ignoring his right to do as he likes with his own estates. Then I argue that for similar reasons the nobleman cannot interact properly with himself—after all, what his younger self is doing is setting a trap for a future self with whose values he disagrees.

To put it in slightly different terms than I did in the book, the story is supposed to show that you cannot regard your later self's values simply as different without falling apart. You must either regard them as irrational—in which case the story is like Odysseus and the Sirens after all—or as giving rise to reasons, in which case you ought to take them into account. But since there is no important difference between your relation to your later self and your relation to other people, that means you should regard other people's values in just the same way—either as irrational or as giving rise to reasons you have to take into account. Values are the kinds of things that, by their nature, must be shared.

3:AM: What are for you the most serious threats to your system of thinking about ethics? Are there philosophical arguments that still give you sleepless nights? Do you find the naturalist challenge to agency and sovereign will, as presented by the likes of Alex Rosenberg, Patricia Churchland, and Brian Leiter, at all problematic for your approach?

KORSGAARD: There are philosophical arguments that give me sleepless nights, but the ones you mention here aren't among them. To see these arguments as a threat would be to make a mistake about what moral philosophy is for. Moral philosophy isn't armchair theorizing about what people are like. It is addressed to problems that arise when we are deliberating about what to do, problems that arise when we are actually attempting to use reason to determine what we ought to do. There's no point in saying, "Oh, you can't do that anyway." I believe that the structure of our self-consciousness makes it necessary for us to attempt to use reason to determine our beliefs and actions. As I said earlier, we are aware of the grounds of our beliefs and actions, and that makes it both possible and necessary for us to evaluate those grounds, to ask whether they provide good reasons for what we believe and do.

I think it is important to realize that there is no more reason to doubt that reason plays a role in guiding human actions than there is to doubt that reason plays a role in forming human beliefs. In fact there is less, since people believe much crazier things than they do. And all of the people you mention are dedicated to the project of working out what we have good reason to believe. If they came to the conclusion that reason doesn't play much of a role in forming most people's beliefs most of the time, they wouldn't give up that project themselves. They are interested in the kinds of questions that arise when we are trying to use reason to figure out what to believe. As a moral philosopher, I'm interested in questions that arise when we are trying to use reason to figure out what to do.

3:AM: Do you see yourself as developing a metaphysical system of morals?

KORSGAARD: It depends on what you mean by "metaphysical." My view is metaphysical if that means that I am concerned to explain why and how values and obligations exist, how there can be such things as values and obligations. As I mentioned above (in reply to your second question), the desire to figure that out is a driving force of my thought. Sometimes by "metaphysical," people mean that you have "nonnaturalistic" ontological commitments—that you believe in the existence of facts or entities that are not part of the physical world. If metaphysics includes explaining how such entities or facts can exist, then my views are metaphysical. If the facts or entities are supposed to be fundamental and incapable of being explained, however, then my views are anti-metaphysical.

3:AM: Peter van Inwagen writes that one of the great risks of anyone involved in metaphysical enquiry is being meaningless. He doesn't see being meaningless as an insult but merely a danger that comes with the metaphysical territory. Any metaphysician worth her salt will probably say meaningless things from time to time. Do you agree with him, and are there things you've argued which now you'd say were meaningless and false?

KORSGAARD: There is a danger of saying something meaningless. I also think that when you help yourself to views that are metaphysical in the last sense I mentioned—believing in entities or facts that are nonnatural but also fundamental and incapable of being explained—there is a very real danger of thinking you've solved a problem when all you've done is give it a name. In response to an earlier question, I talked about how normative concepts actually name, without specifying, the solution to some problem people face. For example, people face the problem of deciding what to aim for, what goals we should have, and that's why we use the concept "good." So here's one kind of thing you find in philosophy: someone wonders how people decide what to aim for, and the philosopher (we could call him G. E. Moore) replies: "Well, some things are intrinsically good! And furthermore, we know by intuition which things are intrinsically good!" Nobody knows what intuition is, so all that's really happened here is that the philosopher has affirmed that there is some (unspecified) solution to the problem, and that we have some (unspecified) way of knowing what it is.

I don't recall having said anything that I now think is meaningless, but that doesn't mean I haven't. I've said some things I now think are false, of course. However, I have to admit that my views haven't changed in major ways. Instead I have developed and elaborated them. Some times this seems odd to me—a lifetime spent thinking, with so little change of mind. On the other hand, when I think of other philosophers who have spent their lives developing some system, and I admire their work even though I disagree with it, I think of them as the guardians of some set of ideas and lines of thoughts that philosophers through time have found it fruitful and illuminating to think through. That seems to me a valuable thing to do, even if in the end I don't think their views are right. But it's a little hard to think of one's own work in that way. After all, I believe the things that I believe.

3:AM: If only knowledge of its philosophical systems and arguments can justify moral behavior, then doesn't that imply that only Kantian philosophers can be moral?

KORSGAARD: No, because Kant's philosophy is just ordinary reflection—in the case of moral philosophy, practical deliberation—pushed to further limits. Kant undertakes to carry to completion a line of thought on which every reflective person takes the first few steps. Anyone who has ever asked herself, "What if everyone did that?" or "How would you feel if someone did that to you?" has started a course of reflection that, when properly articulated, ends in a commitment to the categorical imperative and the idea that every human being (and in my view, every animal) is a source of value. Decent people can act in a way that embodies these commitments even if they can't always articulate them.

20 | Michael Lynch
TRUTH, REASON, AND DEMOCRACY

Michael Lynch is a philosopher interested in theories of truth, democracy, reason, and epistemology working in the University of Connecticut, and at the Northern Institute of Philosophy at the University of Aberdeen. He is also an Associate Fellow of Arché at the University of St Andrews. He is the author of *In Praise of Reason* (MIT, 2012); *Truth as One and Many* (Oxford University Press 2009); *True to Life: Why Truth Matters* (MIT, 2004); and *The Nature of Truth: Classic and Contemporary Perspectives* (MIT, 2001). He co-edited with Patrick Greenough *Truth and Realism* (Oxford University Press, 2006) and with Heather Battaly Roman *Perspectives on the Philosophy of William P. Alston* (Rowman and Littlefield 2005).

3:AM: When did you decide to become a philosopher, and why? Has being a philosopher lived up to your expectations?

LYNCH: I am the youngest in a big family. My sisters are writers and artists, my brother a psychologist and a painter. So I always sort of expected to be an artist of some kind. And I guess I still think of myself as one. For me, philosophy has always been as essentially creative discipline, always drawing and redrawing the boundaries of the possible. That's what drew me to it from the get-go. I remember sitting in a philosophy course in college at 8:30 in the morning, listening to a lecture on Descartes, and thinking I had stumbled onto the secret language of the world. And while I admit that I sometimes weary of the whirligig of academic life, I still have that first sense of finding my creative home. Here's a simpler way of putting it: I couldn't stop thinking about this stuff if I tried.

3:AM: It might seem obvious to some people, but to others the question "What is truth?" doesn't seem quite as important as it once did. Why do you think this is such an important question, not just for philosophy but for the rest of us?

LYNCH: During the Bush administration, Ron Susskind famously reported that one of Bush's top advisors (probably Karl Rove) sneered that the administration's critics were continuing to live in the "reality-based community." That was a mistake, he said, because "we are an empire now, we create our own reality." This is a telling remark. It illustrates not only what was wrong with that administration but why truth is so important a concept—and not just for philosophers. When we ignore the difference between what those in power say is true and what is true, we risk losing not only our rights but the ability to even give ourselves any critical voice. So that is why thinking about truth matters—because the truth matters.

3:AM: You have spent a great deal of your time figuring out what truth is. This is one of the big questions, the kind of question the folk expect their philosophy departments to be thinking about. There are a whole bunch of positions contemporary philosophers take towards this subject, so I wonder whether it would be good if you could give a quick overview of the landscape before I ask where we'd find you. So, can you say something about what the variations are? For example, monism and pluralism and relativism, functionalist and alethic and folk theories, realist and anti-realist theories, correspondence, coherence, deflationism, and so on. Where do we find the most pressing work taking place these days?

LYNCH: Traditionally, philosophers have thought that truth had a single essence. Call this monism about truth. The oldest monist view, traceable perhaps to Aristotle, is that beliefs are true when they correspond to the world. On this way of looking at things, beliefs and sentences are like maps: they are accurate or true when they represent the world as it is. An alternative view, not as old, but not new either, is that beliefs are true when they hang together—when they form a coherent narrative, as it were. This may have started with Hegel. Call it the coherence theory: truths don't need to fit the world, but they need to fit each other. In more recent years, many of us who work on truth for a living have given up on monism of either type. The newly dominant view is that truth has no nature at all. Views of this sort are often labeled deflationary; they deflate the pretensions of the traditional theories. Pluralism about truth, on the other hand, rejects monism not because truth has no nature but because it has more than one. According to this idea, both of the major traditional views of truth are right in their way; they just overgeneralized. (William James thought this was the compulsive habit of philosophers—a great generalization if there ever was one!) Some of our beliefs *are* like maps. Beliefs about our immediate environment, when we are lucky, *do* represent how things are in that environment. Many of our beliefs are not like that, but they can still be true. They can be true because it is possible for them to fit extremely coherent narratives. Moral and political beliefs, for example, can be correct or off-base. But they don't picture a world completely independent of us.

Your other question was about what questions are particularly pressing right now in truth theory. There are four, I think. One concerns the value of truth, why it matters. The second concerns whether its nature is one, many, or none (the points I just talked about). The third concerns the logical paradoxes, a prime example being the liar. Consider a sentence that says, in effect "I'm false." Is it true or false? Both? Neither? Meaningless? Each answer has been tried, and each has its costs. And the fourth concerns the relationship between all these questions. A particularly open and interesting issue—one of the many to which my colleague J. C. Beall has contributed—is the extent to which our logical theories of truth, arrived at after grappling with the paradoxes, should change our metaphysical theories about truth, and vice versa. The answer, I suspect, is "yes," but the "how" is still a work in progress.

3:AM: So, your position about truth in *Truth as One and Many* is one that begins with rejecting that if a proposition is true it must be true in the same way. You say that truth is a functional property that can be made manifest in more than one way. Can you say something more about how this works?

LYNCH: I'm a pluralist; I think that there is more than one kind of truth. Truth, in this sense, is many. But what do all these kinds of truth have in common—what makes them all *kinds* of truth? Pluralists have different answers to this question (Crispin Wright has a different answer, for example). In my view, they all share a common job or function. The basic idea is that a belief's being true consists in its having a particular job in our cognitive economy. Just as one person can sort the mail one day, and another person can perform that function on another day, one feature can perform the truth function for some kinds of beliefs and another feature for other kinds of beliefs. So correspondence or representational properties do the truth job for certain kinds of belief. A type of supercoherence may do it for others. The underlying idea here—that some of the concepts and properties that interest us philosophically are functional properties—is not unusual. It is familiar in the philosophy of mind, thanks to the work of Hilary Putnam and David Lewis, among others. Part of what I'm doing is pointing out that, with a little metaphysical work, we can apply it to basic concepts like truth too.

3:AM: So, why do you think this is better than rivals?

LYNCH: One way to judge philosophical theories is by the work they do, the problems they help to solve, and by this standard a functionalist version of pluralism about truth comes off pretty well. Here's an example. There is a long-standing problem with explaining how some kinds of propositions can be true. At least some propositions about what is right or wrong, for example, seem capable of being true. Most of us believe, for example, that slavery is wrong, and to believe it is to believe that it is true. Yet that proposition doesn't seem to represent any part or feature of the *natural* world. We don't find moral rightness in the lab, so to speak. This observation has led philosophers to say some crazy things, like maybe there aren't any truths about what is wrong or right, for example, or maybe they really do map the world, but the nonnatural or supernatural world. Pluralism allows us a way out: we can say, with common sense, that some propositions are true, but they aren't all true in the same way. Not all propositions have to represent the world in order to be true.

3:AM: Yes, so an interesting theory of truth that also appeals to some is not that truth has a single nature (which is possibly the account that most folk might hold) but that it has no nature at all. These are labeled "deflationary" theories of truth. Can you say something about these ,and why you feel that your theory is superior?

LYNCH: We live in somewhat curious times for truth theory. Business is booming—lots of books being written, dissertations written, etc. Yet the prevailing view about truth is that there is not much to say about it. I find that pretty strange. It's sort of like if those paid to think about the nature of poetry or art or architecture spent a lot of time talking about the fact that there is not much to say about it. The most basic reason I deny deflationism is that such theories rob us of a theoretically useful tool. If deflationism were true, then we could know a priori that we don't need to appeal to truth in order to explain anything philosophically interesting, like content, or meaning, or the norms of belief. After all, if truth has no nature, if there are no facts about it over and above the equivalence principle (the idea that, it is true that p if and only if p), then we can hardly appeal to the nature of truth to explain anything else. (In other words, we can't say: well, since truth is like this, then it follows that property x is like that.)

I think this type of explanatory pessimism is far too hasty. We may well need to appeal to truth, and the properties that manifest it, to give a satisfactory explanation of these things. Indeed, for some cases, like the case of how the content of our mental states gets determined, I think the issue is going to hang on yet-to-be-worked-out theories in cognitive science. So I think it is too early to judge whether we should be deflationary pessimists. What I like about functionalism is that it agrees with the deflationists that our ordinary concept of truth is pretty simple: you understand truth if you understand its job, and that job may not be complicated. But it allows us to appeal to the varying nature (the underlying properties that manifest truth or do the truth job) to help us explain knowledge, meaning, and so on.

3:AM: The theory as you present it is a framework for further investigation, I think. So, questions might be raised about whether it is a framework that inevitably presupposes consistency with other philosophical positions that are not purely about the nature of truth. Is this approach consistent with those philosophers who have realist inclinations, for example? Can you say something about this worry and how you answer it? I guess this is a general question about the scope of your theory and the notion of "supercoherence."

LYNCH: That's exactly right: functionalism about truth is something of a meta-theory of truth. It tells you that truth is a functional property that can be manifested in more than one way. One can agree with that and still disagree with my own views about how truth is or isn't manifested in particular domains of inquiry. Now, "realism" is one of those words in philosophy, like "naturalism," that gets thrown around a lot. But I'm certainly not opposed to realism in most of the interesting senses. Indeed, one might say my overall view requires it. Here's a way of illustrating this: as I said above, I'm inclined to think that in some domains, like the domain of morality, truth isn't a matter of corresponding to the world. Whether a moral proposition is true depends, roughly speaking, on whether it would cohere without defeat with the other moral and nonmoral truths. But I don't think this view would make sense across the board. For one thing, the truths about what coheres with what can't be a matter of coherence.

3:AM: I guess that linked to the last question is how well your approach can accommodate science and maths. I presume you would want to do this. If, for example, a naturalist philosopher is left out in the cold, then this would prove a difficulty for your approach, I suppose. Or is there room for your theory to winnow out philosophical positions that don't cohere? Can you say something about this?

LYNCH: I have always thought that the two hardest test cases for any theory of truth are morals and mathematics. I've got a theory of moral truth, more or less. But I still don't have a settled view on mathematical truth. (So I still have some job security). But nothing about functionalism itself precludes holding some version of high-church Platonism about mathematical truth, although I myself am not deeply attracted to that view. If I were to *have* to go with a theory, it would probably be something like structuralism, but luckily no one is yet holding a gun to my head.

3:AM: The collection you edited with Patrick Greenough, *Truth and Realism,* was largely papers from a conference at which Timothy Williamson presented his (in)famous "must do better" talk, which is the last chapter of his own book, *The Philosophy of Philosophy*. He was critical of the variety of approaches to truth that were current, and thought that many were too imprecise to be good philosophy. Was Williamson right?

LYNCH: Well, yes and no; it is hard to say precisely (ahem). Yes: we must always strive to do better, and be as precise as the subject matter merits. No: because, as that remark indicates, not all theories of truth are constructed for the same explanatory purpose. They all want to tell the truth about truth, as it were, but they do so with other goals in mind as well. Some are concerned with the logical paradoxes, some with the metaphysical nature of truth, and some are more interested in the semantics of the English predicate "true." Each of these explanatory goals has merit, but they may bring with them different requirements on what counts as "precision." Good philosophy, like good art or good science, gets done in a variety of ways. Surely the history of philosophy illustrates this fact. That said, Patrick and I have often regretted not having that particular session—and the firestorm of discussion and debate—taped. Tim's brilliant presentation and the various responses by Williams and Rorty amounted to some exceedingly good philosophical theater. Nowadays, of course, it would have been all put on Facebook five minutes after it happened.

3:AM: You're interested in the history of philosophy and co-wrote a book with Heather Battaly on a figure who to most people is pretty obscure, William Alston. He looks pretty dry on the cover. Why is this guy fascinating?

LYNCH: William Alston was a philosopher's philosopher. He is often associated with traditional views: in epistemology, he revitalized foundationalism, in truth theory, realism. And he was one of the most influential philosophers of religion around. But the thing that always fascinated me about Bill is that if you scratched the surface of his views, radical notions teemed beneath the surface. One of Bill's last (and most overlooked) books argues that there really is no such thing as "epistemic justification," and philosophers should just give up trying to define it. Instead, we should just acknowledge there is a plurality of features a belief can have that make it good from the epistemic point of view. And those features are the ones we should care about. That's a sort of pluralism, and there it is no surprise, I suppose, that it resonates with me. I'm proud to say that Bill was also my friend and mentor (a distinction I share with many others, including Al Plantinga, Bob Audi, Heather Battaly, Alessandra Tanesini, etc.). We never agreed on that much, but he was amazingly encouraging of those with whom he disagreed. He died in 2009, but I find I'm arguing with him still.

3:AM: So, your new book *In Praise of Reason* takes on those who are skeptical about the role of reason. Why do you think reason needs defending?

LYNCH: I think that there are two things that need defending: the value and efficacy of reason giving in a democratic culture, and the idea that the sorts of reasons we should give are those that emerge from broadly scientific methods of inquiry. One of the most pervasive sources of skepticism about reason and its value in our culture is the thought that at the end of the day, reasons always give way to something else, something arbitrary. How many times have you heard someone say "Even science comes down to faith"—that reasons must always hit bedrock, after which there is nothing else to say? This is a very old idea, and there is more than a grain of truth to it. But that doesn't mean it is completely right, either. It encourages the worse sort of dogmatism and conservatism, in my view.

3:AM: So this is very much an argument that links democracy with the "space of reasons," isn't it? Can you explain how you make this link?

LYNCH: Absolutely. Democracy is, or should be—to use Sellars's ringing phrase—a space of reasons. Democratic politics isn't war by other means. In a properly functioning liberal democracy, mutual deliberation proceeds through the exchange of public reasons—reasons that can be assessed by the common point of view. And here we encounter what I think is a very deep and overlooked problem. In order to even have a common point of view, we have to have a shared set of epistemic principles—principles that tell us what methods and sources of belief to trust. Without those shared principles, policy disagreements stall out. After all, if we can't agree on the best methods for identifying the facts, we won't be able to agree on what the facts are, and if we can't agree about what the facts are, we will hardly be able to agree on what to *do* in light of the facts. We won't be able to agree on policy. This is just the situation in the United States. We live in isolated bubbles of information pulled from different sources that only reinforce our prejudices. No wonder that political action grinds to a halt. Increasingly, we lack the common principles of rationality that would allow us to engage in meaningful dialogue.

3:AM: The argument that we need to be more reasonable in order to combat prevailing prejudices and irrationalities is likely to resonate with many people. Dogmatic conservativism is a real enemy. But what do you say to a threat coming from those who find evidence that the role of reason in agency is less powerful than might be expected? We find experimenters in cognitive science and psychology finding that when people tell us why they acted as they did, what sound like cogent reasons are merely *post hoc* rationalizations in order to avoid cognitive dissonance. So Peter Carruthers and Eric Schwitzgebel, for example, seem to have lots of evidence suggesting that the powers of reason are pretty feeble, and reasoned agency is less secure than we like to think. This kind of argument is the sort that Nietzschean naturalists launched against

Kantians, but you defend what Anthony Gottlieb has called "the Enlightenment's best idea." So, what do you say to this threat?

LYNCH: I think some of these conclusions are overblown (if not always by the people you mentioned). But it is certainly something I talk about in the book, in part because it has received so much attention. The funny thing is, we don't really need a study, do we, to know that our reasons for our actions are often *post hoc* rationalizations. Nor do we need much more evidence than we already have for the obvious fact that many people make their political and economic decisions just as much or more on emotional or intuitive considerations. In short, I certainly don't dispute that reasons are often not as efficacious in our decision making as we'd like to tell the world they are.

But do we have evidence to think that reasons *can't* be efficacious? Or even that they never actually are? I know of no studies that show that. Nor do I think it is plausible, in part because the more radical view, were anyone to hold it, would appear to be self-undermining. How do you make a scientific argument for the conclusion that no scientific argument ever convinces anyone? There is of course a ton of really interesting work being done on the relation between intuition, reason, and emotion. In my own view, this work does explode the Platonic myth that reason is and should be the master of the mind. But I also think that we should be just as suspicious of the idea that reason is a simple slave to passion, as Hume sometimes seemed to think. The truth must lie somewhere in between.

3:AM: Linked to this is what you feel about the work of experimental philosophy and its relevance for your arguments. Would you change your mind if there was evidence that skepticism about reason was a better description than yours of what people actually do?

ML: Nope. The reason is that I think that lots of folks (not everyone, but lots) actually *are* skeptical about reason. I want to convince them not to be. That said, I've come around on experimental philosophy. Like most of us who are comfortable in their armchairs, I confess to being initially skeptical. But I now think there is value in much of this data—we just need to be careful about explaining that value. What experimental philosophy can tell us is what folks think about stuff. It can tell us therefore about the scope of "common sense" on certain philosophical topics. And what's disturbing (and interesting) is that that may turn out to be different than what we eggheads thought it was. Yet what x-phi *can't* tell us, or so I believe, is what we *should* think about the relevant topics. That's the job of the philosopher: not just to describe the world, but to change our thinking about it. Sometimes the proposed change can be radical (think Peter Singer or Graham Priest); sometimes it can be a matter of suggesting that we systemize our thought, make it more coherent in one direction or another (think Davidson or Rawls). Philosophy in either case is revisionary; it builds.

3:AM: Recently I was talking to a nonphilosopher and was surprised that she thought that most philosophers were dogmatic and conservative, and she then linked this perspective to their belief in the objectivity of truth and couldn't believe that a politics of the left could be defended from such a position. That's why she liked French philosophers! So, what would you say about this and its inference of reactionary politics linked with objectivity, on the one hand, and left politics being linked with relativism of a French kind (probably Derrida) on the other? It made me realize that something that might be supposed to be neutral regarding one's politics, like a theory of truth, is often supposed to be part of a much wider discourse. Is this something you're aware of? It seems to be the source of some of the difficulties and bad reputation that some Anglo-American philosophy has acquired. I sense that someone like Richard Rorty felt something like this. What do you think?

LYNCH: People like me who grew up intellectually in the nineties were soaked with the idea that those on the left must reject the idea of objective truth. That was a mistake, and one that, as I noted above, the Bush years in the United States made us learn the hard way. The fact is that we on the progressive left have done ourselves a terrible disservice by rejecting the concept of objective truth—if only because it is hard to stand up for your opinions if you think they are no more true than anyone else's. This was something that, at the end of his life, Richard Rorty and I went around about it in several venues. In his view, talk of truth is just like talk of God: it is a metaphysical crux, and one that should be abandoned. I see it differently. I think that giving up on objective truth is giving in to those who would like to convince us that there is no difference between what is right and what they say is right, between lies and reality. It is not just a metaphysical mistake; it is a political one. Having said that, it is unfortunate that so many philosophers tend to think that pluralism is inconsistent with objectivity. That is a mistake too, and it gives us a bad name. There can be more than one true story of the world. That just doesn't mean that every story is equally true.

3:AM: Linked to that last point, do you agree that the distinction between Analytic and Continental philosophy is a phony one? Where do you situate yourself? What are the big questions that are going to be pressing on philosophers' brows in the next decade?

LYNCH: Yes and no. Looked at from the vantage point of inquiry, philosophers should be without borders. In my view, there is no deep and philosophically interesting divide between "Analytic" and "Continental" philosophers in the way there is between, say, "nominalists" and "realists" about numbers, or between utilitarians and Kantians in moral theory. Nor is there much methodological divide either (not all "analytic" philosophers are doing "linguistic philosophy" and not all "continental" philosophers are doing phenomenology or deconstruction). But there is a sociological divide that these unhappy terms can be used to pick out, and we can't ignore it. What marks the divide is as much a matter of which books you were brought up to read as anything else: whether for example your graduate program privileged Husserl over Frege or Derrida over Quine.

And then there is a matter of style too, (which is not the same as method). Marked that way, I'm an Analytic philosopher, no question. But the questions I'm interested in are questions that many "Continental" philosophers are interested in too. What's going to be big in philosophy? That's a dangerous question, like asking what is going to be big in the stock market. ("Plastics," said the guy to Dustin Hoffman in *The Graduate*. "Plastics.") But I'm a risk taker as much as the next guy, so here goes. One issue I think that philosophy is ripe to return to is the nature of the imagination. This was a question that fascinated the heroes of old, but it hasn't been central recently (although folks like Tamar Gendler and Tim Williamson have started us down the path again). What is the relation between imagination and knowledge? They are often seen as opposites, but I think that is a mistake. What we imagine can give us knowledge too. I think the problems of knowledge and reason will continue to be important. The virtual age is changing how we think about both. Most of what we know (or think we know) now is via search engine. As a result, knowledge more than ever relies on testimony, on "book learning." But testimony can classically be terribly unreliable. So what does the fact that we can't seem to rely on it mean for what we know—and for what knowledge is? I don't think we've fully grappled with that fact yet, and so far I think philosophers have been ignoring it—which is a problem, for all sorts of reasons.

3:AM: So, are there any books, art, or films that have been enlightening to you outside philosophy?

LYNCH: Tons. Here's one. I was in Rome recently and spent a lot of time looking at some early and lesser-known (at least to me) pieces by Bernini. What struck me is that he was not afraid of the curve. Philosophers shouldn't be either.

3:AM: And finally, can you recommend five top books, other than your own, which of course we'll all be ordering straight away, that will be mind-blowing for the nonphilosophically trained but smart reader?

LYNCH: First: *Reason, Truth, and History*, by Hilary Putnam. I've been rereading for the 10th time and still find it separates my brain from the rest of my body (in a good way).

Second: *The Reliability of Sense Perception*, by William P. Alston. This tiny little book deserves to be a classic (and in some circles is). It argues that we have no noncircular way of proving that our senses are reliable. That seems like a pretty powerful skeptical argument, no? Alston thought it showed something else. Read it to find out what.

Third: Hume's *Enquiry Concerning Human Understanding*. As Quine said, the Humean condition is the human condition.

Fourth: Richard Rorty, *Philosophy and the Mirror of Nature*. I disagree with much of what he says, but he has the problem nailed. And no matter what he (and everyone else) might have said: this is a man who took philosophy seriously.

Fifth: *Game of Thrones*. Loved it. (And all the other books in that series too). So sue me.

21 | Timothy Williamson
CLASSICAL INVESTIGATIONS

Timothy Williamson is a philosopher of philosophical logic, epistemology, metaphysics, and philosophy of language and is the Wykeham Professor of Logic at Oxford University. He is also an annual Nelson Visitor at the University of Michigan, Ann Arbor. He is the author of *Identity and Discrimination* (Blackwell, 1990, updated edition 2013); *Vagueness* (Routledge, 1994); *Knowledge and Its Limits* (Oxford, 2000); *The Philosophy of Philosophy* (Blackwell, 2007), and *Modal Logic as Metaphysics* (Oxford, 2013).

3:AM: Your two books *Knowledge and Its Limits* and *The Philosophy of Philosophy* are astonishingly radical. Your 1994 book on *Vagueness* has already become a classic of analytic philosophy. Yet outside of professional philosophy circles, they have not become well known. Jerry Fodor once noted that whereas Sartre, Foucault, and Derrida could easily be found in bookstores, his own books (and those of others like yourself) were much more difficult to locate. This seems to be a general tendency for much work in analytic philosophy. So, before discussing specifically what they're about, I'd like to ask about this. Why do you think this is the case? Sartre is no easier than Dummett, say, and yet many self-described intellectuals will have heard of Sartre but not Dummett. Is it to do with the writing, the subject matter, or just that analytic philosophers tend to undersell their radicalism and the alternative tradition overplays their claims? (I tend to think this is the case; so with you, your ideas blow away many so-called radicals such as Foucault, and your conclusions, couched in very cool, precise language, belie their corrosive impact!)

WILLIAMSON: Of course Sartre's high public profile depended on his novels, plays, and political writings as much as on his philosophy, so he is a rather special case. Bertrand Russell is an example of an analytic philosopher who was comparably well known to the wider public, as a result of his provocative writings on marriage and morals, atheism, nuclear weapons, and so on, rather than the brilliant technical work in logic on which his reputation in philosophy is based. Nevertheless, there is obviously something to the contrast you draw. Michael Dummett is a good example, because he was a leading activist in the anti-racism campaign of the 1960s and he has written books on a variety of topics outside philosophy, including voting systems and tarot games, but still without becoming widely known outside philosophy. One reason may be that in his public interventions he did not invoke his authority as a philosopher. He never pretended that his writings on the philosophy of language were crucial texts in the struggle against racism. Maybe if he had done, people would have believed him! Not long ago I had a revealing discussion with a professor of ancient Greek literature, who was convinced that, by contrast with the tradition of Sartre, Foucault, and Derrida, contemporary analytic philosophy had nothing useful to offer the study of poetry—a common view in departments of literature. He claimed that it could not handle phenomena such as meaning more than one says.

I discovered that he didn't know of the analytic philosopher Paul Grice's analysis of just such phenomena, which has had a huge impact on linguistics as well as philosophy. The point is that he had never even looked at Grice's book (*Studies in the Way of Words*); he wasn't reacting negatively to its content or manner of presentation. That's not untypical. Outside philosophy departments, many people are taught that analytic philosophy is sterile logic chopping, so they don't feel the incentive to do the hard work that is needed to master the ideas and see how they can be applied to literary texts and other material. Of course, it doesn't help that since comparatively few analytic philosophers present such applications, it is not immediately obvious that they can be made. Analytic philosophers have a sound methodological instinct to start with simpler, more ordinary cases and build up gradually to the complicated, sexy ones; for advertising purposes, that's a drawback.

3:AM: I think the books of yours I mentioned are all radical and have made a profound impact in the way we have to think about their subjects. For instance, your approach to vagueness is striking because it takes seriously the limits to human knowledge. And it undermines several claims that on the face of it seem plausible, such as the idea that you always know when you're in pain. Can you say a little bit about how you came to this theory? I mean, was it something you suspected before you'd worked out the logic, or was it as startling to you as it has seemed to others? And why were you drawn to vagueness in the first place—was it philosophy or reality that drew you to it?

WILLIAMSON: I was aware of vagueness as a challenging issue from my undergraduate days. It seemed to present the strongest challenge to the classical, realist picture that has always rung true to me, on which the world is largely independent of us, and the principle of bivalence holds—every proposition is either true or false (and not both), even if we do not and perhaps cannot know which—and other standard principles of logic hold too. The problem was that, on an unqualified realist picture, there must be a point at which subtracting just one grain from a heap takes it from being true to being false that there is a heap in front of you, which seems to be incompatible with the vagueness of the concept of a heap, which has no precise definition. For a long time I could see no satisfactory way round that objection.

Then, as I was finishing my first book, *Identity and Discrimination*, I started thinking about the way in which ordinary knowledge requires a margin for error. It dawned on me that the need for a margin for error would explain why, even though ordinary concepts have sharp boundaries, we can't know where those boundaries are located. That explanation solved the main objection to the logical view that I had always wanted to hold. So the hard part was working out the epistemology; the logic was the easy bit. The larger purpose underlying my book *Vagueness* was to argue for realism like this: if realism is wrong about anything, it is wrong about vagueness (that premise was generally agreed); but realism is not wrong about vagueness; therefore it is not wrong about anything.

3:AM: How far is your commitment to the principle of bivalence something that shapes your philosophical outlook, and what are your thoughts about philosophical traditions that tend to dismiss it, such as Hegelianism?

WILLIAMSON: I regard classical logic, in a broad sense that includes the principle of bivalence, as the best guide we have in philosophy. That doesn't mean that I think it crazy to challenge bivalence. Many able philosophers have argued against it in various interesting ways for various domains, including the past, the future, the infinite, and the quantum world, as well as vagueness. I don't dismiss their arguments; I try to show in detail where they have gone wrong. I would put Hegelianism low on the order of challenges to bivalence, because Hegel was writing long before the development of modern logic, at a time when logic was in a terrible state, and so he had no idea of the resources of logic. There are profound things in Hegel, such as the master-slave dialectic in *The Phenomenology of Spirit*, but he was no logician. Although some contemporary advocates of nonclassical logic refer to Hegel from time to time, I have never seen a powerful Hegelian critique of classical logic.

3:AM: Are there fields of inquiry that would benefit from taking vagueness more seriously than they do at the moment? For instance, are there aspects of evolutionary theory that might be less secure once vagueness comes into play?

WILLIAMSON: Cats evolved from animals that were not cats. If you ask when the first cat appeared, you realize that vagueness is involved. As it happens, I discussed vagueness-related problems about the individuation of species in *Identity and Discrimination*. One of the main theories is that two animal populations belong to the same species if and only if they can interbreed with each other. The trouble is that there are chains of populations where each can interbreed with its immediate neighbors but the population at one end of the chain can't interbreed with the population at the other end. The theory seems to imply identity of species at each link of the chain but difference of species between the endpoints, which is a contradiction. I showed how to achieve a logically consistent best approximation to the original inconsistent theory in situations like that. However, that is really just a matter of tidying up loose ends. Vagueness throws no doubt on the spirit of evolutionary theory.

3:AM: I think somewhere you suggest that AI engineers need to consider vagueness if they're to engineer thinking like ours. How far has AI taken up this thought?

WILLIAMSON: Vagueness is a much more serious issue in AI and related fields. If robots are going to have concepts that they apply in real time primarily on the basis of perception, then those concepts are likely to be vague, which raises the question of how they should be reasoning with those concepts—a central issue in philosophical discussion of vagueness. Unfortunately, one of the most influential theories of vagueness in those fields has been fuzzy logic, which is much cruder and more naïve even than the best of the nonclassical theories of vagueness. Fuzzy logic has been applied to the design of washing machines, although I don't think they were using the most distinctive implications of the theory. Recently I looked at a paper for *Artificial Intelligence Journal* that used the framework of my theory of vagueness, so it is having an impact in that area too.

3:AM: Were practical applications important to you, or was it just the fun of working out the theory that drew you in?

WILLIAMSON: I must admit that practical applications were the last thing on my mind when I developed the theory. I was just interested in the theoretical questions. But it is normal in science that theories developed for no practical purpose later turn out to have practical applications. In fact, worrying too much about practical applications may be counterproductive, because it tends to inhibit the kind of radical questioning that in the long run drives major innovations. Turing developed the concept of a computer in response to a purely theoretical question in mathematical logic.

3:AM: The third book, *Knowledge and Its Limits*, puts forward what Tim Crane called "a daring new picture of knowledge," Brian McLaughlin and John Hawthorne considered "the most important contribution to epistemology in many years," and Patrick Greenough called "one of the most important and refreshing books on epistemology written in the past 20 years." In it you argue that knowledge isn't to be understood in terms of a kind of "true belief." Can you briefly say a little bit about this position?

WILLIAMSON: The basic distinction in epistemology is between knowledge and belief. Beliefs can be false, but knowledge can't be. Someone may believe that the earth is flat but they can't know that it is flat; they just believe (falsely) that they know that it is flat. The traditional direction of explanation in epistemology is to start with belief and analyze knowledge in terms of it: knowledge is belief plus truth plus various other factors. The trouble is that there have turned out to be counterexamples to all such analyses that have been proposed. In the book, I reverse the direction of explanation, starting with knowledge and treating belief as a state that aspires to the condition of knowledge. There is a deeper motivation behind this reversal. Knowledge is the success state, whereas belief is neutral between success and failure (it may be true or false).

The idea is to understand malfunctioning in terms of successful functioning, rather than treating them on a par. In the case of action, trying is the thing neutral between success and failure—you try and you may succeed, you may fail. But our analysis shouldn't start with trying, because trying can only be understood in relation to what it is aiming at, that is, succeeding. Similarly, believing can only be understood in terms of what it is aiming at, that is, knowing. *Knowledge and its Limits* is a further step in the development of a tradition in the philosophy of mind known as externalism, which goes back to the work of philosophers such as Hilary Putnam, Tyler Burge, Gareth Evans, and John McDowell in the 1970s. The idea is that mental states are not internal to the brain; their very nature involves relations between the brain and the external environment. Those philosophers were interested in the way that the contents of mental states involve the world: someone on a planet causally disconnected from ours can't want to meet Obama. I'm interested in the way that states like knowing, remembering, and seeing involve the world: you can't see that it is raining unless it is raining (if it is not raining, you can only believe that you can see that it is raining).

3:AM: Were you aware how groundbreaking the argument was? Did you have certain targets in mind when writing the book?

WILLIAMSON: I remember, several years before the book was published, I put forward some of the ideas in it in a lecture at an American university, and someone in the audience said that if he thought I was right, he would give up philosophy! That struck me as a rather extreme reaction. I knew that I was proposing a view of knowledge that challenged the framework within which much of 20th-century epistemology had been done, although I was also building on the ideas of previous philosophers. What I didn't know was what reaction it would provoke. I was afraid that since it didn't fit into the standard terms of debate, it would be marginalized. It has had much more impact than I expected. Maybe the time was right for such a theory.

3:AM: Were there positions being taken and arguments being made, implicitly or explicitly, not just in circles of analytic philosophy, that you were dissatisfied with?

WILLIAMSON: The picture that I was criticizing is not confined to analytic philosophy; it goes back to Plato. Internalism about the mind is extremely common among nonanalytic philosophers and nonphilosophers. Films like *The Matrix* raise all sorts of questions about internalism and externalism.

3:AM: Since writing it, have you reconsidered any of your positions in the book?

WILLIAMSON: I recently had to write replies to 15 critical essays on *Knowledge and Its Limits*, to appear with the essays in a book called *Williamson on Knowledge*. I had to clarify some things I said, but the essays didn't make me change my mind on anything. For independent reasons, I have changed my view on a few things that are peripheral to the main line of argument. There are lots of points on which I now think that the book, although what it says is correct as far as it goes, does not go far enough, and the theory needs to be developed further. I have carried the development forward in subsequent articles.

3:AM: Outside philosophy, are there areas where you think your work would be well learned? It seems that skeptical arguments and much continental philosophy grounded in luminosity, for example, poststructuralism and phenomenology—are seriously challenged by the book. Have there been counterarguments coming from those areas?

WILLIAMSON: Some linguists (and at least one missionary!) have been interested in the ideas about assertion in the book, and some lawyers in the ideas about evidence. It would be interesting to see reactions from poststructuralists or phenomenologists to the book, but most of them don't read any analytic epistemology. In the last years of his life, Richard Rorty started using me as a paradigm of what he regarded as the wrong turning analytic philosophy has taken. I was hoping that he would attack *The Philosophy of Philosophy*, since that would have been good for sales, but he died before it appeared.

3:AM: This book and *Vagueness*, indeed everything you're writing, seem to suggest that human fallibility and the limits to what we as humans can know are a key insight. How far is this a view that has been developed by the philosophy, and how far was it an already established insight that then suggested the contours of your theorizing?

WILLIAMSON: It's pre-theoretically obvious that in almost every domain of human thought our beliefs are fallible and our knowledge limited. Many philosophers have regarded our own minds as some kind of exception, a "cognitive home" as I once called it, in which those limitations did not apply, so that there is no cognitive limitation to knowing one's own present mental states (they are "luminous," in the book's jargon). Theoretical argument was needed to show that the same fundamental limitations apply even to one's knowledge of one's own mind.

3:AM: In your last book you again insinuate yourself into contemporary philosophical thought and say that not only has it made errors but it has actually taken a disastrous wrong turn. You call this the "linguistic turn," which develops into "the conceptual turn." This is radicalism without a hat. Could you briefly outline the main argument, that it's wrong for philosophy to think its sole job is to analyze language/concepts, why this is such an important point?

WILLIAMSON: The linguistic turn and the conceptual turn took many different forms. All of them were, in one way or another, responses to a methodological challenge to philosophy that the development of modern experimental science has made more and more urgent: How can philosophers expect to learn about the world without getting up out of their armchairs to see what it's actually like? The idea was that whatever philosophers have to do, they can do on the basis of their understanding of their native language, or perhaps of some ideal formal language, or their grasp of the corresponding concepts, both of which they already have in the armchair. In some sense, philosophical questions are linguistic or conceptual questions, either because they are about our own language or thought, or because they are the kind of questions that can be answered from principles that we implicitly accept simply in understanding the words or grasping the concepts.

In reply, I argue that the attempts to rephrase philosophical questions as questions about words or concepts are unfaithful to what contemporary philosophers are actually interested in. For example, philosophers of time are interested in the underlying nature of time, not just the word *time* or our concept of time. As for the principles that we implicitly accept simply in understanding words or grasping concepts, I argue that there aren't any. A language is a forum for disagreement; contrary to what many philosophers have thought, it doesn't impose an ideology. People who take wildly unorthodox views, even about logic, are not "breaking the rules of English."

Although the linguistic turn and the conceptual turn involve radical misconceptions of philosophy, in my view, I don't regard them as avoidable accidents. Probably they were stages that philosophy had to go through; we can only determine their limitations if lots of able people are doing their utmost to defend them. But by now we can see their limitations. As an alternative, I show how we can answer the methodological challenge to armchair philosophy without taking the linguistic or conceptual turn. For example, thought experiments, which play a central role in contemporary philosophy, involve offline applications in the imagination of cognitive skills originally developed through online applications in perception. Those skills go well beyond the minimum required for understanding the words or grasping the concepts. Our ability to perform thought experiments is really just a byproduct of our ability to answer nonphilosophical questions of the form "What would happen if...?" Philosophy is much more like other forms of inquiry than philosophers have often pretended.

3:AM: When you wrote the book, did you intend to shake everything up?

WILLIAMSON: I felt that the predominant self-images of philosophy hadn't properly adjusted to its current practice, in part because the "big picture" narratives of philosophy were mainly being written by people like Rorty who were unsympathetic to the most fruitful recent developments. Although our practice can be better than our theory of our practice, if we have a bad theory of our practice it is likely to have some distorting effect on the practice itself. I thought it time to explore a philosophy of philosophy more in tune with philosophy as it is actually being done.

3:AM: Has the book caused analytic philosophy to reimagine itself?

WILLIAMSON: It is too soon to say how much impact the book will have. Some philosophers, especially in the United States, have strongly agreed with it. Others regard it as crazy. Several debates on the book between other philosophers and me have been published or are about to be.

3:AM: Many of my friends are Wittgensteinians, others phenomenologists. Should they stop?

WILLIAMSON: It would be unhealthy as well as boring for philosophy if everyone did it in the same way. We need a wide gene pool of ideas and methods. Nevertheless, some ideas and methods are better than others. When it comes to writing the history of twentieth-century philosophy, the works of

Wittgenstein, Husserl, and Heidegger will presumably remain major texts, given their originality and vast influence. But from a historical point of view, it also seems clear that in recent decades the Wittgensteinian and phenomenological traditions have not adequately renewed themselves. Although books continue to be published in both traditions, they are recycling old ideas rather than engaging with new ones. Part of the attraction of such a tradition for its adherents is that it constitutes an intellectual comfort zone in which they are given pseudo-justifications for not bothering to learn new ways of thinking.

At their best, the Wittgensteinian and phenomenological traditions share the virtue of patient, accurate description of examples. In that respect the analytic tradition has learned from them, I hope permanently. But once the examples started giving results that didn't suit them, Wittgensteinians retreated into their dogmatic theoretical preconceptions while pretending to do the opposite. As for phenomenology, if a phenomenological description of experience is one that mentions only facts the subject knows at the time, fine. But it shouldn't be confused with a description of facts about appearances, since one often knows facts that go beyond them. You can know that you are seeing a computer screen, not just that you seem to be seeing a computer screen. I argue in *Knowledge and Its Limits* that the privileging of appearances results from the fallacy of assuming that we must have a cognitive home.

3:AM: Regarding philosophers' intuitions, you have strong things to say about these in *The Philosophy of Philosophy* when discussing evidence. At one point you say, "The point of such maneuvers is primarily dialectical, to find common ground on which to argue with the opponent at hand." Do you think that this may be a reason for analytic philosophers not having found a broader readership—it hasn't managed to find common ground, its intuitions have been faulty?

WILLIAMSON: I was arguing that the idea of "intuition" is mystifying and unhelpful in discussion of philosophical method. What we are really talking about are philosophers' judgments. There is no special faculty of intuition. When analytic philosophers take their opponents seriously, they go out of their way to find common ground with them; perhaps they sometimes go too far doing that, for example in arguing with extreme skeptics. Of course, analytic philosophers often make faulty judgments—they are human, after all—but that isn't what explains why they haven't found a broader readership. Plenty of books packed with faulty judgments sell well.

3:AM: Returning to the afterword of your last book, where you address us like a head teacher admonishing us all to do better, do you think there is no room for continental philosophy? Given that you argue that so much of the analytic tradition, so called, has been wasting its time taking the linguistic/conceptual turn, might not someone from the continental field suggest that that in itself is a reason for looking for different approaches to philosophy?

WILLIAMSON: The linguistic/conceptual turn wasn't confined to analytic philosophy; it occurs in a different form in "Continental" philosophers like Derrida (of course, the label "Continental philosophy" covers a wide variety of approaches, but it is convenient shorthand). Nor was it a mere waste of time. Analytic philosophy learned much about language and mind in the course of it, and thereby contributed to linguistics and cognitive science too. One philosophical gain is that we have become much better at analyzing the structure of arguments, by thinking about the semantics and syntax of the sentences that make them up; as a result, we have become much better at determining whether they are valid or not, even though the arguments themselves are not about words. As for learning from continental philosophy, analytic philosophy has become a much broader, more varied, and more tolerant tradition than it once was. It is not afraid of learning from nonanalytic philosophers; you can find analytic philosophers discussing Hegel, Nietzsche, Heidegger, Merleau-Ponty, and Derrida from time to time. However, it tends to learn much less from such continental philosophers than it does from nonphilosophers—linguists, psychologists, biologists, physicists, mathematicians. In philosophy in continental Europe (as opposed to "continental philosophy"), the most important development over the past thirty years has been the massive spread of analytic philosophy. "Continental philosophy," by contrast, is stagnating.

3:AM: Are there no writers from this other field who interest you?

WILLIAMSON: When I was a graduate student, I used to go to meetings of a Radical Philosophy group and read Derrida and Foucault because I was curious about whether continental philosophy had intellectual resources that I could use. Although I occasionally found something intriguing in their works, I eventually came to the conclusion that they were not worth the trouble. The texts were obscure and dogmatic. At first I thought other people in the Radical Philosophy group understood them better than I did, but then I discovered that they didn't; they were simply more willing to go on talking in that way, without trying to clarify the obscurity. They couldn't answer my questions. In general, although the rhetoric of liberation is far more prevalent in continental than in analytic philosophy, I've found the world of continental philosophy far more hierarchical and authoritarian than that of analytic philosophy. In a department of analytic philosophy, if the most famous philosopher in the world comes to give a lecture, graduate students are expected to put tough objections to them; if the famous philosopher tries to fob them off, that's noticed and disapproved of. The attitude in continental philosophy tends to be more deferential and fawning. I find it a depressing world. It isn't much fun arguing with people who don't know how to discriminate between sophistry and valid reasoning. I admire Nietzsche as a brilliant writer and culture critic rather than philosopher.

3:AM: Do you think analytic philosophy can change? Do you see yourself as a radical leading such a change?

WILLIAMSON: Analytic philosophy has been changing throughout its history, and will continue to do so. I don't think a radical change in how it operates (as opposed to how it thinks it operates) is needed. What I was suggesting is that by conscious reflection and training we can improve our performance incrementally. Although that sounds dull, the long-term effects can be dramatic. Tycho Brahe was just a bit more accurate and comprehensive in his astronomical observations than his predecessors, but the result was data good enough to discriminate between the Ptolemaic and Copernican systems.

3:AM: Can you say a little about the ontological commitments of your general philosophical position?

WILLIAMSON: My work on vagueness and ontology doesn't really concern ontology. Probably my most distinctive ontological commitment comes from my defense of a controversial principle in logic known as the Barcan formula, named after the American logician Ruth Barcan Marcus, who first stated it. An application of this principle is that since Marilyn Monroe and John F. Kennedy could have had a child (although they actually didn't), there is something that could have been a child of Marilyn Monroe and John F. Kennedy. On my view, it is neither a child nor a collection of atoms, but rather something that merely could have been a child, made out of atoms, but actually has no location in space and time. The argument can be multiplied, so there actually are infinitely many things that could have been located in space and time but aren't. It takes quite a bit of work to show that the Barcan formula is better than the alternatives! That's what my next book will be on. The working title is *Ontological Rigidity*.[1]

3:AM: You wrote a wonderful piece about Barcan. Though the logic is too hard for me to understand, you still managed to indicate to me the intellectual excitement of her discoveries and the journey this remarkable woman has traveled. You also expressed great sympathy and admiration for her; you seemed to be writing almost as a fan.

WILLIAMSON: That piece is the speech I gave when Ruth was awarded the Lauener Prize for a lifetime's achievement in philosophy. I'm glad that

---

[1] Published as *Modal Logic as Metaphysics* (Oxford University Press, 2013).

I managed to communicate something of that achievement. Of course, there are many other philosophers for whom I have a deep respect. For instance, an important experience for me as a first-year undergraduate was listening to Saul Kripke lecture at Oxford: the combination of clarity, logical power, and good judgment struck me then, and continues to strike me, as a model for how to do philosophy.

3:AM: Currently, who or what excites you most, and why?

WILLIAMSON: Intellectually, what excites me most at the moment is an obscure branch of logic known as second-order modal logic, which I'm going to use in *Ontological Rigidity*. It excites me because it is beautiful and rigorous and casts light from unexpected angles on metaphysical disputes that have become rather stuck, and so enables us to move them on.

3:AM: What do you see as the great challenges facing humans, and what role do you think philosophy has in helping us face them?

WILLIAMSON: Obviously, a central challenge facing our species is to survive on this planet for as long as it can. It's hard not to despair when one thinks about the destruction of the environment and the tenacity of irrational belief. Philosophy can help us face these challenges. My colleague John Broome, who is the professor of moral philosophy at Oxford, has a book on *Counting the Cost of Global Warming*. There are difficult philosophical issues about how to take into account the interests of actual or possible future generations in present decision making. There are even logical issues: How can we reason about future individuals who will never exist if we wipe ourselves out first? Interestingly, the Barcan formula provides a solution to the purely logical problem, but unfortunately not to the others.

3:AM: Has the recent credit crunch raised issues that philosophy can address?

WILLIAMSON: I'll leave it to nonanalytic philosophers to pontificate on the credit crunch in ignorance of economics.

3:AM: Are there any nonphilosophers you'd say are worth reading?

WILLIAMSON: I don't know any philosophers who think that only philosophers are worth reading! I know some who seem to think that only nonphilosophers are worth reading. It's frightening to go into a bookshop and realize how many of the books are worth reading and how few of them one will find time to read. In fiction, I like novelists who are as clever and clear-eyed as good philosophers, and as exact in their use of words, but who don't attempt to do philosophy. Jane Austen is an obvious example (my taste in literature, art, and music is as classical as in logic). Those virtues can be found in less-exalted branches of fiction too; Dashiell Hammett has them. The poets I return to most often are Shakespeare and Yeats. I'd be more receptive to "experimental" literature if I knew how to tell whether it refutes the author's theory.

22 | Ernie Lepore
MEANING, TRUTH, LANGUAGE, REALITY

Ernie Lepore is a philosopher and cognitive scientist interested in the philosophy of language and mind, the philosophy of logic, and the philosophy of Donald Davidson. He often writes in collaboration with other philosophers at Rutgers University, where he is the director of the Rutgers Center for Cognitive Science. He was sole author of *Meaning and Argument* (2000); edited with B. Smith *Handbook in Philosophy of Language* (2006); co-authored with Herman Cappelen *Insensitive Semantics: In Defense of Semantic Minimalism and Speech Act Pluralism* (2004); with Kirk Ludwig *Donald Davidson: Truth, Meaning, Rationality in Mind* (2005) and *Donald Davidson's Truth-theoretic Semantics* (2007); with Jerry Fodor *Holism: A Shopper's Guide* (1991) and *The Compositionality Papers* (2002); with Sarah-Jane Leslie *What Every Student Should Know* (2002); with Barry Loewer *Meaning, Mind, and Matter: Philosophical Essays* (2011); with H. Cappelen *Language Turned on Itself* (2007); with H. Wettstein *Philosophy and Poetry* (Midwest Studies in Philosophy, vol. 33, 2009); co-edited with B. Smith *Handbook in Philosophy of Language* (2006); with Z. Pylyshyn *Rutgers University Invitation to Cognitive Science* (1999); with J. Fodor *Holism: A Consumer's Update*, ed. and comments (1994); *The Philosophy of Donald Davidson: Perspectives on Inquires into Truth and Interpretation* (1986, paperback 1989); with B. McLaughlin *The Philosophy of Donald Davidson: Perspectives on Action and Events* (1985); *New Directions in Semantics* (1986, paperback 1989); and with R. van Gulick *John Searle and His Critics* (1990, paperback 1993).

3:AM: What made you become a philosopher? Was it a surprise to anyone?

LEPORE: During my freshman year in college I promised my mom on her deathbed that I would become a lawyer. After a year of mourning I returned to college; the consensus was that philosophy was the best pre-law major. As it happened, UMass-Amherst had an excellent philosophy department, though not in the style I was vaguely familiar with from having read the fiction of Sartre and Camus in high school. Doubts about my prose brought me to ask where I might bone up on grammar; the answer was linguistics.

There I was, 18 years of age, taking metaphysics with Bruce Aune, modal logic with Ed Gettier, math logic with Terry Parsons, and "grammar" (semantics) with Barbara Hall Partee. It was not what I expected. To boot, many of the undergrads in Barbara's class were English majors and I thought that was cheating; they already knew grammar. Little did I know! After the first year, I unofficially adopted both the philosophy and linguistics departments as my new family; it was a splendid arrangement. Did my newfound fascination with philosophy surprise anyone? Well, during regular visits to Amherst, I would suffocate my best friend from high school, Brian McLaughlin, with what I was learning about Quine and Skinner; he went back to Jersey, took a philosophy course with Chris Hill; and so we both sort of backed into the field. I'm still surprised by grad students who tell me that they knew they wanted to become philosophers since high school. I can't imagine either of us entertaining that idea while we were growing up and spending most of our time on the wrestling mat.

3:AM: Are you a philosopher of mind or a philosopher of language, or both? Or is the distinction no longer very useful?

LEPORE: I'm a philosopher of language, not a philosopher of mind. Barry Loewer and Jerry Fodor pushed me into philosophy of mind in the late 1980s, convincing me it made little difference whether language or thought were being investigated, since both were representational. It took me longer than it should have to realize they snookered me. Once I did, I ran back to language. I bailed out right around the time that I was asked whether strong or weak, global or regional supervenience was guiding my judgments about the relationship between the mental and the physical. It wasn't that philosophy of mind had become too scholastic; after all, I've written an entire book on quotation marks. (Fodor once chided me that the semicolon was unsafe from my philosophical purview; and after he complained I shouldn't be working on such a small topic as "that," I turned to "the"; "a" has become a recent interest of mine.)

What drove me back to natural language were the robust intuitions I lacked about supervenience but that I had about linguistic usage. Colin McGinn once counseled me to always ask myself first, "What do I think about this subject?" That was sage advice. In the philosophy of mind, I simply didn't have any intuitions, or least strong intuitions, about a wide range of subjects. Mind you, many philosophers would say (and have said) that my intuitions about language are perverse; those about context sensitivity are particularly so.

It has come as a surprise to me to discover how deep my commitments to intuition run.

When I was younger I thought philosophers adopted certain positions just to be provocative. They wanted to see how far they could defend them. I now appreciate that given the perseverance it takes to endorse minimalism (or eliminativism or solipsism or anomalous monism or the language of thought or paraconsistent logics or a range of other "perverse" views), you'd better believe it; I believe minimalism. A more recent source of concern for me is consistency—my own, that is: I have nine books and nearly 150 published articles; that's a lot of potential inconsistency to worry about. Intuitions and pursuits in one area sometimes clash with those in another. A case in point is my work on quotation; I had published several articles on the topic before the book; and in those articles I advocated contextualism, until once in a seminar, Jason Stanley, John Hawthorne, and Jerry Fodor all pressed the peculiarity of defending contextualism about quotation while rejecting it for gradable adjectives. That encounter caused a year's delay on the book's completion as well as a thorough rethinking of its subject.

I could tell similar sagas about my work on Davidson as well as my current book in progress on the semantic-pragmatic divide. Unfortunately, we sometimes set out to theorize about a subject on the basis of too small a portion of the relevant data. That reminds me of a BBC radio interview I once did with Michael Dummett and Myles Byrnyeat. The host began by saying, rather loudly, "The cat is on the mat." When it became evident we had no idea what he was getting at, he added he had been told this was the most important sentence in philosophy. Dummett corrected him saying that that sentence had been replaced by "Snow is white"; of course, were he speaking now he'd have to say that both sentences have been replaced with "It's raining." We've come a long way!

3:AM: Semantic holism has been a terribly influential approach in philosophy of language and has been contrived and defended by some of the biggest names in modern philosophy, hasn't it? Quine, Davidson, Lewis, Dennett, Block, Brandom, and Churchland, et al. And Wittgenstein of the *Philosophical Investigations.* Can you say what question meaning holism is trying to answer and how it goes about doing so?

LEPORE: When Fodor showed up at Rutgers in the late '80s, we co-taught a graduate seminar on holism versus atomism. He was puzzled how I could reconcile my endorsement of Davidson's holism—the idea that the contents of words in some sense depend on one another—with my criticisms of conceptual role semantics—a rather old idea dating back at least to Ferdinand de Saussure, that the meaning of a word is a function of its inferential relationships to other words. Fodor thought the best (only?) defense of holism would rely on inferential (conceptual) role semantics. (Fodor and I agreed from the start that wherever I used "word" he would say "concept" and vice versa; I don't think natural language has interested him much since his days with Katz in the '60s.)

I thought Davidson had independent arguments for holism; and so, Fodor agreed to co-teach the seminar. It came as an embarrassment—a game changer intellectually—to discover that my "arguments" in defense of Davidson's holism were mere restatements of the thesis; Fodor and other colleagues, e.g., Stich, McLaughlin, Loewer, Klein, and Matthews, pressed me on this weekly. (It's worth noting that the seminar never got to atomism; a number of philosophers over the years have inferred that I had gone Fodorian with the holism book. I doubt there exist any good arguments for atomism either.) I found myself by the end of the term mumbling something like "Holism is a metaphor" (or a picture or a way of life or some other nonsense).

3:AM: Interestingly, Donald Davidson was one of the targets of your attack on holism, but you have returned to him again and again. A reviewer of your first book, about his work with Kirk Ludwig, praised you for laying out the complexity of this difficult philosopher, but nevertheless he considered it "400 pages of rough sledding." Is your fertility partly explained by this oppositional stance to Davidson's work?

LEPORE: One consequence of publishing the holism book was that Davidson did not speak to me for five years beginning with a rather hostile Pacific APA symposium Fodor and I did with him on holism and radical interpretation. That encounter was brutal. Though Fodor and I intentionally moderated our tone and hedged our critical comments, Donald would hear none of what we had to say.

After my five-year exile, Davidson invited me to a workshop on him in Girona. He would speak in the morning, and an invited participant would guide the afternoon discussion. I was assigned the follow-up discussion of holism. Quine, Davidson, and Dreben complained that I had not fully appreciated the role of indeterminacy in defending holism; and that some of my arguments against holism presumed a relational account of belief. That was the substance of their objections. I recall phoning Jerry from Spain to tell him we remained on terra firma.

For the rest of his life, Davidson always referred to the holism book as Fodor's book. He intended this as a compliment. When he died, Marcia Cavell, his widow, gave me what she assumed was a copy of the book I must have given Davidson. When I asked why she thought it was my copy, she replied that there was a dedication to Donald on the first page. I couldn't imagine I had done that. When I looked at the book later I found an inscription in Davidson's own handwriting, "To Don, from the authors, with contempt." After Girona, back in the fold, I began several efforts to implement the Davidson semantic program for a few largely ignored linguistic fragments, for example, quotation and (with Kirk Ludwig) complex demonstratives like "that man."

Davidson appreciated, encouraged, and liked the results; this led to more work on Davidson's semantic program, eventually culminating in Kirk Ludwig's and my fat book on truth theoretic semantics. It also led to an invitation to teach at Berkeley in the winter of 1995. There I met Herman Cappelen at Berkeley; he was my TA in philosophy of language. The following year he moved to New York City and we began a collaboration, which ultimately climaxed in *Insensitive Semantics*.

It started out harmlessly enough; Herman recommended a paper by his tutor from Balliol, Ian Rumfitt, on the semantics of indexicals. Rumfitt argued that each speaker must have a different semantic theory since distinct utterances of for example "I am Norwegian" can differ in truth conditions, depending on who's talking. I thought the view idiosyncratic, but after a little research discovered it was ubiquitous; its impetus was the seemingly innocent thesis that a semantic theory should capture what speakers say when they speak, as well as the correct intuition that what I say when I utter "I'm Norwegian" differs from what Herman says when he utters it. Our attack on this thesis became the basis for what we call speech act pluralism—the view that we say indefinitely many things when we utter a single sentence.

This latter view, interestingly enough, precedes our development of semantic minimalism. Once what's said is separated from semantic content, we need to rethink what the semantic content of an expression is. Minimalism, our answer, was consonant with Davidson's and Fodor's disquotational stories; I am returning to this important question in current research.

3:AM: In your first book with Ludwig, you focus largely on issues in Davidson's *Meaning, Truth, Language, and Reality*, don't you? So you look at Davidson's theory of trying to run a theory of meaning off the application of a theory of truth, Tarski's famous Convention T. You argue that as he constructs it, it fails. You look at Davidson's notion of radical interpretation and interpretative charity, which as you see it Davidson hoped would add a constraint to the theory of truth and help fix meaning. You think this fails. And you look at Davidson's thought that because of his linking a theory of truth to meaning, plus radical interpretation and charity, we could commit to certain positions in metaphysics and epistemology—one in particular is striking, that there couldn't be massive error in our beliefs. Again, you are unconvinced. Of course you can't go through all your reasoning here, but perhaps you could sketch how Davidson goes wrong in these three areas, and why despite this you think his truth conditional semantics approach is still fertile.

LEPORE: We don't advocate truth conditional semantics for natural language, if by that you mean an absolute truth theory as a theory of meaning.

We're convinced by the standard arguments, in particular, by Foster's argument that sentences of the form "S is true iff p" affirm only a material bi-conditional, which is too weak to underwrite an attribution of meaning to S. But, as we've argued several times in print, an appropriately constrained truth theory can deliver a correct meaning theory. If "S is true iff p" is derived from interpretive axioms by means of rules that preserve meaning, then the sentence used on its right hand side will give the meaning (without saying it does) of the sentence described on the left hand side.

Such canonically derived material conditionals provide us with all the information we need to assign meaning. It's my contention that nothing I've just said is incompatible with Davidson's views. The literature is littered with sophomoric critiques of Davidson's philosophy of language, advanced by authors who have read one article and on that basis decided they've understood the motivations for the larger program. They were wrong. Davidson was never a meaning eliminativist (like Quine); nor a meaning reductionist nor an extensionalist. If someone can give an argument to the contrary, please do.

3:AM: An appeal of Davidson's attempt to get meaning out of truth is that it tries to explain a lot using very little. In this respect it seems in the same ballpark as what Fodor was doing with his LOT [Language of Thought] and Chomsky with his UG [Universal Grammar]. In *Meaning, Mind, and Matter,* with Barry Loewer, you say that this approach can explain "one central ability: the ability to acquire justifiable beliefs about the world and about each other's beliefs through our linguistic abilities." Can you explain how it does this? Does this approach imply that a nonlinguistic creature does not have beliefs, or that we do it this way, but that lions have other options?

LEPORE: I steer clear of discussions about animal thought. My intuition is that they obviously do think, and since so many arguments to the contrary rely on an unfounded holism, I tend not to be seriously engaged with this debate, so I'm not currently on top of it. On the role of a meaning theory in explaining belief formation, however, I've had much to say over the years.

It began in my third year of graduate school; I found myself attending courses on Frege, model theory, lexical semantics, language acquisition (with Kenneth MacCorquodale), and psycholinguistics (with J. J. Jenkins). I was puzzled why all these courses were said to be concerned with semantics; as far as I could tell, they had little to do with each other. This put me in a funk over what semantics was all about, and what counted as getting it right. Reading Field's "Tarski's Theory of Truth" the following summer, I was baffled by his portrayal of semantics as a threat to physicalism. I then had an epiphany. A role Field (and, as I realized later, Davidson as well) assigned to a theory of meaning was to account for transitions from heard utterances to beliefs about the world. If you utter "It's raining" and I find you reliable, *ceteris paribus*, I will come to believe that it's raining, whereas someone who doesn't understand English won't. Semanticists are (or should be) asking which knowledge underwrites this linguistic-nonlinguistic transition. This presents a way for evaluating alternative semantic frameworks, one from which my dissertation grew as well as probably a half-dozen of my first publications.

I concluded that many of the then-popular frameworks were ill suited to answer this question and so were quite useless. Davidson himself hedged on my question; sometimes he spoke of linguistic knowledge, but more often he spoke of what a speaker could know that would enable her to make these transitions. I believe, and have argued as much, that the stronger approach is needed. My stand on the psychological reality of semantics theories, linguistic communication, and convention perhaps reveals a commitment to a deeper connection between mind and language than I suggested earlier.

3:AM: Meaning holism still presses its claims, and in *The Compositionality Papers* you and Fodor continue to push back. Could you say what is so important for this dispute?

LEPORE: Compositionality is important. Punkt! Most of us got into semantics worrying about productivity—about how a finite being can understand indefinitely many sentences. Comprehending how this is possible obviously invokes compositionality: the meaning of a complex is built up out of the meanings of its parts. Closely related but distinct motivations include systematicity and innocence. How can you understand a complex without understanding its parts (assuming the complex is not idiomatic)? How can you understand closely related but nonsynonymous sentences without compositionality; for example, since you can't understand "The cook questioned the plumber" without also understanding "The plumber questioned the cook," mustn't we suppose that the meaning contribution of an expression is constant throughout its occurrences?

3:AM: In that collection, prototypes as well as supervaluated approaches to vagueness get slapped down, don't they? Why are they in trouble?

LEPORE: Our paper critical of supervaluations as a technique for explaining vagueness has caused me personally a great deal of consternation. I am not someone who stubbornly endorses a position regardless of its criticisms. I've changed my mind about many issues over the years, even in print. Yet Fodor and I remain convinced that we were right in that paper, even though no one else is. Close friends, and even others equally skeptical about supervaluations, tell us we got it wrong. We listen and invariably conclude that their criticisms place them in one of several niches we attack. It's been frustrating.

Prototypes (stereotypes, conceptual or interferential roles) come in for a shellacking in our essays. Our argument is embarrassingly simple: meaning is compositional; prototypes aren't. So, prototypes aren't meanings. I could belabor the sallies to and fro between us and our critics, but our papers are so transparent that I doubt I could add anything. Brandom is a (nonsolipsistic) meaning/conceptual role theorist. We argue he is therefore stuck with a variety of familiar unhappy consequences: if any change of mind results in a change in every belief, and no two people can assign the same content to their sentences (and thoughts), so disagreement is unlikely.

Churchland, facing these problems, invoked similarity of meaning to try to avoid it. We argued that sense could not be made out of similarity of meaning without a prior robust notion of meaning simpliciter. Brandom took a different tack, embracing meaning holism but saying that because speakers share words conversation can still flow. To be honest, we've never understood this reply.

3:AM: The other book with Cappelen is *Language Turned on Itself*. It's great because it looks at something that sounds as if its subject is terribly technical (metalinguistic discourse) but is really about something we all do from the very start and keep doing forever: quotation. This is a great example of something dead familiar that philosophy opens up and shows how strange it is. Quotation seems to behave in ways many theories of language can't accommodate, doesn't it? So, can you say why this is a subject that raises serious philosophical issues for anyone wanting to understand language and minds, and perhaps give us a taste of the intriguing nature of this phenomenon?

LEPORE: Quotation is special; I can recognize a word as a name or a predicate and never figure out what it names or predicates, but I can't recognize an expression as a quotation without knowing what it quotes. To explain why this is so, we supposed that quotations include the very items they quote as constituents. It's as if a name carried its referent around with it. This idea has many interesting consequences; one is that infinitely many expressions in English cannot be spoken, infinitely many others cannot be written, and so on, for each distinct manner of articulation language affords us. Since we can quote graphemes and pronunciations, and since what we quote must be a constituent of the quotation expression we use, it follows that if we quote a grapheme, for example, we can't say it out loud; and vice versa for the quotation of a sound.

In various published pieces on poetry and metaphor, I exploit my theory of quotation to explain the heresy of paraphrase, arduously defended by the New Critics and their guiding light, T. S. Eliot. The thesis that poetry resists translation (and paraphrase), I argue, is best explained by treating poems, in effect, as quoting their own articulation—by which I mean the vehicles by which the poem is presented, which can run the gamut from its typography, its font, its rhyme, its meter, and sundry other poetic effects. If I'm right, then of course, a poem cannot be translated since its translation (or paraphrase) will result automatically in a different presentation, and therefore in a poem with partly different subject matter.

3:AM: I think quotation hadn't really been the subject of great philosophical reflection until you two waded in. Another subject you've turned to is words. You ask, "What is a word?" So how should we start trying to answer that question?

LEPORE: I got into the topic of what a word is through worrying about quotation individuation. Here's an important distinction, one I just alluded to, that philosophers completely ignore. Suppose there are two people who are equally proficient with English but only one can read and write it, while the other can only speak it. The two thereby cannot communicate even though they share a language. This simple thought experiment makes clear we must distinguish between the vehicles with which we articulate language and the expressions these vehicles articulate.

This immediately entails that Davidson and others were wrong to identify an expression with its shape or sound; doing so conflates words with their vehicles of articulation. My work on word individuation starts there. When I looked around, I was stunned by how little has been written on words.

The main paper was Kaplan's. Around this time, John Hawthorne helped me appreciate that I (as well as Kaplan) was engaged in a familiar metaphysical project. He charted out the possible moves, and we collaborated on figuring out what was wrong with each; in the end, we concluded that our linguistic practices don't settle on exhaustive necessary and sufficient conditions for word individuation. When our interests are historical, intuitions go one way; when they are about communication, they go a different way. We are waiting for replies.

3:AM: It's striking how much collaboration figures in your works. Your collaborators read like a premier division team in the field—including Fodor, Hawthorne, Borg, Cappelen, Loewer, Ludwig, McLaughlin, Stone. Is it your preferred mode of operation? Is collaboration a reflection of the subject matter, or more a reflection of the way you personally like to work?

LEPORE: I believe my collaborations emulate the collaborative nature of cognitive science: good work happens by engaging with others. Still, each collaboration differs from every other; sometimes a philosophical problem spans area boundaries and ultimately requires insights from others disciplines both in and outside of philosophy. In these cases, I require a collaborator who knows something I don't know. This happens more often than I'd like to admit.

And even the style of collaboration varies. Sometimes I write the first draft; sometimes a collaborator does. (If you're entertaining philosophical collaboration, here is some advice: write the first draft for yourself. The person who does this dictates the direction of the rest of the investigation.) With Fodor, we wrote every word together, side by side, fighting over the keyboard, often with Jerry's cat Mr. James, all 50 pounds of him, refusing to move.

3:AM: Looking at the current situation in your field, are we closer now than when you started to understand the relationship of mind and language? Have certain ideas been killed for good, and are others beginning to seem secure?

LEPORE: I believe the philosophy of language is going through a second renaissance. In the '90s, I kept hearing it was dead, that it had peaked in the '70s with Montague, Davidson, Kripke, Lewis, et al., but that was all over. Yet I kept discovering philosophers advancing contextualist theses to dissolve one ancient philosophical conundrum or another. Suspicious from the beginning, I wondered how generations of philosophers could have missed so much context sensitivity. No one missed the context sensitivity of "I," "now," and "here"; can it really be that different with "know" and "heap" and "penguin"? More interestingly, the very same epistemologists, metaphysicians, logicians, ethicists, and aestheticians who told me philosophy of language was dead were now advocating a rather liberal position on the scope of context sensitivity in natural language.

That's philosophy of language, alive and flourishing, after all. What separates the '70s from the present is that young philosophers of language are better informed than their teachers about the nature of language. It will no longer suffice to permit a small range of belief sentences to command an entire philosophy of language. This doesn't mean philosophers should become second-rate linguists. Philosophers have interests in language that linguists don't, and shouldn't, but we can still learn from them. Ignore them at your own peril.

In 1997, after becoming director of cognitive science at Rutgers, I sponsored several small interdisciplinary workshops in semantics and pragmatics. There have now been nearly 20 of them. They are no longer small; the last one included nearly 70 participants. They bring together young and old philosophers, linguists and computer scientists. Some tend to be more philosophical than others, some more linguistic, but the one constant is that no participant is advocating isolationism. When philosophers advocate a priori that their research cannot be informed by anyone else, the jig is up.

3:AM: And finally, are there five books you could recommend that will help people understand more about this area of philosophy?

LEPORE: Different books have had an impact on me at different times in my career. Probably the first to have a great impact on me was Quine's *Word and Object*; at one point I knew it so well that you could read a passage and I could tell you which page you were reading from. Hey, I was a graduate student. Sadly, it may not have stood the test of time; or perhaps it's just my presentational skills. I taught it in a graduate seminar two years ago, and Gil Harman and I worked through it in our NEH Summer Seminar two summers ago; the reaction both times was "This is just behaviorism." I'm still puzzled.

Interestingly, both seminars reacted differently to Davidson's work; though largely critical, they recognized Davidson's work as important and philosophical. Davidson's writings were hard to come by when I was an undergraduate and a graduate student. They were scattered in relatively unknown and not easily accessible journals. This added to their mystique. I recall the excitement when "Radical Interpretation" or "Belief and the Basis of Meaning" surfaced. It wasn't until 1980 and 1984, when OUP published the first two volumes of Davidson's collected papers, that I had books by him. I must have taught those collections a dozen times over the years. Trying to pull together a cohesive project or program has taken up a substantial chunk of my professional life. I think it was worth it; over and over again, I came to realize that some idea of Davidson's that I found too unclear to defend or too peripheral to worry about would end up taking center stage. This is certainly true of his event-based semantics and his paratactic accounts of direct and indirect quotation.

Kripke's *Naming and Necessity* is an obvious choice; anyone who doesn't list this book is either insincere or just not thinking. I say this as someone weaned on the opposition—Davidson and Quine. Their books are also significant, but if you are looking to engage a young student, I doubt there's a better book than this one.

Dummett's first book on Frege I remember devouring as a young faculty member at Notre Dame. I couldn't put it down. I found it mesmerizing. I had no one to discuss it with at the time; but my engagement with the book was enough for me.

More recently, Lewis's *Convention* has captivated me. It took me a long time to appreciate its significance. Philosophers have a reputation for not answering the questions they ask, but Lewis answers his questions and his answers are correct. I once asked Fodor why Lewis's book isn't more widely discussed; he replied, "What are we going to say, 'Lewis got it right'?" Under Lewis's influence, I've begun to see that if you intend to separate semantics from pragmatics along familiar Gricean linguistic versus psychological lines, Lewis's work will make you rethink hard about where you draw that line.

There is a lot more conventionality in linguistic practice than philosophers typically acknowledge; for example, Kripke (following Grice) tells us there are psychological reasons to infer a speaker disagrees with his interlocutor when he replies to her utterance of "He put a red handkerchief on the table" with "It looked red." But the intonation pattern with which one utters this second sentence conventionally determines whether there is disagreement or not. Psychology has nothing to do with it. Reading Lewis helped me see why this must be so.

23 | Jerry Fodor
MEANINGFUL WORDS WITHOUT SENSE, AND OTHER REVOLUTIONS

Jerry Fodor is a philosopher working in the field of the philosophy of mind and cognitive science, philosophy of language, rationalism, functionalism, and cognitivism at Rutgers University. He is a leading contributor to the field of philosophy of mind and cognitive science. He has written with Massimo Piattelli-Palmarini *What Darwin Got Wrong* (2010); *LOT 2: The Language of Thought Revisited* (2008); *Hume Variations* (2003); with Ernie Lepore *The Compositionality Papers* (2002); *The Mind Doesn't Work That Way: The Scope and Limits of Computational Psychology* (2000); *In Critical Condition* (1998); *Concepts: Where Cognitive Science Went Wrong, the 1996 John Locke Lectures* (1998); *The Elm and the Expert: Mentalese and Its Semantics, the 1993 Jean Nicod Lectures* (1994); with Ernie Lepore (eds.) *Holism: A Consumer Update* (Grazer Philosophische Studien, Vol 46, 1993); with Ernie Lepore (eds.), *Holism: A Shopper's Guide* (1992); *A Theory of Content and Other Essays* (1990); *Psychosemantics: The Problem of Meaning in the Philosophy of Mind* (1987); *The Modularity of Mind: An Essay on Faculty Psychology* (1983); *Representations: Philosophical Essays on the Foundations of Cognitive Science* (1979); *The Language of Thought* (1975); with T. Bever and M. Garrett *The Psychology of Language* (1974); *Psychological Explanation* (1968); with Jerrold Katz (eds.) *The Structure of Language* (1964).

3:AM: What made you become a philosopher? You've been one for a long time. Has it been what you expected, and has the profession changed a lot since you started?

FODOR: It was because my parents wanted me to be a lawyer. I actually did take a constitutional law course in order to please them; but when I'd read some judicial decisions, it seemed to me I could make equally bad arguments without bothering to get a law degree. Hence philosophy, since, being very young, I thought of philosophers as particularly rational sorts of people, a view of which faculty meetings soon disabused me.

3:AM: You're famous for your work on the *Language of Thought (LOT)*. This is the thesis that thinking is explained using a theory of mind that describes a modular representational computerized system. You wrote about it in 1975, but then in 2008 wrote *LOT2* to update us on how your thinking had moved on in the intervening years. For readers not up on this, could you quickly give a rundown of the basics of how your theory works? Also, a key issue is that you have to come up with a theory that isn't just running a random string of thought following thought, but rather the theory has to explain how we can have meaning coherence, that is, we must be able to semantically and epistemically causally connect the thoughts, or else we wouldn't have a theory of "making sense," which is what thinking is. How have you done this?

FODOR: LOT is a throwing together of ideas, some borrowed from Empiricists, some from Rationalists, and some from theories about computers. The book was an attempt to connect these bits and pieces. I arrived at a view that was already much in the air, albeit less than explicitly: the mind gets at the world by representing it, and cognitive processes are operations that the mind performs on mental representations. In fact, I think what I recommended taking out was distinctly more original than what I recommended putting in: associationism (which made an utter mystery of the coherence of mental life) and behaviorism (which favored a cavalier rejection of the commonsense view that people do the things they do because they want what they do and believe what they do). At the time, behaviorism and associationism permeated both psychology and the philosophy of mind, though in somewhat different forms. They still do, here and there.

The main change in my views over the (many, many) intervening years is that I now think we should also discard a thesis that most philosophers hold explicitly and that cognitive science has never considered denying: that words, concepts, and the like have "senses" (meanings, contents, etc.) as well as referents. Zenon Pylyshyn and I are just finishing a book about why other philosophers and cognitive scientists should abandon it too.

3:AM: One of the things you think this commits us to is that learning concepts is impossible and that everything is innate, isn't it? This is what philosophers label an innatist position. There are some LOT theorists who don't think this, aren't there? So why do you think the innatist position is plausible? And how could we have an innate concept for Wednesday, say, or doorknob, given that our brains have not changed much for about 200,000 years?

FODOR: There is certainly a paradox lurking somewhere in these bushes. The question, however, is how(/whether) it can be avoided. For a long while, I thought it couldn't be, indeed, that it followed directly from what practically everybody agrees: that concept learning, if there were such a thing, would have to be some sort of hypothesis formation and confirmation. So, the argument went: learning the concept BACHELOR requires learning that the hypothesis "bachelors are unmarried men" is true. But this hypothesis already contains the concept BACHELOR, since (by assumption) the concept UNMARRIED MAN is the concept BACHELOR. Conclusion: you can't learn any concepts that you don't already have; which is to say that you can't learn any concepts. Paradox.

I now think there is, after all, a way out, though it requires rejecting the (more or less Fregian) doctrines that concepts and the like are individuated by their "senses": what makes BACHELOR the concept that it is, is its having the same sense as the concept UNMARRIED MAN. Frege likewise held that "sense determines reference," so what makes John a bachelor is his being a man and unmarried.

If, however, Frege was wrong about that, the innateness paradox disappears. Suppose, for example, that what determines the reference (the "extension") of a concept is some sort of causal relation between the (mental) representation that expresses it and the things belonging to its extension. Then, even assuming the hypothesis-formation-and-confirmation story about concept acquisition, the precondition for learning BACHELOR is only that the learner has some concept that is coextensive with BACHELOR. Since this requirement is very weak, there is no residual paradox.

3:AM: How much is this an empirical thesis, and so a branch of the natural sciences, that kind of stimulates its own research program, and how much of it is rather like a basic map that can then be utilized by different theories of mind, as the Atomic thesis stands in relation to a bunch of theories not all of which are compatible? I mean, apart from people thinking they have a folk psychology, is there any other evidence supporting the existence of mentalese and RTM [Representational Theory of Mind]? Or is it that what you're really doing is a kind of metaphysics, looking at what must be for any kind of mind, and so is in some sense a priori?

FODOR: I think the LOT thesis is a priori only in the sense that it's hard to think of an alternative that seems remotely plausible. I'll gladly give it up if somebody were to find one. It's the usual story: most empirical argument is "inference to the best explanation."

3:AM: The commitments of RTM, particularly compositionality and productivity, lead to disaster for many big philosophical attempts to understand meaning and the mind. So Wittgenstein's "meaning is use" gets the order of explanation wrong, and thus is hopeless, and connectionist views of Paul Churchland and other "holist" positions held by esteemed philosophers such as Brandom, McDowell, and Block are also in big trouble. Even your old supervisor, Hilary Putnam, gets it wrong. Why is holism such a bad idea?

FODOR: It depends on what, exactly, it's holism about: whether it's an epistemological or a semantic thesis. I take epistemological holism (essentially, the "Quine-Duhem 'thesis'") to be correct in spirit and historically accurate to boot. Scientific method assumes that evidence for the (dis)confirmation of an empirical theory can come from anywhere, including not just "observations" but also considerations of simplicity, economy, and other such "global" properties of belief systems. Anything can be given up (though, of course, you can't give up everything at once, skeptics to the contrary notwithstanding). This sort of epistemological holism is an essential corrective to the hyper-empiricism that was, for a while, the main obstacle to progress in the behavioral sciences (which turn out, on reconsideration, to be not about behavior but rather about its mental causes).

But holism makes hopeless semantics; it simply can't be true that the content of each of one's beliefs depends on the content of each of the others. Since the reasons are familiar, I won't review them here; suffice it that, if there is to be a belief-desire psychology at all, it must leave room for the piecemeal alterations of beliefs and desires. This is to say that epistemological holism (which I take to be more or less true) is incompatible with semantic holism (which I take to be false root and branch). It is therefore unsurprising that semantic holists (Quine, Davidson, Dennett), the Churchlands, many others (including, alas, even Putnam in some of his moods) refuse to take "propositional attitude" psychology to be ontologically serious. (It's sometimes suggested, as a way out, that semantics should endorse some sort of partial holism. If that's not an oxymoron, what would be?) The muddling of epistemological with semantic and ontological theses was, of course, pursued as a matter of policy by empiricists; they thought they could refute skepticism by showing that empirical claims translate to claims about one's experience, which they supposed to be incorrigible. In the event, this project did not succeed. I wonder why anyone still cares whether it does.

3:AM: What's neat about your thesis is that it takes a strong naturalistic view of the mind and also endorses folk psychological theories such as beliefs and desires and so on. This is kind of essential for you, isn't it? Because if we don't start with the big problem—how could anything material be conscious?—then we're ducking the actual problem. Is this right? Along the way, Dan Dennett's arguments about the realism of these mental representations gets clobbered, don't they?

FODOR: I'm increasingly unconvinced that the fuss about consciousness being the "hard problem" has the stick by the right end. Consciousness is itself an intensional state; you can't be just conscious *tout court*; if you are conscious at all, there must be something you are conscious of; and this "of" is intensional and exhibits the usual substitution ambiguities. This is to say that the familiar claim (see Searle) that materialist theories of intentionality beg the problem of consciousness gets things back-to-front. Still, even if, as I rather suppose, consciousness turns out to be more or less the same thing as attention, the questions about sensory content ("qualia") have to be faced; but it's at best unclear that they bear much on theories of cognition.

3:AM: One of the targets of your work initially was Skinner and Watson's behaviorism. It was the mechanism of associationism that they used that had to be replaced because it was too weak-assed to work. Yet there are still behaviorists about, aren't there? So how come?

FODOR: I don't know why there are still behaviorists. The explanation may lie in the maxim that, in science, progress is made one funeral at a time. Behaviorism is verificationism applied to psychological explanation; and verificationism is the philosophy of science that's generally taken for granted in Psych 101. A little philosophy is a dangerous thing and inclines a freshman to behaviorism.

3:AM: Your book on Hume was great on so many levels; one was that you claimed not to have read any Hume before you set off. (And didn't read so much by the time you'd finished either.) This is often leveled against you as a criticism, that you're oblivious to the history of philosophy and this means that you're not able to join in with a philosophical conversation that might have been going for centuries. So is this a deliberate strategy of yours, to work it out for yourself from first principles? And what do you say to those who say you'd gain through reading historical predecessors?

FODOR: This does surprise me, since I think of my views as embedded in a tradition of "representational" theories of mind that includes, among others, empiricists (notably Hume), rationalists (notably Frege and Kant), certain of the scholastics (notably Ockham) and Aristotle; in fact, practically everybody of major philosophical significance prior to the 20th century. (When I was still at MIT, I had occasional arguments with Chomsky about which of our ideas had been anticipated first. I won. Though Chomsky is, understandably, proud of his indebtedness to Descartes and Port-Royal, I trace my ancestry to the fifth century BC.) My major departures from this tradition are urging that it should keep its semantics and ontology clear from its epistemology, and that it cut its traditional entanglement with associationism in favor of a computational account of mental processes. On the other hand, it's true that I don't care much about the history of philosophy when it is practiced as the explication of text; and I regard the "If only he'd tried a bit harder, Aristotle might have been Quine" school of historiography as a giggle.

3:AM: And linked to this, I guess, is the observation that you're a great fan of Wagner but have never engaged with philosophers like Hegel and Heidegger or anyone from the so-called continental tradition. There's been some discussion recently about whether the divide between analytic and continental philosophers identifies anything significant. What's your take on this? Is it that you just think there's nothing of value in the stuff from what you've heard, or is it just that you've already got enough to be thinking about?

FODOR: As a matter of principle, I refuse to read philosophers who write that badly; anyhow, for what it's worth, I think that being reconciled with "analytic philosophy" is a blessing that philosophers are well advised to forgo.

3:AM: Your recent incursion into the Darwin wars caught some people by surprise, but really it shouldn't have. You basically were arguing the same case against a version of natural selection that you used against behaviorism, weren't you? The pesky intension-intention distinction was something you realized lay at the heart of a hidden piece of fallacious thinking in the Darwinian camp, and although disguised it was a potentially devastating element. Can you say why the mechanism for natural selection used by Darwinists is flawed?

FODOR: That's easy. Darwinism doesn't have a mechanism for natural selection; in particular, the "theory of natural selection" doesn't provide one. That was the main theme of my book with Piatelli *What Darwin Got Wrong*. Darwin, like Skinner, is a "black box" theorist; both insist that the nonrandom variables in explanations of biological traits are environmental. In consequence, Darwin is left with the hopeless problem, of (for which the "linkage" of traits is a parade example) how environmental variables could account for the effects of a creature's internal organization in determining its phenotype. Hence the familiar loose talk about Mother Nature's role in guiding trait selection. Dawkins (among others) keeps assuring us that such talk is metaphorical. But he never does explain how to cash the metaphor. Skinner's problem is exactly the same, except he's interested not in innate phenotypes but in acquired "behavioral repertoires."

3:AM: The backwash was unusually intemperate and at times personal. I got the sense that the scientists were pretty upset that you'd called them out. Perhaps your style was something they got all prim about: you're always very funny in the way you ridicule philosophical ideas you think are bogus, and never pull punches, but perhaps the science lot aren't used to that kind of knock-about mode. Clearly you weren't part of the usual anti-Darwinian creationist crowd, but I wondered if they thought that they couldn't afford to lose any ground at all because of the extra-curricular politics surrounding Darwin in the United States. Were you shocked by the nature of the criticism, or is it what you get a lot of the time?

FODOR: I wasn't surprised that the biologists missed the point; for better or worse, evolutionary biology is now a largely statistical science, so its practitioners generally don't think much about the explanatory adequacy of other kinds of empirical theories. But that the philosophers missed the point too struck me as really shocking; contemplating issues about explanatory adequacy is a lot of what they're supposed to do for a living. It should be kept in mind, however—both in biology and in the philosophy of biology—a lot of careers are built on firm adherence to (Neo-)Darwinism. So it's hardly surprising that serious criticism of *The Theory of Natural Selection* (as distinct from the Creationist kind) provokes spasms. God save us from true believers on either side.

3:AM: It was Alex Rosenberg, a philosopher, who seemed to mount the best counterattack on your theory rather than any of the biologists. So, what do you say to his criticism of your position? It seems that, were his idea to work, then there would be implications for the arguments against associationism. Is that right?

FODOR: Alex says (rightly) that selection for/against are contraries, not contradictories. (There are neutral traits as well as adaptive and anti-adaptive ones). I think Alex thinks we miss this logical point in *What Darwin Got Wrong*, but we didn't. Since it is tautological that there can't be selection for or against a neutral trait, it follows that, if there is selection at all, then it is selection for a trait iff it isn't selection against it. Still, let's assume, for the sake of argument, that whiteness wasn't selected for in polar bears. What, in that case, was selected against? Being pink? Being green with orange stripes? Do Darwinists believe that there used to be green polar bears with orange stripes, but they all got eaten up by predators? If not, what does Alex think is gained by rejecting selection for in favor of selection against?

3:AM: You don't agree with people like Steven Pinker that your LOT thesis is the final word on thought. He thinks modularity potentially explains everything, but you are less optimistic. What's the reason for your disagreement?

FODOR: I take it seriously that the cognitive psychology of belief formation should be continuous with the philosophy of theory confirmation in empirical science. Science works so well because it's just the application of rational practice to questions about how the world works (as opposed to, say, questions about why the family car has stopped running). Among the most important insights in the theory of confirmation in the last hundred years or so is the "Quine-Duhem" thesis: the (dis)confirming evidence for an empirical theory can come (not only from experiments and observations but) from anywhere in the network of received scientific beliefs, including, in particular, global considerations like the overall simplicity, conservatism, plausibility, etc., of the theory under evaluation (including, notably, whether there is a plausible alternative). This is to say that there are criteria of evaluation at work in scientific confirmation that are global rather than modular; hence there are no principled limitations on what may turn out to be relevant to what.

The trouble with endorsing an entirely modular theory in psychology is that you would then be forced to not take global constraints on thought into account. It's worth noting that "expert systems" (that is, modular attempts) to simulate human problem solving at large quite strikingly don't work. (If you don't believe that, try explaining to the computer on the other end of the line just why it is that you want to return the article that you ordered last week.) It's an open secret that the reason that computers can't pass the Turing test is that they lack "common sense"; and "common sense" is nonmodular by definition. Cognitive psychology ignores such patent truths at its peril.

3:AM: Philosophers rarely change their minds. What would it take for you to abandon your approach to the mind? Could Chalmers or McGinn or Dennett or Churchland ever find something to convince you that you were in the wrong ball park?

FODOR: All that's required is that someone suggest a serious (hence not verificationist and not reductionist) theory of cognition that is reasonably sensitive to empirical data. I'm betting that is not going to happen. Any takers?

3:AM: You're known as an opera man. What's the appeal for you, and what's your favorite? If you were to recommend a recording, what would you offer?

JF: Usually my favorite opera is the last one I've listened to; but if I must choose, I think I'd opt for Debussy's *Pelleas*. (Last week, it would have been Gluck's *Orpheus*; or maybe Verdi's *Falstaff*.) There is a fine recording of *Pelleas* conducted by the always-reliable Haitink, with von Otter singing Melisande. (The competition has von Karajan conducting and von Stade, for whom I have, for decades, been consumed by an asymmetric passion.) Still, the Haitink by a close call.

3:AM: And are there five books you could recommend that would help us further understand this area of philosophy?

FODOR: Five is a lot; but here's four: any of Chomsky's nontechnical/ nonpolitical books (*Language and Mind* is a good place to start); the anthology *Concepts: Core Readings* (Margolis and Laurence editors); *Things and Places* (Zenon Pylyshyn); *Contemporary Philosophy of Mind* (Georges Rey).

24 | Huw Price
WITHOUT MIRRORS

Huw Price is Bertrand Russell Professor of Philosophy at Cambridge
University, interested in the philosophy of pragmatism and science. He is the
author of *Expressivism, Pragmatism and Representation* (Cambridge University
Press, 2013); *Naturalism Without Mirrors* (Oxford University Press 2011);
Causation, Physics, and the Constitution of Reality: Russell's Republic Revisited
ed. with Richard Corry (Oxford University Press 2007); *Time's Arrow and
Archimedes' Point: New Directions for the Physics of Time* (Oxford University
Press 1996); and *Facts and the Functions of Truth* (Blackwell 1988).

3:AM: You argue in *Facts and the Function of Truth* that usual ways of
making a distinction between factual truths and nonfactual truths fail. Before
looking at your own position, can you outline the main difficulties with the
alternatives?

PRICE: At this distance it's hard not to be anachronistic, but what I was criticizing was the common view that there is a "bifurcation" in language between
those declarative utterances that are genuinely "descriptive," or "fact-stating,"
and those that have some other function. Traditional noncognitivists employed
this distinction, arguing, say, that moral claims lie on the latter side of the line,
not the former (and hence that there is no metaphysical issue about the nature
of moral facts). I was (and am) sympathetic to that anti-metaphysical move,
but I think the bifurcation thesis turns out to be unnecessary to it, confusing,
and ungrounded. In *FFT* I argued that the various ways in which people try to
draw this distinction tend just to take in each other's washing, and that attempts
to find a firm place to stand don't work.

For example, it was a common idea that the notion of direction of fit would
do the job. Beliefs were said to have "mind-to-world" direction of fit, meaning
that we try to conform our beliefs to the way the world is; whereas desires

were said to have "world-to-mind" direction of fit, meaning that we try to conform the world to our desires. But apart from the fact that this distinction is no use at all for drawing the distinction needed in nonnormative cases—that of noncognitivism about probability claims, for example, to mention one case that I was interested in at an early stage—it turns out to be completely unhelpful even where it is supposed to work.

In order for it to work, we need to exclude the possibility that there could be a proposition Val(P) such that believing that Val(P) could be compatible, even identical, with desiring that P. And the direction-of-fit test doesn't tell us that. Having world-to-mind direction of fit about Val(P) might be entirely compatible with having mind-to-world direction of fit about P, simply because P and Val(P) are not the same proposition. In order to apply the direction-of-fit test, in other words, you need to already have an answer to the question whether there is such a proposition Val(P)—and that's just the original issue.

3:AM: You argue that we should understand truth in terms of a functional analysis. You argue that truth has a central normative function, and that is to get people to argue. You link this with arguing that there is no sharp boundary between factual and nonfactual uses of language. Is this a version of deflationism?

PRICE: Yes. It shares several features with more familiar versions of deflationism, such as those of Quine, Horwich, Brandom, and many others. Like those writers, I think that asking "What is truth?" is asking the wrong question—a question that mistakenly assumes that truth is the kind of thing that has a nature, as it is sometimes put. Instead, we should be asking explanatory questions about the term, or concept: Why do we have a truth predicate? What is its function, and how would matters be different if we didn't have it? My view diverges at this point, since I link truth to a central norm of our assertoric practice rather than to the kind of logical role (in generalizations such as "Everything that Fred says is true") central to other deflationary views. But I agree with other deflationists completely about what questions we should be asking.

3:AM: Since you wrote that book, back in 1989, there have been other functionalist approaches to truth. So Beall argues that truth is merely a mechanism that allows us to generalize, a shortcut mechanism required because of our medical limits (so god wouldn't need truth in her vocabulary). How has your view developed over the subsequent time?

PRICE: Beall's view is another version of the "transparent," deflationary account of truth I just associated with Quine, Horwich, Brandom. I haven't changed my mind about that kind of deflationism not being the whole story.

On the contrary, I have defended my own version again more recently in a couple of papers, including "Truth as Convenient Friction." Roughly, I think that my view trumps the other kind of deflationism in this sense: our conversational practice needs a norm of the kind I associated with truth; but once we have one, and a means of making it explicit, as Brandom would say, then we have something that will do the logical job, too. But the same doesn't work in reverse, so the normative notion is the more basic one.

I don't have much to say about philosophers changing their minds, but I do have an anecdote. When I was in Edinburgh in the early 2000s I once had the pleasant task of introducing Michael Dummett, who was there to give a named lecture. He told me that he had once done the same thing for Putnam. Putnam's advertised title was something like "Theory Change in Science," and Dummett said that in his introductory remarks he commented on what a suitable title this was for Professor Putnam, who was famous for his readiness to change his own mind. He said that Putnam then got up and said, "It's funny you should say that, Michael, because I've decided to give you a different paper!"

3:AM: You're a metaphysician and you've taken a look at all the big themes. One of them is time's arrow. When discussing this, you suggest that we step back and look at the idea from a point of view outside of time. But before you tell us your thoughts about time's arrow, could you say something about the block universe theory of time? Because it is very peculiar, isn't it? It conceives of time as being tenseless, which to many folk will seem paradoxical. How could there be time without past, present, and future? It sounds like a redefining of the concept to avoid agreeing with McTaggart that time is unreal. How can time be tenseless? Is this just another case of folk talk being totally cut off from theories of physics?

PRICE: Well, just to disagree with a couple of bits of the first claim, I'm not a metaphysician (at least not in what's now the familiar sense—more on this below), and I'm sure I haven't looked at all the big themes! But about time, if someone wants to insist that time can't be tenseless I'd be very happy to give them the term, leave them to the mercy of McTaggart, and use a different term for the notion associated with the block view.

I'd expect to be able to reclaim the term, eventually, when the lessons of McTaggart, Mellor, and many others finally sink in on the other side of the fence—or, more likely, when that degenerating research program finally fizzles out. And even if that never happens, no matter. One of the advantages of not being a metaphysician is that I'm not in the grip of the idea that there's a thing, Time, whose nature it is our job as metaphysicians to figure out. So it's easy for me to walk away ... though that's not incompatible with nipping over the fence occasionally to join McTaggart, Mellor, et al. in exposing the internal difficulties in that program. (Nor would it be incompatible with talking to physicists about whether something was missing from the block view for the purposes of physics, if someone came up with a plausible argument of that kind.)

3:AM: You argue that there is an asymmetry in how we think about the world that contradicts the block universe idea, or that at least looks strange from that view. Can you tell us about this and your theory of time's arrow?

PRICE: Time itself doesn't have an arrow, in my view. Someone creating a world like ours from scratch (and from outside, of course!) wouldn't have to make a choice between two versions, one the exact temporal mirror image of the other. Those are the same world, differently described. (This is the temporal equivalent of disagreeing with what Kant says about a world containing only one hand: he thinks there is a fact of the matter about whether it is a left hand or a right hand.) Indeed, I think it is very difficult to make sense of what it would be for these to be different worlds, in the intended respect.

There's lots of temporal asymmetry with the world as we know it, of course, but I see no reason to think of any of that as an indication that time itself has a direction. (As I said, I find it hard to see what that would mean.) But there are fascinating questions about the nature and source of these various asymmetries—which of them are fundamental, and in what sense, for example. Another fascinating kind of question, in my view, is which of these apparent asymmetries are entirely objective, and which might in some sense be merely projections of our own temporally asymmetric viewpoint.

But to get these questions into focus, you need a clear sense of the background, the base from which the project starts. One reason for starting with the undirected block universe—apart from the fact that it's what physics gives us!—is that if you're sure that you've stripped all the asymmetry out, it's not so hard to keep a close eye on how it gets back in. That way, we can hope to avoid what I call double standard fallacies: illicitly assuming a time asymmetry in some subtle form, in the course of trying to explain another one.

3:AM: Philosophers have had a pretty torrid relationship with physicists recently, but you were hammering away at Stephen Hawking's views about the direction of time in public when his bestseller came out in the early 1990s. What did Hawking get wrong, and more generally, why should philosophers and scientists listen to each other?

PRICE: Hawking was interested in the question whether cosmology could explain why entropy was so low around the time of the Big Bang. By that stage, thanks especially to the work of Roger Penrose, that question was clearly in view as the one to which the task of explaining the time asymmetry of the second law of thermodynamics was pointing. The second law says that entropy goes up asymmetrically towards the future, and as Penrose saw perhaps more clearly than anyone at that time, the real puzzle is why it goes down towards the past. (In a sense this is the same thing, but focusing on the past directs our attention at the anomaly: statistically speaking, as had been clear since the late nineteenth century, one would expect entropy to be high in both directions. The puzzle is why the statistical inferences don't work towards the past.)

Penrose also saw that there's a problem with explaining why the Big Bang has low entropy in terms of a time-symmetric fundamental physics (which is essentially what we have). In such a physics, any argument applicable to the Big Bang ought to be equally applicable at the other end of the universe, in a "Big Crunch"—or even in the kind of mini big crunches that produce black holes. But that would mean that the second law would reverse direction, as one approached such a final singularity. Penrose thought that that was unacceptable, and proposed instead that cosmology must invoke some time-asymmetric law (what he calls his "Weyl curvature hypothesis").

Hawking thought he could do better than this, using an alternative hypothesis called the Hawking-Hartle "No Boundary Proposal." As Hawking explained in *A Brief History of Time*, he believed initially that this hypothesis would imply that entropy would reduce towards a "Big Crunch"—in other words, he accepted the consequences of symmetry that Penrose found unacceptable. But then he became convinced that he had made a mistake—he calls it his greatest mistake—and retracted this part of the view. That left him in the situation of claiming to get an asymmetrical result out of symmetrical theory—the very thing that Penrose, like many others, had decided was impossible—without telling us how the trick works.

A natural thought, at least for a suspicious philosopher like me, was that he hadn't pulled off the trick at all. Instead, he'd slipped in an asymmetry at some point (for example, by relying on statistical arguments in one direction but not the other), thereby committing a double standard fallacy (and ending up in the same position as Penrose, only without being aware of his asymmetric assumption).

That's what I wrote about in my little commentary article in *Nature* in 1989. I haven't changed my mind about that one, either. Indeed my confidence went up considerably when I sent a copy of it to Penrose (I think this was couple of years later), and he said that he had been saying that kind of thing to Hawking for years.

On the general issue—why should philosophers and scientists listen to each other?—I think there's a sense in which they don't have a choice. There are questions that arise in relation to most (probably all) of the special sciences that are by nature philosophical questions. (It's hard to say what that means, but you know them when you see them.) Of course, no one in either field needs to engage with these questions, if they don't want to. But the questions are there, and interesting from both sides, to thinkers with particular predilections. At that point, each side is simply shooting itself in the foot, if it refuses to listen to the other.

3:AM: Is asking whether the past exists, or any tensed portion of reality, a badly formed question because it presupposes a bad metaphysics? Is there a general lesson here about how ignoring the metaphysical foundations of any statement can lead to hot water? Does your idea of metaphysical and semantic quietism help here?

PRICE: The main problem with the debate about ontological issues between presentists and the like, on the one side, and B-theorists on the other, is that it looks like they are simply talking past one another, by meaning different things by "exists": one side means it in a tensed way, the other in an untensed way. The participants on both sides try to meet this charge by agreeing with each other that the issue turns on some "fundamental" notion of existence, whose nature is in dispute between them. Metaphysical and semantic quietists like me can simply tune out at this point, as for "time" above, because "fundamental" is not one of our words (at least as it is being used here). The same goes for "reference" and other semantic terms that tend to be pressed into service—interpreted in a "thick," nondeflationary sense—in trying to identify some real point of disagreement in these debates.

3:AM: Causation is another big topic you've grappled with. At the start of your book *Causation, Physics, and the Constitution of Reality*, you and co-editor Richard Corry cite Bertrand Russell saying that causation was like the monarchy, a relic of a bygone age erroneously thought of as being harmless. Should we be republicans about truth, as Russell suggested?

PRICE: Richard Corry and I develop Russell's metaphor a bit. We point out that in the political case, there are two ways of disagreeing with the traditional view that political authority is vested in kings by god. You can be an anarchist, and reject the idea of political authority altogether, but there's also a more moderate option: republicans don't seek to reject political authority, but just to bring it down to earth—to think of it as constructed by us, rather than instituted by god. By analogy, we suggest, a "causal republican" doesn't seek to eliminate talk of causation but regards it as partly anthropocentric, not simply an element of the preexisting "furniture of reality." (Causation is regarded as a secondary quality, in other words, as I put it in an early paper with Peter Menzies.)

It is not really clear whether Russell should count as a causal anarchist or a causal republican, by these criteria. I think a charitable way to read him is as a kind of armchair anarchist, much like Hume, who thinks that talk of causation is fine when we're out in the real world. We just need to avoid the mistake of thinking that it is something we should be investigating when we are looking for the fundamental constituents of reality. And that's much the same as causal republicanism.

One of the great attractions of the republican view, I think, is that it makes it easy to explain the difference between cause and effect, and the fact that, at least most of the time, this causal "arrow" lines up past-to-future. The former stems from the asymmetry between means and ends, from an agent's point of view (I think Ramsey was the first to see this, incidentally). While the latter turns on the fact that all human agents happen to face the same way, as it were: we all deliberate past-to-future. Creatures elsewhere in the universe may do things in the opposite direction, and if so then they take the causal arrow to point in the other direction—and there's no objective sense in which one of us gets it right, of course, any more than it is an objective fact that Australia is on the top half of the planet.

3:AM: The idea of practical deliberation being "open" or "settled" is a key to how you go about answering the issue of the asymmetries of causality. Can you explain this and say whether, as with your views about time's arrow and truth, your metaphysics link functional explanation to why we think about the world as we do (even though science tells us that there are no asymmetries in their theories)?

PRICE: Suppose you are deliberating about whether to do something—whether to stop reading your email and go out for lunch, say. There are some things you know, like what time it is, whether you are hungry, and so on, and other things that you may not know but think of as "available for knowing," before you make your choice. All that counts as settled, in the terminology you mention to here. But there are some things you don't know before you make up your mind, starting, obviously, with whether you're going to go out to lunch or not. (If you thought you knew that, you couldn't think of yourself as still deciding whether it would happen.) Things in the latter category are open, in this terminology.

Just as with our immediate choices (like whether to go for lunch), anything we take ourselves to be able to influence by our choices (like whether we are hungry in midafternoon) must also be in this open category, and for the same reason. To think you can control it is to think that your present choice "trumps" any existing evidence you might have, as Jenann Ismael puts it. Ramsey was the first to appreciate this point, too, I think. He puts it like this: "Any possible present volition of ours is (for us) irrelevant to any past event. To another (or to ourselves in the future) it can serve as a sign of the past, but to us now what we do affects only the probability of the future."

As I noted earlier, Ramsey proposes that this is the basis for the distinction between cause and effect. He doesn't go into the question why this distinction seems to line up past-to-future, but as I said above, I think that that is plausibly explained by a contingent fact about us, namely that we also deliberate about later actions. As I noted, creatures elsewhere might do it differently, and in that case they would divide up the world differently into what was settled and what open, from their point of view.

Another interesting possibility, which Ramsey misses, is that not everything in the past need count as settled, from our point of view. It isn't incoherent to think of some of it as open and under our control (as an indirect consequence of some future action), so long as we don't think we could find out about it before we decided whether to perform the action in question. This possibility was first noticed by Michael Dummett in the 1960s. It amounts to admitting a bit of retrocausality, even in a world in which the prevailing forward direction of causality reflects our contingent temporal perspective, in the way I have described. I think it is going to be big news in quantum mechanics, incidentally.

3:AM: In *Naturalism Without Mirrors* we get a further look at how you do (or don't do, depending on how we look at this) metaphysics. You don't so much ask, "What are we looking at?" but rather, "What are we talking about?" What is the difference between the two questions in terms of what answers we might give and what we might suppose metaphysics is really about? You say it's not just, "as an Australian apostle might have put it, that language shows us the world 'as through sunnies, darkly'..." but that "the glassy metaphor itself is entirely empty." So, are you a kind of pragmatist? The metaphysics suggests that perhaps Peirce might be your kind of pragmatist, but the title of your book and this language-oriented approach to the subject is kind of solid with Rorty, Wittgenstein, and Brandom, and that's where many people seem to put you. Are you doing metaphysics, or are you deflating metaphysics so far that it doesn't count as metaphysics anymore?

PRICE: The alternative question isn't "What are we talking about?" That leaves us just where we were, trying to think about the things. I want to recommend that we think instead about the language, by asking, "Why are we talking this way—what role do these concepts play in the lives of creatures like us?" That's why I say that I'm recommending that we do anthropology, in place of metaphysics.

Yes, certainly I'm a pragmatist. In my view, the most helpful way to characterize pragmatism is to say that it approaches a range of philosophical issues in the way I just mentioned, by asking about the practical role that philosophically interesting concepts (for example, that of causation) play in our lives—by looking for explanations, and genealogies, in broadly naturalistic terms (by starting with the assumption that we are natural creatures in a natural environment).

I don't know much about Peirce, so I'm not sure whether I'm his sort of pragmatist, but I'm happy to be seen as kind of solid with Rorty, Wittgenstein, and Brandom, as you put it. (We're, you know, like that.)

3:AM: The "without mirrors" is your way of signaling a major theme in the book, which is your rejection of the view that language mirrors nature, isn't it?

PRICE: The context for my use of this metaphor is the issue whether, if you start off asking questions about language, you can nevertheless end up asking the usual kind of metaphysical questions about (nonlinguistic) things. On the face of it, the answer is yes. If you start with something you take to be a referring term, say X, and then ask the question, "What does X refer to?" it looks as though a question about language—about the term X—is directing your attention to the world.

But if you are a deflationist about semantic notions like truth and reference then, as Quine pointed out, this is a kind of illusion. In this case the question "What does X refer to?" is just another way of saying "What is X?"—which isn't a question about language at all. So deflationary semantic notions can't provide a ladder to take you from genuinely linguistic issues to metaphysical issues. That was my point.

Simon Blackburn makes a similar point in terms of what he calls "Ramsey's ladder," that takes us from P to "P is true" (and back again, of course). He points out that Ramsey's redundancy theory of truth—an early version of what we now call deflationism—implies that this ladder is "horizontal," in the sense that it doesn't take us anywhere new. Again, as Quine says, we have the same subject matter in view at both ends. (Blackburn himself complains about philosophers who take advantage of the fact the ladder is horizontal in order to climb it, and then announce a better view from the top.)

3:AM: You make a distinction between two species of expressivism: local and global types. Simon Blackburn's quasi-realism is the acme of the local expressivist position, but you think even this fails, and that it's global expressivism that we need. Can you say what this distinction separates, and why only the global species is useful?

PRICE: Local expressivists rely on the idea I mentioned in my answer above, that there is a bifurcation in language between descriptive and nondescriptive uses of declarative utterances. They take expressivism to be appropriate on the nondescriptive side of the line, and some sort of representationalist story on the other side of the line. (Blackburn's quasi-realism is distinctive in paying a lot of attention to the question why some declaratives that are not descriptive—"Cruelty is wrong," say—nevertheless behave as if they were.)

That combination of expressivism on one side of the line, representationalism on the other, is off-limits for me, because I reject the idea that there is such a line—I reject the bifurcation thesis, as I put it above. In principle, this would be compatible with being either a global expressivist or global representationalist, depending on who wins when the wall comes down. But in my book, both figuratively and literally, it's the expressivists who win. The sorts of questions that local expressivists ask about what they take to be nondescriptive claims—questions about use and function, cast in something other than the semantic terms that their representationalist opponents employ—turn out to be good questions to ask everywhere. Hence global expressivism, as I call it.

3:AM: Your view is both deflationary and expressivist, and for philosophers like Crispin Wright and John McDowell this is simply not done. How come you think you can make it work? Why are they mistaken?

PRICE: One way in which local expressivists cashed out what it was supposed to mean to be nondescriptive was in terms of the idea that nondescriptive utterances "don't have truth conditions," or are not "truth-apt." But writers such as McDowell and Wright pointed out that that if we are deflationists about truth, having truth conditions and being truth-apt is cheap; anything that meets the basic syntactical criteria gets to qualify, more or less. This was thought to be a big problem for expressivists (who did tend to want to be deflationists themselves, on the whole).

The solution is to note that expressivists typically made two proposals about their target vocabulary—moral claims, say—one negative and one positive. The negative thesis was that moral claims lack truth conditions, or are not truth-apt. The positive thesis was whatever nonrepresentationalist story expressivists proposed instead about what the target vocabulary is "for"—that its function is to express affective attitudes. Deflationism undermines the negative thesis, but it doesn't touch the positive thesis. On the contrary, it implies that we need such non-representationalist stories everywhere, because the representationalist's semantic vocabulary—truth, references, and the like—has been ruled too "thin" to do any theoretical work in telling us about the function of various bits of language.

So in a sense the old objection got things exactly backwards, in my view. Deflationism is indeed a problem for local expressivists such as Blackburn, but the problem is not with their expressivism, but with their residual representationalism about what they regard as the genuinely descriptive vocabularies. Deflationism supports global expressivism, not global representationalism.

3:AM: If an anthropologist were to discuss the issues you do, conceptions of time, causation, and so on, would he or she be looking at anything different from you, only with more field work? So firstly, is it philosophy you're doing here, or is it converging with anthropology? And secondly, if what you think we should be doing is thinking about what we're saying, then is there a role for x-phi who look and see if what philosophers say the folk are saying is actually what they are saying?

PRICE: It's converging with anthropology, certainly, or perhaps some mix of biology, psychology, and anthropology. Does that mean that it's not philosophy? Not in my book, but if someone wants to be precious about the use of the term *philosophy*, that's not going to bother me. I certainly think that experimental work is relevant. For example, I think that the recent fascinating work on development of causal concepts, both in human infants and in primates, is helpful in bringing into focus questions about the functions of these concepts—what they are for, as it were. (We learn about this by learning about what difference it makes if creatures don't have them.)

I'm less clear about whether my approach has something to learn from some distinctively philosophical kind of empirical work. Since I'm not wedded to the idea that there's any sort of interesting metaphysical fact of the matter about what the folk are locking on to, in using a particular term, I'm a little bit skeptical about whether there's something for x-phi to investigate, that's not already investigated somewhere else. (It would be compatible with this that some of the work called x-phi is the same kind of thing done elsewhere—my kind of anthropology, for example—but with a sharper eye for the philosophically interesting questions.)

3:AM: Is there no room for, say, a Frank Jackson analytic metaphysics in your view? And what would you say to people who say that you've changed the subject?

PRICE: Well, I do want to change the subject, but not in most cases by just walking away from the old one. I try to say what I think is wrong with it, first. For example, I've argued that at least some versions of the Canberra plan are problematic because they rely on semantic or representational presuppositions that turn out not to be amenable to analysis by the program's own lights. Again, I have offered McTaggart-style objections to A-theoretic conceptions of time, and I could give more examples of this kind.

More generally, I try to identify common ground with my opponents—common explananda, for example—so as to be able to argue that a pragmatist approach provides better explanations, in the cases in question. (Accounting for our sense of the direction of causation is a case in point here.) So I haven't just changed the subject. I've tried to explain why it seems to me that it should be changed.

Most people won't change their minds, or their philosophical spots, of course, and you get to the point where there's nothing to say. Does that matter? Probably not, in my view. We need some stubbornness and intellectual inertia to sustain our research programs, and it's only philosophy, after all. The scope for any serious harm is rather limited!

25 | Gary Gutting
WHAT PHILOSOPHERS KNOW

Gary Gutting holds the Notre Dame Endowed Chair in Philosophy at the University of Notre Dame. He is interested in French philosophy, philosophy of science, and the philosophy of religion. He is the author of *Thinking the Impossible: French Philosophy Since 1960* (Oxford University Press, 2011); *What Philosophers Know: Case Studies in Recent Analytic Philosophy* (Cambridge University Press, 2009); *Foucault: A Very Short Introduction* (Oxford University Press, 2005); *French Philosophy in the Twentieth Century* (Cambridge University Press, 2001); *Pragmatic Liberalism and the Critique of Modernity* (Cambridge University Press, 1999); *Michel Foucault's Archaeology of Scientific Reason* (Cambridge University Press, 1989); and *Religious Belief and Religious Skepticism* (University of Notre Dame Press, 1982).

3:AM: What made you become a philosopher?

GUTTING: The problem of skepticism. My first philosophical thought—when I was ten or eleven—was that, if you gave a reason for some claim, someone could still ask for a reason for your reason—an infinite regress, as I would later learn it was called. This led to an interest in Descartes and, later, foundationalists such as Husserl and the logical empiricists. Fairly soon, I concluded that radical, global skepticism was an impossible attitude and not worth worrying about (Hume was a big help here—and, later, Wittgenstein and Rorty). But I still took seriously "regional" skeptical challenges to specific areas of thought that claim cognitive authority. Here my first focus was on the challenge to science that many people found in Kuhn. I also became interested in the idea, which I found in Husserl and Merleau-Ponty, that the scope of scientific knowledge was limited by its empirical methodology.

Later, I developed a strong interest in Foucault's historical critique of various social sciences. Also I was very taken up with the cognitive claims of religion. I had a Jesuit education from high school on, and at that time there was an insistence that Catholicism was a rationally grounded religion. My teachers especially emphasized the power of Aquinas' philosophical system, which, however, they believed needed to be somehow integrated with modern science and philosophy. I pretty quickly concluded that Aquinas wasn't the answer, but was left with the dual conviction that religion couldn't be dismissed as simply not in accord with modern scientific thought and that, at the same time, it needed much more than a facile appeal to faith. My first book was *Religious Belief and Religious Skepticism*.

Finally, I have always been interested in skeptical challenges to philosophy itself. Here Richard Rorty has been a major influence, though my book on the topic, *What Philosophers Know*, turned out to be much less Rortyan than I had expected. Of course, philosophy as a discipline doesn't know the answers to the fundamental questions (God, freedom, morality) that define its cognitive enterprise. But why think that our beliefs on such topics require a philosophical foundation? To take Rorty's example, we don't need a philosophical guarantee that democracy is a value worth fighting for. The same is true for our deepest ethical and religious (or secular) commitments. If we need philosophical justifications, then we aren't entitled to any such beliefs, since the justifications aren't there. But it would be absurd to think that we have no right to the fundamental convictions that define our moral self-identity—our souls, if you will. Rorty's conclusion from this seems to be that philosophy isn't important for most people but is more a specialized interest for certain types, perhaps like an interest in fine wine or avant-garde literature. I disagree. Our fundamental beliefs don't need intellectual justification, but they do need intellectual maintenance. We need to understand their implications, modify them to eliminate internal contradictions, and defend and perhaps modify them in response to objections.

Over its history, philosophy has accumulated an immense store of conceptual distinctions, theoretical formulations, and logical arguments that are essential for this intellectual maintenance of our defining convictions. This constitutes a body of knowledge achieved by philosophers that they can present with confidence to meet the intellectual needs of nonphilosophers. Consider, for example, discussions of free will. Even neuroscientists studying freedom in their labs are likely to offer confused interpretations of their results if they aren't aware of the distinction between caused and compelled, the various meanings of "could have done otherwise," or the issues about causality raised by van Inwagen's consequence argument. Parallel points apply for religious people thinking about the problem of evil, or atheists challenged to explain why they aren't just agnostics. Philosophers can't show what our fundamental convictions should be, but their knowledge is essential to our ongoing intellectual engagement with these convictions.

3:AM: Were you from very early on finding dialectical relationships between so-called Analytics and so-called Continentals? I'm thinking that even when studying in Belgium (at the end of the 1960s) on a Fulbright you were examining the link between phenomenology and Analytic philosophy in your paper "Husserl and Logical Empiricism." There you took phenomenology away from ordinary language philosophy, where the connections were already being made between Husserl and Wittgenstein (which wasn't too great a leap given Wittgenstein's "floating" status as both an Analytic and a Continental) and into the realm of the eidetic and phenomenological reduction of logical empiricism. Was this a conscious move on your part to develop a link with Continental philosophy from the Analytic side, or was that divide one that you either hadn't noticed or didn't worry about?

GUTTING: I was very aware of the divide and did have some idea that I might build a bridge over it. At that point, Analytic philosophy for me meant mainly the philosophy of science, which was my specialty in graduate school. (I didn't know much about the rest of Analytic philosophy until I took a job at Notre Dame, right after my Fulbright year. At Notre Dame I got a great education in Analytic philosophy as part of a group of young faculty interested in Wilfrid Sellars, who became a very important philosopher for me.) The idea of going to Louvain was to complement my training in philosophy of science with a study of Husserl's phenomenology. I'm no longer happy with the project of "bridging the gap" between Analytic and Continental philosophy. I now think that, overall, they are two quite different ways of doing philosophy. They can learn from one another, but there's no good way of combining them into a single enterprise. Still, Husserl (like a number of others) did have a place in the early history of both Analytic and Continental philosophy—that's what made my paper on him and logical empiricism possible—although the two enterprises have diverged more and more since then.

3:AM: Much of your early work concerned issues of the methodology, epistemology, and ontology of the natural sciences. Is it fair to say that your interest in phenomenology and Husserl and Habermas was due to your suspicion about the claim that "science is great, and if we can find out how it works we can improve other discussion enormously," which Philip Kitcher worries about too? Also, does the paper you wrote in the form of a dialogue between a scientific realist *à la* Wilfrid Sellars and a constructive empiricist *à la* Bas van Fraassen illustrate one of your continuing philosophical preoccupations? You thought of the issue then as a dialectic in your own mind. Where do you now stand on the issue? Has it changed over time? Is it still one of your philosophical preoccupations?

GUTTING: The skeptical thought that science might have important cognitive limitations was important in my early work. But an even stronger influence was Sellars's idea that science has an ontological primacy (as he put it, "science is the measure of what there is, that it is, and the measure of what there is not, that it is not"). Like Sellars, I never took this to mean that science was the only way of knowing. There is normative knowledge (about meanings and values) that is not about what exists in the primary sense of exercising causal power in the world. Science tells us nothing about this domain of non-ontological truth. Nowadays, though, I'm less willing to push the hard Sellarsian line that science is the sole arbiter of ontology. I'm not sure, in particular, that science can handle the "hard problem" of phenomenal consciousness—or, in terms of Sellars's famous example, that he can melt the pink ice cube. I've also become more sympathetic to Rorty's pragmatic take on different ontologies as corresponding to different interests we have in engaging with the world. But I still think there's a special role for the interest in causal control, which maintains a certain ontological privilege for science.

3:AM: And when did you discover that setting up dialogues between competing positions in a certain philosophical sphere of interest was a useful way for you to grapple with issues, and why is it a literary philosophical form that attracts you?

GUTTING: Dialogues are just something I find myself naturally falling into every so often. I found them attractive in cases where I held strong views on an issue but had a deep respect for people on the other side and wanted to give a full hearing to their views. This was true of Rorty on Kuhn, van Fraassen on scientific realism, and Plantinga on religious belief.

3:AM: Am I right in thinking that another issue that haunts much of your work and has motivated many of your various research interests is the question, "Can philosophical beliefs be rationally justified?" Doesn't this become part of the theme that you expand on in your book *Pragmatic Liberalism and the Critique of Modernity* through the voices of Richard Rorty, Alasdair MacIntyre, and Charles Taylor? Are these three still important to you?

GUTTING: Right. I called an *APQ* article "Can Philosophical Beliefs Be Rationally Justified?" to echo the question standardly asked about religious beliefs. The issue comes up in *Pragmatic Liberalism* but is central in *What Philosophers Know*, and I'm currently pursuing the topic in a paper on philosophical progress. I wrote *Pragmatic Liberalism* as a treat for myself, after many years of working on Foucault and other difficult Continentals. I was tired of having to strain every intellectual muscle just to see what the texts I was reading might mean. So, when I thought about what my next book should be about, I said, "Who are the philosophers I most look forward to reading?" My immediate answer was Rorty, MacIntyre, and Taylor (also Bernard Williams, though he turned out to have a less central role). It was the book I've had the most fun writing and the one that best expresses my own views on the central issues of metaphysics, epistemology, and ethics. I defend what I see as the best of the Enlightenment: a commitment to reason and to liberal values, but freed from the philosophical foundationalism, dismissal of history and tradition, and facile atheism associated with its positivist versions. Despite the disagreements among them, I see Rorty, Taylor, and even MacIntyre as contributors to the Enlightenment project.

3:AM: In "Paradigms and Hermeneutics: A Dialogue on Kuhn, Rorty and the Social Sciences" it seems you were continuing with that question about rational justification and beliefs. This paper again works as a kind of dialectic between philosophy of science (Kuhn) and pragmatism (Rorty). Can you say how this dialectic worked for you, and why you chose Rorty as the representative of pragmatism rather than say Quine, or Pierce, who might have been pragmatists more obviously concerned with science?

GUTTING: I was trying to work out a position that combined a consensus account of justification with scientific realism. Rorty makes a good case for consensus but also thinks that consensus is inconsistent with realism. I wanted a Rorty-like voice in the dialogue, first to support a pragmatic epistemology of justification and second to serve as a foil to my claim that such an epistemology doesn't exclude a realistic ontology of science. The position I defended was roughly that of Sellars (without the difficulties of his picture theory of truth). Also, a primary example I wanted to use was the Galileo-Bellarmine debate over the cognitive authority of scripture and of science. Rorty had a stimulating treatment of that.

3:AM: You also use the dialogue form to discuss Alvin Plantinga's philosophical arguments about the existence of God and the general issue of the relationship between faith and reason. What are the key philosophical arguments you discuss here? Do you think faith is philosophically respectable?

GUTTING: I sat in on Plantinga's early, very exciting seminars at Notre Dame, where he was developing his idea that religious belief could be epistemologically respectable without being justified by evidence. His claim was that we could plausibly regard, say, belief in God the way we (should) regard belief in other minds, the validity of inductive inference, or the reliability of memories. On his view, these were all examples of properly basic beliefs: claims that we are entitled to hold without evidence. The way to refute this surprising view would seem to be to find a definition of "properly basic" that covers belief in other minds, etc., but excludes belief in God. But Plantinga showed that at least the more obvious ways of doing this didn't work. His suggestion was that to define "properly basic beliefs" we needed to generalize from some obvious examples of such beliefs. But once we embark on this project, he claims, there's no answer to a religious believer who thinks (as many in effect do) that "God exists" is obviously properly basic.

The dialogue you mention (from 1985) was one of several efforts I've made over the years to come to terms with this defense of religious belief. My most recent publication on the topic is in chapter 5 of *What Philosophers Know*. There my conclusion is that, even if there's no reason in principle why religious belief couldn't be properly basic, most thoughtful adults in the epistemic situation of our secular and pluralistic world cannot claim that most of their religious beliefs are properly basic. My current work on philosophy of religion tries to move beyond traditional discussions, which strike me as having little relevance to the reasons why actual people (even philosophers) do or do not believe. To keep in some touch with religious reality, I've been working with several books of "testimonials" from believing and nonbelieving philosophers. My current thought is that neither traditional atheists nor traditional theists are in a very strong epistemological position. Atheists, I think, should move to a more humble agnosticism: there simply are no decisive reasons for denying the existence of God (where's the compelling case for atheism in the philosophical literature?). But to meet the objections of atheists (for example, the problem of evil) believers need to give up anthropomorphic conceptions of God and regard God as fundamentally mysterious in a way that moves them to their own sort of religious agnosticism. My idea is not that belief and nonbelief should converge to a neutral middle ground. Rather, I think that there are significantly different varieties of agnosticism that include viable views for both believers and nonbelievers.

3:AM: Michel Foucault was a thinker that you have found important and interesting. Can you sketch out what you understand Foucault's central contributions to philosophy to have been, in particular his ideas of "discourse," of an "archeology of knowledge," and a "genealogical method"?

GUTTING: I see Foucault as more a philosophically informed and oriented historian than as a philosopher in any traditional sense. He typically writes what he calls "histories of the present," meaning that he starts from what he sees as an ethically intolerable practice of contemporary life (the treatment of the mad or the system of imprisoning criminals) that, despite its obvious flaws, we tend to see as necessary given certain general views our society holds (that madness is a medical condition, that prison is the only humane form of punishment). His histories are genealogies showing that the view allegedly justifying the practice is a contingent feature of our society that does not impose a genuinely normative limit on what we think and do. (A genealogy is a diachronic causal story, usually also accompanied by synchronic archeological analyses of the conceptual structure at various key temporal points.)

Foucault's histories are philosophical in that they require critical discussion of philosophical views, but he does not put forward his own philosophical views in any traditional sense. At most, he sometimes constructs an ad hoc theoretical apparatus (a "theory" of power) designed to expose the limitations of a view he is criticizing. But once the critical points are made, he is happy to abandon the apparatus, which functions like a scaffolding that's removed when the work is done. Toward the end of his life, Foucault did move toward a conception—akin to that of the ancients—of philosophy as a way of life. But he does not seek a body of theoretical truth.

3:AM: Doesn't his reading of Nietzsche misconstrue Nietzsche in a way that recent scholarship now would find disastrous? And doesn't this point to a larger criticism about Foucault, that his work is parochial (so his work on prisons for example generalizes from specifics of French penal systems that aren't true in, say, England of the period); that his historical ideas are prisoners of his theory and so only hold the imagination so long as we ignore actual historical details; that at heart he's committed to a corrosive form of relativism; and that he writes deliberately obscure prose?

GUTTING: Foucault was quite happy to offer "creative misreadings" of Nietzsche and other thinkers. He specifically says, "The only valid tribute to thought such as Nietzsche's is precisely to use it, to deform it, to make it groan and protest." His engagement with Nietzsche (and Heidegger, for another example) is often more a matter of appropriation than of explication (although there is explication in "Nietzsche, Genealogy, History"). As to historical accuracy, Foucault does paint with a broad brush, often with a limited palette of data. On the other hand, his goal is not, as it is for many historians, a meticulous delineation of "exactly how it was." Rather, he's after a general interpretative framework that will shed critical light on current practices. Such large-scale work must still answer to the facts, but it is less vulnerable to simple counterexamples. So, for example, when Foucault claims that confinement of the mad in asylums expresses the Classical Age's distinctive conception of madness, we can't refute him by simply pointing out that there were cases of confinement well before the Classical Age.

Foucault's relativism and skepticism is always very specifically local. His critiques are aimed at certain psychological and social scientific disciplines and associated practices. He does not try to undermine knowledge or reason in general (for example, in math, physics, chemistry) and even allows that disciplines thoroughly implicated in the network of social power (economics) still produce bodies of objective knowledge. As to obscurity, Foucault has his faults, particularly in some literary essays and when (as in parts of *The Order of Things*) he's channeling Heidegger. But he's overall much more accessible than, say, Deleuze or Derrida, especially from *Discipline and Punish* on. His last two books, on ancient sex, are quite lucid—he was ill and may have realized he didn't have time to be obscure.

3:AM: You've written about French philosophy in the last century. You make several claims in that book, that existentialism is French philosophy's major achievement, but that structuralism and poststructuralism are also important. You've recently been worrying that no one takes existentialism seriously anymore, but then you rethought that and think that it still casts a large, if only implicit, shadow. So firstly, can you tell us what you think existentialism is? Why is it so important an achievement, and what is your own relationship to it? Are you, or have you ever been, an existentialist?

GUTTING: I'm not an existentialist—just a fellow traveler. In the narrow and probably most useful sense, existentialism is Sartre's philosophy—not just *Being and Nothingness* but also the *Critique of Dialectical Reason* (an attempt at an existential assimilation of Marxism) and everything else. But the theme of engaged freedom and the atmosphere of metaphysical drama occur in other philosophers, at least since Kierkegaard, so a broader understanding of the term is sometimes helpful. In the end, though, what you think of existentialism should depend on what you think of Sartre.

3:AM: So is Sartre an impressive philosopher in your opinion? De Beauvoir?

GUTTING: Sartre continues to impress me. First, I think he's a very original philosopher, not a second-hand dealer in the ideas of Hegel or Heidegger. Second, at his best, he achieves a rare integration of literary and philosophical expression (trailing, I'd say, only Plato, Kierkegaard, and Nietzsche). Of course, he's not always at his best—his philosophical books are far too long, lack discipline, and try too hard to build a system. But they are filled with striking arguments and brilliant philo-literary vignettes. And his plays, novels (especially *Nausea*), biographies, and autobiography are superb literary expressions of ideas. I would suggest, in fact, that Sartre is a writer first and philosophizes mainly as a way of enriching his literary expression. I admit, however, that he could be remarkably silly in his political postures. I have also learned a lot from Simone de Beauvoir. Sartre was obviously a strong influence on her thinking, though we need to remember that the two of them were in constant discussion of one another's ideas. She had, in any case, a distinctive ability to present existentialist thought with a clarity, balance, and nuance that often escapes Sartre. Also, there's nothing in Sartre to match the wisdom of her work on feminism and on aging. She wrote excellent novels and her autobiography, especially in the opening volumes, before it becomes more a log of her travels with Sartre, is wonderful.

3:AM: You devote a chapter to Derrida. Lee Braver recently corrected my ignorant skepticism and told me to buck up, stop being a prejudicial prig, and take Derrida seriously! Braver is right, isn't he, in saying that there's a lot of prejudice about Derrida in certain circles (not that I'm in any circle, unless going round and round getting nowhere counts)? What makes Derrida important for you, and why does he have such a negative reputation?

GUTTING: To some extent, Derrida deserves his negative reputation. He's a serious and valuable philosopher, not a charlatan, as some maintain. But much of his writing is needlessly obscure and repetitive. More important, he often pretends to a logical rigor—which he indeed needs, to make his points—that he falls far short of achieving. I also think that his writing often has far less intellectual density than its difficulty suggests. There's a continuous deployment of ever-new convoluted terminology to make pretty much the same points about the essential instability of discourse. But he's an intelligent and creative reader of texts and often worth the irritations you encounter. I agree that you should take Derrida seriously, but I'd advise thinking carefully before committing large amounts of time to reading him. He's especially frustrating if you try to pay him the complement of a rigorous close reading.

3:AM: What's the relationship between existential phenomenology and structuralism and the emergence of poststructuralism?

GUTTING: Conceptually, I think existentialism was capable of incorporating much of what structuralist social science had to offer. Merleau-Ponty (a good friend of Lévi-Strauss) was on his way to doing this but died too early. Sartre, in the *Critique*, developed existentialism in a structuralist direction, but the rivalry between him and Lévi-Strauss made any rapprochement impossible. Things might have been very different if Merleau-Ponty (to whom Lévi-Strauss dedicated the book in which he denounced Sartre) had lived.

Poststructuralism is a different matter. It began as a reaction against the scientific objectivism of structuralism, and could, in principle, have found a lot in common with Sartre's existentialist critique of structuralism. Even Sartre's view of subjectivity needn't have been foreign to, say, Derrida. (As Mary Howells has shown, Sartre's analysis of self-presence in some ways anticipates Derrida's deconstruction of Husserl's phenomenology.) But the parricidal drives of the new generation of philosophers allowed no fruitful dialogue with Sartre. They needed to eradicate their adolescent devotion to existentialism. This may have been for the good. Sharpening differences often produces creative leaps that respectful negotiation could never achieve.

3:AM: You thought Brian Leiter's *Future of Philosophy* collection did accurately reflect the naturalistic bias in current philosophy. But you thought this meant that it omitted contemporary metaphysics—which is a flourishing area. Your major concern was that it omitted Continental philosophy. You say:

> I agree that there is no fruitful Analytic-Continental division in terms of substantive doctrines distinctively characteristic of the two sides. But it seems to me that we can still draw a significant distinction between Analytic and Continental philosophy in terms of their conceptions of experience and reason as standards of evaluation. Typically, Analytic philosophy reads experience in terms of common-sense intuitions (often along with their developments and transformations in science) and understands reason in terms of formal logic. Continental philosophy, by contrast, typically sees experience as penetrating beyond the veneer of common-sense and science, and regards reason as more a matter of intellectual imagination than deductive rigor.
>
> Do you still think this is the case?

GUTTING: Yes. It's fashionable to say that the Analytic-Continental divide is outdated, and it's certainly true that there are more and more philosophers who read and work across any borders we may try to designate. The fact remains that you can be an eminent metaphysician in the anglophone world and never have read a word of Heidegger, Deleuze or Badiou, or be famous on the Continent for your philosophy of language and have no interest in Quine or Putnam. Is it just that the two styles of philosophizing are different, that Continentals can't understand the complexities of rigorous logical analysis and argument and that Analytics can't penetrate the thickets of a philosophical version of literary modernism? This isn't likely: there are too many smart and good-willed philosophers on each side.

In my view, the mutual befuddlement goes much deeper. Philosophy is the deployment of experience and reason to answer deep human questions. But Analytic and Continental philosophers have different understandings of experience and reason. Analytics appeal to the obvious truths of common human experience (and its extension via science) and then reason to further conclusions using standard rules of inference. Some Continentals appeal in various ways to phenomenological or transcendental modes of experience that penetrate beneath or go beyond ordinary experience; others see reason as a creative power that leads to radically new ways of thinking. There can occasionally be fruitful local interactions between these approaches, but I think there's little hope of any sustained and comprehensive convergence.

3:AM: Your *New York Times Stone Opinionator* blog shows that you are someone keen to bring philosophy into the mainstream discourses. This is something that figures in the Continental tradition seem to do really well—Zizek is everywhere, it seems, as is Badiou. And we think of Sartre and de Beauvoir and Camus and Foucault and Derrida in the past—they have an aura of sexy, worldly, lefty cool. How do you explain this foregrounded public intellectual role that philosophers have in the Continental tradition, and why do you think it's so difficult in the Anglo-American setting? Is it because Anglo-American philosophy tends not to think the impossible, and so lacks the dramatic risky performance qualities?

GUTTING: The French in particular have a long cultural tradition of public philosophizing, supported since the 19th century by universal philosophical education in the last year of secondary school. Other European countries, at least to some extent, similarly support public philosophy. We Americans lack such a tradition and also tend to think of democracy as requiring a certain anti-intellectualism. There are, however, a number of recent developments that are giving philosophers a much higher public profile. Ever since Rawls, ethicists have increasingly engaged topics of political and social interest, a turn intensified by the explosion of work in applied ethics and the acceptance of philosophers as essential contributors to discussions of ethical issues raised by professions such as medicine and law. Work in the social sciences, psychology, neuroscience, evolutionary biology, and fundamental physics has raised issues about consciousness, freedom, the origin and nature of ethics, and the origin of the universe that can't be adequately discussed without invoking philosophical distinctions. And a new militancy among both conservative Christians and "new atheists" has brought philosophical discussions of religion and science to the fore.

The internet has allowed a much wider range of people access to philosophical discussions and revealed, beneath the crust of anti-intellectualism, a substantial popular interest in philosophy. The *New York Times* blog, *The Stone*, publishes about two philosophical essays per week, each typically attracting often quite intelligent comments from 200 to 800 subscribers. Each of the forty or so columns I've written for *The Stone* over the last year or so has been read by far more people than have read all of my books and articles together. I've also found that writing philosophy for a nonprofessional adult audience demands a focus and clarity that improves my own philosophical thinking and writing. Martha Nussbaum's current book, *The New Religious Intolerance*, derived from a piece she wrote for *The Stone* and the comments responding to it. Internet philosophy is rapidly making obsolete the old saw that philosophy has no meaningful presence in the general culture. Finally, I would mention the internet's invigorating effect on philosophy just as an academic discipline. There are countless blogs that facilitate professional interactions, and *PhilPapers* has become an essential gathering of current work in all areas. *Notre Dame Philosophical Reviews*, the book review journal I co-edit with Anastasia Friel Gutting, could not publish so many reviews so quickly if it weren't online. And, of course, your *End Times* series has been one of the best ways we philosophers have of learning about one another.

3:AM: The world is in crisis—politically, economically, socially, environmentally. Are you pessimistic or optimistic about what's going to happen, and do you think philosophy has a role?

GUTTING: I learned long ago from *Candide* that both optimism and pessimism are just ways of avoiding the work of improving the world. For optimism, improvement is unnecessary; for pessimism it's impossible. But it always makes sense to do what we can to make things better in our immediate locale, where we have some reasonable chance of alleviating what Voltaire rightly saw as the three great evils of vice, poverty, and boredom. It might seem that philosophy would have little relevance to such immediate and mundane concerns, and it's true that theory, high or deep, won't tell us how to work in our gardens. But effective action requires accurate thought, and in our culture at least, the basic ideas we need for thinking trickle down from philosophy, as do the methods of thinking well.

3:AM: Of the new Continentals, who do you find important and stimulating?

GUTTING: I have to admit I haven't found much in any of them. It may be that philosophy on the European continent is in an interregnum, waiting for Being to speak again. There are also signs of a move, even in France, to Analytic philosophy, which may become a new international scholasticism. On the other hand, it may well be that, for now, I'm a bit burnt out on the Continentals. Certainly, my current interests are much in Analytic work and in the possibilities of public philosophy.

INDEX

"3am Asia" strand, 3
3ammagazine.com, 1, 2–4
"3 Quarks Daily," 3

abortion, 117
abusive power, 182–183
academia, pharmaceutical/biotechnology
    industries, 185
academic philosophy, 159
action, 11
    intentional, 80–81, 88
    intentionality in, 82–83
    self-constitution, 203–2
action theory, 33, 82
activism, bioethics, 187
Afghanistan war, 196
Alcoff, Linda, 190
Al Jazeera, English site, 24
Almeder, Robert, 191
Alston, William, 11, 216
Alston, William P., 221
amalgamated cognition, 51–52
American Apartheid, Massey and
    Denton, 198
Analysis (journal), 66
"Analytic" philosophy, 11, 12, 13, 16,
    219–20, 229, 232, 270, 277, 279
Anarchy, State, and Utopia, Nozick, 174
Anderson, Elizabeth S., 10, 188–99
androcentrism, 180
animalism, 7, 57

personal identity, 58
personal identity over time, 60–61
psychological-continuity views, 60
animals
    animal rights, 48–49
    interests of, 49
    Rowlands and Brenin (wolf), 46–47
Anscombe, G. E. M., 6, 8, 16, 53, 80–81,
    83, 84, 85
anthropology, 103, 161
anthropomorphism, 164
anti-naturalists, 16, 17, 23, 161
anti-realist, 93, 212
Antony, Louise, 190
Appiah, Kwame Anthony, 112
Aquinas, Thomas, 66, 269
Arab Spring, 197, 198
Arendt, Hannah, 25
Aristotle, 9, 21, 42, 66, 80, 95, 96, 102,
    112–13, 136, 148, 212, 251
Arrow, Keith, 98
artificial intelligence, 62
Artificial Intelligence Journal
    (journal), 225
artists, 26
associationism, 253
atheists, 273, 278
atom, Bohr's theory, 153
atomism, 237
At the Mountains of Madness, Lovecraft, 89
attitudes, 106–7

Audi, Bob, 216
Aune, Bruce, 236
Austen, Jane, 187, 234
austerity measures, 198
Austria, 158
avant-garde, 3
avian brain, 106

Bach, J. S., 177
Badiou, Alain, 277
Baggini, Julian, 4
Baier, Annette, 183, 184
Barber, Stephen, 3
Barcan Marcus, Ruth, 232
Barnes, Julian, 56
Battaly, Heather, 216
Bayle, Pierre, 42
Beall, J. C., 213, 257
behaviorism, 251
behaviors, 106–7
belief, 11
    cognitive psychology of, formation,
        253–54
    conceptualizing, 38–39
    contradictions, 150–51
    direction of fit, 256–57
    false, 23
    God, 90
    intentionality, 51
    moral and political, 212–13
    religious, 22–23, 130, 134, 152, 269,
        271–73
    true justified, 102
belief box, 154–55
Bell, John, 75, 78
bias, 26
biased towards the truth, 87
bifurcation, language, 256–57
Big Bang, 259–260
"Big Crunch," 260
Big Questions in Free Will (BQFW)
    project, 137, 145
BigThink interview, 138
bioethics, feminism and, 178–79, 186–87
biology, 75, 83, 102, 103, 189, 253,
    266, 278

birds, 105–6
black-and-white dreaming, 37
Blackburn, Simon, 264
Blair, Tony, 19
Block, Ned, 237, 250
Bloggingheads tv, 2
Blum, Lawrence, 183
Blustein, Jeffrey, 183
Bohr, Niels, 75
Bohr's theory of atom, 153
Boltzmann, Ludwig, 71
boomerang effect, 127
Borges, Jorge Luis, 45, 156
Bracewell, Michael, 3
brain
    mammalian and avian, 106
    scanning content, 61–62
    sleep and dreaming, 103–4
    transplant, 59, 67
Braintrust: What Neuroscience Tells
        Us About Morality, Churchland,
    101, 106
Brandom, Robert, 237, 250, 257, 263, 264
Braver, Lee, 276
Brenin (wolf), 46, 47
Brennan, Jason, 192
Broome, John, 233
Büchner, Ludwig, 16
Buddhism, 9, 109, 152, 153
Burge, Tyler, 226
Burra, Arudra, 134
Bush, George W., 15, 195, 219
Byrne, Richard, 48
Byrnyeat, Myles, 237

Callender, Craig, 7, 68–79
Camp, Elizabeth, 29
Camus, Albert, 55, 56, 236, 277
Cappelen, Herman, 12, 235, 242, 243
Carnap, Rudolf, 16, 23
Carroll, Sean, 2, 8, 73
Carruthers, Peter, 1, 9, 121–30, 217
Cartesian dualism, 58, 84
Cashmore, Anthony, 140, 141
Catholicism, 269
causal republican, 261–62

causation, 261–62, 266
Causation, Physics, and the Constitution of Reality, Price, 256, 261
cause and effect, 262, 263
Cavell, Marcia, 238
Chalmers, David, 27, 50, 51, 52, 104, 105
change of mind, 89–90
character, human, 22
cheating, 154
Chicago University's "Eludications," 4
Childish, Billy, 3
Children of the Sky, Vinge, 43
Chinese philosophy, 7, 41, 42
Chomsky, Noam, 1, 251, 255
Christianity, 109, 147, 150, 153, 278
Churchill, Caryl, 187
Churchland, Patricia, 8, 101–10, 208, 237, 242
Churchland, Paul, 250
civil rights, 170, 193
Clark, Andy, 50, 51, 52
classical logic, 11, 149, 224. *See also* logic
Clemens, Samuel, 28
Clinton, Bill, 15, 19
Code, Lorraine, 190
coercive distribution, 174
cognitive dissonance, 125, 126
cognitive psychology, 149–50, 217
    belief formation, 253–54
cognitive science, 9, 122, 171
    collaborations, 243–44
    free will, 138–139
    philosophy and, 129, 130, 132, 135
    psychology, 217
Cohen, G. A., 18
Cohen, Hermann, 9–10, 160–62
Cohen, Jerry, 169
Cohen, Jonathan, 140, 141
coherence theory, truth, 212–13
collaborations, cognitive science, 243–44
Collins, Patricia Hill, 190
colored dreaming, 37
color vision, science, 66
combat model, soul, reason and passion, 205, 207

common sense, 39, 52, 77, 218, 254
communication
    linguistic and nonlinguistic, 31
    science, 76
communitarianism, 173
compositionality, 241
The Compositionality Papers, Lepore, 235, 241
The Computational Brain, Sejnowski, 109
computer-generated life, 62–63
Conant, James, 84
conception of selves, 129
concept learning, 249
conceptual analysis, 53–54
conceptual turn, 228–29
Confucians, 109
Confucius, 42
congenital adrenal hyperplasia (CAH), 184
conscience, liberty or freedom, 23
consciousness, 27, 44–45, 103, 104–5, 251
consequentialism, 85–86
conservatism, 217, 254
The Constitutional Model, Korsgaard, 205
constitutional rights, 10
constitutional social rights, 170–71
The Constitution of Agency, Korsgaard, 200, 205
constructivism, 205–6
contemporary moral philosophy, 119–20
content, 29
Continental Philosophy, 6, 11, 12, 16, 219–20, 230–31, 270, 277, 279
continental tradition, 252
contradictions, 150, 152, 154–55
Convention, Lewis, 245–46
Corry, Richard, 261
cosmology, 7–8, 65–66, 100, 259–60
counterattitudinal essays, 126–27
counterstories, 10, 182–83
Counting the Cost of Global Warming, Broome, 233
Crane, Tim, 226
crazyism, 7, 39, 40, 44, 97–98
Creating the Kingdom of Ends, Korsgaard, 200

creativity, 124–25
crisis, 25, 33, 279
"The Crisis of Philosophy," Stanley, 25
Critchley, Simon, 177
Critique of Pure Reason, Kant, 66,
    159, 160
Crow, Jim, 196
Cudworth, Damaris, 187
cultural history, 103
Current Biology (journal), 139

Daily Telegraph, 3
Damaged Identities, Lindemann, 178, 181
Dancy, Jonathan, 87, 183, 184
Darwall, Stephen, 199
Darwin, Charles, 12
Darwinism, 252–53
"Darwin Wars," 1, 252
Davidson, Donald, 12, 32, 80, 81, 83, 84,
    89, 219, 237, 238, 239, 240, 243,
    244, 245
Dawkins, Richard, 2, 22, 23, 252
de Beauvoir, Simone, 275, 277
defending family values, 15
defense mechanism, reaction formation, 15
deflationary pessimism, truth, 214
deflationary theory, truth, 214
deflationism, 257–58, 265
Deleuze, Gilles, 274, 277
deliberation, 262–63
democracy, 10, 19, 169–70, 196, 198,
    217, 278
de Negroni, Barbara, 168
Dennett, Dan, 1, 22, 53, 122, 237, 250
Denton, Nancy, 198
deprivation of opportunity, 181
Derrida, Jacques, 1, 13, 17, 219, 220, 222,
    223, 231, 274, 276, 277
de Saussure, Ferdinand, 237
Descartes, Rene, 36, 39, 42, 52, 84, 140,
    164, 167, 187, 211, 251, 268
Describing Inner Experience?
    Schwitzgebel and Hurlburt, 35
determinism, 133
Dewey, John, 6, 10, 191, 192
dexamethasone, 184–85

dialetheism, 9, 148, 149, 151, 154,
    155–56
Dialogues Concerning Natural Religion,
    Hume, 75
Diamond, Cora, 84
Diaspora, Egan, 43, 45
Dickens, Emily, 65
direction of fit, beliefs, 256–57
discussions about mental, 164
distributive equality, 193–94. *See also*
    equality
distributive justice, 169–70, 171, 172, 173
dogmatism, 217
Doris, John, 119
Dorr, Cian, 89
Dostoevsky, Fyodor, 156
Doubt Truth to Be a Liar, Priest, 147, 148
Dowker, Fay, 78
dreaming, brain, 103–4
Dreben, Burton, 238
Du Bois, W. E. B., 26
Dummett, Michael, 149, 222, 223, 237,
    245, 258, 263
Dupré, John, 76
Dworkin, Ronald, 17, 20, 170
dynamics, 150

economics, 188–89, 199
Economics in One Lesson, Hazlitt, 188
education, philosophical, 278
Effective Intentions, Mele, 136, 139, 141
egalitarianism, 10, 193–95, 197
egalitarian liberals, 10, 172–73
Egan, Andy, 29
Egan, Greg, 43, 45
Einstein, Albert, 2, 74, 75
Eleatic monism, 163, 166
electromagnetism, 74
eliminativism, 93, 117–18
Eliot, T. S., 177, 242
"Eludications," Chicago University, 4
embedded cognition, 50
embodied cognition, 52
empirical philosophy, 119
enaction, 50
enactiveness, 55

engineers, 134
England, philosophy in, 158
England, Paula, 189
Enlightenment, 13, 272
entropy, 73–74
epistemic egoism, 86
epistemology, 6, 7, 10, 29, 251, 270
    Alston's, 216
    Cohen's logics, 161–62
    Descartes', 164
    epistemological holism, 250
    feminist, 188, 190–91, 196–97
    justification, 30, 272
    knowledge and belief, 11, 226–27
    metaphysics and, 239
    moral theorist, 87, 88
    virtue, 33
equality, 38, 177, 188, 193–94, 196,
    197, 198
essays, freedom of choice, 126–28
Essays on Anscombe's Intention, 32, 89
eternity, 165
ethics
    anthropology, 161
    bioethics, 178–79, 186–87
    feminist, 10, 179, 181, 186
    justification, 87
    moral behavior, 40, 41
Ethics, Spinoza, 161, 163, 164, 166
Evans, Gareth, 226
evolutionary biology, 102, 103
evolutionary theory, vagueness, 224–25
existence
    free will, 137–138
    god, 108–9
    quantifier vs. predicate, 93
existentialism, 275, 276
experience, 35–36, 277
    stream of, 36–38
    theory of, 160
experimental philosophy (x-phi), 21, 67,
    98, 118–19, 122–23, 131–32,
    135, 141, 144, 152, 171, 186,
    218, 266
Experimental Philosophy, Knobe and
    Nichols, 9

expert systems, 254
explanatory pessimism, truth, 214
extended cognition, 52, 54–55
extended mind, 50, 51
extended mind hypothesis, 7
externalism, 52, 226, 227

Fabre, Cecile, 10, 168–77
Facts and the Function of Truth,
    Price, 256
factual knowledge, 32–33
false advertising, 154
families, 15, 184, 187
feminism, 179–80, 192, 196–97
Feminism and Families, Lindemann,
    178, 184
feminist bioethics, 178–79, 186–87
feminist ethics, 10, 179, 181, 186
feminist epistemology, 190–91, 196–97
Fermat's Last Theorem, 97, 98
Feuerbach, Ludwig, 16
Fey, Tina, 110
Feyerabend, Paul, 102
Feynman, Richard, 75
fiction writers, 35
financial deregulation, 197–98
Fine, Kit, 8, 89, 91–100
Firestone, Shulamith, 184
A Fire Upon the Deep, Vinge, 43
Flanagan, Owen, 108
flash ontology, 78
Fodor, Jerry, 5–6, 12, 16, 75, 81, 236, 237,
    238, 239, 241, 243, 244, 245,
    247–255
folk conceptions, free will, 143–44
Formula of Humanity, Kant, 200, 201
Foucault, Michel, 17, 222, 223, 231, 268,
    271, 273–74, 277
The Foundations of Arithmetic, Frege, 27
Fox News, 24
Frankfurt, Harry, 89
Frankfurt School, 17
freedom, 10, 23, 24, 192, 197, 199, 269
freedom of choice, 126–28
freedom of movement, 172
freedom of speech, 169, 172

free will, 105, 13
    cognitive science and neuroscience,
        138–139
    folk conceptions, 143–44
    grant of $4-plus million, 136–37
    intentions, 139–43
    libertarianism, 143
    reality and existence of, 137–38
Free Will and Luck, Mele, 136, 138,
    140, 146
Frege, Gottlob, 16, 27, 55, 91, 98, 149,
    220, 240, 245, 249, 251
French constitution, 169
French philosophy, 275
Freud, Sigmund, 14, 16, 18, 21, 36
Fricker, Miranda, 199
functionalism, truth, 215
Future of Philosophy, Leiter, 276

Galix, Andrew, 3
Gallagher, Shaun, 50
Gamow, George, 76
Garfield, Jay, 153
gay marriage, 15
The Gay Science, Nietzsche, 19
Gazzaniga, Michael, 140, 141, 142
gender, feminist ethics, 179–80
gender symbolism, 189
Gendler, Tamar, 220
Genealogy of Morality, 19
genital surgery, 184–185
geometrical method, Spinoza, 162–63
Geroch, Bob, 75
Gettier, Ed, 102, 236
Geuss, Raymond, 17
Ghirardi–Rimini–Weber theory (GRW), 78
Gibbard, Alan, 119
global broadcasting, 128
Glymour, Clark, 108
God, 194, 269
    belief in, 150, 151
    contradictory object, 152
    existence of, 108–9
    love of, 166
    morality, 90
    religious belief, 272–73

Gorgias, Plato, 85
Gormley, Antony, 89
Gottlieb, Anthony, 218
grant ($4-plus million), free will study,
    136–37
Great Depression, 198
Greenberg, Gabriel, 31
Greene, Brian, 76
Greene, Joshua, 140, 141
Greenough, Patrick, 215, 226
Grice, Paul, 223, 245
Groundwork, Kant, 201
group minds, 43
Guardian (newspaper), 3
Gutting, Anastasia Friel, 278
Gutting, Gary, 1, 2, 12, 268–79

Haak, Susan, 191
Habermas, Jürgen, 18, 270
Haidt, John, 111, 113
Hammett, Dashiell, 234
hand complement, 63
Haraway, Donna, 190
Harding, Sandra, 190
Hartsock, Nancy, 190
Harvard, 27
Haslanger, Sally, 190
Hastings Center Report (journal), 178, 183
Hawking, Stephen, 8, 12, 100, 259, 260
Hawthorne, John, 29, 226, 237, 243
Haybron, Dan, 119, 120
Hazlitt, Henry, 188
health care, 15, 193
health insurance, 192–193
Hegel, G. W. F., 9, 16, 43, 66, 149, 152,
    155, 212, 231, 252, 275
Heidegger, Martin, 17, 40, 55, 56, 230,
    231, 252, 274, 275, 277
Heisenberg, Werner, 75
Hell, Richard, 3
Hepburn, Audrey, 199
hermeneutics of suspicion, 14, 16, 154
Hertz, Heinrich, 71
hierarchy, 172, 193, 194
Hill, Chris, 236
Hitchens, Christopher, 22

Hobbes, Thomas, 167
holism, 237–39, 240–41, 250
Home, Stewart, 3
homosexuality, 15
Hornsby, Jennifer, 32, 33
Horton, John, 169
Horwich, Paul, 257
Howells, Mary, 276
How Judges Think, Posner, 20
How to Live Safely in a Science Fictional Universe, Yu, 79
Hudson, Hud, 64, 65
humanities, philosophy in, 6–7, 26
humanity, 10–11, 176–77, 200–201
humans
    action, 203–5
    free will, 105, 133. *See also* free will
    making up their minds, 116–17
    nature, 42, 58, 114–15
    personal identity, 58–60
    types, 22
    weakness, 129–30
Hume, David, 8, 11, 12, 16, 26, 42, 66, 75, 89, 101, 102, 113, 115, 129, 218, 221, 251
Hurlburt, Russell, 35, 36
Hursthouse, Rosalind, 120
Husak, Doug, 25
Husserl, Edmund, 16, 55, 56, 220, 230, 268, 270, 276
hypocrisy, 9, 154, 155

identity, 58–61, 94, 183
Identity and Discrimination, Williamson, 222, 224, 225
imagery, experience, 38
imagination, 165, 220, 229, 274, 277
The Imperative of Integration, Anderson, 188, 196
improvisation, creativity, 125
"in-between," believing, 38
Incidents in the Life of a Slave Girl, Jacobs, 183
Indian philosophers, 42
inequality, 192, 196, 197–98
infiltrated consciousness, 181

innatist position, 248–49
innativism, 164
Insensitive Semantics, Lepore, 235, 239
Inside Higher Education, Stanley, 26
intelligence
    artificial, 62–63
    humans and animals, 46, 47, 49
intension-intention distinction, 252
intention, 32
    action, 80–81, 82–83, 88
    free will, 139–143
    intentionality, 51, 52, 53, 54, 251
    intentional psychology, 83
Intention, Anscombe, 80–81
internalism, 227
internet, 2, 13, 24, 278
interviews, 4–6
introspection, 7, 123–24
intuition, 9, 70, 71, 98, 119, 133, 174, 209, 218, 230, 239, 240, 243
    common sense, 67, 277
    dualist and libertarian, 140
    free will, 141
    logic, 149
    moral, 9, 86–87, 134, 140, 161
Iraq war, 44, 196
Ishiguru, Kazuo, 119
Islamic philosophers, 42, 43
Ismael, Jenann, 262

Jackson, Frank, 266
Jacobs, Harriet, 183
Jaggar, Alison, 179, 180
James, William, 212
Jenkins, J. J., 240
John Templeton Foundation, 137
journalistic objectivity, 24
Journal of the History of Philosophy prize, 158
Joyce, James, 35
justice, 117, 174, 175, 177, 181, 199, 206
    distributive, 10, 169, 170, 171, 172, 173
    moral virtues, 85
    social, 170
Justice in a Changing World, Fabre, 168, 171–72

Kane, Robert, 146
Kant, Immanuel, 9, 10, 11, 16, 17, 18, 19,
    21, 22, 43, 66, 159, 160, 177, 200,
    201, 202, 210, 251, 259
Kasser, Tim, 119
Keller, Evelyn Fox, 190
Kennedy, John F., 232
Kierkegaard, S., 132, 134, 275
Kingsolver, Barbara, 119
Kitcher, Philip, 76, 106, 270
Klein, Peter, 238
Knobe, Joshua, 2, 9, 21, 22, 122, 131–35,
    144, 186
"Knobe Effect," 9, 131
Know How, Stanley, 25, 29, 30
Knowing Right From Wrong, Setiya, 80,
    87, 88, 90
knowledge, 29–30
    meaning, 32, 33
    practical and theoretical, 32
    testimony, 162, 220
Knowledge and Its Limits, Williamson,
    222, 226, 227, 230
Knowledge and Practical Interests,
    Stanley, 25, 31
Koertge, Noretta, 191
Korsgaard, Christine, 10–11, 89, 119,
    200–210
Kraut, Richard, 120
Kripke, Saul, 7, 28, 102, 233, 244, 245
Kuhn, Thomas, 45, 268, 271, 272
Kukla, Rebecca, 182
Kundera, Milan, 55, 56
Kurzweil, Ray, 43

Labour Party, 18, 19
laissez-faire, 188
language, 12, 27
    bifurcation, 256–57
    linguistic representation, 31
    philosophy of, 27–29, 236–37,
        240, 244
    possible worlds, 95–96
Language in Context, Stanley, 25, 31
Language of Thought (LOT), Fodor, 247,
    248, 253

Language Turned on Itself, Lepore,
    235, 242
Laozi, 42
Last and First Men, Stapledon, 43
law of non-contradiction, 148
Leibniz, Gottfried, 16, 39, 167
Leiter, Brian, 2, 6, 14–24, 116, 208, 276
Leiter Reports (blog), 2, 14, 182
Lenin, 168
Lepore, Ernie, 12, 235–46
Levellers, 194, 198
Leviathan, Hobbes, 177
Lewis, David, 39, 156, 213, 237, 244, 245
Lib-Dem Party, 18
liberalism, 9, 13, 19, 172, 173, 177, 197
libertarianism, 140, 143, 172,173, 174,
    175, 193, 197
Libet, Benjamin, 139, 142
light, speed of, 74–75
The Limits of Abstraction, Fine, 91, 92
Lindemann, Hilde, 10, 178–87
linguistic communication, 31
linguistics, philosophy of language, 28–29
linguistic turn, 228–229
Lloyd, Elisabeth, 190, 191
Locke, John, 36, 187
Loewer, Barry, 235, 236, 238, 240, 243
logic, 5, 6, 64, 72, 77, 96, 149, 150, 154,
    161, 232, 277
    androcentrism, 180
    classical, 11, 149, 224
    fuzzy, 225
    mathematical, 27, 147, 225, 236
    paraconsistent, 9, 148, 149, 151, 152,
        237
    philosophical, 9, 25, 91, 222, 223, 235
    second-order modal, 233
Logic, Hegel, 152
logical possibility, 150
Longino, Helen, 190, 191
Lovecraft, H. P., 89
Lucretius, 89
Ludlow, Peter, 27
Ludwig, Kirk, 238, 243
Lugones, Maria, 190
Lynch, Michael, 11, 211–21

MacArthur prize, 108
McCall, Dan, 88
MacCorquodale, Kenneth, 240
McDowell, John, 16, 81, 83, 84, 115, 226, 250, 265
McGee, Bryan, 4
Machianism, spacetime, 72
Machiavellian Intelligence Hypothesis, 7, 48
MacIntyre, Alasdair, 271, 272
McLaughlin, Brian, 226, 238, 243
McTaggart, John, 258, 266
Magee, Bryan, 156
mammalian brain, 106
mammals, 105–6
manifest time, 72–73, 78
Mann, Charles, 198–99
Marr, David, 53
Martin, Virginia, 180
Marx, Karl, 6, 9, 14, 16, 17, 18, 19, 134, 149, 155
Marxism, 275
Massey, Douglas, 198
Material Beings, van Inwagen, 65
materialism, 5, 18, 44, 45, 119
mathematics
    logic, 27, 147, 225, 236
    metaphysics, 91–92
    philosophy of, 147
    philosophy of language, 27–28
    truth, 11, 215
The Matrix (film), 227
Matthews, Robert, 238
Maxwell, James, 71
Maynard–Smith, John, 75
meaning, 32, 33, 250
    meaningful, 15, 99–100, 217, 278
    meaningless, 11, 99, 209–10, 213
    prototypes, 242
    truth theory as theory of, 239–240
Meaning, Mind, and Matter, Lepore, 235, 240
media, 3, 22, 24, 37, 44, 195
Meinong, 152, 153
Mele, Alfred R., 9, 136–46
Mellor, D. H., 258

Mencius, 42
Mendus, Susan, 169
mental process, 7, 50, 52, 252
mental states, copying, 61
Menzies, Peter, 261
mereological metaphysics, 69
mereology, wholes and parts, 94–95
Merleau–Ponty, Maurice, 231, 268, 276
meta-ontology, 93–94
metaphysical, 209
metaphysical and semantic quietism, 261
metaphysicians, 258–59
metaphysics, 7, 8, 39, 65
    contemporary, 68–69
    mathematics and, 91–92
    meaningfulness, 99–100
    mereological, 69
    mereology, 94–95
    philosophy of mind and, 163, 164
    possible worlds, 95–96
Metaphysics, Gamma, Aristotle, 148
methodological naturalism, 76
middle classes, mobility, 18
Milgram studies, 22
Mill, John Stuart, 111, 134, 188
Miller, David, 170
Mills, Charles, 190
mind
    changing one's, 89–90
    humans making up their, 116–17
    mind-body dualism, 164
    mind-body relationship, 44
    mindreading, 9, 123, 124, 128
    understanding selves, 128
Mind (journal), 66
Mind and World, McDowell, 81
Mindwarp, Zodiak, 3
Ming, Sexton, 3
minimalism, 12, 237, 239
Modal Logic as Metaphysics, Williamson, 222, 232
money, research programs and, 185–86
monism, 163, 212, 237
monotheism, 109, 194
Monroe, Marilyn, 232
Montague, Read, 139–40, 141, 244

Montaigne, Michel de, 42
Montello, Martha, 182
Moorcock, Michael, 3
moralists, 17, 20
morality, 21
    Chinese philosophers, 42
    humans and animals, 46, 47
    naturalism, 111–12
    obligation, 201–2
morals
    behavior, 7, 40, 41, 42, 109, 186, 210
    education of, 118
    intuitions, 86–87
    knowledge, 87, 186
    moral philosophy, 8–9, 21, 119–20,
        208, 210
    particularism, 8, 85–87
    principles, 117–18
    psychology, 22
    truth, 11, 215
    virtues, 85, 115
    worth, 202
motives, 36, 203, 205
Mozi, 42
Murdoch, Iris, 88, 89
Murdoch, Rupert, 24
My Dinner with Andre (film), 45
myth of the given, 9, 159

Nagel, Thomas, 89, 122, 170
Naming and Necessity, Kripke, 245
narrative repair, counterstories, 182–83
narrative theory, 183–84
National Center for Education Statistics,
    182
naturalism, 6, 17, 19, 161–62, 215
    epistemic normativity, 161–62
    ethics, 161–62
    morality, 111–112, 117–118
Naturalism Without Mirrors, Price, 256, 263
naturalists, 16, 200–201
Naturalized Bioethics: Toward
        Responsible Knowing and Practice,
    Lindemann, 178, 186
natural philosophy, 71–72
natural world, 214

Nature (journal), 260
Nature Neuroscience (journal), 142
Nazism, 40, 41
negation, 154–55
negative liberty, 192
Nelson, Lynn, 190
Neo-Marxism, 177
nervous system, 103–4
neurophilosophy, 8, 101
neuroscience, 8, 102, 103
    behaviors and attitudes, 106–7
    consciousness, 104–5
    free will, 138–39
    intentions, 140
    vision, 103
New British Philosophy: The Interview,
        Baggini and Stangroom, 4
The New Religious Intolerance,
        Nussbaum, 278
The New Science of the Mind, Rowlands,
    46, 54
Newton, Isaac, 2, 71
Newtonian dynamics, 150
New York Times, 2, 24, 25, 33, 277, 278
Nicholas of Cusa, 152
Nicholson, Peter, 169
Nietzsche, Friedrich, 6, 14, 16, 17, 18, 19,
    21, 22, 23, 26, 39, 40, 55, 56, 89,
    106, 117, 129, 132, 134, 217, 231,
    274, 275
Nisbett, Richard E., 36
Nixon, Richard, 15
normativity of self-constitution, 202–3
Notre Dame Philosophical Reviews
        (journal), 278
noumenal world, 201
Nozick, Robert, 174
Nurses Recognition Day, 180
Nussbaum, Martha, 17, 115, 278

Obama, Barack, 15, 191, 195, 196, 226
objective truth, 219
Observer (newspaper), 3
Occupy movement, 10, 19, 20, 173, 197
Ockham, 251
Odysseus and Sirens, 207, 208

Olson, Eric T., 7, 57–67
On Bullshit, Frankfurt, 89
On Liberty, Mill, 188
"on-line Fitzrovia," 3
Ontological Rigidity, Williamson, 232, 233
ontology, 92, 93, 94, 232
opacity of mind, 125
The Opacity of Mind, Carruthers, 121,
    123, 130
opera, 156, 254
optimism, 114, 279
organ transplants, 174–175
ornithology, 75–76
Orwell, George, 199
oxytocin, 107

paraconsistent logic, , 9, 148, 149, 151,
    152, 237. *See also* logic
Parfit, Derek, 11, 106, 207
Parsons, Terry, 236
Partee, Barbara Hall, 236
particularism, moral, 86–87
partism, 7, 64–65
parts of the body, 63
Pascal's Wager, 32
passion
    self-constitution, 205
    slaves of our, 113–114
past-to-future, time, 262, 263
Patchett, Ann, 119
The Patient in the Family, Lindemann,
    178, 179
Peirce, Charles, 263, 264
Penrose, Roger, 259, 260
perception, 25, 30, 53, 105, 115, 123, 124,
    129, 165, 197, 198, 225, 229
Permutation City, Egan, 43, 45
Perplexities of Consciousness,
    Schwitzgebel, 35, 37, 40
personal identity, 58–60, 60–61. *See also*
    identity
personal integrity, 175–176
pessimism, 214, 279
pharmaceutical and biotechnology
    industry, academia and, 185
phenomenal world, 201

phenomenology of meaning, 32
The Phenomenology of Spirit, Hegel, 224
The Philosopher and the Wolf, Rowlands,
    46, 47, 48, 56
philosophers
    history, 1–2
    interviews, 4–6
philosophical histories, Foucault, 273–74
Philosophical Investigations,
    Wittgenstein, 84, 184, 237
philosophical logic, 9, 25, 91, 222, 223,
    235. *See also* logic
philosophy
    academic, 159
    cognitive science and, 129, 132, 135
    critics of contemporary, 66–67
    judging theories, 213214
    of language, 236–37, 240, 244
    of law, 6
    of mind, 163, 164, 248
    political, 10, 166, 171
    psychology and, 121–22, 134–35
    radical, 231
    science and, 65–66
    term, 266
"Philosophy Bites," 4
The Philosophy of Philosophy,
    Williamson, 53, 215, 222, 227, 230
"Philosophy TV," 2
PhilPapers (blog), 278
"PhilPapers" site, 2
physics, 7–8
Pinker, Steven, 12, 253
Plantinga, Alvin, 13, 16, 216, 271, 272
Plato, 17, 42, 65, 101, 111, 136, 151, 172,
    177, 188, 227, 275
Platonic myth, 218
Platonism, 215
pluralism, 197, 212, 213, 214
plutocracy, 16, 19, 173, 193
political correctness, 191
political philosophy, 10, 166, 171
political rights, 170
political science, 103
Pol Pot, 87, 116
Popper, Karl, 76

Port–Royal, 251
Posner, Richard, 17, 20
The Possibility of Altruism, Nagel, 89
possible worlds, 95–96
postmodernism, 17, 190
poststructuralism, 227, 275, 276
"potshot" approach, 6
power, feminism, 179–80
Pragmatic Liberalism and the Critique of Modernity, Gutting, 268, 271
pragmatics, linguistics, 28
pragmatism, 263–64, 272
precision, 216
pregnancy, 117
Price, Huw, 12, 256–67
Priest, Graham, 9, 147–56, 218
principle of bivalence, 224
Principle of Non-Contradiction (PNC), 148–49, 152, 153
privacy, 84, 195
private property rights, 192–93
prostitution, 10, 174–76
prototypes, 242
Proust, Marcel, 35
psychological-continuity views, 59–60, 67
psychology, 9, 102, 103, 104
    cognitive science, 217
    experimental philosophy, 141
    philosophy and, 40, 121–22, 132, 134–35
psychotherapy, 166
The Pursuit of Unhappiness, Haybron, 119, 120
Putnam, Hilary, 16, 213, 220, 226, 250, 258, 277
Pylyshyn, Zenon, 248, 255

quantification, 92–93
quantum logic, 77
quantum mechanics, 72, 78, 153
quasi-realism, 264–65
Queen Christina of Sweden, 187
quietism, 261
Quine, W. V. O., 8, 16, 92, 102, 191, 220, 221, 236, 237, 240, 245, 257, 264, 277

"Quine–Duhem thesis," 250, 254
quotation, theory of, 242–43

racism, 10, 192, 194, 196
radicalism, 222, 223, 228–29
radicalness, 167
radical philosophy, 231
Ramsey, Frank, 262–63, 264
rape, 180–181
rationality, 7, 9, 40, 41, 115, 138
    rational acceptability, 150
    rationalization, 217, 218
    science and, 83–84
    truth and, 148
    thinking, 9
Rawls, John, 10, 17, 86, 115, 171–72, 177, 219, 278
Rawlsian contractualists, 48
Raz, Joseph, 170
reaction formation, 15
Reagan, Ronald, 20
realism, 6, 13, 18, 19, 20, 21
    quasi-, 264
    scientific, 160, 161, 271, 272
    truth, 215–216
    vagueness, 224
realists, 17, 20, 93
reality, 93, 137–38, 212, 261
reason, 216–217, 218, 277
    descriptively, 206–7
    human nature, 115
    intentional action, 80–81
    morality, 115–16
    normatively, 206
    self-constitution, 205
Reasons Without Rationalism, Setiya, 80, 85, 87
recognition, 180–81
Reconstruction era, 26
reductionism, 83, 84, 93, 117–18
reflective equilibrium, 86–87
The Reflective Life, Tiberius, 111, 112
reflective wisdom, 114, 116
Reid, Thomas, 39
relativism, 9, 90, 148, 212, 219, 274–75
relativity, 78–79, 153

religion, 194
   philosophy of, 147–48
   religious belief, 22–23, 130, 134, 152,
      271–73
   skepticism, 268–269
Religious Belief and Religious Skepticism,
   Gutting, 268, 269
Renz, Ursula, 9–10, 157–67
representational theory of mind (RTM),
   249–50
Republic, Plato, 172, 177, 188
research programs, money and, 185–86
retrocausality, 263
Rey, Georges, 255
Ricardo, David, 199
Richardson, Bob, 108
Ricoeur, Paul, 14, 154
Ripley, Dave, 152
Robbins, Trevor, 105
Romano, Carlin, 25
Rorty, Richard, 191, 216, 219, 221, 227,
   229, 263, 264, 268, 269, 271, 272
Rosenberg, Alex, 16, 83, 108, 171, 208, 253
*The Routledge Companion to Philosophy
   of Language*, Routledge, 27
Rove, Karl, 212
Rowlands, Mark, 7, 46–56
Ruddick, Sara, 184
Rumfitt, Ian, 239
Running with the Pack, Rowlands, 56
Russell, Bertrand, 1, 58, 89, 111, 149,
   222, 261
Rust, Joshua, 41

Sacks, Oliver, 45
same-sayers, 96, 97
sarcasm, 29
Sartre, Jean Paul, 1, 16, 21, 56, 156, 222,
   223, 236, 275, 276
Satz, Debra, 199
Sayers, Dorothy L., 187
Schmidtz, David, 192
Schopenhauer, Arthur, 39
Schrödinger's cat, 77
Schwitzgebel, Eric, 7, 27, 35–45, 77, 97,
   152, 217

science
   faith, 217
   knowledge, 270–71
   living good life, 118
   metaphysics and, 69–70
   philosophy and, 65–66
   philosophy of, 148, 190
   physics and cosmology, 7–8
   rationality, 83–84
science fiction
   computer-generated life, 62–63
   "Strange Baby," 43
ScienceNow Daily News (journal), 143
scientific methodology, 76
scientific realism, 160–61
scientism, 17
Searle, John, 88, 89
segregation, 196
Sejnowski, Terry, 109, 110
self-concept, 129
self-constitution, 11
   action, 11, 203–5
   normativity of, 202–3
Self-Constitution, Korsgaard, 200, 203,
   207
self-deception, 144–45
Self-Deception Unmasked, Mele, 136,
   144–45
self-image, 107
Sellars, Wilfred, 84, 160, 161, 270, 271,
   272
Sellars, Wilfrid, 16
semantic minimalism, 12
semantic relationism, 8, 96–97
Semantic Relationism, Fine, 91, 96
semantics, philosophy of language,
   28–29
Sen, Amartya, 188, 199
sensation, 165
sense, 55
sense of mortality, humans and animals, 47
sensory content, 159–160
separation, philosophy of science and
   science, 75–76
September 11, 195
Setiya, Kieran, 8, 80–90

Sextus Empiricus, 42
sexual harassment, 182
sexual identity, 183
The Significance of Free Will, Kane, 146
The Silence of Bartleby, McCall, 88
Sinclair, Iain, 3
Singer, Peter, 218
Sirius, Stapledon, 43, 45
skepticism, 26, 45, 99, 268–69, 274–75
skill, knowledge and, 29–30
Skinner, B. F., 236, 251, 252
slaves of passions, 113–14
sleep, brain, 103–104
Smith, Adam, 199
social brain hypothesis, 48
social insurance, 192
social issues, 16
social justice, 170
social rights, 10, 170–171
Social Rights Under the Constitution,
    Fabre, 168, 169
Socrates, 25, 73
Soon, Chun Siong, 142, 143
Sorenson, Roy, 154
Sorkin, Rafael, 78
Sosa, Ernest, 30
soul sickness, 84
The Sources of Normativity, Korsgaard,
    89, 119
The Sovereignty of Good, Murdoch, 88
spacetime, 69–70, 72, 78–79
specialization, philosophy, 71–72
speed of light, 74–75
Spinoza, Baruch, 6, 9–10, 158
    ethics, 161–62, 165–67
    philosophy of mind, 163, 164
    systematicity, 162–63
Stalinism, 177
Stalnaker, Robert, 29
Stanford Encyclopedia of Philosophy, 2,
    191
Stangroom, Jeremy, 4
Stanley, Jason, 6–7, 25–34, 65, 237
Stanovich, Keith, 119
Stapledon, Olaf, 43, 45
Stich, Stephen, 16, 238

Stocker, Michael, 183
Stone, Matthew, 243
The Stone (blog), 278
Stoppard, Tom, 187
*Stories and the Limits: Narrative
    Approaches to Bioethics*,
    Lindemann, 178, 183
Stoutland, Frederick, 89, 90
"Strange Baby," science fiction, 43
Strawsonian metaphysics, 69
stream of experience, 36–38
structuralism, 275, 276
Studies in the Way of Words, Grice, 223
substance dualism, 139, 140
Sumner, L. W., 119, 120
supercoherence, 215
supernatural world, 214
supervaluations, 241
supreme principles, 106
surrogacy, 176
survivor, victimization vs., 180–81
Susskind, Ron, 212
Switzerland, 158
Sylvan, Richard, 156
Sylvan's Box, Priest, 156
systematicity, Spinoza's work, 162–63

Tanesini, Alessandra, 216
Taoists, 109
"Tarski's Theory of Truth," Field, 240
Taylor, Charles, 115, 271, 272
Taylor, Richard, 55
Tea Partyers, 198
Temkin, Larry, 193
terrorism, 10, 191, 195. *See also* war
testimony, 162, 220
theological concepts, 165–66
theory of affects, 161
Theory of Justice, Rawls, 10, 171–72, 177
theory of obligations, 10–11
theory of the concept of man, 161
therapy, philosophy as, 166
thermodynamics, second law of, 260
Theseus, 64, 65
Thing and Space, Husserl, 55
Thomson, J. J., 71

thought, language of, 7, 12, 237, 240, 280
Thucydides, 17
Tiberius, Valerie, 8–9, 111–20
Tibetan University, 153
time, 7, 68–69, 266
    asymmetry, 259–60
    block universe theory of, 258, 259
    manifest time, 72–73, 78
    spacetime, 69–70, 72, 78–79
time travel, 79
titanic influence, Kripke, 7, 28
toleration, 170
Tolstoy, Leo, 177
Tractatus, Wittgenstein, 84
traditional marriage, 15
transhumanism, 61–62
Treatise, Hume, 66, 119
*The Tristan Chord: Wagner and
        Philosophy*, Magee, 156
true, 216
true belief, 226
true justified belief, 102
truth, 11, 101–2, 148, 211–12
    coherence theory, 212–13
    deflationism, 257–58
    objective, 219
    truth-seeking, 26
    truth theory, 214, 215, 239–40
Truth and Realism, Lynch, 211, 215
Truth as One and Many, Lynch, 211, 213
Tuana, Nancy, 190
Tufts, James, 192
Tumulka, Roderich, 78
Tversky–Kahneman conjunction
        fallacy, 43
Twain, Mark, 28

underground, 3
unexplained explainers, 71, 74
United Kingdom, politics, 18–19
United States, consciousness, 44–45
universe
    entropy, 73–74
    fine-tuned nature, 74–75
    space and time, 78–79
University of Alabama, 47

University of Notre Dame, 2
U.S. Supreme Court, 20, 170
utilitarianism, 85, 220

vagueness, 223–25, 232, 241
Vagueness, Williamson, 222, 224, 228
Value in Ethics and Economics, Anderson,
        188, 193
values
    changing, 207–8
    meaningless, 209210
    truths, 213
van Inwagen, Peter, 65, 209, 269
victimization *vs.* survivor, 180–81
Vinge, Vernor, 43, 44
virtue epistemology, 30, 33
virtue ethics, 33, 120
vision, neuroscience of, 103
Voltaire, 279
von Herbert, Franz Paul, 158

Waldro, Jeremy, 171
Walker, Margaret Urban, 183, 184
Walzer, Michael, 177
war, 23, 32, 139, 168, 170, 179, 183, 196
    terrorism, 10, 191, 195
    World War II, 18, 125, 169, 177
Warner, Marina, 3
Wason Card Test, 149
Wason selection task, 43
Watson, John B., 251
Weatherson, Brian, 29
Weber, Max, 17
Wedgwood, Ralph, 89
well-being, 8, 24, 112
What Darwin Got Wrong, Fodor, 247,
        252, 253
What Philosophers Know, Gutting, 268,
        269, 273
White, Tony, 3
Whiten, Andrew, 48
*Whose Body Is It Anyway? Justice and
        Integrity of the Person*, Fabre,
        168, 173
*Who's in Charge? Free Will and the Science
        of the Brain*, Gazzaniga, 140

Why Tolerate Religion? Leiter, 23
Williams, Bernard, 89, 183, 184, 272
Williamson, Timothy, 4, 11, 33, 53, 89,
    215, 220, 222–34
Williamson on Knowledge, 227
Wilson, Timothy, 119, 120
wisdom, 114, 115
Wittgenstein, Ludwig, 1, 12, 84, 122,
    184, 229, 230, 237, 250, 263, 264,
    268, 270
wolf, Brenin, 46, 47
Wolff, Robert Paul, 19
women, 109–10
    feminism, 179–80
    philosophy, 181–82, 189–90
Woolf, Virginia, 35, 187
Word and Object, Quine, 102, 245
working memory, 128–29

world, witness and locus, 95–96
World War II, 18, 125, 169, 177.
    See also war
Wright, Crispin, 213, 265
www.philpapers.org, 2
Wylie, Alison, 190

X-ons, 70
x-phi, 21, 67, 152. *See also* experimental
    philosophy
Xunzi, 42

Yale University, 2, 9
Youngsteadt, Elsa, 143
Yu, Charles, 79

Zhuangzi, 42
Zizek, Slavoj, 1, 177, 277